JOURNAL FOR THE STUDY OF THE NEW TESTAMENT
SUPPLEMENT SERIES
93

Executive Editor
Stanley E. Porter

JSOT Press
Sheffield

Isaiah and Prophetic Traditions in the Book of Revelation

Visionary Antecedents and their Development

Jan Fekkes III

Journal for the Study of the New Testament
Supplement Series 93

Copyright © 1994 Sheffield Academic Press

Published by JSOT Press
JSOT Press is an imprint of
Sheffield Academic Press Ltd
343 Fulwood Road
Sheffield S10 3BP
England

Typeset by Sheffield Academic Press
and
Printed on acid-free paper in Great Britain
by Bookcraft
Midsomer Norton, Somerset

British Library Cataloguing in Publication Data

Fekkes, Jan
    Isaiah and Prophetic Traditions in the
    Book of Revelation.—(JSNT Supplement
    Series, ISSN 0143-5108; No. 93)
    I. Title II. Series
    224

ISBN 1-85075-456-X

CONTENTS

ACKNOWLEDGMENTS

It is inevitable that the production of a work of this nature owes a great deal to the support and guidance of others. Consequently, a variety of thanks are in order for those who have helped in the course of this study, whether financially, intellectually, or through emotional support.

First of all, I wish to acknowledge my debt to the late Professor Barnabas Lindars, who first encouraged me to study the use of the OT in Revelation, and provided evaluation throughout the course of research.

I am also grateful to those who read portions of the manuscript and offered not only helpful criticisms, but timely encouragement as well. I am especially indebted to the comments of Dr George Brooke and Professor Richard Bauckham, who gave me much of their time and helped clarify my thinking on many points. I am particularly grateful to the latter for suggesting that this study should be published and putting forward his recommendation to Sheffield Academic Press.

For unexpected yet very welcome financial support, my family and I would like to thank the Committee of Vice-Principals of the Universities of the United Kingdom, and the University of Manchester Research Studentships program, who together provided assistance for the years 1985–1987.

My thanks also go to Professor John J. Collins, editor of *JBL*, who graciously allowed me to include material previously published in the Journal.[1]

The final note of recognition must be reserved for my family, who patiently waited, encouraged, and provided mind-clearing diversions from research. I am particularly grateful to my wife Lori for the time and careful attention she devoted to typing the original manuscript and undertaking various editorial tasks.

1.   J. Fekkes III, '"His Bride has Prepared Herself": Revelation 19–21 and Isaian Nuptial Imagery', *JBL* 109 (1990), pp. 269-87.

ABBREVIATIONS

AB	Anchor Bible
AJBI	*Annual of the Japanese Biblical Institute*
AnBib	Analecta biblica
ANCL	Ante-Nicene Christian Library
ANRW	*Aufstieg und Niedergang der römischen Welt*
ANTJ	Arbeiten zum Neuen Testament und Judentum
APOT	R.H. Charles (ed.), *Apocrypha and Pseudepigrapha of the Old Testament*
ATA	Alttestamentliche Abhandlungen
ATANT	Abhandlungen zur Theologie des Alten und Neuen Testament
AUSS	*Andrews University Seminary Studies*
BAGD	W. Bauer, W.F. Arndt and F.W. Gingrich, *Greek–English Lexicon of the New Testament*
BDB	F. Brown, S.R. Driver and C.A. Briggs, *A Hebrew and English Lexicon of the Old Testament*
BDF	F. Blass, A. Debrunner and R.W. Funk, *A Greek Grammar of the New Testament and Other Early Christian Literature*
BETL	Bibliotheca ephemeridum theologicarum lovaniensium
BFCT	Beiträge zur Förderung christlicher Theologie
BGBE	Beiträge zur Geschichte der biblischen Exegese
Bib	*Biblica*
BKAT	Biblischer Kommentar: Altes Testament
BTL	H. Cremer, *Biblico-Theological Lexicon of New Testament Greek*
BWANT	Beiträge zur Wissenschaft vom Alten und Neuen Testament
BZ	*Biblische Zeitschrift*
BZNW	Beihefte zur ZNW
CBC	Cambridge Bible Commentary
CBQ	*Catholic Biblical Quarterly*
CBQMS	*Catholic Biblical Quarterly*, Monograph Series
CHB	*Cambridge History of the Bible*
CIG	*Corpus Inscriptionum graecarum*
ClassJ	*Classical Journal*
CNS	*Cristianesimo nella storia*
CNT	Commentaire du Nouveau Testament
CT	Cahiers Théologiques

Abbreviations 9

DBAT	*Dielheimer Blätter zum Alten Testament*
DBSup	*Dictionnaire de la Bible, Supplément*
DEB	*Dictionnaïre Encyclopédique de la Bible*
DJD	Discoveries in the Judaean Desert
EncJud	*Encyclopaedia judaica* (1971)
EspVie	*Esprit et Vie*
EstBib	*Estudios biblicos*
ETL	*Ephemerides theologicae lovanienses*
ETR	*Etudes théologiques et religieuses*
EvT	*Evangelische Theologie*
ExpTim	*Expository Times*
GCS	Griechische christliche Schriftsteller
HDR	Harvard Dissertations in Religion
Herm	Hermeneia
HNT	Handbuch zum Neuen Testament
HSS	Harvard Semitic Studies
HTR	*Harvard Theological Review*
ICC	International Critical Commentary
IDB	G.A. Buttrick (ed.), *Interpreter's Dictionary of the Bible*
IDBSup	K. Crim (ed.), Supplementary Volume to *IDB*
IEJ	*Israel Exploration Journal*
ISBE	G. Bromiley (ed.), *International Standard Bible Encyclopedia* (3rd edn, 1979–)
Jastrow	M. Jastrow, *A Dictionary of the Targumim, the Talmud...*
JBC	R.E. Brown *et al.* (eds.), *The Jerome Biblical Commentary*
JBL	*Journal of Biblical Literature*
JEH	*Journal of Ecclesiastical History*
JR	*Journal of Religion*
JSJ	*Journal for the Study of Judaism*
JSNT	*Journal for the Study of the New Testament*
JSNTSup	*Journal for the Study of the New Testament*, Supplement Series
JSOTSup	*Journal for the Study of the Old Testament*, Supplement Series
JSS	*Journal of Semitic Studies*
JTS	*Journal of Theological Studies*
KB	L. Koehler and W. Baumgartner, *Lexicon in Veteris Testamenti libros*
KJV	*King James Version*
LCL	Loeb Classical Library
LD	Lectio Divina
LR	*Lutherische Rundschau*
LS	H.G. Liddell and R. Scott, *A Greek–English Lexicon*
LTK	*Lexikon für Theologie und Kirche*
LuViSup	*Lumière et vie, Supplément biblique*
MG	J.H. Moulton, W.F. Howard and N. Turner, *A Grammar of*

	the Greek New Testament (vols. I–IV)
MM	J.H. Moulton and G. Milligan, *The Vocabulary of the Greek New Testament*
N²⁶	Nestle–Aland, *Novum Testamentum Graece*, 26th edn
NCB	New Century Bible
NEB	*New English Bible*
NedTTs	*Nederlands theologisch tijdschrift*
Neot	*Neotestamentica*
NICNT	New International Commentary on the New Testament
NIDNTT	C. Brown (ed.), *New International Dictionary of New Testament Theology*
NIV	*New International Version*
NKZ	*Neue kirchliche Zeitschrift*
NovT	*Novum Testamentum*
NovTSup	*Novum Testamentum*, Supplements
NovVet	*Nova et Vetera*
NRT	*La nouvelle revue théologique*
NTApoc	W. Schneemelcher (ed.), *New Testament Apocrypha*
NTM	New Testament Message
NTS	*New Testament Studies*
OLD	P.G.W. Glare (ed.), *Oxford Latin Dictionary* (1982)
ÖTK	Ökumenischer Taschenbuch-Kommentar zum Neuen Testament
OTL	Old Testament Library
OTP	J.H. Charlesworth (ed.), *The Old Testament Pseudepigrapha*
OTS	*Oudtestamentische Studiën*
PG	J. Migne, *Patrologia graeca*
RB	*Revue biblique*
RevExp	*Review and Expositor*
RevQ	*Revue de Qumrân*
RevThom	*Revue thomiste*
RHPR	*Revue d'historie et de philosophie religieuses*
RivB	*Rivista biblica*
RNT	Regensburger Neues Testament
RSV	Revised Standard Version
RV	Revised Version
SBLASP	Society of Biblical Literature Abstracts and Seminar Papers
SBM	Stuttgarter biblische Monographien
SC	Sources chrétiennes
Schürer	E. Schürer, *The History of the Jewish People in the Age of Jesus Christ* (rev. edn (1973–1987, vols. I–III.2)
SE	*Studia Evangelica*, I, II, III (= TU 73 [1959], 87 [1964], 88 [1964], etc.)
SJLA	Studies in Judaism in Late Antiquity
SJT	*Scottish Journal of Theology*

SNT	Studien zum Neuen Testament
SNTSMS	Society of New Testament Studies Monograph Series
SPB	Studia postbiblica
StudNeot	Studia neotestamentica
TDNT	G. Kittel and G. Friedrich (eds.), *Theological Dictionary of the New Testament*
TDOT	G.J. Botterweck and H. Ringgren (eds.), *Theological Dictionary of the Old Testament*
THKNT	Theologischer Handkommentar zum Neuen Testament
TLZ	*Theologische Literaturzeitung*
TRE	*Theologische Realenzyklopädie*
TS	*Theological Studies*
TU	Texte und Untersuchungen
TZ	*Theologische Zeitschrift*
UBS	United Bible Society
UBSGNT	*United Bible Societies Greek New Testament*
VC	*Vigiliae christianae*
VT	*Vetus Testamentum*
VTSup	*Vetus Testamentum*, Supplements
WMANT	Wissenschaftliche Monographien zum Alten und Neuen Testament
WUNT	Wissenschaftliche Untersuchungen zum Neuen Testament
ZAW	*Zeitschrift für die alttestamentliche Wissenschaft*
ZBK	*Zürcher BibelKommentar*
ZNW	*Zeitschrift für die neutestamentliche Wissenschaft*
ZRGG	*Zeitschrift für Religions–und Geistesgeschichte*
ZTK	*Zeitschrift für Theologie und Kirche*

INTRODUCTION

In his study on the formative background of early Christianity,
Christopher Rowland put forward the following programmatic
statement:

> The use of Scripture in the apocalypses is a subject which is only just
> being investigated in any detail. Preliminary results suggest both that it is
> a field which demands further study and that many apocalyptic visions
> may have their origin in the study of Scripture.[1]

Despite the considerable attention which critical scholars have devoted
to the use of the OT in the NT in the past one hundred years,[2] what is
today true of the Jewish apocalypses in general is still true of the NT
Apocalypse in particular. Therefore, as recently, as 1986, E. Schüssler
Fiorenza could say, 'A thorough study of the use of the OT by the
author of Revelation is not available'.[3]

Because John's use of the OT is so thoroughly pervasive, and yet at
the same time so consistently allusive in character, it is not really
surprising to find that no single author, let alone a single book, has yet
to do justice to this important subject. The ambiguous nature of John's
use of Scripture requires a systematic and comprehensive approach,
whereby each supposed allusion can be evaluated in detail, in order to
determine its level of substantive influence.

An obvious starting place for such an investigation is with those OT
traditions which are widely recognized as dominant in the prophet's
visionary consciousness and expression, including the books of Ezekiel,
Daniel, Isaiah, Exodus and Jeremiah. In recent years, individual
studies have appeared on each of these OT books and their use in

1. *Christian Origins* (London, 1985), p. 62.
2. Details and bibliography of past research are given in the introduction to
Chapter 2.
3. *The Book of Revelation: Justice and Judgment* (Philadelphia, 1985), p. 28
n. 39.

14   *Isaiah and Prophetic Traditions in the Book of Revelation*

Revelation—each, that is, except Isaiah.[4] The present study aims to fill this gap.[5]

A further incentive for this research topic comes from the recognition that the book of Isaiah was one of the most influential biblical forces behind the formation of both Jewish and early Christian eschatology. As a result of this controlling influence, the modern scholar has inherited a wealth of primary material, both textual and literary, which relates to Isaiah and its interpretation. And naturally these resources are invaluable as a basis for comparison with John's own use of Isaiah.

The specific goals of this study can best be described by first summarizing the aims of the body of the work (Part II, Chapters 3–7), and then explaining its relationship to the supporting framework (Chapters 1–2; Chapter 8).

In Part II, where the use of Isaiah in Revelation is explored, the agenda is controlled by two main objectives:

1. *To determine the validity of each proposed allusion to Isaiah.* The ultimate goal of this aspect of the inquiry is to be able to rank each suggested Isaiah allusion according to three general levels of probability:

4.   A. Vanhoye, 'L'utilisation du livre d'Ezéchiel dans l'Apocalypse', *Bib* 43 (1962), pp. 436-76; G.K. Beale, *The Use of Daniel in Jewish Apocalyptic Literature and in the Revelation of St John* (Lanham, 1984); D. Mollat, 'Apocalisse ed Esodo' in S. Giovanni, *Atti della XVII settimana biblica* (Brescia, 1964), pp. 346-61; J.S. Casey, 'Exodus Typology in the Book of Revelation' (PhD dissertation, SBThS, 1981); C. Wolff, *Jeremia im Frühjudentum und Urchristentum* (TU 118; Berlin, 1976), pp. 166-74. Three works which do discuss in one way or another the influence of Isaiah in Revelation are J. Comblin, *Le Christ dans l'Apocalypse* (Tournai, 1965); B. Marconcini, 'L'utilizzazione del T.M. nelle citazioni isaiane dell' Apocalisse', *RivB* XXIV (1976), pp. 113-35; and A. Gangemi, 'L'utilizzazione del Deutero-Isaia nell' Apocalisse di Giovanni', *Euntes Docete* 27 (1974), pp. 109-44; 311-39. But the first cites Isaiah texts at random with no obvious concern for establishing the validity of proposed allusions. The second study is limited to a discussion of textual sources (Hebrew vs. Greek OT), and the work of Gangemi, though helpful, is restricted to allusions to Second Isaiah.
5.   C. Brütsch also recognizes the need for further study on John's use of the Prophets, 'Wie es Vanhoye getan hat... [i.e. with Ezekiel], sollten noch weiter Einzelvergleiche zwischen den prophetischen Schriften des AT und der Apok. unternommen werden'. (*Die Offenbarung Jesu Christi, Johannes-Apokalypse* (ZBK; Zürich, ²1970) 3, 133 n. 9b).

      a. Certain/virtually certain
      b. Probable/possible
      c. Unlikely/doubtful

In this endeavor I have tried to counteract the tendency of scholars to view the discovery of OT references in Revelation as a sort of open-ended exercise in concordancing, with the objective being to raise the tally as high as possible. Each new entry becomes just as important as another, and the whole homogeneous collection is held up as testimony to John's remarkable knowledge of the Scriptures. Needless to say, such an approach contributes little to the interpretation of the book, since it indiscriminately lumps together primary, secondary, and even, at times, non-existent allusions. In my opinion it is just as important to weed out dubious parallels as it is to substantiate which OT texts are clearly being employed. By reducing the options to a workable core of certain texts, it is hoped that we may be in a better position to discern patterns in John's choices and devote more attention to the texts that form the fundamental matrix of his visionary expression. While I have tried to be inclusive in my treatment of proposed allusions, it is inevitable that a few examples claimed by various commentators will have either been overlooked or omitted.

2. *To assess the purpose and significance of each certain allusion to Isaiah.* After concluding that a particular Isaiah text has been used, it is necessary to ask how it is being used and to what extent this affects the interpretation of the passage where it appears. The intention here is to illuminate the *process* as well as the *result* of a particular use of Isaiah. This includes trying to get beyond the visionary setting of an allusion to the pre-visionary exegetical praxis which underlies its application. To this end, a variety of methods may be employed in the analysis of any given passage, but these will usually include at least:

1.   a comparison with the original language and context of Isaiah
2.   tracing (where possible) the tradition history of a particular text or motif
3.   studying both the immediate and wider context in Revelation

Throughout this investigation, I have purposely refrained from categorizing John's use of the OT with conventional labels, such as typological, midrashic, and the like. Not only are such rubrics commonly subject to various definitions, but more fundamentally, they tend to cause one to compartmentalize an author's approach to

Scripture, rather than treating each example as a phenomenon in its own right.[6] Therefore, I will use broad terms for describing John's overall approach, and try to explain in individual cases what it appears he is doing with a text. In addition, a summary of the exegetical techniques employed by the prophet in his use of Isaiah will be provided in Chapter 8.

But while the main concern of this study is to discern the extent and manner of John's use of Isaiah, the results of Part II have wider implications for the prophet's OT applications in general. Therefore, John's overall approach to the OT is discussed in Chapter 2, where it is argued that the majority of certain allusions to the OT in Revelation fall into a limited number of well-defined thematic classifications. It is suggested that these OT texts are consciously selected according to topic (rather than book), and correspond closely to John's purpose and subject matter in a given passage.

Because these proposals are based on a general overview of biblical allusions in Revelation, the special focus on Isaiah in Part II can also function as a test case to determine whether the thematic patterns outlined in Chapter 2 correctly reflect a fundamental authorial strategy, or whether they simply stem from a superficial reading and arrangement of the evidence. Thus the relationship between the first and second parts is taken up in the summary and conclusion (Chapter 8), and leads naturally into the question of how much John is interpreting Scripture as opposed to merely borrowing conventional language and image patterns.

In relation to these chapters (2–8) and their focus on John's literary and exegetical activity, Chapter 1 serves as an introduction to the man himself and his office. The special concerns of this preliminary section, in particular John's prophetic status, self-understanding and authority, provide the background necessary for setting his use of previous prophetic materials in context.

It should be noted that the present study is relatively unconcerned with the issue of textual sources—that is, John's use of a Hebrew or Greek OT.[7] The verdict of R.H. Charles that the prophet invariably

---

6.   'The NT exegesis of the OT was extraordinarily varied, and any attempt to classify it as one type of exegesis is doomed to failure' (R.E. Brown, *JBC*, II, 611).

7.   I would concur with M.P. Miller that text-form is of secondary importance in the study of OT allusions. See 'Targum, Midrash and the Use of the Old Testament in the New Testament', *JSJ* 2 (1971), p. 61.

'draws his materials directly from the Hebrew (or Aramaic) text' has been corroborated in a variety of subsequent studies,[8] and my own analysis has yielded nothing to weaken this opinion. Anyone wishing to settle the question in their own mind can do so by working through the catena of OT allusions in Revelation 17–18 with a Hebrew and Greek Bible.

There are occasions where John may be in touch with a Greek tradition (either directly or indirectly),[9] and, likewise, a few examples which appear to reflect targumic and rabbinic traditions.[10] But for the most part, it seems clear that John is working from a knowledge of the Hebrew text, and unless otherwise stated, this is the presupposition adopted in individual lexical comparisons.

Finally, it will be helpful to provide a few definitions of basic terminology employed throughout the thesis. Three words that recur repeatedly in the course of this investigation deserve some explanation: the adjective *eschatological*, and the nouns *judgment* and *salvation*. My point of departure for the understanding and application of these and related terms is in general dictated by John's own theological perspective—especially his expectation of the imminence of the parousia and his prophetic self-consciousness—rather than modern scholarly distinctions (however valid they may be).[11]

According to the prophet's own christological view of history,

8. *A Critical and Exegetical Commentary on the Revelation of St John* (Edinburgh, 1920), I, lxvi-lxviii); *Lectures on the Apocalypse: The Schweich Lectures 1919* (London, 1922), pp. 29-40; *Studies in the Apocalypse* (Edinburgh, 1913), pp. 79-102. Vanhoye, 'L'utilisation du livre d'Ezéchiel'; A. Lancellotti, *Sintassi ebraica nel greco dell' Apocalisse. I. Uso delle forme verbali* (Assisi, 1964); G. Mussies, *The Morphology of Koine Greek as Used in the Apocalypse of John: A Study in Bilingualism* (NovTSup, 27; Leiden, 1971); S. Thompson, *The Apocalypse and Semitic Syntax* (Cambridge, 1985); Marconcini, 'L'utilizzazione'; Gangemi, 'L'utilizzazione'.

9. P. Trudinger, 'Some Observations concerning the Text of the Old Testament in the Book of Revelation', *JTS* NS 17 (1966), p. 85 n. 2; G. Beale, 'The Origin of the Title "King of Kings and Lord of Lords" in Revelation 17.14', *NTS* 31 (1985), pp. 618-20.

10. A. Schlatter, *Das Alte Testament in der johanneischen Apokalypse* (BFCT XVI/6; Gütersloh, 1912); M. McNamara, *The New Testament and the Palestinian Targum to the Pentateuch* (AnBib, 27; Rome, 1966), pp. 97-125, 189-237, 255-56; Trudinger, 'Observations', pp. 82-88; and 'The Text of the Old Testament in the Book of Revelation' (PhD dissertation, Boston University, 1963).

11. Schüssler Fiorenza, *Revelation*, pp. 48-50.

which he shared with the early church in general, the starting point of eschatology is not the parousia or Day of the Lord, but the first coming of Christ.[12] It follows from this that the peripheral boundary of eschatological events extends from the incarnation to the universal establishment of God's kingdom. On this basis, I use the word *eschatological* in a very broad sense to describe divinely ordered events both in and beyond history which contribute to the fulfilment of this goal. The emphasis then is not so much on the content or categories of eschatology (e.g. judgment, rewards, etc.), as it is on the *temporal relationship* between the events so described and the prophetic expectations of the author describing them.[13]

But as will be evident in Chapter 2, I do subsume the *content* of John's eschatology to a great extent under the heading of judgment and salvation, and elsewhere apply these terms loosely to the negative and positive spheres of divine activity vis-à-vis the world and the church, respectively. The justification for this follows largely from the specific aims of the present study, and is thus determined by John's own paradigmatic selection of OT texts, the bulk of which correspond to the general OT form-critical categories of oracles of judgment and salvation.[14] Because of this predilection, and his overall affinity with the prophetic ethos of his biblical predecessors, I have found it useful to adopt these two terms (judgment and salvation) as broadly representative of John's dualistic conceptual framework and prophetic expression.[15]

And since the actualization of threats of judgment and promises of salvation is consistently seen as polarized between the wicked and the righteous in Revelation, with the fulfilment of the righteous being deferred until the parousia, I see no need to invest these categories

---

12. Schüssler Fiorenza, *IDBSup*, pp. 271, 274.

13. For divisions of eschatology (in both OT and NT criticism) according to *content* (e.g. national, individual and universal), and *time perspective* (e.g. transcendent, consistent, realized, etc.), see C. Steuernagel, 'Die Strukturlinien der Entwicklung der jüdischen Eschatologie', in *Festschrift für Alfred Bertholet zum 80* (ed. W. Baumgartner, O. Eissfeldt, K. Elliger and L. Rost; Tübingen, 1950), pp. 479-87; T.C. Vriezen, 'Prophecy and Eschatology', *VTSup* 1 (1953), pp. 199-229; E. Jenni, *IDB* 2, pp. 126-33; Schüssler Fiorenza, *IDBSup*, pp. 272, 276-77; L. Hartman, *Prophecy Interpreted* (Lund, 1966), pp. 3, 15-16.

14. C. Westermann, *Basic Forms of Prophetic Speech* (Philadelphia, 1967), pp. 95-98.

15. Schüssler Fiorenza, *Revelation*, pp. 47-48, 55-56.

with the sort of ambiguity associated with so-called 'inaugurated eschatology' in general, and 'Johannine' theology in particular. As Schüssler Fiorenza has rightly observed, 'It is clear that Rev. and the Fourth Gospel represent opposite eschatological options'.[16]

16. *Revelation*, p. 107, cf. 106.

Part I
METHODOLOGICAL UNDERPINNINGS

Chapter 1

JOHN AS A JEWISH-CHRISTIAN PROPHET

A. *The Role of Prophets in Early Christianity*

Introduction

Critical studies on the subject of prophecy in early Christianity were generally sporadic until the 1970s, when interest in this area surged and reached a definite high-water mark towards the end of the decade. In this period alone over thirty journal articles and at least eight major works on early Christian prophecy appeared in print. Much of the momentum for this renaissance was provided by an SBL seminar on early Christian prophecy which met six years running (1972–77) and which was consecutively chaired by M.E. Boring and D.E. Aune. Though differing in scope and purpose, both scholars subsequently produced major contributions on the subject of early Christian prophecy. Aune's work in particular, published in 1983 under the title *Prophecy in Early Christianity and the Ancient Mediterranean World*, received very positive reviews and has already been touted by some as the standard treatment of the subject. Yet other important works which helped to form a continuum of scholarly dialogue and which paved the way for Aune's book must be recognized.[1]

----

1.   These are: the various articles on προφήτης in *TDNT*, VI, particularly R. Meyer on the early Jewish period, and G. Friedrich on the Christian sources; the article by E. Cothenet in *DBSup*, VIII, cols. 1222-1337; G. Dautzenberg, *Urchristliche Prophetie: Ihre Erforschung, ihre Voraussetzungen im Judentum und ihre Struktur im ersten Korintherbrief* (Stuttgart, 1975); U.B. Müller, *Prophetie und Predigt im Neuen Testament: Formgeschichtliche Untersuchungen zur urchristlichen Prophetie* (Gütersloh, 1975); E.E. Ellis, *Prophecy and Hermeneutic in Early Christianity: New Testament Essays* (WUNT, 18; Tübingen, 1978); D. Hill, *New Testament Prophecy* (Richmond, 1979); W. Grudem, *The Gift of Prophecy in 1 Corinthians* (Washington, DC, 1982); M.E. Boring, *Sayings of the Risen Jesus* (SNTSMS, 46; Cambridge, 1982); and the collection of essays edited by

The major issues confronted in these various treatises may be summarized in the form of three basic questions:

a. From a history-of-religions point of view, what effect did antecedent and contemporary prophetic traditions, both Jewish and Pagan, have on the rise and development of prophecy in early Christianity?

b. From a sociological perspective, what was the role and function of the prophet in the early Christian community, and how did this relate to and differ from the roles of other important figures such as apostles, teachers, evangelists, and the like?

c. From the standpoint of theology, what were the dynamics of Christian prophetism—its human element, its relationship to the divine Spirit, and its continuity or discontinuity with previous revelation, oral and written?

Although it is not my purpose to address these issues systematically, some of the problems and solutions involved in them will necessarily be given attention in the following pages. As a basis for discussion, three periods of prophetic activity commend themselves:

1. The beginnings of Christian prophecy
2. Prophecy in the Pauline churches
3. Prophecy in the post-apostolic church

1. *The Beginnings of Christian Prophecy*

The rise and decline of early Christian prophecy is generally set within a time frame of c. 120 years (30–150 CE), although the 'New Prophecy' movement (Montanism) which arose after this period maintained some scattered influence until its virtual disappearance after 500 CE.[2] But it must be emphasized at the outset that the paucity

---

J. Panagopoulos in *Prophetic Vocation in the New Testament and Today* (NovTSup, 45; Leiden, 1977).

2. *LTK*, VII, pp. 578-80; Aune, *Prophecy*, pp. 313-16. In its early stages, Montanism was accepted as a valid renewal movement within the churches. Only later did its ecstatic excesses bring on charges of heresy and foster organized opposition from church officials. Cf. J.L. Ash, 'The Decline of Ecstatic Prophecy in the Church', *TS* 37 (1976), pp. 237-43; H. von Campenhausen, *Ecclesiastical Authority and Spiritual Power in the Church of the First Three Centuries* (London, 1969), pp. 187-91; E. Nestler, 'Was Montanism a Heresy?', *Pneuma* 6 (1984), pp. 67-78.

of literary material relating to prophecy in this historical period makes much of any reconstruction tentative. Apart from scattered references and allusions, only three authors actually discuss Christian prophets or prophecy in any length: Paul in 1 Corinthians 12–14, the author(s) of *Didache* 10–15, and Hermas in *Mandate* 11.

The most critical gap is the first fifteen years (30–45 CE) in which almost nothing is known concerning the establishment of Christian prophets and prophecy among the first Palestinian Christians. Some detailed treatments of prophecy (e.g. Friedrich) leave out discussion of this foundational period altogether and begin with the Pauline material or the few short notices in Acts. Others give it only a brief and often vague mention. Nevertheless, several theories have been advanced in an attempt to fill in the picture.

J. Reiling follows H. Greeven in the opinion that the first stage of Christian prophecy was congregational or group prophecy.[3] These scholars hold that the special recognition of individual prophets was a natural, though secondary, development, and remained the exception rather than the rule. Yet apart from Acts, where Luke consistently portrays group prophecy and tongues as a confirmatory sign of the initial infilling of the Spirit, there is little evidence for this phenomenon in the early stages of Christianity.[4]

E.E. Ellis and others have seen a connection between the rise of early Christian prophets and the practice of so-called 'charismatic exegesis'.[5] In this view the early Christian prophets and teachers were inspired interpreters of the OT writers whose message was a mystery which could only be unlocked by a revelation of the Spirit. Aune shows little interest in this view and relegates it to a short appendix in his book.[6] While admitting that charismatic exegesis was indeed a

3.   'Prophecy, the Spirit and the Church', in Panagopoulos, *Prophetic Vocation*, pp. 66-67.

4.   Aune, *Prophecy*, pp. 199-200; Ellis, *Prophecy*, pp. 129-30; R.J. Dillon, *JBC*, II, pp. 171-72; Boring, *Sayings*, pp. 38-43. An experience of group enthusiasm in a Christian gathering may lie behind the description in *Asc. Isa.* 6, but this is later. Cf. P.C. Bori, 'L'estasi del profeta: Ascensio Isaiae 6 e l'antico profetismo cristiano', *CNS* 1 (1980), pp. 367-89.

5.   Ellis, 'Prophecy in the New Testament Church—and Today', in Panagopoulos, *Prophetic Vocation*, pp. 46-47; *Prophecy*, p. 172.

6.   *Prophecy*, pp. 339-46, where he states (345), 'of the many studies of the use of the OT in the NT, only one—that of E.E. Ellis—suggests that OT exegesis was a task carried out by early Christian prophets'. This is a little unfair, for a similar

common practice in early Christianity, he sees no evidence to connect it with the ministry of Christian prophets in particular.

More significant are those theories which explore the role of the Twelve as bearers of tradition, who continued the prophetic ministry of Jesus According to G. Theissen, the post-Easter Apostles and others carried on a peripatetic mission to Israel which had its Gentile counterpart in the mission inaugurated at Antioch in Acts 13.[7] These wandering apostles and prophets adopted a radical lifestyle modeled after the earthly Jesus and preached and delivered oracles in the name of the risen Jesus. Of great importance for Theissen's view is the belief that many of these prophecies in the name of the risen Jesus were indiscriminately combined with pre-Easter Jesus traditions, both of which are said to be reflected in the Gospels.[8]

Theissen's reconstruction of the social matrix of earliest Palestinian Christianity is in many ways illuminating, but his opinion that the office of prophet was closely connected with a missionary purpose is problematic. While it is evident that some who are specifically called prophets were engaged in missionary work,[9] did this activity constitute them prophets? What revelatory skills were necessary to preach the Kerygma? If we accept the definition of a Christian prophet as a

view is expressed by E. Cothenet, 'Les prophètes chrétiens comme exégètes charismatiques de l'Ecriture', in Panagopoulos, *Prophetic Vocation*, pp. 77-107; *DBSup*, VIII, col. 1287; and L. Gaston, *No Stone on Another: Studies in the Significance of the Fall of Jerusalem in the Synoptic Gospels* (Leiden, 1970), pp. 439-43, both of whom Aune uses elsewhere. Boring also favours this view (*Sayings*, pp. 95-110).

7.   *Sociology of Early Palestinian Christianity* (Philadelphia, 1978) pp. 8-16, and in more detail, 'Wanderradikalismus: Literatursoziologische Aspekte der Überlieferung von Worten Jesu im Urchristentum', *ZTK* 70 (1973), pp. 245-71; cf. Cothenet, *DBSup*, VIII, cols. 1285-86; Aune, *Prophecy*, p. 193.

8.   'Wanderradikalismus', pp. 252-55; Aune, *Prophecy*, pp. 214, 243; Boring, *Sayings*, p. 77. Boring's work in particular is a more recent and detailed presentation of the view that the Gospels contain post-Easter Jesus sayings transmitted by early Christian prophets. See the negative appraisals of Aune, *Prophecy*, pp. 233-46; and Hill, *Prophecy*, pp. 160-85. On the Jesus traditions in Revelation and their relation to prophetic activity, see L.A. Vos, *The Synoptic Traditions in the Apocalypse* (Kampen, 1965), esp. pp. 110-11, 193-95, 223-24; and Boring, 'The Apocalypse as Christian Prophecy: A Discussion of the Issues Raised by the Book of Revelation for the Study of Early Christian Prophecy', in *SBLASP* (1974), II, pp. 43-62.

9.   E.g. Silas=Silvanus, Acts 15.31, 40; Barnabus and Saul(?), Acts 13.1.

type of inspired preacher, what is there to distinguish him or her from the apostle or the evangelist? No doubt, some of the problem lies in the anachronistic use of such titles, but the main issue remains the prophet's function. The evidence from Paul's letters, *Revelation*, the *Didache* and the *Shepherd of Hermas* consistently describes the Christian prophet's sphere and role in cultic rather than evangelistic terms. The primary context of the Christian prophet is not the marketplace or streetcorner but the gathered community.[10] Thus Paul is not simply expressing his own charismatic theology when he says 'prophecy is not for unbelievers but for believers' (1 Cor. 14.22b). Therefore, it would seem necessary to make a distinction between the itinerant preachers of the early Christian communities and the prophets who ministered among them, on the basis of both the content of the message and the sphere of operation.

In the search for possible factors which may have contributed to the emergence of prophets among the early Christians, one item is often overlooked: the presence of Jewish charismatics and apocalyptic prophets in late second temple Judaism. The rise of prophets within the earliest Hebrew Christian communities did not take place in a vacuum. The popular misconception that attributes to second temple Judaism the belief that prophecy had ceased with Malachi has been thoroughly treated and dismissed by modern scholars. On the contrary, in the period encompassing the life and death of Jesus and the emergence of the church, Palestine and its environs abounded in interest groups who claimed charismatic leaders and members, including prophets. In addition to apocalyptic visionaries and prophetic messianic figures, individual prophets, groups of prophets and other charismatics are recorded among the Essenes, the Zealots and the Pharisees.[11]

10. Cf. Boring, *Sayings*, pp. 70-71; Aune, *Prophecy*, pp. 196, 211.

11. Meyer, *TDNT*, VI, pp. 812-28; P. Vielhauer, *NTApoc*, II, pp. 601-607; Aune, *Prophecy*, pp. 106-53; and 'The Use of PROPHĒTĒS in Josephus', *JBL* 101 (1982), pp. 419-21; M. Hengel, *The Charismatic Leader and his Followers* (New York, 1981), pp. 20-24; R.A. Horsley with J.S. Hanson, *Bandits, Prophets, and Messiahs: Popular Movements at the Time of Jesus* (San Francisco, 1985); O. Michel, 'Spätjüdisches Prophetentum', in *Neutestamentliche Studien für Rudolf Bultmann* (ed. W. Eltester; Göttingen, 1954), pp. 60-66; O. Plöger, 'Prophetisches Erbe in den Sekten des Frühen Judentums', *TLZ* 79 (1954), cols. 291-96; E.E. Urbach, 'מתי פסקה הנבואה?' ('When did Prophecy Disappear?'), *Tarbiz* 17 (1945–46), pp. 1-11; Gaston, *No Stone on Another*, pp. 443-44. Cf. the discussion

It is not surprising then that we find prophets among the earliest Palestinian Christians and it is not unlikely that some of these charismatic individuals had formerly exercised their gifts in other contexts before joining the Jesus movement.

2. Prophecy in the Pauline Churches

In the closing exhortations to the newly founded church at Thessalonica Paul writes, 'Do not quench the Spirit, do not despise prophesying, but test everything; hold fast what is good, abstain from every form of evil' (1 Thess. 5.19-22). These four verses form a unit of thought which closes a paraenetic section begun in 5.12.[12] They reveal that the charismatic gifts which later play such a prominent role in the Corinthian congregation are also in evidence in the Thessalonian church and appear to have occasioned problems there as well.

If we accept the view that 2 Thessalonians is in fact prior to 1 Thessalonians (and authentic),[13] then it provides a possible background for understanding Paul's exhortation not to reject prophesying. 2 Thess. 2.1-12 reveals that the church had been upset by a *spirit* (πνεῦμα) or *word* (λόγος) which claimed that the Day of the Lord had already passed.[14] The manner of revelation and eschatological content suggest that this crisis came about as a result of a prophetic word given in their assembly.[15] Paul is quick to point out the error of such teaching and reminds them to test all eschatological revelations

of the contradictory evidence in Grudem, *Prophecy*, pp. 21-32. The idea of the cessation of prophecy is closely related to the concept of the withdrawal of the 'Spirit of Prophecy'. Both of these beliefs were not fully developed and disseminated until the rabbinic period: A. Unterman, *EncJud*, XIV (1971), cols. 264-65; W. Foerster, 'Die Heilige Geist im Spätjudentum', *NTS* 8 (1961–62), pp. 117-34; P. Schäfer, *Die Vorstellung vom Heiligen Geist in der Rabbischen Literatur* (München, 1972), esp. pp. 143-46.

12. B. Henneken, *Verkündigung und Prophetie im 1 Thessalonicherbrief* (Stuttgart, 1969), pp. 107-11. D. Hill discusses the view set forth by R.P. Martin that 1 Thess. 5.16-22 contains the principal order and content of an early Christian worship service (*Prophecy*, pp. 119-20).

13. Perhaps the latter was sent with Timothy (1 Thess. 3.2); F.F. Bruce, *1 & 2 Thessalonians* (Waco, 1982), pp. xxxix-xlvi.

14. The example of Hymenaeus and Philetus in 2 Tim. 2.17-18 reflects a similar situation, though there it is not associated with prophetic utterances.

15. So also Aune, *Prophecy*, p. 220.

by what he has previously taught them.[16] The anxiety which this mistaken prophecy produced was certain to provoke a measure of antipathy towards prophets and their utterances. In this light, the exhortation in 1 Thess. 5.19-22 not to quench the Spirit, not to despise prophecy, and to test all charismatic manifestations is more intelligible.

But regardless of the order of the letters, both passages reveal that prophetic activity was an integral part of these early Christians' experience and Paul wanted it to stay that way, despite the conflicts which it occasionally provoked.[17]

The charismatic tensions hinted at in the Thessalonian correspondence provide a preview to the full-scale conflicts being waged on the same grounds at Corinth. While 1 Corinthians 12–14 comprises the only systematic treatment of spiritual gifts, and prophecy in particular, in the NT, it would be hazardous to presume that Paul's teaching here is characteristic of the universal status of prophecy in early Christianity. Although the Apostle includes many general principles with regard to *charismata*, the entire discourse (chs. 12–14) is set within a strong apologetic framework. The special problems at Corinth in many ways control the manner and content of Paul's approach, and one may wonder how much of his teaching here reflects wider traditions.[18]

One important tradition which Paul shares with the church in general is the belief that prophets and prophecy play a fundamental role in the Christian community. In the three places where Paul discusses spiritual gifts (1 Thess. 5.18-22; 1 Cor. 12–14; Rom. 12.4-8) the only consistent member is prophecy. And the fact that Paul assumes prophetic gifts to be active in the Roman church, to which he has not been, furnishes implicit testimony to their established position.[19]

---

16. In places where a conflict arises between his teaching and a charismatic word given in the churches, Paul, as an apostle (and prophet), always claims the higher authority—2 Thess. 2.1-15; 1 Cor. 14.37-38; cf. Gal. 1.8-9, Acts 21.11-14; cf. Aune, *Prophecy*, pp. 221-22.

17. According to Paul in 1 Cor. 13.8-10, prophecy may be imperfect, but it is to be a part of community experience until the parousia; cf. Grudem, *Prophecy*, pp. 211-19.

18. Despite this caveat, Paul is aware of and concerned with the continuity of church tradition (1 Cor. 11.16), and cannot always be portrayed as an innovator or *ad hoc* theologian.

19. Hill, *Prophecy*, p. 122; Friedrich, *TDNT*, VI, p. 850; Boring, *Sayings*, pp. 30-31.

Furthermore, Paul's estimate in 1 Cor. 12.28 that prophets are to be ranked in importance only second to apostles finds confirmation in a variety of witnesses. The juxtaposition of apostles and prophets (always in that order) occurs in Eph. 2.20; 3.5; 4.11; Rev. 18.20; and *Did.* 11.3.[20] This consistent tradition makes it unlikely then that Paul is merely exalting prophecy in 1 Corinthians 14 because he intends to contrast it to tongues-speaking.

In 1 Cor. 14.3 Paul states, 'he who prophesies speaks to men for their upbuilding and encouragement and consolation'. Paul here describes the end goal of prophecy with three similar terms, οἰκοδομή, παράκλησις and παραμυθία. Throughout the rest of the discussion he confines himself to the first word οἰκοδομή (*upbuilding*),[21] and the building up of the church is presented as the guiding principle for all community manifestations of the Spirit, not just prophecy (14.12, 26). That the goal of edification should characterize a variety of speech activities within the community (e.g. singing, teaching, revelations, and the like, 14.26) shows that this function cannot be used to distinguish prophetic speech from other forms of charismatic expression.[22] Consequently 1 Cor. 14.3 is no more a definition of prophecy than it is of a number of spiritual gifts. It reveals nothing about the content of prophetic speech.

This distinction between the function and content of prophecy is usually lost in modern attempts to define early Christian prophecy on the basis of this passage. In his book on NT prophecy, D. Hill includes a lengthy discussion of how prophecy is little more than 'pastoral preaching', and similar evaluations can be found in the works of a

---

20. Lk 11.49 has 'προφήτας καὶ ἀποστόλους', but the context is primarily concerned with the common motif of the 'violent fate of the prophets' (= OT Prophets), and the similar reception accorded Jesus and his apostles. For a discussion of this theme see Aune, *Prophecy*, pp. 157-59. For the Ephesian passages, see the lengthy discussion of Grudem (*Prophecy*, pp. 82-105), who understands the καί as epexegetical, equating the apostles with the prophets. While such an interpretation is possible for Eph. 2.20 and 3.5, the grammatical construction in 4.11 is unambiguous, and suggests that the author considered apostles and prophets as two distinct gifts in the church. Cf. also Boring, *Sayings*, pp. 36-37.

21. In doing so, Paul now expands on a theme which he had earlier mentioned in passing (1 Cor. 8.1; 10.23).

22. Grudem, *Prophecy*, p. 183; Reiling, 'Prophecy', p. 59; Boring justly criticizes Hill's use of 1 Cor. 14 as a basis for a general definition of Christian prophecy (*Sayings*, p. 16; cf. Aune, *Prophecy*, pp. 9-10).

number of scholars.[23] Often closely associated with this view is the claim that the Christian prophecy that Paul describes is not predictive. Even H. Conzelmann falls into this when he comments on 1 Cor. 14.3 that 'the working ascribed to prophecy makes plain that it is not the foretelling of the future'.[24] A similar attempt to reduce prophetic speech to a homiletic clone is found in W. Grudem's statement that 'prophecy of the type found in 1 Corinthians will not include any claims to divine authority (such as "thus says the Lord")'.[25]

All of these definitions of early Christian prophecy fall into the same error of taking Paul's terms for what prophecy should result in and making them a static definition of a dynamic manifestation. Does 1 Cor. 14.3 mean that prophecy cannot be prediction? Cannot prediction result in building up? Paul himself appears to think so when he tells the Thessalonians to comfort one another (παρακαλέω) on the basis of an eschatological forecast (1 Thess. 4.15-18).[26]

Even if we limit 1 Cor. 14.3 to describing the *function* rather than the *content* of early Christian prophecy, this is not adequate. For this does not take into account those examples of Christian prophecy where the paraenetic element is missing, or at best, secondary. This is true for the two Agabus oracles in Acts (11.28, 21.11) and for several of the prophetic oracles in Revelation 2–3. Even in 1 Corinthians 14

23. Hill, *Prophecy*, pp. 126-33; and 'Christian Prophets as Teachers or Instructors in the Church', in Panagopoulos, *Prophetic Vocation*, pp. 113-19, where he mentions many other scholars who have made similar statements relating prophecy and preaching. Cf. also R.J. Dillon and J.A. Grassi, *JBC*, II, pp. 173, 347.

24. H. Conzelmann, *1 Corinthians: A Commentary on the First Epistle to the Corinthians* (Philadelphia, 1975), p. 234 (cf. 243); likewise F.J. Leenhardt, 'Le prophète n'est pas l'homme des prédictions, mais de la prédication qui insère la Parole de Dieu dans l'existence d'une communauté', (quoted by Hill, 'Christian Prophets as Teachers', p. 114; on p. 118 n. 32 Hill states his agreement with Conzelmann).

25. Grudem, *Prophecy*, p. 229 (cf. also p. 67). The use of messenger formulas equivalent to 'Thus says the Lord' (e.g. 'Thus says the Spirit'), or other formulas claiming divine authority consistently accompany early Christian prophetic oracles. To say that this was not a feature of prophecy in the Pauline churches is an argument from silence. Note Acts 13.2; 21.11; Rev. 2.7, 11, 17, 29; 3.6, 13, 22; 14.3; 1 Tim. 4.1; Ign. *Phld.* 7.2; Aune, *Prophecy*, pp. 263-64, 328-30. Cf. Heb. 3.7; 2 Pet. 1.21.

26. While the origin of this 'λόγος κυρίου' is debated, Aune presents a good case for it being a Pauline revelation (*Prophecy*, pp. 253-56; cf. Boring, *Sayings*, p. 114).

itself, Paul discusses an application of prophecy in which the secrets of someone's heart are exposed before the gathered community (14.24-25). Here prophecy goes beyond exhortation or even warning and approaches judgment.[27] The prophets' role as vehicles for divine revelation was unpredictable and, at times, unconventional. Their duty was not to tailor their words to the social or spiritual expectations of their hearers, but to deliver God's message, regardless of the consequences. Thus, simply to portray early Christian prophets as inspired preachers is to institutionalize them.

3. Prophecy in the Post-Apostolic Church
If there is any one thing which characterizes the discussion of prophecy in post-apostolic literature, it is the increase of prophetic conflict. From the beginning, the problems associated with prophetic authority and its legitimacy were recognized and certain controls or procedures for testing a prophet were occasionally suggested.[28] But with the increase of false prophets, or in some cases competing brands of Christianity, the credibility of a prophet and his or her message came under greater scrutiny. The problem of the delay of the parousia, the crisis of 70 CE, and the gradual disappearance of the foundational figures of first generation Christianity were only some of the factors which led to a greater instability in this period and nurtured various new interpretations of Christianity.[29]

27. An unbeliever is the subject here. In Ign. *Phld.* 7.1-2, the work of the Spirit of prophecy as a revealer of secrets (τὰ κρυπτὰ ἐλέγχει) is connected with believers. Cf. Acts 5.3-5; 8.20-24; Aune, *Prophecy*, p. 292; Hill, *Prophecy*, pp. 124, 126-27; and 'Christian Prophets as Teachers', pp. 112-13 n. 13; Boring, *Sayings*, p. 118. However, this function of the prophetic Spirit is not unique to Christian circles, for in *Jos. Asen.* 22.13; 23.8; 26.6, Levi is portrayed as a prophet who 'used to read what was written in the heart of men' (*OTP*, II, p. 240); cf. Tertullian, *De Anima* 9.4.

28. It appears that there never was a universal early church procedure for evaluating prophets and their messages—even two generations after the beginning of Christianity. Where some chose moral or behavioural criteria (e.g. Paul in 1 Thess. 5.21; Matt. 7.15-20; *Did.* 11; Hermas, *Man.* 11; Rev. 2.20-22), others preferred doctrinal tests (e.g. Paul in 1 Cor. 12.3 and Rom. 12.6; 1 Jn 4.1-6). Cf. Aune, *Prophecy*, pp. 217-29; Grudem, *Prophecy*, pp. 62-66; Boring, *Sayings*, pp. 64-69.

29. W. Bauer, *Orthodoxy and Heresy in Earliest Christianity* (London, 1972),

In some cases theological conflicts led to new movements forming from a single community, as is seen in the Johannine epistles. In other cases, various factions seem to coexist within the community, as in Revelation 2–3; 2 Tim. 2.14-26; Matthew, and probably 2 Peter. The loose system of churches hosting visiting prophets, teachers and other itinerants hardly served to improve doctrinal continuity, and it is no wonder that church leaders gradually imposed stricter doctrinal and moral guidelines on itinerant charismatics. Some leaders, like Diotrephes of 3 John, simply refused to grant a hearing to those with whom they differed.[30] Others tried to discredit their opponents by depicting them as the eschatological fulfilment of the false prophets predicted in apocalyptic timetables. In this latter category, it is sometimes questionable whether those so accused actually ever claimed to be prophets or whether they are simply branded ψευδοπροφῆται because of their teaching.[31]

A case in point is 1 Jn 4.1-6. In discussions of Christian prophecy, these verses are generally taken to be John's test to distinguish true and false prophets.[32] But few commentators recognize that John's discussion here is contextually determined. Those whom the Elder labels 'false prophets' in 4.1 he also calls 'antichrists' in 2.18-22, and simply 'deceivers' in 2 John 7-10. In each case John is almost certainly referring to the same group of opponents, who are depicted as the

esp. pp. 77-103, 212-15; S.G.F. Brandon, *The Fall of Jerusalem and the Christian Church* (London, 1957), pp. 249-51; H. Conzelmann, *Primitive Christianity* (London, 1973), pp. 122-26. See more generally J.D.G. Dunn's response to Bauer's work, *Unity and Diversity in the New Testament* (London, 1977); and J.L. McKenzie, *JBC*, II, p. 105.

30. Cf. R. Brown, *The Epistles of John* (AB, 30; London, 1982), pp. 715-20; and the interesting discussion of A.J. Malherbe, 'The Inhospitality of Diotrephes', in *God's Christ and his People: Studies in Honour of Nils Alstrup Dahl* (ed. J. Jervell and W.A. Meeks; Oslo, 1977), pp. 222-32, though he argues against any recognized leadership role for Diotrephes.

31. The use of such polemical tags is often indicative of a specific theological and social conflict, depending on the opposition group whom the writer wishes to warn his readers about. They are rarely incidental general warnings—'By the way, if you happen to encounter any false prophets...' Cf. Aune, *Prophecy*, p. 229; Boring, *Sayings*, pp. 118-20.

32. B. Vawter, *JBC*, II, p. 410; Ellis, 'Prophecy in the New Testament Church', p. 52; J. Panagopoulos, 'Die urchristliche Prophetie: Ihr Charakter und ihre Funktion', in Panagopoulos, *Prophetic Vocation*, pp. 19-20, 27; Grudem, *Prophecy*, p. 283; Hill, *Prophecy*, p. 151; Aune, *Prophecy*, pp. 224-25.

embodiment of eschatological evil (2.18-26).

Rather, it appears that 1 Jn 4.1-6 is not specifically concerned with prophets and the testing of their oracles within the community, but with true and false doctrine, through whatever medium it is received. It is rooted in the dualistic concept of a cosmic spiritual battle in which every true doctrine comes from the Spirit of God, while every false teaching is a 'doctrine of demons'.[33] The true doctrine which forms the basis of John's test in 4.1-6 is determined by the theological deficiencies of his specific opponents and therefore would serve only a limited function in testing prophets in general. John's main concern is to legitimate his own teaching and to keep his community's focus sharp on what separates them from their former brethren.[34]

The remaining literary sources of the post-apostolic period which contain significant information on Christian prophecy are Matthew, Revelation, the *Didache*, and the *Shepherd of Hermas*. Of these four, Revelation will be treated separately, and *Hermas* only incidentally.[35]

Matthew is of particular interest because of redactional elements which suggest that the issue of Christian prophets and their role was of special concern to the writer and his community. Many scholars have noted Matthew's inclination to present the disciples as prophets rather than apostles.[36] More debatable is whether Matthew, in depicting

33. 1 Tim. 4.1-2; Ign. *Eph.* 16–17; cf. Rev. 13.2, 11; 16.13-14; C. Spicq, *Les Epitres Pastorales* (Paris, 4th edn, 1969), pp. 495-96; R. Schnackenberg, 'Zum Begriff der "Warheit" in den beiden kleinen Johannesbriefen', *BZ* N.F. 11 (1967), pp. 253-58.

34. Aune (*Prophecy*, pp. 224-25) recognizes the problems raised by John's polemical intentions and language, but decides that 'the polemic in 1 John 4.1-3, 6 is leveled against those prophets who *lend support to the deviant form of teaching opposed by the Elder through prophetic utterances*' (emphasis Aune's). Cf. Brown, *Epistles*, pp. 489-91, 496-506.

35. For a detailed discussion of prophecy in *Hermas*, see J. Reiling, *Hermas and Christian Prophecy: A Study of the Eleventh Mandate* (Leiden, 1973). While the growing formalization of office and canon in the second century contributed to the quenching of the dynamic spirit of prophecy and its vital place in the worship service, prophetic activity in the churches continued well after the testimony of Hermas. Note Justin Martyr, *Dial.* 82, 'For the prophetical gifts remain with us, even to the present time' (*ANL*, II, p. 202); similarly Irenaeus, *Adv. Haer.* 2.32.4; 3.11.9; 5.6.1; *Dem.* 99; Eus. *H.E.* 4.18.8. See further Ash, 'Decline', pp. 227-36.

36. A comparison of the mission charges in Mt. 10.1-42 and 28.16-20 with the closing words of the woe discourse of 23.34-39 seems to make this clear. Cf. P. Minear, 'False Prophecy and Hypocrisy in the Gospel of Matthew', in *Neues*

the disciples as prophets, adapts imagery and traditions associated with the Christian prophets of his own day.[37] Rather than draw inferences from these doubtful connections, we will focus our attention on other passages.

Mt. 7.15-20 contains a warning to the community against false prophets and criteria for recognizing them. In this section Matthew has taken over a logion about discerning good and bad fruit in general and applied it to a specific context of discerning false prophets. This is accomplished by the redactional addition of v. 15.[38] The passage betrays Matthew's opinion that some of those who exercise prophetic gifts within the community are hypocrites, whose inner spiritual poverty cannot be deduced from the outward manifestation of their gifts.

If the following section of Mt. 7.21-23 is meant to complement 7.15-20, an even clearer picture emerges of the prophetic conflicts with which Matthew is concerned.[39] These false prophets are recognized

Testament und Kirche (ed. J. Gnilka; Freiburg, 1974), pp. 76-78; E. Cothenet, 'Les prophètes chrétiens dans l'Evangile selon saint Matthieu', in *L'Evangile selon Matthieu: Rédaction et théologie* (ed. M. Didier; Gembloux, 1972), pp. 293-99; A. Sand, *Das Gesetz und die Propheten: Untersuchungen zur Theologie des Evangeliums nach Matthäus* (Regensburg, 1974), pp. 168-77; Boring, *Sayings*, pp. 45-46; Aune, *Prophecy*, pp. 214-15.

    37. But note the discussion of Minear, 'False Prophecy', pp. 76-93; Cothenet, 'Les prophètes chrétiens', pp. 299, 306-307; Boring, *Sayings*, pp. 46-47, 63-64; E. Schweizer, 'Observance of the Law and Charismatic Activity in Matthew', *NTS* 16 (1969-70), pp. 219-21.

    38. Only a few of the many treatments of this passage can be cited: D. Hill, 'False Prophets and Charismatics: Structure and Interpretation in Matthew 7.15-23', *Bib* 57 (1976), pp. 327-48 [who gives a useful review of the literature]; M. Krämer, 'Hütet euch vor den falschen Propheten. Eine überlieferungsgeschichtliche Untersuchung zu Mt. 7, 15-23/Lk. 6, 43-46/Mt. 12.33-37', *Bib* 57 (1976), pp. 349-77'; Minear, 'False Prophecy', pp. 80-86; Aune, *Prophecy*, pp. 222-24; Cothenet, 'Les prophètes chrétiens', pp. 299-305.

    39. Admittedly, the emphasis shifts in v. 21 from a specific application to prophets (vv. 15-20), to charismatic activity in general (vv. 21-23), though the exorcism and mighty works of v. 22 are characteristics associated with Matthew's disciple-prophets in Mt. 10.8. But this is partly traceable to Matthew's adaptation of existing materials. It is unlikely that Matthew's redaction of Q material in vv. 21-23 (Lk. 13.25-27) is to be separated in purpose from his editorial addition of v. 15 to vv. 16-20. See further Minear, 'False Prophecy', p. 82; Aune, *Prophecy*, p. 223; Boring, *Sayings*, pp. 43, 208; Cothenet, 'Les prophètes chrétiens', p. 300;

Christian prophets who speak in Christ's name (v. 22), but whom Matthew characterizes as those who bear no fruit or bad fruit (vv. 17-19), who do not do God's will (v. 21) and who are evildoers (v. 23).

Attempts to discover more precisely what opponents Matthew has in mind here—if a specific adversary is even in view—have not generally been deemed successful.[40] Equally vague is how such a test was to be practically applied. We are left in the dark as to what bad fruit Matthew has in mind, though of course this is somewhat determined by his adaptation of an existing logion which could be equally as vague in whatever context it might appear.[41]

Perhaps part of the answer lies in seeing a relationship between this passage and the predictions concerning false prophets in Matthew 24. Besides a reference to false christs and false prophets in 24.24 which he has taken over from his Markan source (Mk 13.22), Matthew adds a second mention of false prophets alone in 24.11: 'And many false prophets will arise and lead many astray'. He connects this proliferation of false prophets with a time of trouble and persecution in the church, when the community is beset with various internal conflicts (24.9-12).

If the Matthean addition of 24.10-12 reflects the circumstances of the writer's community, as some have suggested, it is likely that these verses provide a background to Matthew's discussion of false prophets in ch. 7.[42] While this connection brings us no closer to identifying the false prophets themselves, it does perhaps shed some light on the extent of influence which these prophets had within the community. Those whom Matthew depicts as 'ravenous wolves' appear to be successful in leading many astray. And, as with other Christian

R.A. Guelich, *The Sermon on the Mount* (Waco, 1982), pp. 383-85, 397-98; *contra* Hill, 'False Prophets', pp. 327-30.

40. Guelich lists the various views (*Sermon*, p. 391). I would agree with Schweizer against the popular opinion that they are Pharisees, for these opponents 'are certainly Christians' ('Observance', pp. 216-17), although we cannot rule out altogether a group of Christian Pharisees.

41. Minear, 'False Prophecy', p. 81.

42. W.G. Thompson, 'An Historical Perspective in the Gospel of Matthew', *JBL* 93 (1974), pp. 243-63; E. Schweizer, *Matthäus und seine Gemeinde* (Stuttgart, 1974), p. 127; G. Stanton, *The Interpretation of Matthew* (London, 1983), p. 120 n. 18; Guelich, *Sermon*, p. 391; Cothenet, 'Les prophètes chrétiens', pp. 302-303; Aune, *Prophecy*, p. 223; Hill, 'False Prophets', pp. 334-36, 339.

writers, he sees these false prophets as the fulfilment of eschatological prophecy.

That the test which Matthew provides is based on moral rather than doctrinal grounds may suggest that the divisions caused by these rival Christian prophets had no clear theological definition. But it is more likely that the test of behaviour is meant to be a warning against the teaching of the prophets. Matthew is telling them how to identify *false* prophets, not true prophets with spiritual problems.

Matthew's test for prophets in 7.15-23 appears to provide the inspiration for the prophetic code of ethics contained in *Did.* 11.8, 'But not everyone who speaks in a spirit is a prophet, except he have the behaviour of the Lord. From his behaviour, then, the false prophet and the true prophet shall be known.' The final phrase is simply a passive paraphrase of Mt. 7.16a.[43]

Mt. 7.16a	*Did.* 11.8
ἀπὸ τῶν καρπῶν αὐτῶν	ἀπὸ οὖν τῶν τρόπων γνωσθήσεται
ἐπιγνώσεσθε αὐτούς	ὁ ψευδοπροφήτης καὶ ὁ προφήτης

Having established behaviour as the basis for testing prophets, the *Didache* goes on to translate this into practical procedures by which the community can evaluate prophets and their utterances. For example, if a prophet orders a meal in a spirit, or anything else for his own personal benefit, he is a false prophet (11.9, 12). Likewise, any prophet who speaks the truth but does not do it is to be rejected (11.10).

Yet despite all these cautions, the *Didache* holds prophets in high regard, and its testimony with regard to the sociological and cultic role of early Christian prophets is invaluable. In 10.7 we find that the prophets often provided the benediction to the Eucharist while in the

---

43. Scholars are divided on the question of the *Didache*'s use of written Gospel sources. W. Rordorf and A. Tuilier agree with Köster, Audet and Glover that the *Didache* uses no NT exemplar (*La doctrine des douze apôtres* [SC, 248; Paris, 1978], p. 91). Yet almost all of these scholars admit that the *Didache* contains many parallels with traditions peculiar to Matthew. The many allusions of language and subject matter, plus the explicit statement in *Did.* 11.3 that the guidelines for receiving apostles and prophets should be 'according to the teaching of the Gospel' (κατὰ τὸ δόγμα τοῦ εὐαγγελίου, cf. also 8.2) suggest, in my opinion, a knowledge and use of a redacted form of Matthew. See further J.M. Court, 'The Didache and St Matthew's Gospel', *SJT* 34 (1981), pp. 109-20; E. Massaux, *Influence de l'Evangile de saint Matthieu sur la littérature chrétienne avant saint Irénée* (Gembloux, 1950), pp. 604-46.

Spirit.[44] And *Did.* 13.1-7 states that prophets who desire to settle in the community are to be held in honour as the *high priests* (ἀρχιερεῖς 13.3) of that community, and thus are to receive the firstfruits of all possessions in appreciation for their ministry (cf. 15.1-2). This cultic role is important to keep in mind for the subsequent evaluation of John's prophetic status among the Asian churches, particularly in view of his emphasis on believers as priests.

One final passage reveals much concerning the kind of authority and inspiration associated with prophetic speech. *Did.* 11.7 warns, 'Do not test or examine any prophet who is speaking in a spirit, "for every sin shall be forgiven, but this sin shall not be forgiven"'. Here the difficult logion of the unpardonable sin, taken from Mt. 12.31, is interpreted to mean blasphemy of the Spirit when it speaks through a prophet.[45] The utterances themselves were not to be tested in case one might accidentally call the Holy Spirit into question. This caution perhaps accounts for the *Didache*'s strong emphasis on a prophets' behaviour as an indicator of the genuineness of their speech.

B. *John as a Jewish-Christian Prophet*

Introduction
Despite the growing mass of literature which deals with the genre of Apocalypse in general, and the Book of Revelation in particular, the question of what to call the visions of John of Patmos has been and

---

44. K. Lake translates 10.7, 'But suffer the prophets to hold Eucharist as they will' (*The Apostolic Fathers* (LCL; London, 1912), I, p. 325). His rendering of 'εὐχαριστεῖν' assumes that prophets sometimes presided over the Eucharist and adopted their own distinctive liturgy. But while 'to hold Eucharist' is a possible translation of εὐχαριστεῖν in 10.7, the more common rendering is 'to give thanks'. If the latter is adopted, the Didachist is exempting prophets from strict adherence to the formal Eucharistic benediction which he suggested in 10.1-6, and allowing them more charismatic freedom (cf. 1 Cor. 14.6). Such an interpretation is accepted by Aune, *Prophecy*, p. 209; R.A. Kraft, 'Barnabas and Didache', in *The Apostolic Fathers: A Translation and Commentary* (ed. R.M. Grant; New York, 1965), III, pp. 168-69; cf. J.-P. Audet, 'Literary Forms and Contents of a Normal εὐχαριστία in the First Century', *TU* 73 (1959), pp. 643-62.
45. Aune, *Prophecy*, pp. 225-26; Boring, *Sayings*, pp. 162-63, and 'The Unforgivable Sin Logion Mark III 28-29 (Matt. XII 31-32/Luke XII 10): Formal Analysis and History of Tradition', *NovT* 18 (1976), pp. 258-79.

remains a divided issue.[46] In determining the message of this book, too much weight has sometimes been placed on John's use of apocalyptic tradition and not enough on his self-understanding as a prophet.[47] While the apocalyptic character of Revelation should not be underestimated, it must be kept in mind that John's use of previous prophetic and apocalyptic tradition is almost exclusively limited to the OT.[48] Unlike his contemporary, the apocalyptist of *4 Ezra*, who values the '70' esoteric books more highly than the '24' common works (14.42-47, cf. v. 26), John's theological and eschatological concepts are firmly rooted in the OT, which he clearly regards as the prime locus of God's revelation. His exploitation of apocalyptic device and symbol may provide the colour, but it does not always necessarily provide the fabric of his message. John is not only concerned with

46. J.J. Collins, 'Pseudonymity, Historical Reviews and the Genre of the Revelation of John', *CBQ* 39 (1977), pp. 329-43; J. Kallas, 'The Apocalypse—An Apocalyptic Book?', *JBL* 86 (1967), pp. 69-80; B.W. Jones, 'More about the Apocalypse as Apocalyptic', *JBL* 87 (1968), pp. 325-27; E. Schüssler Fiorenza, 'Composition and Structure of the Book of Revelation', *CBQ* 39 (1977), pp. 344-66; J.L. Blevins, 'The Genre of Revelation', *RevExp* 77 (1980), pp. 393-408; D. Hellholm, 'The Problem of Apocalyptic Genre and the Apocalypse of John', [bibliog.], in *SBLASP* 21 (1982), pp. 157-98.

47. J. Roloff comments, 'Die Forschung der letzten 100 Jahre war so einseitig auf die Zusammenhänge zwischen der Offenbarung und den jüdischen Apokalypsen fixiert, dass sie einen anderen Aspekt völlig ausser acht liess', *Die Offenbarung des Johannes* (Zürich, 1984), p. 15. Roloff mentions in particular the epistolary character of Revelation, and to this might be added liturgical, mythical, and dramatic elements. However, it is John's prophetic consciousness and the relation of prophecy to apocalyptic in Revelation which is fundamental to the question of its literary genre, as Schüssler Fiorenza rightly observes ('Composition', pp. 352-58). Further helpful discussions of this issue are found in W. Hadorn, *Die Offenbarung des Johannes* (THKNT, 18; Leipzig, 1928), pp. 8-9; A. Wikenhauser, *Die Offenbarung des Johannes* (RNT, 9; Regensburg, 3rd edn, 1959), pp. 10-11; L. Morris, *Apocalyptic* (Grand Rapids, 1972), pp. 91-95; and esp. Schüssler Fiorenza, *Revelation*, pp. 133-56.

48. M. Kiddle and M.K. Ross, among others, have noted that there are no conclusive allusions to non-canonical Jewish apocalyptic books (*The Revelation of St John* [London, 1940], p. xxviii). But John does adopt shared apocalyptic traditions not found in the OT: e.g. the figure of blood flowing as high as a horse's bridle (Rev. 14.20; *1 En.* 100.3; *4 Ezra* 15.35), and chains prepared for Satan (Rev. 20.3; *1 En.* 53.3-3; 54.3-5; *2 Bar.* 56.13; Jude 6; 2 Pet. 2.4). Cf. A. Farrer, *A Rebirth of Images* (Glasgow, 1948), p. 19.

images, but with promises, and their fulfilment.[49]

Having said this, it is certainly not my intention in this study to displace the apocalyptic elements of Revelation, but only to give John's prophetic consciousness the emphasis it deserves. Scholarly arguments which attempt to categorically label Revelation as either apocalyptic or prophetic (e.g. Collins, Kallas, Jones and others) are misguided, as Schüssler Fiorenza and Boring have rightly observed.[50] Roloff's conclusion approaches the right balance: 'Die Offenbarung ist ein prophetisches Schreiben, das zahlreiche apokalyptische Motive und Stilelement enthält, dessen Form aber vorwiegend durch den Zweck brieflicher Kommunikation geprägt ist'.[51]

1. *John's Sphere of Prophetic Authority*
John's Status in the Churches
John's vocation as a prophet was inseparably connected with the life of local gatherings of Christian believers. The message of John through the Spirit is for the churches. Besides the seven letters themselves, both the prelude and epilogue emphasize this fact (Rev. 1.4, 11, 20; 22.16).

Furthermore, the attachment of an epistle format to the visions, along with the personal identification of John, lifts the book out of the realm of the pseudonymous apocalypses and places it within the context of real churches with specific problems in a fairly limited local setting.[52] With the faithful of these communities John counts himself a

49. Schüssler Fiorenza remarks, 'The apocalyptic language and imagery of the book serve prophetic interpretation' ('Composition', p. 358; cf. also pp. 356-57). Cf. J.M. Schmidt, *Die jüdische Apokalyptic* (Neukirchen, 1969), pp. 96-97; Boring, *Sayings*, pp. 27-28; Aune, *Prophecy*, pp. 274-75. Note also the major commentary of H. Kraft, *Die Offenbarung des Johannes* (Tübingen, 1974), who tends to subordinate John's apocalyptic influence to his prophetic purpose; cf. Boring, *Sayings*, pp. 126-27.

50. 'Composition', p. 356; *Sayings*, pp. 27-28.

51. *Offenbarung*, p. 16.

52. The epistolary framework of Revelation is hardly a 'secondary' or 'superficial' element, as A. Yarbro Collins suggests, *The Combat Myth in the Book of Revelation* (HDR, 9; Missoula, 1976), pp. 5-8; cf. Roloff, *Offenbarung*, pp. 15-16; Schüssler Fiorenza, 'Composition', p. 366. For the relationship of epistle formats to apocalyptic in general, see K. Berger, 'Apostelbrief und Apostoliche Rede—Zum Formular Frühchristlicher Briefe', *ZNW* 65–66 (1974–75), pp. 207-19; and to Revelation in particular, M. Karrer, *Die Johannesoffenbarung als Brief: Studien zu ihrem literarischen, historischen, und theologischen Ort* (Göttingen, 1986). The problem of composite literary genre, particularly involving epistolary and apocalyptic

brother, a fellow-sharer, and a priest in God's kingdom (1.4-6, 9). His detailed knowledge of the geographical, historical, political and religious circumstances of the Asian churches reflects a longstanding association with these communities and suggests that he served as a sort of circuit prophet rather than an itinerant.[53]

The question of John's official status among the churches is more difficult to answer, and complicated by the fact that he omits any references to local church officials, unless of course one understands the ἄγγελοι of the seven churches to represent such leaders.[54] Because of this silence, and John's high opinion of prophets as a special class of God's servants, some scholars have suggested that he functioned as the prophetic shepherd of these congregations, or that he was a master prophet within a local band of prophets.[55]

The main objection to such a theory is that it would seem to conflict with the testimony of Pauline tradition and the letters of Ignatius that by this period (late first century CE) the church order of Asia Minor

elements, is also found in the Coptic *Apocryphon of James* (and other Gnostic works); cf. F.E. Williams in *Nag Hammadi Codex I: Introduction, Texts, Translations, Indices* (ed. H.W. Attridge; Leiden, 1985), pp. 17-20; Aune, *Prophecy*, p. 72.

53. Note esp. C.J. Hemer, *The Letters to the Seven Churches of Asia in their Local Setting* (JSNTSup, 11; Sheffield, 1986); H.B. Swete, *The Apocalypse of St John* (London, 3rd edn, 1911), pp. ccxvii-ccxviii. On the question of itinerancy, see Aune, *Prophecy*, pp. 212-15; Boring, *Sayings*, pp. 58-59; Schüssler Fiorenza, *Revelation*, pp. 144-45. The oracle of judgment against the prophetess 'Jezebel' in Rev. 2.20-23 implies that a previous prophetic warning had been issued by John (v. 21), and the evidence of the letters in general to ongoing conflicts between John and various interest groups further reinforces the assumption that he had taken up prophetic residency among the Asian churches. Cf. Schüssler Fiorenza, *Revelation*, pp. 144-45; Aune, *Prophecy*, p. 278; Roloff, *Offenbarung*, p. 57.

54. Aune, *Prophecy*, p. 205; on the interpretation of the ἄγγελοι in Rev. 2-3, see A.T. Nikolainen, 'Der Kirchenbegriff in der Offenbarung des Johannes', *NTS* 9 (1962-63), p. 353; Hemer, *Letters*, pp. 32-34; Schüssler Fiorenza, *Revelation*, pp. 145-46. This and related questions concerning church leaders and structure are covered in more detail in the influential study of A. Satake, *Die Gemeindeordnung in der Johannesapokalypse* (WMANT, 21: Neukirchen, 1966).

55. Hill, *Prophecy*, pp. 87-88; Boring, *Sayings*, p. 29; Schüssler Fiorenza, *Revelation*, pp. 106-108. Aune (*Prophecy*, pp. 206-208) is hesitant to accord John any leadership role, but cf. pp. 197-98. In another article ('Prophecy and Prophets in the Revelation of St John', *NTS* 18 [1971-72], pp. 401-18, 415-16), Hill goes a little too far in emphasizing John's unique relationship to the community. See the comments of Grudem, *Prophecy*, p. 106; Aune, *Prophecy*, pp. 206-207.

was episcopal rather than prophetic in nature. But in fact, the evidence from both Ignatius and the Didache indicates that authority structures and patterns of church office at the end of the first century were as yet neither fixed nor uniform. While there was certainly a movement towards an established ecclesiastical hierarchy, the authority of the bishop and deacon had not yet everywhere supplanted that of the prophet and teacher.[56] Even if such a process had begun already in John's day, it is not thereby necessary to conclude that this involved a transition from a charismatic to a non-charismatic form of leadership. Could not a leading community prophet become a bishop, or a bishop exercise prophetic gifts? The association of prophetic gifts with recognized church officials, particularly bishops, is not uncommon even in the second century. Ignatius himself includes several prophetic oracles in his letters, and both Polycarp of Smyrna and Melito of Sardis display prophetic qualities.[57]

Whether or not John himself exercised such a dual role among the Asian churches is more debatable. In any case, he understands himself first and foremost as a prophet and takes very seriously the responsibility of his calling in relation to the seven churches. And his isolation on Patmos 'for the word of God' may be indicative of the high profile which he maintained within the Christian communities of Asia Minor.[58]

56. Schüssler Fiorenza, *Revelation*, pp. 140-46.

57. Ash, 'Decline', pp. 234-36; Schüssler Fiorenza, *Revelation*, p. 143; Aune, *Prophecy*, pp. 196, 291-96. In 1 Tim. 1.18 and 4.14, church elders are also associated with prophetic gifts. Clement of Alexandria relates an oral tradition he received from others concerning John the Apostle, who, after returning from Patmos to Ephesus, 'used to journey by request to the neighbouring districts of the Gentiles, in some places to appoint bishops, in others to regulate whole churches, in others to set among the clergy some one man, it may be, of those indicated by the Spirit'. Leaving aside the problem of the identification of this John with the Apostle, the tradition mediated by Clement upholds a regional or circuit ministry for an Asian figure by the name of John, who also possessed charismatic abilities. G.W. Butterworth, *Clement of Alexandria* (LCL; London, 1939), p. 357. The pointing out of potential church leaders by means of the gift of prophecy is found also in 1 Tim. 1.18.

58. Hemer rightly emphasizes that the tradition of John's political banishment (*relegatio*) to Patmos is probably no more than an inference from Rev. 1.9 (*Letters*, pp. 27-29). But it is still a likely interpretation. The assertion made by many commentators (e.g. Beckwith, Charles, Brütsch) that Patmos is specifically mentioned by the elder Pliny (*H.N.* 4.12.23) as a place of banishment is in error. Cf. G.B. Caird, *A Commentary on the Revelation of St John the Divine* (New York and London, 1966), pp. 21-22.

Cultic Prophecy and Apocalyptic Vision
As was emphasized earlier, the natural habitat of the early Christian prophet was the gathered community. And this is no exception in John's case, even though he is physically separated from the intended recipients of his oracles. The influence of early Christian worship on John's thought is evident throughout his book, which is saturated with hymnic and liturgical elements.[59] His visions are set within the context of the heavenly sanctuary, complete with temple imagery and a divine service. This cosmic worship setting is the heavenly counterpart to the cultic activity of the gathered earthly community. Both spheres ultimately coalesce to form the eschatological priesthood and temple which unites the worshiping community with the glorious presence of God. It is no accident then that John's prophecy for the churches receives its inspiration on the Lord's day (Rev. 1.10), when the community would be gathered for worship, for it contributes to the legitimation and authority of the message and partially compensates for his physical absence.[60]

John's isolation from the community also brings to attention another question concerning the content of his book and its reception by the churches. As a prophet, how would he have mediated his visions orally in a cultic setting? Certainly the prophetic letters to the seven churches in Revelation 2 and 3, and possibly some isolated oracles, reflect the more typical sort of prophetic speech, and it is not hard to imagine John standing up among the believers and relaying such oracles 'in the Spirit'. But the vision(s) of Revelation 4–22 (at least in their present form) could hardly have been given in a cultic setting. There is little reported precedent for such a lengthy apocalyptic prophecy being related directly in the assembly, and the public revelation of private apocalyptic experiences in general is frowned upon by various early Christian writers.

When Paul mentions his own apocalyptic encounter in 2 Cor. 12.1-4

---

59. M.H. Shepherd, *The Paschal Liturgy and the Apocalypse* (London, 1960), pp. 77-97; P. Prigent, *Apocalypse et liturgie* (CT, 52; Neuchâtel, 1964); S. Lauchli, 'Eine Gottesdienstruktur in der Johannesoffenbarung', *TZ* 16 (1960), pp. 359-78; L. Thompson, 'Cult and Eschatology in the Apocalypse of John', *JR* 49 (1969), pp. 330-50.

60. Boring, *Sayings*, p. 69; Hill, *Prophecy*, p. 90; but J. Panagopoulos goes beyond the evidence when he states that John probably received his visions 'während der Eucharistie-versammlung' ('Die urchristliche Prophetie', p. 22).

he acknowledges that the content of such visions could not be adequately communicated to others and appears to conclude that this revelation was received for personal rather than corporate benefit.[61] Col. 2.18 likewise warns against those who would want to regulate the beliefs and behaviour of others on the basis of their private visionary experiences.[62] Ignatius of Antioch, who is not shy about proclaiming his own prophetic gifts, writes in his letter to the Trallians that sharing his own revelations of heavenly mysteries with them would be inappropriate, and remarks, 'Am I not able to write to you heavenly things? Yes, but I am afraid that I should do you harm "seeing you are babes"' (*Trall.* 5.1; cf. 4.1–5.2).[63]

Perhaps the most relevant parallel is found in the *Shepherd of Hermas*. This work by a Christian visionary in the church at Rome encompasses a series of revelations spanning a period from about 100 to 140 CE.[64] When Hermas discusses Christian prophecy in *Mandate* 11, the locus of prophetic revelation is plainly described as the gathered community.[65] Yet Hermas' own apocalyptic visions always

61. This judgment is confirmed by Paul's statement earlier in 2 Cor. 5.13, εἴτε γὰρ ἐξέστημεν, θεῷ. While some scholars understand this verse in the context of Paul's sanity, see the detailed discussion of R. Bultmann, who comments, 'Insofar as he [Paul] experiences ecstasies, he has them for himself and God alone (1 Cor. 14.2, 18-19!)', *The Second Letter to the Corinthians* (Minneapolis, 1985), pp. 149-50; cf. A.T. Lincoln, *Paradise Now and Not Yet* (Cambridge, 1981), pp. 71-86; H. Saake, 'Paulus als Ekstatiker', *NovT* 15 (1973), pp. 153-60; R.P. Spittler, 'The Limits of Ecstasy: An Exegesis of 2 Corinthians 12.1-10', in *Current Issues in Biblical and Patristic Interpretation* (ed. G.F. Hawthorne; Grand Rapids, 1975), pp. 259-66; C. Rowland, *The Open Heaven* (London, 1982), pp. 379-86. But one might well ask why Paul chose to keep this vision private, while other revelations were made public (cf. Gal. 1.12, 16; Eph. 3.3; Acts 16.9)?

62. F.O. Francis, 'Humility and Angelic Worship in Col. 2.18', in *Conflict at Colossae* (ed. F.O. Francis and W.A. Meeks; Missoula, 1975), pp. 173-76; E. Schweizer, *The Letter to the Colossians* (London, 1982), pp. 160-62.

63. Lake, *Apostolic Fathers*, I, p. 217; cf. W.R. Schoedel, *Ignatius of Antioch* (Herm; Philadelphia, 1985), p. 143-45; Aune, *Prophecy*, p. 294; C. Trevett, 'Prophecy and Anti-Episcopal Activity: A Third Error Combatted by Ignatius?', *JEH* 34 (1983), pp. 5-13.

64. Reiling, *Hermas*, pp. 22-24; Aune, *Prophecy*, p. 299; Boring, *Sayings*, pp. 50-51.

65. The true prophet receives his inspiration in the assembly and 'speaks to the congregation as the Lord wills' (*Mand.* 11.9); the false prophet avoids the righteous assembly and 'prophecies to [men] in a corner' (11.13).

take place in private, usually following fasting and prayer.[66] As in John's case, Hermas is told to write down the visions and send copies to other churches, while he himself is to read the visions to the Roman church 'along with the elders that preside over the church'.[67] On the basis of these two different descriptions Reiling recognizes a contrast between the revelatory process of Hermas's visions and the community prophet described in *Mand.* 11. He concludes that Hermas is a 'visionary', not a 'word-prophet', and argues that such a distinction was clearly understood by Hermas himself.[68]

While there is little or no evidence in early Christianity for vocational or titular distinctions between so-called 'word prophets' and 'visionaries',[69] there does appear to be some justification for believing that *visions* and *prophecy* were recognized as two different types of revelatory phenomena.[70] It may be granted that, from a phenomenological point of view, such a distinction must not be unduly pressed, for the experiential boundary between the two manifestations

Cf. also 11.14, Reiling, *Hermas*, pp. 122-23.

66. *Vis.* 2.2.1; 3.1.2; 3.10.6-7; *Sim.* 5.1.1-3; cf. Reiling, *Hermas*, pp. 163-64. Fasting and prayer are common acts of piety which prelude visions: Dan. 9.3, 20-23; *4 Ezra* 5.13, 20; 6.31, 35; 9.23-28; 12.50; *Apoc. Ab.* 9.7-10; 12.1-2; *3 Bar.* 4.14-15; *Gr. Apoc. Ezra* 1.1-5; *T. Isaac* 4.1-8; *Hist. Rech.* 1.1-5; cf. Acts 13.1-3.

67. *Vis.* 2.4.3; cf. also 2.1.4; 3.8.10-11; 4.3.6; 5.5-7; *Sim.* 10.2.2-4; Reiling, *Hermas*, p. 161. On visionaries recording their own revelations, see H. Weinel, *Die Wirkungen des Geistes und der Geister im nachapostolischen Zeitalter bis auf Irenäus* (Freiburg, 1899), pp. 103-105; Aune, *Prophecy*, pp. 330-31. Cf. Rev. 10.4.

68. *Hermas*, pp. 155-70, esp. 156-57, 163-64, 169-70.

69. Cf. Schüssler Fiorenza, *Revelation*, pp. 139-40.

70. In the *Passio Perpetuae*, a North-African martyrdom account (c. 200 CE), the distinction between prophecies and visions is clearly maintained, 'So too we hold in honor and acknowledge not only new prophecies but new visions as well' (1.5) [*visiones* (5a) = *revelationum* (5b) = Gr. MS ἀποκαλύψεων); H. Musurillo, *The Acts of the Christian Martyrs* (Oxford, 1972), p. 106. The *Apocryphon of James* relates that although prophecy ended with John the Baptist (6.21–7.1), apocalyptic visions are still possible (15.5-25). In 1 Cor. 14.6 Paul appears to mention ἀποκάλυψις and προφητεία as separate gifts manifested in the community, but the context of ἀποκάλυψις here (and in vv. 26, 30) is revelation in general, not apocalyptic visions in particular. Note D. Lührmann, *Das Offenbarungverständnis bei Paulus und in Paulinischen Gemeinden* (WMANT, 16; Neukirchen, 1965), p. 39, 'Die scheinbar näheliegende Interpretation dieses Charismas im Sinn der ekstatischen Offenbarungsvision von 2 Kor. 12.1, 7 erweist sich als unmöglich'. *Contra*: Schüssler Fiorenza, *Revelation*, p. 151; cf. Grudem, *Prophecy*, pp. 138-39.

is arguably fluid, with elements of one at times crossing over into the other. Nevertheless, it is still possible to discern a general pattern of contrasting characteristics.

1. *Revelatory Setting*. Vision experiences are typically presented as private affairs in which the recipient, either by chance or design, is isolated from other individuals and the community of faith. Early Christian prophetic speech, on the other hand, is generally conceived of as an activity which takes place within a context of social and cultic interaction. Both types of revelation may be shared with the church, but the 'word-' prophet's inspiration and utterance comes in the course of community worship,[71] while the 'visionary' experiences a private revelation which he records or remembers and subsequently mediates to the gathered saints.[72] This does not mean, however, that the prophet's message was always extemporaneous, or delivered in an ecstatic state, or that visions were never received during a worship service or in the company of others.[73] But such variations appear to be the exception rather than the rule.

71. Acts 11.28; 1 Cor. 14.24-25, 29-33; Ign. *Phil.* 7.1-2; *Did.* 11.7-12; *Asc. Isa.* 6.6-9a; Herm. *Mand.* 11.9-15.

72. Acts 10.9–11.18; ?Col. 2.18; Rev. 1.9-11; Herm. *Vis.* 1–4; *Pass. Perp.* 11.1; 14.1; 16.1.

73. OT prophets commonly received auditions privately and then related them publicly with the addition of a messenger formula. Visions experienced in a group setting are found in Ezek. 8.1–11.24a (followed by a vision-report in 11.24b-25); *Asc. Isa.* 6.10-17 (followed by a vision-report in chs. 7–11); Tertullian *De Anima* 9.4 (c. 210–213 CE), 'We have now amongst us a sister whose lot it has been to be favoured with sundry gifts of revelation, which she experiences in the Spirit by ecstatic vision amidst the sacred rites of the Lord's Day in the church: she converses with angels, and sometimes even with the Lord; she both sees and hears mysterious communications. Whether it be in the reading of the scriptures, or in the chanting of psalms, or in the preaching of sermons, or in the offering up of prayers, in all these religious services matter and opportunity are afforded to her of seeing visions'. The most significant aspect of this account is not that such visions come during the worship service, but that they were only shared *after* the service had finished, 'After the people are dismissed at the conclusion of the sacred services, she is in the regular habit of reporting to us whatever things she may have seen in vision' (ANCL, XV.2, pp. 427-28). The account of Kenaz relating his own vision while in ecstasy found in *LAB* 28.6-10, though irregular, may reflect contemporary visionary experience. But the change from present to past tense in the vision-report renders the example somewhat suspect. One might compare with this the trance experiences of some Merkabah mystics (*Hekalot Rabbati* 18.4, cf. P.S. Alexander, *OTP*, I, p. 234).

2. *Revelatory State.* While the prophet can be the immediate channel for divine speech and retains a certain measure of self-awareness and control, the visionary experiences such an altered state of being that often any personal consciousness, let alone a consciousness of others in the earthly sphere, is precluded. So Paul could say that even he did not know whether his own vision took place 'in the body or out of the body' (2 Cor. 12.2-3). Both activities may be said to be 'in the spirit', but in the latter case, the discontinuity between the seer and his or her environment is heightened.[74] And it is often the case that the vision comes while the individual is already in an enhanced state of spiritual awareness and concentration, such as prayer or praise.

3. *Revelatory Content.* Whereas the prophet receives and transmits primarily auditory messages, the spiritual encounter of the visionary combines both auditory and visual elements.[75] Both types of revelation

74. According to Paul in 1 Cor. 14, a prophet—even while in the middle of delivering an oracle—could be conscious of those nearby and break off speaking at his or her own discretion, for 'the spirits of prophets are subject to prophets' (14.29-32; cf. 14.15-19). This is directly contrasted by the previously mentioned vision of Kenaz, 'a holy spirit came upon Kenaz and dwelled in him and put him in ecstasy, and he began to prophesy... and when Kenaz had spoken these words, he was awakened and his senses came back to him. But he did not know what he had said or what he had seen' (28.6, 10; *OTP*, II, pp. 341-42). A striking example of the difference between oracular and visionary ecstasy is found in *Ascension of Isaiah.* It has been argued by Bori ('L'estasi del profeta', pp. 367-89) that the account of Isaiah's prophecy and vision in ch. 6 is patterned after actual early Christian revelatory experiences. The descriptions clearly distinguish between Isaiah's prophesying in the Spirit (6.6-10a, cf. 7.2) and his entrance into a vision trance (6.10b-12): 'And while he was speaking by the Holy Spirit in the hearing of all, he (suddenly) became silent and his consciousness was taken from him and he saw no (more) the men who were standing before him: his eyes were open, but his mouth was silent and the consciousness in his body was taken from him; but his breath was still in him, for he saw a vision'. (*NTApoc*, II, p. 652; cf. *Ap. Jas* 15.9, 15, 25).

75. The distinction between '"Visionen" und "Auditionen", das Geschaute und das Gehörte', noted by H. Gunkel (*Die Propheten* [Göttingen, 1917], p. 121), has received abundant attention by scholars within the context of OT prophecy, and some of these studies are of help in the present discussion: cf. esp. J. Lindblom, *Prophecy in Ancient Israel* (Oxford, 1962), pp. 122-37; B.O. Long, 'Reports of Visions among the Prophets', *JBL* 95 (1976), pp. 353-65; Aune, *Prophecy*, pp. 112-14; and note the discussion and bibliography of R.R. Wilson, 'Prophecy and Ecstasy: A Reexamination', *JBL* 98 (1979), pp. 321-37. Important works which deal with these issues in relation to early Christian tradition are Lindblom, *Gesichte und Offenbarung: Vorstellungen von göttlichen Weisungen und übernatürlichen Erscheinungen*

may carry a similar purpose (e.g. paraenesis) and application (e.g. to individuals, special groups or the community as a whole), but the prophetic oracle tends to be shorter and more direct, while the vision-report is more involved and equivocal. This greater complexity of the vision-experience over the simple audition makes it more susceptible to reflective analysis and often adds an interpretative stage to the revelatory process.[76] In other words, between the reception of the vision and the actual vision-report, the content of the vision may undergo varying degrees of mental and literary redaction.

Individually, these three contrasting characteristics (revelatory setting, state and content) may not always be formally determinative. But taken together they can be used to differentiate between two distinct mediums of revelation: oracular prophecy and visions. However, it must be emphasized again that both types of revelation could be experienced by a single charismatic individual, as appears to be the case with John's Revelation. His book contains both oracular speech and vision experiences (both earthly, 1.10-20, and heavenly, 4–22), but it is all understood and designated as προφητεία.[77] A comparison of the various formal elements of revelatory praxis found throughout the book gives a clearer picture of its dual character.

visionary formulae	*oracular formulae*
statement of provenance (1.9)	the word of God (1.2, 9; 19.9)
entrance to ecstasy (1.10; 4.2)	thus says... (2.1 etc.)
command to write (1.11, 19; 19.9)	hear what the Spirit says (2.7 etc.)
door opened in heaven (4.1; cf. 19.11)	first person oracles (2–3; 16.15; 22)
ὅρασις (9.17; ?ὄψις, 1.16)	says the Spirit (14.13)
I heard/saw; after this, etc.	isolated oracles (13.9-10, 18; 14.13;
transportation in the	16.15; ?18)
Spirit (17.3; 21.10)	

im ältesten Christentum (Lund, 1968), pp. 32-67, 218; and Rowland, *The Open Heaven*, pp. 358-402.

76. As Fishbane has observed, the dissonance of esoteric visions and dreams comes immediately upon reception and is only resolved on interpretation. But the dissonance of oracles increases only in the delay of its predictive fulfilment, because at first its meaning is generally understood (*Biblical Interpretation in Ancient Israel* [New York, 1985], pp. 508-11).

77. Cf. Justin, *Dial.*,81.4: Ἰωάννης... ἐν ἀποκαλύψει... προεφήτευσε᾿ (PG, VI, p. 669). Schüssler Fiorenza's remark, 'Early Christian prophecy is expressed in apocalyptic form and early Christian apocalyptic is carried on by early Christian prophets', is along the right lines, but it is certainly incorrect to suggest that early Christian prophecy was *only* expressed in apocalyptic form (*Revelation*, p. 149).

It follows from all this that the superscription which stands over the contents of the book—ἀποκάλυψις Ἰησοῦ Χριστοῦ—is not for John a technical term referring to the manner of revelation or even a specific type of vision experience; it is best understood as a general description of all that follows as divine *revelation*.[78] Moreover, it is somewhat imprecise to label John an *apocalyptic* prophet.[79] According to his own self-understanding he is simply a prophet, who communicates God's word through a variety of revelatory media, including visions and oracles, both written and oral.[80]

If we may compare John with contemporary Jewish seers (e.g. *4 Ezra, 2 Baruch*) and those Christian visionary traditions which come closest to Revelation (e.g. Hermas, *Passio Perpetuae*), it appears probable that he typically sought and received his visions in private rather than in the context of the gathered community. At the very least, it seems highly unlikely that, had he been present in the assembly, John would have mediated his visions while in ecstasy.[81] His knowledge and use of traditional formulae, together with his obvious skill in fashioning a vision-report, suggests rather that this was his customary method for relaying a vision to the community.[82] This

---

78. Cf. T. Zahn, *Die Offenbarung des Johannes* (Leipzig, 1924–26), I, p. 43: 'All prophetic speech, acts, and writings have an ἀποκάλυψις as a prerequisite'. Schüssler Fiorenza cogently argues that John's use of the title ἀποκάλυψις Ἰησοῦ Χριστοῦ consciously builds on Pauline vocabulary and authority (*Revelation*, pp. 150-51).

79. Thus Schüssler Fiorenza puts the cart before the horse when she says that 'early Christian prophecy belongs to the context of early Christian apocalyptic' (*Revelation*, p. 149).

80. In contrast to *1 Enoch, 4 Ezra* and other visionary works, John never refers to dream visions. While we may concur with J.S. Hanson that 'as far as form or content is concerned, dreams and visions cannot readily be separated', such a distinction may have been important to the prophet, on the view that dreams represented an inferior level of inspiration ('Dreams and Visions in the Graeco-Roman World and Early Christianity', *ANRW*, II.23.2, pp. 1395-1427, 1409). Note in this connection the comment of Lindblom (*Gesichte und Offenbarung*, p. 217, cf. 32-33, 125): 'Der klassiche [sic] Prophetismus des AT, wenigsten auf seinen Höhepunkten, verwirft,... bewusst den Traum als ein Mittel für göttliche Offenbarungen'.

81. *Contra* Boring, *Sayings*, p. 84.

82. K. Koch has argued that the apocalyptic vision-report goes back to prophetic speech-forms, 'Vom profestischen zum apokalyptischen Visionsbericht', in *Apocalypticism in the Mediterranean World and the Near East* (ed. D. Hellholm; Tübingen, 1983), pp. 413-46.

activity would complement rather than contrast with his role as a cultic prophet who undoubtedly also delivered oracles in the Spirit within the worship gathering. John's vocation as a prophet thus encompassed both categories of divine revelation.

2. *John's Prophetic Consciousness*

Although John never explicitly calls himself a prophet (Rev. 22.9 comes close), but rather a brother and fellow-servant, such an understanding of his role by his readers is taken for granted. For his own prophetic consciousness is clearly attested throughout the book in a variety of ways.[83] This prophetic awareness can be illustrated by means of four lines of evidence: testimony related to the word group προφητ-, the significance of John's prophetic commission, formal elements of prophetic speech, and the absolute authority of John's prophecy.

Testimony Related to the Word Group προφητ-[84]

1. προφητεία. This word occurs seven times in Revelation (1.3; 11.6; 19.10; 22.7, 10, 18, 19). Of these seven occasions, five are reserved for the introduction and conclusion to the collection of visions, where they serve to identify the content of the book. In Rev. 1.3 John writes 'Blessed is he who reads aloud the words of this prophecy', and in 22.10 the revelatory angel says, 'Do not seal up the words of the prophecy of this book'. Clearly the product of John's visionary experience is understood to be prophecy, and this description is intended to characterize the entire book, not merely chs. 2 and 3.[85]

2. προφητεύω. Not only is the product of John's visions called *prophecy*, but the activity in which he is engaged is called *prophesying*. In Rev. 10.11, which is dependent on the prophetic call narrative of Ezek. 3.1-4, John is commissioned by the theophanic angel and told, 'you must again (πάλιν)

83. Cf. Boring, *Sayings*, p. 27; Hill, 'Prophecy and Prophets', p. 406; Cothenet, *DBSup*, VIII, cols. 1322, 1324-25.

84. For a more detailed discussion of this word group in Revelation, see Satake, *Gemeindeordnung*, pp. 47-74.

85. For questions relating to the unity of the book, cf. Schüssler Fiorenza, 'Composition', pp. 346-50; Aune, *Prophecy*, p. 74; Boring, *Sayings*, pp. 26-27.

prophesy about many peoples and nations and tongues and kings'. And in 11.3 John presents the two witnesses as prophets who are endowed by God with the 'power to prophesy'.

3.   προφήτης. This noun occurs eight times in Revelation, always in the plural. The 'prophets' are regarded as a distinct brotherhood among the people of God who act as God's mouthpiece to the community.[86] In most cases John makes no attempt to distinguish between OT and Christian prophets, and in view of his philosophy of history and understanding of the kingdom of God, such ambiguity is no doubt intentional.[87] In this way he accents the continuity of the prophetic role in salvation history. For John there is no distinction because the guiding principle of all prophecy, whether past or present, is the 'testimony of Jesus' (19.10).[88] That he himself is part of the prophetic fraternity is confirmed by the words of the angel to John in 22.9: 'I am a fellow servant with you and *your brethren* the prophets'.[89]

4.   προφῆτις. Further evidence of John's active prophetic role can be adduced from his involvement in prophetic conflict. Like Elijah against the prophets of Baal, he faces strong opposition from a rival prophetess and her circle of followers in the church at Thyatira (Rev. 2.20-24). Having ignored a previous warning by him to repent, John delivers an oracle of judgment against her and her disciples in the name of the risen Lord. Other groups with which he is in competition,

86. 'Als Prophet ist Johannes nur eine Sprachrohr des Geistes, von dem er erfüllt ist. Was er an die kleinasiatischen Gemeinden schreibt, bezeichnet er als Worte des Geistes (2, 29; 3, 6 usw.). Das ist ganz im Sinne der alttestamentlichen Propheten gesprochen' (Lindblom, *Gesichte und Offenbarung*, p. 213). Cf. Hill ('Prophecy and Prophets', p. 414), who thinks John considers the whole church 'potentially a community of prophets'; but cf. Aune, *Prophecy*, pp. 200-201, 206; I.T. Beckwith, *The Apocalypse of John* (New York, 1919), p. 610.

87. Grudem, *Prophecy*, pp. 107-108; Justin, *Dial.* 82.1; Cothenet, *DBSup*, VIII, cols. 1326-27; Beckwith, *Apocalypse*, p. 610.

88. For discussion of this ambiguous phrase see Cothenet, *DBSup*, VIII, cols. cols. 1323-24; Grudem, *Prophecy*, pp. 107-108 n. 195; Hill, 'Prophecy and Prophets', pp. 411-13.

89. Cf. Boring, *Sayings*, pp. 27, 29. On the basis of 22.9 and the plural pronoun ὑμῖν in 22.16, Schüssler Fiorenza concludes that 'a circle of prophets is named as the recipient of the prophecy for the churches' (*Revelation*, p. 146).

such as the Nicolaitans (2.6, 15) and the followers of 'Balaam' (2.14), may likewise have been associated with the authority of a prophetic figure.[90]

The Significance of John's Prophetic Commission

Both Rev. 1.10-20 and 10.8-11 contain a prophetic commission scene. Whereas the latter is a reaffirmation of John's prophetic call which forms a prelude to a new phase of revelation with the sounding of the seventh trumpet,[91] the commission of ch. 1 serves to underline the authority of the book as a whole. Because John is already an established prophet, Rev. 1.10-20 should not be taken as a prophetic call based on OT call narratives. It would be better described as a commissioning ceremony with OT call elements.[92] A comparison of John's inaugural commission with the call narratives in Isaiah 6 and Ezekiel 1–3 in particular reveals that all three share a common core of auditory and visual components.[93]

1. The divine voice and its intensity (Rev. 1.10; Isa. 6.4, 8; Ezek. 1.24-25, 28; 2.2).
2. Apocalyptic descriptions of the divine glory (Rev. 1.13-16; Isa. 6.1-3; Ezek. 1.4-28).[94]

90. So Schüssler Fiorenza, *Revelation*, pp. 144-45.

91. Cf. Cothenet, *DBSup*, VIII, cols. 1325-26; Beckwith, *Apocalypse*, pp. 576-77.

92. Thus H. Wildberger's term 'prophetische Legitimationsausweis' (*Jesaja* (Neukirchen, 1965–72), I, p. 238) is more appropriate than Kraft's "Berüfungsvision' (*Offenbarung*, p. 38). Aune notes 'There is scant evidence that early Christian prophets claimed to receive inaugural visions or commissions which launched them into their prophetic careers. Early Christian prophets did claim to have received commissions *for particular tasks*, however, such as the writing of a prophetic book' (*Prophecy*, pp. 202-203, emphasis Aune's).

93. The following list is not intended to serve as a precise form-critical analysis of prophetic call visions, but merely illustrates major elements common to each vision-pericope. For more detailed studies see N. Habel, 'The Form and Significance of the Call Narrative', *ZAW* 77 (1965), pp. 309-14; W. Zimmerli, *Ezekiel* (Herm; Philadelphia, 1979), I, pp. 97-100; the bibliography in B.O. Long, 'Reports', pp. 358-59 n. 19; and T.Y. Mullins, 'New Testament Commission Forms, Especially in Luke–Acts', *JBL* 95 (1976), pp. 605-606, 613-14; Aune, *Prophecy*, pp. 97-99; Roloff, *Offenbarung*, p. 38.

94. In the description of the exalted Christ, John depends heavily, though not exclusively, on Dan. 7 and 10. See the detailed discussion of Beale, *Daniel*,

3.   Physical or emotional distress at the divine presence followed by divine reassurance and restoration (Rev. 1.17a; Isa. 6.5-7; Ezek. 1.28–2.1).
4.   A statement of the commission (Rev. 1.10, 19; Isa. 6.9-13; Ezek. 2.3-7).

John's literary dependence on Isaiah 6 and Ezekiel 1–3 in later parts of the book (Rev. 4, 10) makes it likely that the conceptual affinities between his commission in ch. 1 and the call narratives of Isaiah and Ezekiel are intentional and serve to emphasize to his readers the continuity of his own role with official prophetic tradition.[95]

Within the whole commission narrative of Rev. 1.10-20, vv. 12-18 play an especially vital role. Because the commission has been fully stated already in v. 11 and is then restated in v. 19, vv. 12-18 appear to form a special unit in John's construct. Theoretically Rev. 1.11 could be followed by 1.19 or 2.1. But the section 1.12-18 functions to identify the voice of v. 10 and reveal the divine origin of John's message. The Christophany goes beyond providing assurance to John and makes clear to his readers that the *revelation* which he brings them is from Jesus Christ himself, the Lord of the church (1.1).[96]

The importance of this scene in John's mind for the authority of the book as a whole is stressed by the constant reminders that are taken from this commission and used in later visions to reinforce their divine character.[97] A significant example occurs in 4.1, where John is careful to note that the same voice like a trumpet that he previously

pp. 154-77. But Beale overestimates the influence of Daniel in this passage, and fails to see that Rev. 1.10-20 as a whole, and in its constituent parts, is first and foremost a preparatory statement of legitimation—a divine commission, on which the authority of the rest of the book depends. Cf. M. Black, 'The Throne-Theophany Prophetic Commission and the "Son of Man": A Study in Tradition-History', in *Jews, Greeks, and Christians* (ed. R. Hamerton-Kelly and R. Scroggs; Leiden, 1976), pp. 57-63. Both Beale and Black overlook the fact that the theophanies of Dan. 7 and 10, unlike Isaiah, Ezekiel and Revelation, do not contain a call or commission.

95.   Aune, *Prophecy*, p. 206; cf. 202, 391 n. 85, 'Call narratives in OT prophetic books were primarily means of legitimating prophetic status'. Hadorn also points out the influence of OT call narratives on John (*Offenbarung*, pp. 6-7, 12).

96.   So also Roloff, *Offenbarung*, p. 38; Aune, *Prophecy*, p. 206.

97.   Noted by Kiddle and Ross, *Revelation*, p. 14; R.H. Mounce, *The Book of Revelation* (Grand Rapids, 1977), pp. 83-84; Aune, *Prophecy*, pp. 275, 432 n. 165.

heard (and whose authority lay behind the commission to the seven churches, Rev. 2–3) is also the authority for the visions of chs. 4 and following.[98]

Formal Elements of Prophetic Speech
Up until now, little has been said concerning the stylistic features of John's prophecy and their similarity or dissimilarity with Hebrew prophetic tradition. A fair amount of evidence suggests that he regarded himself, and Christian prophets in general, as forming a continuum with God's OT messengers. To what extent then has John's prophetic style been influenced by OT models? This is perhaps seen most clearly by studying the formal characteristics of his oracles and their antecedents.[99]

Introductory and Concluding Formulas. Each of the oracles to the seven churches in Revelation 2–3 begins with a similar introductory formula which includes the expression τάδε λέγει ('thus says'), followed by a short descriptive phrase identifying the risen Jesus as the speaker.[100] For example, to the church at Smyrna in Rev. 2.8 John writes, 'Thus says the first and the last, who died and came to life'. Here the christological title is borrowed from the commission scene of ch. 1.

The phrase τάδε λέγει occurs just eight times in the NT—seven times in Revelation 2–3 and once in the Agabus oracle of Acts 21.11. In the Septuagint it generally translates כה אמר and is used chiefly as a messenger formula introducing prophetic speech. Whether or not the

98. Cf. Schüssler Fiorenza, 'Composition', p. 362; Roloff, *Offenbarung*, p. 15, 'Man darf keineswegs, wie das häufig geschieht, diese brieflichen Elemente als unwesenliche Beigaben zu der "eigentlichen" Apokalypse des zweiten Hauptteils (4, 1–22, 5) oder gar als sekundäre Zutaten betrachten. Bei genauerem Zusehen zeigt sich vielmehr, dass sie durch vielfältige thematische Bezüge untrennbar mit dem zweiten Hauptteil verknöpft sind.'
99. I have limited the following comparison to the formal elements of oracular speech, but it should be kept in mind that visionary and apocalyptic traditions are no less a part of John's overall *prophetic* heritage. For an outline of these traditions see Lindblom, *Gesichte und Offenbarung*, pp. 214-16, and the list above, p. 47.
100. Cf. F. Hahn, 'Die Sendschreiben der Johannesapokalypse', in *Tradition und Glaube: Das frühe Christentum in seiner Umwelt* (ed. G. Jeremias, H.-W. Kuhn and H. Stegemann; Göttingen, 1971), pp. 366-67; Aune, *Prophecy*, pp. 275, 328; Hill, *Prophecy*, p. 77.

use of this OT messenger formula is indicative of Christian prophets in general, it reveals something of John's own prophetic consciousness and serves to invest his proclamations with the highest authority.

Each of the seven letters also shares a similar concluding formula, 'He who has an ear, let him hear what the Spirit says to the churches'. This formulaic call to attention or *Weckformel* is found also in Rev. 13.9, while variations on the first clause appear seven times in the Synoptic Gospels as a summons to consider a cryptic saying of Jesus.[101] Aune suggests that the use of this phrase in Revelation is functionally equivalent to OT proclamation formulas such as 'Hear the word of Yahweh!'[102] It is interesting—and unlikely to be coincidental—that John's introductory and concluding formulas exhibit a pattern similar to that given to the prophet Ezekiel by Yahweh, 'But when I speak with you, I will open your mouth, and you shall say to them, "Thus says the Lord God"; he that will hear, let him hear' (Ezek. 3.27a).

Oracles Delivered in the First Person. Another important feature of John's prophetic style is the delivery of oracles in the first person.[103] In this prophetic mode of speech the prophet assumes the divine ego, and speaks not merely in the name of the divine being, but as the divine being.[104] Since the revelatory discourse of apocalyptic literature generally adopts a third-person perspective, John's use of the first person makes it possible to isolate specific prophetic oracles in Revelation from their apocalyptic framework.[105] Though oracles

101. Also called a *Weckruf*; cf. Hahn, 'Die Sendschreiben', pp. 377-81.

102. *Prophecy*, p. 278.

103. While common in OT prophetic oracles, Revelation is the only NT book that includes first person oracles in the name of the deity. Cf. Origen, *Contra Celsum* VII.9; *Odes. Sol.* 42.6, 'Then I arose and am with them, and will speak by their mouths' (*OTP*, II, p. 771). The Odist frequently speaks as if he were Christ, in the first person, and without any indication of a change of speakers. Cf. 8.8-19; 10.4-6; 17.6-16; 22.1-12; 28.9-20; 31.6-13; 36.3-8; 41.8-10; 42.3-20. Also, five out of the fifteen extant Montanist oracles are given in the I-form (*NTApoc*, II, p. 686).

104. On the psychological state of the prophet, and its relation to the Deity and the people see T. Polk, *The Prophetic Persona* (JSOTSup, 32; Sheffield, 1984), pp. 58-59, 80-81, 96-97, 125.

105. E.L. Dietrich, 'Das religiös-emphatische Ich-Wort bei den jüdischen Apokalyptikern, Weisheitlehrern und Rabbinen', *ZRGG* 4 (1952), pp. 289-93, 308-10.

spoken in the name of the Lord God are rare—occurring only in Rev.
1.8 and 21.5-8—oracles delivered in the name of the risen Lord or
the christophanic angel are scattered throughout the book.[106] Besides
the seven Jesus speeches in chs. 2 and 3, other first person oracles are
found in Rev. 1.17-20; 16.15; 22.7a (?b), 12-13, (?14-15), 16-20.[107]
While John's use of the first person is likely an extension of OT
models, this prophetic manner of speech is not unique to Hebrew or
Christian prophecy in the ancient world.[108]

Symbolic Prophetic Actions. One final stylistic device which is a
common feature of the Hebrew prophets is the use of symbolic prophetic actions.[109] A familiar example from the OT is Jeremiah 27–28,
where the prophet is told to wear a yoke to signify how Judah should
submit to the Babylonians.[110] Likewise it appears that the oracles of
some Christian prophets were occasionally accompanied by dramatic
illustrations, as is seen in Acts 21.11.[111]

The question of whether and to what extent John himself adopted
such methods in his own prophetic ministry is complicated by the fact
that his book is a literary record of visionary experiences rather than

106. Boring, *Sayings*, pp. 128-30; Hill, *Prophecy*, pp. 81-82. It is these
oracles in the name of the risen Jesus which are a main feature of the debate over
whether the Gospel sayings of Jesus contain assimilated prophetic oracles. Along
with the references on p. 25 above, see J.D.G. Dunn, 'Prophetic "I"—Sayings and
the Jesus Tradition: The Importance of Testing Prophetic Utterances within Early
Christianity', *NTS* 24 (1977–78), pp. 175-98; Aune, *Prophecy*, pp. 233-35.

107. Aune discusses these and other possible oracles in Revelation (*Prophecy*,
pp. 279-88).

108. Boring, *Sayings*, pp. 128-29; cf. Aune, *Prophecy*, pp. 333-34, 372 n. 116.

109. Other formal features which have been put forward as indicative of
prophetic speech are the use of '(amen) I say to you'; 'Behold' (ἰδού); the presence
of makarisms; etc. (Boring, *Sayings*, pp. 132-35). But none of these elements are
limited to prophetic oracles (Aune, *Prophecy*, pp. 164-65, 279). However, 'woe
oracles', which occur at Rev. 8.13, 12.12, and 18.10, 16, 19, are characteristic of
OT prophecy, and John twice uses the OT *perfectum propheticum* in 14.8 and 18.2-3
(Aune, *Prophecy*, pp. 96-97, 434 n. 210).

110. For this prophetic device see further G. Fohrer, *Die Symbolischen Handlungen der Propheten* (ATANT, 54; Zürich, 1953); Lindblom, *Prophecy*, pp. 165-
73; Aune, *Prophecy,* pp. 100, 161-63; Boring, *Sayings*, pp. 90-91.

111. The enigmatic passage in *Did.* 11.11 probably has in mind prophetic
actions; J.-P. Audet, *La Didaché: Instructions des Apôtres* (Paris, 1958), p. 452;
Boring, *Sayings*, p. 91; *contra* Aune, *Prophecy*, p. 413 n. 214.

an account of prophetic activity in a cultic setting. In Rev. 10.8-11 John is told to eat the scroll, while in 11.1-2 he is instructed to measure the temple, both motifs which are adapted from Ezekiel. In Rev. 18.21 it is an angel who performs the symbolic act in which Babylon's destruction is foreshadowed by the casting of a stone into the sea, inspired by Jer. 51.63-64.

The incorporation of all these symbolic acts into John's book of prophecy' suggests that his use of prophetic illustrations was probably not limited to his literary activities. Such actions as removing the church's lampstand in Rev. 2.5, or knocking on the gathered community's door in 3.20 may well have been dramatizations which John the prophet would have undertaken had he delivered his message in person.[112]

The Absolute Authority of John's Prophecy. Much of what has already been presented has revealed John's concern for providing his words with the highest accreditation. Not only does the commission narrative of Rev. 1.10-20 emphasize that this is the *revelation of Jesus Christ* to John (not the revelation of John),[113] but the revelatory chain of 1.1 traces the initial source of these visions back to the mandate of God himself. It is therefore God whom John is told to worship in 19.10 and 22.9, not the revelatory angel who is just a fellow mediator. John is merely the servant of God who fulfils the role of the human agent who brings God's message to his people—the final link in the catena of divine disclosure.

Like the prophets of old, he does not hesitate to speak in the name of the deity and to bestow divine sanction on his utterances, even if in written form.[114] So it comes as no surprise that he proclaims his book to be 'The Word of God' (τὸν λόγον τοῦ θεοῦ, 1.2), placing it on a

112.   'A Christian prophet whose thinking is so thoroughly permeated with such an understanding of the nature of prophecy probably engaged in such symbolic acts himself' (Boring, *Sayings*, p. 90).

113.   Compare how the various translations (e.g. RSV versus NEB) deal with this issue.

114.   It is in the area of authority that Revelation's lack of pseudonymity has the greatest significance. John does not borrow some past figure's authority, but strongly asserts his own divine inspiration—'Nicht die fiktive, weil geborgte Authorität eines grossen Gottesmannes der Vergangenheit gibt ihrer Botschaft gewicht, sondern die reale Authorität des erhöhten Jesus Christus, der durch das prophetische Zeugnis des Johannes zu seiner Kirche spricht' (Roloff, *Offenbarung*, p. 15).

level with inspired Scripture.[115] John is convinced that his words are not only authoritative—they are essential. And they represent God's interim message until the parousia, as Rev. 22.6-7 intimates, 'And he said to me, "These words are trustworthy and true. And the Lord, the God of the spirits of the prophets, has sent his angel to show his servants what must soon take place. And behold, I am coming soon." Blessed is he who keeps the words of the prophecy of this book.'

If this is not enough, the subsequent warning against those who would add or subtract anything from God's revelation in Rev. 22.18-19 stresses in no uncertain terms the inviolability which John accorded his visions. This prophetic word for the churches possesses plenary inspiration, extending to all parts equally. Unlike the Christian prophets known from the Pauline writings and other sources, John has no interest in having his prophecy tested or evaluated by others and leaves no room to do so.[116] The recipients of this prophecy are not told to 'test all things and hold fast to what is good' (1 Thess. 5.21), but to 'hear what the Spirit says to the churches' and 'keep what is written therein; for the time is near' (Rev. 2.7; 1.3b).

Conclusion

Thinking back to the first part of this chapter, we may ask how John's role as a prophet compares to what we know of early Christian prophets in general. To what extent did other prophets align themselves with Israelite-Jewish prophetic traditions? Some scholars have seen John the prophet as an idiosyncratic figure, whose style and self-understanding cannot be representative of early Christian prophets and prophecy in general.[117] Certainly the level of prophetic authority assumed by John is significantly different from what we know of the

115. Boring, *Sayings*, p. 88.

116. 'There can be no question of testing the correctness of his sayings' (Friedrich, *TDNT*, VI, p. 849); cf. Aune, *Prophecy*, p. 221; Grudem, *Prophecy*, pp. 106-107. Interestingly, Rev. 2.2b witnesses to the fact that the testing of spiritual authority was practiced in these churches, which John commends, while deeming his own authority beyond reproach. But Aune rightly points out that we do not know what kind of response John's book received in the churches (*Prophecy*, p. 206).

117. So Friedrich, *TDNT*, VI, pp. 849-50; Hill, 'Prophecy and Prophets', pp. 410, 415-16; *contra* Aune, *Prophecy*, pp. 6, 206-208; cf. Grudem, *Prophecy*, pp. 106-107.

prophets discussed in the first half of this chapter. But we should be careful against pressing such distinctions too far, since the book of Revelation is our only complete example of first century Christian prophecy.

In any case, the understanding of John as a Christian prophet is not nearly as important for the meaning of the book as is the recognition that he is a Jewish-Christian prophet. John not only takes it for granted that the prophetic heritage of Israel has become the inheritance of the church, but that with the revival of the prophetic office in Christianity, and the imminence of the parousia, the mantle has been passed on for the last time.

But there is more involved in this succession than simply the passing on of prophetic authority. We shall see that John not only takes up *where* the Prophets left off—he also takes over *what* they left behind. He is not only part of a prophetic circle, but stands in a prophetic continuum which carries on and brings to final revelation the living words of God entrusted to the care of the brotherhood (Rev. 10.7). The presupposition of continuity is supremely christological: 'for the testimony of Jesus is the spirit of prophecy' (19.10).

This brings us then to an evaluation of John's use of the OT, and especially the Prophets. In what ways does he handle the legacy of oral and written traditions handed down to him? In the next chapter I will attempt to answer this question by setting out John's *general* approach to the OT Scriptures. This will in turn provide the necessary background for examining his use of Isaiah in particular.

Chapter 2

JOHN AND THE INFLUENCE OF THE OLD TESTAMENT

Introduction

In 1912, Adolph Schlatter, in his seminal study of the use of the OT in Revelation, made the remarkable statement that there was no need to seek for any other source behind John's prophecies beyond the OT.[1] More recently, H. Kraft has taken up a similar view and made it the guiding principle of his (1974) commentary. There he asserts that 'In those passages of Revelation where we have failed to point out the OT source for the apocalyptic prophecy, we have likewise failed to interpret them'.[2]

Until recently these somewhat exaggerated claims were simply given a place among the multitude of other so-called 'keys' to the Apocalypse, such as the liturgical, dramatic and mythological approaches. Only in the last decade has John's use of biblical traditions begun to receive the detailed investigation which it deserves, though even now much remains to be done.

Of course, there is no denying that Revelation is a complex of various traditions and even multiple genres, and this should warn any who would attempt to build an interpretation on the basis of one tradition alone. Yet the sheer magnitude, variety and consistency of John's use of the OT certainly constitutes this area as a fundamental starting place for the exegete.

A. Special Nature of Old Testament Traditions in Revelation

1. Methodological Considerations
Any study of John's use of OT traditions must necessarily take into account previous scholarly research on the subject of early Christian

---

1. *Das Alte Testament*, p. 105.
2. *Offenbarung*, p. 16.

employment of the Jewish Scriptures. Yet any hope of finding some methodological direction or even the barest of paradigms which might facilitate an approach to John's use of the OT is often frustrated by the monotonous assertion that the Book of Revelation 'does not contain a single quotation from the OT'. As one reads through study after study of 'How the NT Uses the Old', it becomes evident that most of these analyses should rather be titled 'How the Gospels Use the OT', or, 'How the NT (except Revelation) Uses the OT'.[3]

A singular fault with many such studies is that they attempt to evaluate and define early Christian biblical exegesis primarily on the basis of citations which are accompanied by introductory formulae or similar contextual indicators. While such self-defined limitations are convenient for research, they automatically exclude the more numerous and equally important instances of OT allusions, concepts, characters and institutions.[4] Consequently, the results of these investigations may be valuable for describing certain functions and stages of Christian OT interpretation, but it would be misleading and unwise to make sweeping generalizations about early Christian attitudes to the OT as a result of this evidence alone. That one NT writer presents a three line word-for-word citation is of itself no more or no less important or illuminating than an author who retains only a few key words of an OT *topos*, which are imbedded in the passage. They are merely different ways of using the same source. Both examples may in turn reveal something of the presuppositions and purposes of the author, and of the social and religious environment in which early Christian Bible interpretation took place.[5]

3.   Full bibliographies of such studies can be found in C.H. Toy, *Quotations in the NT* (New York, 1884), pp. xxxviii-xliii [lists the older works with annotations]; R.H. Gundry, *The Use of the Old Testament in St Matthew's Gospel* (NovTSup, 18; Leiden, 1967), pp. 235-40; and most recently the bibliographic essay of H.G. Reventlow, *Problems of Biblical Theology in the Twentieth Century* (London, 1986), esp. pp. 20-23.

4.   C.K. Barrett notes, 'The use of the OT in NT is thus a much larger matter than direct, indicated question' (*CHB*, I, pp. 390-91). Similarly L. Goppelt, *TYPOS* (Grand Rapids, 1982), p. 198. K. Grobel gives 150 quotations versus 1100 allusions for the NT, but the first number is too low (*IDB*, III, p. 977). I count at least 200 formal quotations.

5.   An interesting example of imbedded OT interpretation is found in Rev. 12.1-17. The exegesis of this crucial passage has suffered repeatedly from *parallelomania*, in which almost every conceivable history-of-religions analogy has been attested as

Even when one one turns for help to the literature on Revelation itself, adequate treatments of John's use of OT traditions are few and far between.[6] Of course, like the more general NT studies mentioned above, most commentators mention somewhere that the book of Revelation—more than any other in the NT—is virtually saturated with OT texts and traditions. Yet remarkably, after having acknowledged this fact, few authors then go on to discuss the implications of John's debt to the OT in individual passages, consistently and methodologically throughout the book. In many of these works, the OT in Revelation is first defined as a prime literary-critical source, but then it is treated as no more than an overworked religious thesaurus.[7]

Therefore, a preliminary task in our investigation lies in defining more clearly the special nature of OT allusions in Revelation and the criteria used for isolating these texts. The need for systematic methodological guidelines in delimiting John's use of specific OT texts

the background to its thought. While some mythological development must be allowed for, one of the leading traditions is undoubtedly the so-called 'Protoevangelium' of Gen. 3.15, along with motifs from Daniel, Exodus and Isaiah. Not only are the main *dramatis personae* represented (the Serpent, the Woman and the Seed), but the arena of conflict between the Serpent and the Woman, and between the Serpent and her Seed is what would be expected of a messianic application of Gen. 3.15. Christian speculation on this OT text can already be found in Rom. 16.20 and in 1 Jn 3.8-10. The whole becomes highly illustrative for John's purpose of revealing the primal origin of the church's conflict and persecution. See the detailed discussion of L. Cerfaux, 'La vision de la femme et du dragon de l'Apocalypse en relation avec le Protévangile', *ETL* 31 (1956), pp. 21-33; J. Cambier, 'Les images de l'Ancien Testament dans l'Apocalypse de Saint Jean', *NRT* 77 (1955), p. 119; and E.C.S. Gibson, *The Old Testament in the New Testament* (London, 1907), p. 146.

6.   French scholars, and to a lesser degree the Germans, have contributed the most to this area of study, while British and American offering are scarce. Some of the more important general studies are those of Schlatter; Cambier, 'Les images'; Comblin, *Le Christ*, esp. pp. 80-91; R. Halver, *Der Mythos im letzten Buch der Bibel* (Hamburg, 1964), pp. 11-17; A. Lancellotti, 'L'Antico Testamento nell' Apocalissa', *RivB* 14 (1966), pp. 369-84; and S. Giet, *L'Apocalypse et l'histoire* (Paris, 1957), pp. 186-92, 193-208.

7.   The comment of Schüssler Fiorenza is indicative of the general attitude: 'The author of Rev. does not interpret the OT but uses it in employing words, images, phrases, and OT patterns in order to make his own theological statement' (*Revelation*, p. 102; cf. also pp. 135-36). Notable exceptions are Kraft, and L. Cerfaux and J. Cambier, *L'Apocalypse de Saint Jean lue aux chrétiens* (LD, 17; Paris, 1955).

is evident simply from the multitude of disparate enumerations of OT allusions in Revelation.[8]

Charles	Swete	Tenney	Marty	Gelin	*UBSGNT*	Staehelin
250	278	348	453	518	634	700

A differential of 50 or perhaps even 100 suggested allusions between scholars is not unreasonable to expect in a book such as Revelation, but one of 450 (250 versus 700) is unacceptable. Unfortunately, the common Greek editions help to perpetuate an inexact attitude towards OT quotations and allusions in the NT. The UBS index of *quotations* is in fact a listing of all the OT cross-references given in the margins of the text. This is never explained in the introduction. Even the policy of N^{26} (p. 72), of listing 'direct quotations' in italics and 'allusions' in normal type, is often arbitrary. This procedure results in 25 'direct quotations' in the Book of Revelation, a figure no one would accept in these terms.

Furthermore, a better understanding of John's use of the OT will not come by merely citing parallels. In my opinion, very little substantial progress can be made by postulating allusions wherever similar ideas occur. This only leads to a multiplicity of theories which can hardly be verified, and vast discrepancies in the totals of allusions, as noted above. On the surface, the language and images of Revelation offer opportunity for comparison with a multitude of traditional texts, models, symbols and so on. But does a detailed historical and exegetical analysis bear out a proposed connection? Does John really use tabernacles imagery here and there? Is there any real basis for seeing a specific allusion to Isaiah, Daniel or Ezekiel in a particular passage?

8.   Charles, *Revelation*, pp. lxviii-lxxxi; Swete's calculation (*Apocalypse*, pp. cxl-cliii) that there are '278 OT allusions out of 404 verses' is often quoted by scholars. This total is based on the appendix of OT quotations in Westcott–Hort. L. Vos points out that there are actually 405 verses (not 404), but fails to note that Rev. 12.18 is included with 13.1 in some editions and translations (e.g. Souter, RV, RSV), though, oddly enough, not in Swete's own text (*Synoptic Traditions*, p. 18). See also M.C. Tenney, *Interpreting Revelation* (Grand Rapids, 1957), p. 101; J. Marty, *DEB*, I, pp. 213-14; A. Gelin, *L'Apocalypse dans Bible Pirot* (Paris, 1938), pp. 589-90; 'Index of Quotations', *UBS Greek New Testament* [!] (London, 2nd edn, 1966), pp. 897-920; J. Staehelin, *700 Parallelen, die Quellgründe der Apokalypse* (Bern, 1961). This last work actually contains 748 parallels, but this includes the OT Apocrypha and a few random references to the Pseudepigrapha. This brings the OT total down to c. 638.

Despite the fact that Kraft takes seriously John's use of the OT, his approach suffers from a lack of objective criteria for determining the validity of proposed allusions. And similar deficiencies can be found in the works of other commentators. It is not enough merely to be sympathetic to the presence and influence of possible OT texts. Because of the imbedded nature of allusions in Revelation, one must dig deeper and look closer at apparent biblical links. Each supposed tradition must be scrutinized from various angles—language, context, tradition history and so on—to see what substantive role, if any, it plays in the author's construct. Some progress along these lines is now being made, and one must welcome detailed studies on the influence of individual OT books such as D. Mollat on Exodus, G. Beale on Daniel, and the older treatise on Ezekiel by A. Vanhoye.[9]

2. *Criteria for Quotations and Allusions*

It is clear from the outset that the principles used to classify and identify OT quotations and allusions in other NT books cannot be rigidly imposed on John's book. Just as Revelation has its own special grammar, so also its use of the OT must be evaluated on its own terms, independent of canonical standards. For example, it may be that some texts which have usually been considered as allusions should in the wider background of John's method and purpose be regarded as quotations. Or, in passages where allusive clusters from a particular OT source are present, further previously undiscovered or doubtful parallels may rise to become clear allusions.[10]

At this point it becomes necessary to define terminology, and to make clear what principles and procedures are employed in distinguishing OT quotations and allusions in Revelation.

By *formal quotation* I understand *any* portion of OT text accompanied by *any* additional word or phrase which the author uses to

---

9. Cf. the references in n. 4 of the Introduction.

10. Little methodological work has been done in this area. Helpful discussions of allusive clusters and isolating allusions in general can be found in Beale, *The Use of Daniel*, pp. 307-111; and S. Holm-Nielsen, *Hodayot: Psalms from Qumran* (Aarhus, 1960), pp. 301-15. A. Pohl is certainly correct in maintaining that 'Die Zahl der Anklänge mag noch weit höher liegen, weil sich in den Winkeln und Hintergrund der Visionen immer neue Beziehungen entdecken lassen', although his example of Isa. 56.1-2 in Rev. 1.1-3 is not particularly convincing (*Die Offenbarung des Johannes* [Wuppertal, 1969], p. 31 n. 29).

introduce that text. This may involve elaborate introductory formulae such as are found in Mt. 1.22 or Jn 15.25, or it may simply consist of a single conjunction, as when γάρ introduces a nine-line quote in 1 Pet. 3.10-12, or δέ before a single line in 2 Cor. 10.17.[11] These formal indicators usually precede the text quoted, but can occasionally follow the text, as in Rom. 2.24. No two NT authors are alike in their use of introductory formulae, and even Paul is not consistent book by book.[12] Indeed, it is evident from the great variety of methods adopted by NT writers in indicating OT quotations that there were no accepted rules for citing Scripture, and that an author was guided more by personal preference and literary purpose than by convention. It is therefore arbitrary to insist that formal quotations should be limited to the use of the more common introductory phrases and words.

Informal quotations, on the other hand, are simply OT citations without introductory formulae. Every major NT book which contains formal quotations also includes informal quotations, and these may be used by a writer in many of the same ways as formal quotations.

However, the difference between an *informal quotation* and an *allusion* is not always clear. For this reason the term *allusion* itself can only be accepted as a broad definition, for it conveys little information about an author's use of Scripture, except to indicate that it is not a quotation. Any added connotations which imply randomness or a reduction of authorial consciousness are inappropriate, for these must be determined by the context and not be dictated by a descriptive rubric.

In the end, the distinction between an informal quotation and an allusion must be based on perceived authorial motive. This will include an estimate of the function of an OT text in a given passage and particularly its interrelationship with the surrounding context. To be more precise, the boundaries between an informal quotation and an

---

11. The most common formulaic verb is λέγω (c. 100×), followed by γράφω (c. 70×). Less common formulae include 'Have you not read...?', and words such as γάρ, ἀλλά, ὅτι, διό, διότι, and others. The longest quote with formula is Heb. 8.8-12, which gives 20 lines from Jer. 31. The shortest formal quote is Rom. 7.7, ὁ νόμος ἔλεγεν· οὐκ ἐπιθυμήσεις.

12. The most uniform usage is found in the writer to the Hebrews, who consistently uses λέγω, but never γράφω. Yet even here, of the 77 formal quotations which do not use λέγω, 6 are different. For a comparison of NT introductory formulae with examples from Qumran literature, see J.A. Fitzmyer, 'The Use of Explicit Old Testament Quotations in Qumran Literature and in the New Testament', *NTS* 7 (1960–61), pp. 297-333.

allusion depend on the level of consciousness or visibility attached to an OT text by an author, and consequently, on the degree of recognition which that author expects of the reader.[13] This may be discerned to some extent from the immediate context—for example, in the degree to which an OT text has been integrated or assimilated into the context. The more a text is broken up and woven into the passage, the less likely it is to be a quotation. A quotation must in some way be distinguishable from its supporting text and not be overshadowed by the author's own additions or modifications. Further illumination of a particular passage may also be obtained by studying the author's overall use of OT texts and traditions.[14]

But besides the immediate context, other less accessible factors are usually also involved, such as the prominence of the OT Scriptures generally in the author's social and liturgical environment, and the possibility that a specific text may belong to local or conventional *testimonia*.[15] Whether or not a passage and its current interpretation is known to a writer's audience will probably affect the way in which it is presented. It is thus essential for the exegete to trace the history of each OT text in previous Jewish and Christian interpretation, if possible.[16]

Before considering whether Revelation may offer any possible examples of quotations, there is the preliminary question of whether its apocalyptic genre automatically excludes the use of *any* quotations, formal or otherwise. This is a common explanation put forward by interpreters to account for the apparent absence of 'quotations' in John's

---

13. Though the degree of recognition might vary between individual readers, a community reading and evaluation of John's prophecy would certainly increase the continuity between author-intention and reader-perception. Cf. the discussion of sender–receiver signals in L. Hartman, *Asking for a Meaning* (Uppsala, 1979), p. 100.

14. Some of the methodological insights and warnings of M. Fishbane are relevant to the above discussion: *Biblical Interpretation*, pp. 286-91.

15. The comments of Holm–Nielsen, *Hodayot*, p. 306 are helpful in this matter.

16. Two especially helpful resources for this task are the appendix III of N[26], and W. Dittmar, *Vetus Testamentum in Novo* (Göttingen, 1903), esp. the appendix, pp. 285-362, which is much more extensive than N[26]. The purpose of such a tradition-historical search is not so much to 'find' the meaning of a specific text as to 'situate' it in its social-exegetical context and set up a *field of meaning* by which it can be evaluated, as Hartman observes (*Asking for a Meaning*, p. 97).

book.[17] The force of this argument depends much on the apocalyptic convention of pseudonymity, and particularly on the chronological *mise en scène* of the specific personality employed by an apocalyptic author. It is self-evident that an author writing under the guise of Enoch would avoid making explicit citations from 'later' biblical revelation. However, there is no such difficulty in the author of Daniel making explicit reference to the earlier prophecy of Jeremiah (Dan. 9.2), or the apocalypticist of *2 Baruch* giving a formal quotation from the prophet Isaiah (4.2).[18]

The Revelation of John is of course not bound by such pseudonymous or anachronistic limitations.[19] If an explanation is needed for John's overall lack of interest in making quotations, it should not be sought in supposed genre restrictions, but in John's prophetic consciousness.[20] He does not commend his visions on the basis of apostolic authority conferred by the *earthly* Jesus. Nor is his book a personal word of exhortation which derives its authority from quoting past divine revelation. John is foremost a προφήτης, not an ἀπόστολος or διδάσκαλος. His commission gives birth to a new prophecy—a fresh revelation—which is authorized simultaneously by God, the *risen* Christ, and the divine Spirit.[21]

Yet even this intense conviction of prophetic authority does not *a priori* exclude the possibility that John might occasionally wish to emphasize a particular OT text.[22] He openly acknowledges the abiding

17. E.g. A. Feuillet, *L'Apocalypse: Etat de la question* (StudNeot, 3; Paris, 1963), p. 65; F. Jenkins, *The Old Testament in the Book of Revelation* (Grand Rapids, 1972), pp. 72-73; Schüssler Fiorenza, *Revelation*, pp. 135-36.
18. Cf. Fishbane, *Biblical Interpretation*, pp. 482, 515. Of course, even the various strands of *1 Enoch*, like most other Jewish apocalypses, are heavily indebted to the OT. Most of these contain numerous allusions to the Hebrew Scriptures, particularly the Prophets. On the apocalyptic handling of Scripture, see D.S. Russell, *The Method and Message of Jewish Apocalyptic* (Philadelphia, 1964), pp. 178-202; Hartman, *Asking for a Meaning*; Giet, *L'Apocalypse*, pp. 193-208.
19. *Contra* J. Becker, 'Erwägungen zu Fragen der neutestamentlichen Exegese', *BZ* NF 13 (1969), pp. 101-102. C.C. Torrey, *Documents of the Primitive Church* (New York, 1941), p. 150.
20. Boring comes to a similar conclusion (*Sayings*, p. 99).
21. Note θεός with λέγω: 1.8; the voice from the throne (*passim*), cf. 1.1; 19.9; Christ with λέγω: 21.1, 8, 12, 18; 3.1, 7, 14; πνεῦμα with λέγω: 2.7, 11, 17, 29; 3.6, 13, 22; 14.13; 22.17.
22. So also Trudinger, *Text*, pp. 11-12; *contra* Boring, *Sayings*, p. 99.

relevance of God's previous testimony through the Prophets (10.7; 22.6), and everywhere reveals his debt to them and other OT tradents. His knowledge and particular use of the OT cannot have been completely new to the communities in which he had previously worshipped and exercised his prophetic gifts. Is it not possible then that amidst the sacred florilegia scattered throughout his book there are certain texts and traditions especially important to John which he would expect his readers to know and recognize? While it is not my concern in this study to provide an exhaustive list or detailed treatment of the question, it would seem to me necessary to dispute the common notion that John never 'quotes' the OT. He does not use Scripture monolithically, and there are several places where John allows a passage to retain a high visibility and close correspondence to the original text. I offer a few examples.

Rev. 2.26b-27	*Ps. 2.8a, 9*	
δώσω αὐτῷ ἐξουσίαν ἐπὶ	ואתנה גוים	δώσω σοι ἔθνη τὴν κληρο-
τῶν ἐθνῶν καὶ ποιμανεῖ	נחלתך...תרעם	νομίαν σου...ποιμανεῖς
αὐτοὺς ἐν ῥάβδῳ σιδηρᾷ	בשבט ברזל	αὐτοὺς ἐν ῥάβδῳ σιδηρᾷ,
ὡς τὰ σκεύη τὰ κεραμικὰ	ככלי יוצר	ὡς σκεῦος κεραμέως
συντρίβεται	תנפצם	συντρίψεις αὐτούς

Regardless of whether John is promising participation in eschatological judgment or merely a share in governing the nations in the future kingdom, the Psalm on which this messianic promise is based is probably a part of early Christian *testimonia*.[23] In the closing sections of other letters in Revelation 2–3, a variety of messianic blessings and motifs have been integrated into a relatively consistent redactional pattern. But here the Psalm text stands out, not only by its length and faithfulness to the original[24] but also by the addition of the problematic and unnecessary final clause (ὡς τὰ σκεύη τὰ κεραμικὰ συντρίβεται), which is not included when John uses this psalm text again in Rev. 12.5 and 19.15. In addition, another important signal directing the reader to Psalm 2 is provided in the Christological title

23. *Pss. Sol.* 17.21-25 uses Ps. 2.9 messianically, while other parts of the Psalm are similarly understood in early Christian interpretation: 2.1 in Acts 4.25-26; 2.2 in Rev. 11.15b; 19.19?; 2.7 in Lk 3.22?, Acts 13.13, Heb. 1.5; 5.5 (cf. 4QFlor). Many studies accept Ps. 2.9 in Rev. 2.27 as the only 'quotation' in the book. It is certainly more than an 'echo', as Caird describes it (*Revelation*, p. 45).

24. The prevalent view that this quotation is one of the clearest evidences of LXX usage has been challenged by Trudinger, 'Observations', pp. 84-85.

'Son of God' that opens this Psalm (Ps. 2.7; cf. Heb. 1.1-5). Thus the contextual visibility of this messianic promise based on a messianically understood OT text is undoubtedly intentional and goes beyond the bounds of an allusion.

A second example is to be found in Rev. 3.7. In Revelation 2 and 3, many of the τάδε λέγει statements contain selections from the OT. While most of these are recapitulations of the christological titles and descriptions given in John's commission scene (1.10-20), there is a notable exception in 3.7c, where a passage from Isaiah is adapted messianically.

Rev. 3.7c	Isa. 22.22
Thus says... the one having the key	And I will place the key of the house
of David,	of David upon his shoulder
who opens and no one will shut,	and he will open and no one will shut
and who shuts and no one will open.	and he will shut and no one will open.

The expansion of the introductory title with this uncharacteristically long and faithful reference to Isaiah 22 is directly related to the circumstances of the Philadelphian Christians. It serves as a proof text—an apologetic testimony against the 'synagogue of Satan...who say they are Jews, but are not' (3.9). To a church that is evidently experiencing the hostility of local Jews who reject the messiahship of Jesus, John gives assurance to his readers that it is those who steadfastly worship Jesus as Christ who have access to the messianic kingdom (cf. 3.12), while the erstwhile children of the kingdom are shut out.[25]

Certainly John expected his readers to recognize this prophetic vindication and to appropriate it—perhaps not only for personal comfort, but also as apologetic ammunition in the current religious conflict.

A third example is to be found in ch. 7:

Rev. 7.16, 17	Isa. 49.10/25.8
They shall hunger no more, neither	They shall not hunger nor
thirst any more;	thirst;
neither shall the sun strike them	neither shall the heat nor sun
nor any heat.	strike them.
For... [the Lamb] will shepherd them,	For... [God] will lead them,
and he will guide them to springs	and by springs of water will he
of living water.	guide them.
And God will wipe away every tear	And the Lord God will wipe away
from their eyes.	tears from all faces.

25. 'Judaic opposition to Christian claims is an evident factor in the situation' (Hemer, *Letters*, p. 161). Cf. Beckwith, *Apocalypse*, p. 479.

This short catena describes the inheritance of those who have faithfully endured the great tribulation, and forms part of a paraenetic preview which anticipates the glories of the New Jerusalem in Revelation 21, where Isa. 25.8 is reused and expanded (21.4a). Apart from minor modifications, John leaves these OT salvation oracles relatively intact and conspicuous.

In view of the fact that the paraenetic value of these verses increases in proportion to their recognition as divine promises, it is unlikely that he is merely borrowing these texts for their poetic effect or metaphorical force. It seems more likely that John highlights these particular OT consolations because he wants the readers to appreciate the prophetic foundation of his statements.[26]

While I have presented only a few examples of possible 'quotations', an emphasis on individual texts in Revelation constitutes only a minute sample of John's approach to the OT.[27] The bulk of OT usage which remains can be divided between general OT terminology and traditions, and allusions, though the latter term is not entirely satisfactory in describing John's method, as we shall see.

3. *General Old Testament Terminology and Traditions*

This category of OT application encompasses a variety of biblical motifs which transcend a particular textual source, being drawn from a general OT milieu or being attributable to a variety of texts. John's use of such traditions can be arranged under four general headings:

a.   *Dramatis personae*: Balaam, Balak, Jezebel, David, the Prophets, Moses, Elijah, Michael, the Lamb, the Serpent, the Beast, the Harlot, Gog and Magog, the four living creatures, Abaddon.

b.   *Divine institutions*: the temple and its cultic accessories, for example, the priesthood, altar of sacrifice, golden altar of

---

26. Isa. 49.10 also appears to lie behind Jn 6.35 (cf. 4.14-15), though there it has a *realized* application (Goppelt, *TYPOS*, pp. 182, 186). Isa. 25.8 is also used in 1 Cor. 15.54-55.

27. Vos discusses other alleged quotations, but offers only negative conclusions. This is determined to a large extent by his presupposition that John always quoted from memory and employs only OT language, not its substance or meaning (*Synoptic Traditions*, pp. 109-27).

           incense, horns of the altar, ark of the covenant, outer court; the tabernacle of testimony; the twelve tribes, the tribe of Judah.

c.   *Holy and mythic geography*: Paradise, Mount Zion, the abyss, Babylon, Jerusalem, Sodom, Egypt, the Euphrates, river of life, tree of life.

d.   *Religious vocabulary and concepts*: sons of Israel, song of Moses, manna, Day of the Lord, book of life, OT numerology, shekinah glory of God, cosmic manifestations of theophany, holy war.

B. *Old Testament Allusions and Thematic Analogues*

While more could be said about methodology, particularly regarding the categories of quotations and allusions and their relevance for John's book, the main concern of this chapter is with the presence of clear OT allusions in Revelation and their function. Accordingly, the results of the majority of my research are not based on the number of *possible* allusions in Revelation, but on those passages where it is certain or virtually certain that a specific OT text or tradition lies behind John's usage. On the basis of detailed evaluation, I count approximately 150 such OT texts. Many of these are further reused from one to seven times in the book for a total of c. 72 recapitulations.

A form-critical analysis of these OT traditions reveals that John's use is in general consciously systematic and purposeful. Rather than discovering a conglomerate of divergent texts, one continually encounters various clusters of tradition which can be arranged according to the theme and purpose of the author in a given context. Thus, of the 150 texts identified, c. 125 fall naturally into thematic clusters. This special use of Scripture in Revelation I will refer to as *thematic analogues*. A compilation of these allusive patterns in Revelation yields the following theological inventory.

1.   *Visionary experience and language*
      a. Prophetic commission scenes
      b. Throne-room theophanies
      c. General revelatory language

2.   *Christological titles and descriptions*
      a. OT messianic titles or descriptions applied to Jesus
      b. Divine titles or descriptions transferred to Jesus
      c. Christological application of non-titular phrases
      d. Christological descriptions using OT language

3.   *Eschatological judgment*
        a. OT language of holy war and the Day of the Lord
        b. OT motifs of serial judgment
        c. OT traditions describing the eschatological enemies
           of God and his people
        d. OT oracles against the nations

4.   *Eschatological salvation*
        a. OT salvation oracles in anticipation of eschatological glory
        b. Oracles of renewal and presence
        c. New Jerusalem oracles:
           i. Architectural traditions
          ii. The temple-city

An extended analysis of these categories, though necessary, is
beyond the scope of this study. But a presentation of the biblical
evidence which accompanies these thematic classifications, along with
some general observations, will suffice to show the contours and
patterns of John's method, and will provide a useful background for
evaluating his use of Isaiah in particular.

1. *Visionary Experience and Language*

a. *Prophetic Commission Scenes* (Rev. 1.10-20; 10.1–11.2)[28]

Revelation	Description	Source
1.10	becoming in the Spirit—a voice behind	Ezek. 3.12
10.1	revelatory angel with a cloud and rainbow	Ezek. 1.28a
10.1b	angel's face as the sun—feet as fire	Ezek. 1.27
10.2a	a book in his hand	Ezek. 2.9
10.5-6a	angel lifting his right hand to heaven and swearing by him who lives forever	Dan. 12.7
10.9-11	command to eat the book which is sweet then bitter and a command to prophesy	Ezek. 3.1-4
11.1-2a	John given a rod and told to measure the temple, altar, but not the outer court	Ezek. 40.3; 41.1; 42.1; 43.13

---

28. The use of Dan. 7.9b, 13; 10.5-6; Isa. 44.6; 49.2 in the commission scene of
Rev. 1.10-20 is included under the category of christological descriptions.

b. *Throne-Room Theophanies* (Rev. 4–5)

Revelation	Description	Source
4.2a	throne in heaven	Ezek. 1.26a; 10.1
4.2b-3a	the divine figure on the throne	Ezek. 1.26b
4.3b	rainbow around the throne	Ezek. 1.27b-28a
4.5a	lightning proceeding from the throne	Ezek. 1.13
4.6a	the sea of glass	Ezek. 1.22; cf. Exod. 24.10
4.6b	four living creatures	Ezek. 1.5
4.6c, 4.8	full of eyes before and behind	Ezek. 1.18; 10.12
4.7	faces of a lion, ox, man and eagle	Ezek. 1.10; 10.14
4.8a	having six wings	Isa. 6.2
4.8b	crying holy, holy, holy	Isa. 6.3
5.1	scroll written within and without	Ezek. 2.9-10
5.11b	myriads of angels around the throne	Dan. 7.10

c. *General Revelatory Language*

Revelation	Phrase	Source
1.1, 19; 4.1; 22.6	that which must take place	Dan. 2.28
1.8	says the Lord God...the Almighty	?Amos 3.13
4.1a	after these things I saw, and behold	Dan. 7.6
7.14a	'and I said to him "Lord, you know"'	Ezek. 37.3b
22.10	sealing of the words of the book	Dan. 12.4, 9

It is well known that the book of Revelation has much in common with the prophecies of Ezekiel. What is less often noticed is that John's use of Ezekiel is restricted to certain clearly defined areas of interest. These are:

i.   The visionary narrative of Ezekiel 1–3
ii.   The New Jerusalem prophecy of Ezekiel 40–48
iii.   Oracles against foreign nations: Tyre in chs. 26–27, and Gog in chs. 38–39

As is evident from the thematic paradigms above, John's sense of personal communion with Ezekiel is strongest in the area of the revelatory experience itself,[29] and it is the pre-prophetic overture of Ezekiel 1–3 which has made the greatest impact on him in this regard. But while it appears that the call narrative of Ezekiel 1–3 holds the lead in verifiable allusions, similar visionary traditions such as Isaiah 6 and Daniel 7 (and probably the Sinai theophany of Exodus 19) lie close to the surface.

a. *Prophetic Commission*
The function of John's prophetic commission has already been discussed in the previous chapter. There it was seen that both Rev. 1.10-20 and 10.1–11.2 contain a prophetic commission scene. Whereas the latter is a reaffirmation of John's prophetic call, which forms a prelude to a new phase of revelation with the sounding of the seventh trumpet, the commission of ch. 1 serves to underline the authority of the book as a whole. A comparison of John's inaugural commission with the call narratives in Isaiah 6 and Ezekiel 1–3 revealed a common pattern of auditory and visual elements. But the dominant influence is clearly the call narrative of Ezekiel 1–3, which provides a variety of motifs for John's presentation of his prophetic commission in Revelation 1 and 10.

b. *Throne-Room Theophanies*
When we turn to Revelation 4 and 5, it is important to note that although Ezekiel 1 appears to form the primary inspiration for the narration of John's own throne-room vision, he also adds elements from the other major OT throne-room theophanies in Isaiah 6 and Daniel 7, and probably the Sinai theophany of Exodus 19 as well.[30] By

---

29. Brütsch recognizes a similar predilection (*Offenbarung*, III, p. 133).

30. Cf. Halver, *Mythos*, p. 15. P.S. Alexander (*OTP*, I, p. 246) notes the fundamental role of Ezekiel's visions in Merkabah tradition, and *1 En.* 14.8-25 and 4QŠirŠabb are examples of such applications before John's time. Alexander also discusses the inclination of mystics to include elements of Isa. 6 and Dan. 7, and presents *1 En.* 14.8-25 as an example of such a synthesis (p. 247). In my opinion, however, it is questionable whether any distinctive elements of Isa. 6 occur in this text. Compare this with the prominence of Isa. 6 (often over Ezekiel) in *2 En.* 20–21; *Ques. Ezra* A29-30; *T. Adam* 1; *Lad. Jac.* 2.7-18. This last text is based primarily on Isa. 6, but appears to include motifs from Ezek. 1–2 (Cherubim and fire, v. 7) and Dan. 7 (lightning eye, v. 17). Isa. 6 and Dan. 7 are combined in *1 Clem.* 34.6; cf. Beale, *Daniel*, p. 225 n. 154. Beale proposes more connections to Dan. 7 in Rev. 5,

identifying himself with authoritative visionary tradition John again reveals the depth of his own prophetic self-understanding and a consciousness of his own role in the continuum of revelatory history. His exploitation of each of the prominent OT theophany accounts would suggest that his use of the OT may sometimes be determined less by special books than by particular themes or traditions in which he has an interest. Such is the case with John's use of prophetic call narratives, which transcends a particular prophetic antecedent (though Ezekiel is dominant). A similar pattern will emerge in the material that remains to be analyzed.

2. *Christological Titles and Descriptions*

a. *OT Messianic Titles or Descriptions Applied to Jesus*

Revelation	Titles/Descriptions	Source
1.5b	the first-born/ruler of kings of the earth	Ps. 89.28
1.13a; 14.14b	like a son of man	Dan. 7.13
2.18 (cf. 27)	the Son of God	Ps. 2.7
5.5a	the lion of the tribe of Judah	Gen. 49.9a
5.5b; 22.16	the root of David	Isa. 11.10
11.15b; 12.10	(the) Christ	Ps. 2.2b
12.5b; 19.15b	(Christ) shall rule with a rod of iron	Ps. 2.9
19.11b	with righteousness he judges	Isa. 11.4a
19.15aß	he will smite the nations	Isa. 11.4b
22.16b	the bright morning star	Num. 24.17

b. *Divine Titles or Descriptions Transferred to Jesus*

Revelation	Titles/Descriptions	Source
1.14a	his head and his hair were white as white wool, white as snow	Dan. 7.9b
1.17b; 2.8; 22.13	the first and the last	Isa. 44.6; 41.4; 48.12
2.23b	he who searches mind and heart	Jer. 11.20
3.7	the Holy One	Isaiah (*passim*)
3.14a	the Amen	Isa. 65.16
5.6b	having...seven eyes	Zech. 4.10
17.14b 19.11	lord of lords and king of kings	Dan. 4.37 (LXX)
19.13a	he is clad in a robe dipped in blood	Isa. 63.1-3
19.15c	he himself will trample the winepress	Isa. 63.1-3

and concludes that Daniel rather than Ezekiel is dominant in Rev. 4–5 (pp. 179-228, esp. 224).

c. *Christological Application of Non-Titular Phrases*

Revelation	Title	Source
1.5a; 3.14	the faithful witness	Ps. 89.38b
3.7b	the one having the key of David	Isa. 22.22

d. *Christological Descriptions Using Old Testament Language*

Revelation	Description	Source
1.13b	clothed with a long robe and with a golden girdle round his breast	Dan. 10.5
1.14b; 2.18b; 19.12a	his eyes were like a flame of fire	Dan. 10.6a; 7.9b
1.15a; 2.18b	his feet were like burnished bronze, refined as in a furnace	Dan. 10.6b
1.15b	his voice was like the sound of many waters	Ezek. 43.2
1.16a; 2.12, 16; 19.15a, 21	from his mouth issued a sharp two-edged sword	Isa. 11.4; 49.2

The thematic element in John's christological applications would appear at first glance incidental and heterogenous. Admittedly, this category is the weakest of the four in presenting a conscious blueprint of scriptural architecture. In spite of this, some patterns of authorial selectivity and arrangement can be discerned. At the outset, it is important to observe that most of the christological development takes place in the epistolary sections (Rev. 1–3), in contrast to the apocalypse proper (Rev. 4–21), where the 'Lamb' dominates the christological spotlight.[31]

The number and variety of OT messianic titles used by John (list 2a above) is without parallel in early Christian literature and approaches the collections of *testimonia* found in the second-century Apologists.[32] Many of these titles derive from OT passages which were prominent

31. Important exceptions are to be found in the complex of messianic *testimonia* in Rev. 5.5-6 and the cluster of christological designations in Rev. 19.11-16. A listing of the remaining christological titles in Revelation with no clear OT source includes: *the living one* (1.18a); *the true one/faithful and true* (3.7b; 19.11); *the beginning of God's creation* (3.14b); *the Word of God* (19.13).

32. E.g. Justin, *Dial.* 126.1, 'even He who is [called] like a Son of man by Daniel, and Child by Isaiah, and Christ and God by David... and Stone by many, and Wisdom by Solomon, and Joseph and Judah and Star by Moses, and Rising by Zechariah, and Suffering One and Jacob and Israel again by Isaiah, and Rod and Flower... and Son of God' [My own translation—*PG*, VI, pp. 768-69].

in both Jewish and Christian messianic speculation and expectation.[33] And among these messianically understood OT texts, John gives a high priority, or at least visibility, to Davidic promises.

The accumulation of such testimonies can hardly be explained on the basis of didactic or liturgical interests alone, but almost certainly reflects a missionary context in which the central issue is the messiahship of Jesus, and in which OT testimonies function as the main platform for dialectic.[34] This can be seen particularly in the letters to Smyrna and Philadelphia, and in the special application of Isa. 22.22 in the latter. Such a background helps to explain the fact that in Revelation χριστός is still current as a messianic title in addition to its use as a personal name.[35]

The second group of titles (list 2b above) consists of divine appellations which have been taken over and applied to Jesus. Several christological descriptions also fit this category. For example, qualities of the 'Ancient of days' in Daniel 7 are applied to Christ in Rev. 1.14. This is one of several ways in which John presents his unusually high Christology. The theological progression of chs. 4–5, moving from the throne-room of God to the enthronement of Christ, makes clear that his exalted christological perspective is a fundamental rather than

33. *Ps. 89*—Acts 13.22b; *b. Sanh.* 97a, 99a; cf. 4Q236; *Gen. 49*—*4 Ezra* 12.31; 4QPBless 3; Heb. 7.14?; *1 Clem.* 32.2; *Targ. Onq.*; *Targ. Ps.–J.*; *Gen. R.* 98.8; *b. Sanh.* 98b; *Ps. 2*—*4 Ezra* 7.28 (*passim*); Acts 4.25-27; 13.33; Heb. 1.5a; 5.5; Mt. 3.17/Lk. 3.22 (cf. *Gos. Eb.* frag. 4); *1 Clem.* 36.4; *Dan. 7*—(son of man) in Gospels, *passim*; Acts 7.56; (Dan. 7.9) in Mk 9.3; *1 En.* 46.1-4; 48.2; *Sib. Or.* 5.256, 414?; *Isa. 11*—*1 En.* 49.3-4; 62.2; 4QpIsa^a 8–10; *Pss. Sol.* 17; 1QSb 5; 2 Thess. 2.8; *4 Ezra* 13.10; Rom. 15.12; Mt. 2.23 (*nezer* ?); Justin, *Apol.* 1, 32.12 (which conflates Isa. 11.1 with Num. 24.17); *Targ. Isa.*; *Num. 24.17*—Mt. 2.2?; 1QM 11.5-7; CD 7.18-20; 4QTest; *T. Levi* 18.3; *T. Jud.* 24.1; *Targ. Onq.*; *Targ. Ps.–J.*; *Isa. 22.22*—Mt. 16.19? The judgment of D. Moody Smith that Revelation shows little contact with early church apologetic is clearly unjustified ('The Use of the Old Testament in the New', in J.M. Efird (ed.), *The Use of the Old Testament in the New and Other Essays: Studies in Honor of W.F. Stinespring* (Durham, NC, 1972), p. 62.

34. Justin's *Dialogue* with the Jew Trypho in Ephesus reflects a similar methodology and reveals how scripturally prepared even Gentile Christians were for such encounters. On Jewish–Christian relations in the Asia Minor communities, see Hemer, *Letters*, pp. 8-12 and *passim*.

35. As a title in Rev. 11.15 and 12.10; and as a personal name in Rev. 1.1, 2, 5; 22.21. Cf. V. Taylor, *The Names of Jesus* (London, 1953), pp. 18-23; T. Holtz, *Die Christologie der Apokalypse des Johannes* (TU, 85; Berlin, 1962), pp. 5-9.

an incidental part of the book. For John, ch. 4 could never stand alone and is incomplete without ch. 5, with its revelation that another divine figure occupies the throne-room and shares control of all history: the Lamb.[36] The cumulative effect of Revelation 4 and 5 is thus highly dramatic and goes a long way towards explaining how John can present both God and Christ as 'the Alpha and the Omega' (1.8; 22.13).

Moving to the last category of christological descriptions (list 2d above), one will notice the recapitulation of various descriptine details attached to Christ in Revelation 2 and 19. The prophetic commission scene of Rev. 1.10-20 serves as the primary matrix for these traditions. The analysis of this commission pericope in the previous chapter yielded a twofold purpose for this section.

1.   Based on OT call narratives, the entire unit of Rev. 1.10-20 describes John's divine commission and provides legitimation for the publication and circulation of his visions.

2.   Within Rev. 1.10-20, vv. 12-18 provide assurance to John and his readers that the authority of the whole book rests on nothing less than the direct testimony of the exalted Lord Jesus.

On the basis of the above list (2d), a third function of the Christophany in Revelation 1 can be added. Several elements in the description, in particular the motifs of the eyes as a flame of fire and the sword coming from the mouth, in combination with other ingredients of authority and majesty, appear to anticipate the judicial role of Christ.[37] This presentation of Christ with forensic authority stands as an intentional prelude to the strong warnings of Revelation 2–3 and to the Epiphany of the messianic Judge in ch. 19.[38]

36. The development is clear: 4.11—'Worthy art thou...' (= God); 5.9–'Worthy art thou...' (= the Lamb); and then in 5.13 the hymns of praise coalesce to form a single doxology to God and to the Lamb: 'To him who sits upon the throne *and* to the Lamb be...' Such a culmination was likely conceived and designed from the beginning of ch. 4. An enlightening discussion of the relationship between these two chapters can be found in P.S. Minear, *New Testament Apocalyptic* (Nashville, 1981), pp. 67-72.

37. Fire is a common symbol of purification, and the association of πῦρ and φλόξ with Christ is already connected with the parousia in 2 Thess. 1.7-10.

38. The emphasis in Rev. 1 on Christ as the imminent Judge is further heightened by the presence of the advent promise of 1.7, and by the inclusion of the 'son of

3. *Eschatological Judgment*

Not surprisingly, the subject of judgment is the single most dominant interest in Revelation, and accordingly the use of *thematic analogues* from the OT likewise finds its greatest development in this area. These judgment texts can be broken down into four categories of application, each related to a distinct circle of tradition.

a. *Old Testament Language of Holy War and the Day of the Lord*

Revelation	Description	Source
6.12b	sun darkened, moon as blood	Joel 3.4
6.13	stars fallen from heaven	Isa. 34.4b
6.14a	heaven rolled up as a scroll	Isa. 34.4a
6.15b	attempts to hide from God's wrath	Isa. 2.19; 10a, 21
6.16a	calling the mountains to fall on them	Hos. 10.8; cf. Lk 23.30
6.16b	(hiding) from the face of God and the Lamb	Isa. 2.19
14.15b-16	reaping the harvest of the earth	Joel 4.13
14.18b-19a	gathering the vintage of the earth	Joel 4.13
14.19b-20a	trampling the winepress of God	Isa. 63.1-3; Joel 4.13
19.13a	clothed in a robe dipped in blood	Isa. 63.3
19.15c	trampling the winepress of God	Isa. 63.1-3; Joel 4.13
19.17, 21b	calling the birds to God's feast	Ezek. 39.17
19.18a	eating the flesh of kings, captains...	Ezek. 39.18, 20
20.8-9	Gog and Magog's attack and defeat	Ezek. 38–39

The opening of the sixth seal in Rev. 6.12-17 sets into motion a series of cosmic catastrophes which culminate in an eschatological confrontation between God and the Lamb on one side and earthly sinners on the other. This passage anticipates the climactic encounter between the armies of heaven led by Christ, and the demonically assembled earthly forces at Armageddon (Rev. 16.12-16; 19.11-21). A fundamental structural and thematic relationship exists between this unit and those of 14.14-20 and 19.11-21. Together they describe the same eschatological event—the parousia—from various perspectives and in increasing detail. The general sketch of the Day of the Lord found in Rev. 6.12-17 is given sharper focus in the harvest metaphors of

man' tradition (1.13), which John later associates with the eschatological harvest (14.14-20; 19.13-15). Holtz (*Christologie*, pp. 122, 127-28) discusses the relation between the Christological titles and descriptions and Christ as Judge in more detail. Cf. Comblin, *Le Christ*, p. 85.

14.14-20, which in turn anticipate the ultimate intervention of the messianic warrior and judge in 19.11-21.
A variety of evidence corroborates the relationship between Rev. 6.12-17 and these later presentations of judgment.

1. First, it is crucial to understand that the parousia pericope of Rev. 19.11-21 follows on chronologically to 16.21, and that all of 17.1–19.10 belongs to an expanded interlude. This will be argued in more detail later.

2. Secondly, the identification of those judged in Rev. 6.15 is the same as those of 19.18:[39]

Rev. 6.15	*Rev. 19.18*
οἱ βασιλεῖς τῆς γῆς	σάρκας βασιλέων
καὶ οἱ μεγιστᾶνες	
καὶ οἱ χιλίαρχοι	καὶ σάρκας χιλιάρχων
καὶ οἱ πλούσιοι	
καὶ οἱ ἰσχυροι	καὶ σάρκας ἰσχυρῶν...
καὶ πᾶς δοῦλος	καὶ σάρκας πάντων
καὶ ἐλεύθερος	ἐλευθέρων τε καὶ δούλων

3. Both Revelation 6 and 16 include a great earthquake (σεισμὸς μέφας) (6.12; 16.18), and the removal of islands and mountains (6.14; 16.20).

4. The use of the military technical term χιλίαρχος in Rev. 6.15 and the motif of hiding among the rocks and caves both anticipate the eschatological battle of ch. 19.[40]

5. Finally, both events constitute the final outpouring of God's wrath and are associated with the 'Day of the Lord':[41]

Rev. 6.17	*Rev. 16.14*
ἡ ἡμέρα ἡ μεγάλη τῆς ὀργῆς αὐτῶν	τῆς ἡμέρας τῆς μεγάλης τοῦ θεοῦ

---

39. The omission of μεγιστᾶνες and πλούσιοι in the second list is not significant. John consistently repeats traditions in various forms and order, e.g. Rev. 5.9b ἐκ πάσης φυλῆς καὶ γλώσσης καὶ λαοῦ καὶ ἔθνους is reused six times, each differing from the others. Other examples abound.

40. The second element, inspired by Isa. 2, was a common feature of battle scenarios, in which the defeated forces would flee and attempt to conceal themselves from the pursuing victors (cf. 2 Sam. 13.6; Tacitus, *Hist.* 1.68).

41. The phrase יום יהוה in the OT is frequently expanded to include the idea of wrath, e.g. Zeph. 1.18 ביום עברת יהוה; cf. 2.2; Ezek. 7.19.

In each of these sections (Rev. 6; 14; 19; 20) the final encounter between evil people and a holy God is conceived in terms of a military conflict and developed to a large extent according to biblical traditions of the Day of the Lord and holy war. Every one of the OT passages which John adopts in 6.12-17 derives from Day of the Lord contexts in which the concept of holy war is present. This is explicit in Joel 3, Isaiah 2, Isaiah 34, and can be implied from Hosea 10. The same is true of Joel 4, Isaiah 63 and Ezekiel 38–39.[42] John's own presentation of the Day of the Lord consciously begins on the foundation of these OT precedents, and by means of this tradition the prophet interprets his own vision of the final eschatological battle.[43]

b. *Old Testament Motifs of Serial Judgment*

Revelation	Description	Source
8.7	hail and fire mixed (with blood) trees and grass destroyed	Exod. 9.24-25
8.8b, 9a	sea turned into blood and sea creatures die	Exod. 7.20-21
9.2-11	plague of demonic locusts	Exod. 10.12-15
9.2c	the sun was darkened	Joel 2.10
9.7a	locusts appearing as horses	Joel 2.4a
9.7aß	prepared for battle	Joel 2.5b
9.8b	teeth as lions	Joel 1.6
9.9b	sound of their wings as the sound of many horses running unto battle	Joel 2.4-5
16.2	boils coming upon men	Exod. 9.10
16.3-4	waters turned to blood and sea creatures die	Exod. 7.19-21
16.10	darkness over the kingdom	Exod. 10.22
16.21	exceedingly great hailstones	Exod. 9.24; cf. vv. 14, 23-25

42. Cf. *IDB*, IV, p. 800. Some of these OT passages will be discussed in more detail below.

43. I would agree with many commentators that John's content and order in Rev. 6 bears some relation to the synoptic apocalypse, but in 6.12-14 there are significant differences: (a) the sun and moon motifs of 6.12 are drawn from Joel 3.4, while the Gospels (Mk 13.24; Mt 24.29) presuppose Isa. 13.10; (b) the stars tradition of 6.13 is expanded, giving it a firmer foundation in Isa. 34.4; (c) in 6.14a, the rolling up of the heavens, also from Isa. 34.4, is absent from the Gospel accounts, as are the mountain and island motifs of 6.14b. One might ask whether John is trying to provide a firmer OT basis to the synoptic agenda or whether he is merely developing a common tradition according to his own biblical and eschatological understanding. The latter seems more likely.

For John, no less than for other Jews and earlier prophets, the Exodus constituted the primary event of salvation history under the old covenant. To a Jewish-Christian it served as a natural analogue to the Christ event, and offered a wealth of typological parallels for the illustration and development of Christian soteriology, ecclesiology and eschatology.[44] It is not surprising, then, that John appropriates images from various stages of the Exodus tradition—from plagues to passover, from the Red Sea to the wilderness—emphasizing its manifestation of both divine judgment and salvation.[45]

His adaptation of various plague motifs in the trumpet and bowl series goes deeper than the mere borrowing of imagery or the apocalyptic heightening of biblical models of judgment.[46] John sees the Roman Imperator and his empire as the spiritual reincarnation of Pharaoh and Egypt, persecuting God's people and replacing the duties of their divine calling and citizenship with forced allegiance to the state. Thus, when he comes to describe those who have conquered the 'beast', they are standing beside the sea of glass and singing 'The song of Moses, the servant of God, and the song of the Lamb' (Rev. 15.2-3).[47] As the spiritual and physical bondage of Egypt was abolished through the

44. 'For the whole exodus... out of Egypt... was a type and image of the exodus of the church... and if any one will devote a close attention to those things which are stated by the prophets with regard to the [time of the] end, and those which John... saw in the Apocalypse, he will find that the nations [are to] receive the same plagues universally, as Egypt then did particularly' (Irenaeus, *Adv. Haer.* 4.30.4, *ANCL*, V.I, pp. 479-80).

45. For the wider use of Exodus traditions in Revelation, see Casey, 'Exodus Typology', pp. 135-220.

46. *Contra* Halver, *Mythos*, p. 15. The recounting of the Egyptian plague-judgments is common in later Jewish writings, and esp. in Hellenistic Jewish authors of *Egyptian* provenance: Wis. 11.5-8, 15-16; 17.1–19.22; *Artapanus* 3.27.33; 3 Macc. 2.3-9; *Ezek. Trag.* 133-74; ?Jannes and Jambres; cf. *Jub.* 48.5-19; *LAB* 10.1; *4 Ezra* 15.5-15 (prob. dependent on Revelation); *Sam. Pent.*; 4QpaleoExod^m. The prominence of the plague story complete with haggidic embellishments among (?Asia Minor) Christians is suggested by the (unexplained) mention of Jannes and Jambres in 2 Tim. 3.8-9. Predictions of eschatological plagues occur in *1 En.* 91.7-11; *Apoc. Ab.* 29.15, 30.3-8; cf. Deut. 28.58-61.

47. P. Lestringant, *Essai sur l'unité de la révélation biblique* (Paris, 1942), pp. 149-50; Cambier, 'Les images', pp. 115, 119; Caird, *Revelation*, p. 197; cf. Rev. 18.4 and the symbolic use of 'Egypt' in 11.8, which some interpret as Rome (e.g. Comblin, *Le Christ*, p. 88). Beckwith argues strongly against Exodus typology in Rev. 15 (*Apocalypse*, pp. 676-78).

leadership and divine empowering of the man Moses, so the Christians overcome their oppressors 'by the blood of the Lamb' (12.11), who, like Moses, 'will guide them to springs of living water' (7.17).

In the formation of the trumpet and bowl schemes, John has not only taken up individual details of the Exodus plagues account, but has also been influenced by its literary structure.[48] Like the Exodus sequence, his plague series moves in progressive levels of intensity and records at appropriate stages the continued negative response of those afflicted (Rev. 9.20; 16.9, 11, 21).[49]

The shift from Exodus traditions to Joel in Rev. 9.2-11 bridges one passage of locust judgment with another and provides John with some of the symbolic imagery necessary to transform an original nature plague into an ominous apocalyptic nightmare. The ready metaphor of locusts as an invading army, and Joel's fusion of locust anatomy and military features thus presented a fitting model for the hellish legions of the fifth trumpet.

c. *Old Testament Traditions Describing the Eschatological Enemies of God and his People*

Revelation	Description	Source
11.7b; (13.7a; cf. 17.14a)	beast wars against and overcomes	Dan. 7.21
12.3	ten horns	Dan. 7.7b
12.4a; cf. 12.9	heavenly stars cast down to earth	Dan. 8.10b
12.14b; cf. 13.5c	time, times and half a time	Dan. 7.25
13.1a; (11.7; 17.7c)	the sea beast	Dan. 7.3a

48. As H.P. Müller has shown by a form-critical analysis, noting five structural and linguistic parallels between Revelation and the Exodus plague sequence, including authorization formulas, delineation of spheres affected, and the use of καὶ ἐγένετο ('Die Plagen der Apokalypse. Eine formgeschichtliche Untersuchung', *ZNW* 51 [1960], pp. 268-78). He concludes that 'Die Exodustexte und die Plageberichte der apokalypsis sind, soweit ich sehe, seine einzigen Belege' (276). But this judgment is a little too exclusive and ignores the use of Joel.

49. This progressive development between the trumpet and bowl series creates difficulties for the recapitulation theory. Various lines of evidence point to a linear movement of intensification rather than a cyclic structure. Philo's understanding of the Egyptian plagues expresses well John's approach. 'First, God wished to admonish...rather than to destroy' (*Mos.* 1.110, cf. 95, 123, 134); see further Caird, *Revelation*, pp. 104-106, 201; Mounce, *Revelation*, pp. 178, 291; cf. Beckwith, *Apocalypse*, pp. 555-56, 669-73.

13.1b; (17.7c, 12a, 16a)	ten horns	Dan. 7.7b
13.2	beast like a leopard, bear and lion	Dan. 7.4-6
13.5a	a mouth speaking great things	Dan. 7.8
13.5b; (13.4a)	authority given the beast	Dan. 7.6c
13.6	blasphemy against God and his temple	Dan. 8.10-12 (cf. 7.25; 11.36)
13.7a; (11.7b; cf. 17.14a)	war with and overpowering of the saints	Dan. 7.21
13.7b, 8a (cf. 13.15)	every tribe, people, tongue and nation worship him	Dan. 7.14
17.12a	ten horns are ten kings	Dan. 7.24
19.20; cf. 20.10	beast thrown into the lake of fire	Dan. 7.11

Although the crisis which prompts John's visions clearly involves Christian conflicts with emperor and empire, it is his burden to show that the contest is only superficially political or historical. Revelation 12 and 13 in particular reveal that persecution (or the threat of persecution) is not merely political or local, but is spiritual, suprahistorical, and part of an ongoing struggle between God and Satan, and their followers (cf. Rev. 2.10, 13; Eph. 6.10-12).[50] Even though the extent of evil's influence has been determined by God (Rev. 6.9-11; 12.12; 13.5), the spiritual war has accelerated with the inbreaking of the Messiah and his kingdom (12.10-12; cf. 11.15-17). It is this

50. Note the connection of earthly political and religious opposition with Satan already in Rev. 2.9-10, 13; 3.9. Rev. 12 and 13 are apparently to be understood as the antithetic parallel to chs. 4–5. Convincing form-critical evidence for this has been set forth by H.P. Müller, 'Formgeschichtliche Untersuchungen zu Apc. 4f.' (PhD thesis, Heidelberg, 1962); and by Beale, *Daniel*, pp. 245, 302, who expands on Müller's thesis. Both sections present authorization scenes with a similar pattern: (a) presentation of an agent; (b) authorization of an agent; (c) effects of the agent's authority. Other parallels could be noted, such as the use of θρόνος (4.2ff. // 13.2); the response of worship and hymns (4.11; 5.9-14 // 13.4), and the use of ὁ κύριος καὶ ὁ θεὸς ἡμῶν (Vulg. = *Domine et Deus noster*) in 4.11, which may be in response to the 'blasphemous names' of 13.1, and alluding to Domitian's title *dominus et deus noster* (Suet. *Dom.* 13); S. Scherrer, 'Revelation 13 as an Historical Source for the Imperial Cult under Domitian' (PhD dissertation, Harvard, 1979), p. 190. Cf. Beale, *Daniel*, p. 254.

eschatological flurry of antigodly activity which John is concerned to expose.

The dualistic drama which he portrays revolves around a central cast of characters, set in conscious antithetic parallel.

The ultimate antagonists:	*God versus Dragon*
(Personal) authorized agents:	*Lamb versus Beast*
(Corporate) representatives:	*Woman/Bride versus Harlot*

To describe these characters, again and again John turns to traditional images and texts. We have already seen that behind his portrait of God lies a core of OT throne-room theophanies, and that the figure of Christ (the Lamb) is invariably characterized by traditional messianic testimonies. Later examination of the Harlot-Babylon image will reveal that John depends almost exclusively on OT oracles against Babylon and other nations to depict Rome's character and judgment.

Such a thematic pattern is even clearer in the present example (List 3c above), where John uses Daniel as a *Vorbild* for his presentation of the eschatological enemies of God. In John's understanding, Daniel's picture of a pagan ruler in opposition to God and his people serves as a natural prophetic parallel to the political and religious circumstances surrounding himself and his readers.[51]

Out of all the Daniel elements which he employs here (Dan. 7.3-8, 11, 14, 21, 24, 25; 8.10-12), the only non-contextual application is Rev. 13.7b-8a, which uses Dan. 7.14 and applies a 'son of man' text to the beast. But one must keep in mind that John continually presents the eschatological enemy as a parody of divine authority. His dualistic

---

51. Two factors contributed to this association: (1) The widespread contemporary belief that the fourth kingdom of Daniel symbolized the Roman empire (not Greece): *4 Ezra* 12.11; *2 Bar.* 39.5-6; Jos. *Ant.* 10.10.4; *Barn.* 4.2-6; (2) The ambiguous nature of the beast symbolism, so that almost any political or religious opponents could be identified: *Sib. Or.* 3.395-400; *4 Ezra* 11.40b-44; 12.11-14, 13.5-6; Mt. 24.15; 2 Thess. 2.3-4; and later, Islam, the Papacy, etc. J. Ernst remarks, 'Dieser (Antiochus) wird zum Vorbild und Prototyp aller Gottesfeindschaft... Die Gestalt des Widersachers ist also ganz wesentlich der nationalen Religionsgeschichte entsprungen. Politische und religiöse Bedruckung und Verführung spiegeln sich in dieser Figur, und es wird vom Gang der Geschichte und der Eigenart der späteren Autoren abhängen, welch Züge hinfort jeweils am meisten hervortreten und mit anderen Prophetien, mit mythischen Erinnerungen und neuen Geschehnissen sich verbinden, um das alte Bild immer wieder neu zu nuancieren' (*Die eschatologischen Gegenspieler in den Schriften des Neuen Testaments* [Regensburg, 1967], p. 197).

program lends naturally to dramatic irony, and thus there is often a
fluid, but conscious and limited, dialectical relationship between text
and context, lamb and beast, which is moving towards resolution. A
clear example occurs in Rev. 17.14, where the motif of 'warring with
and overcoming' (taken from Dan. 7.21) is applied to Christ in an
intentional reversal of Rev. 11.7 and 13.7a, where the same phrase is
used of the beast.[52]

While Revelation 13 is the main explication of the beast in Danielic
terms, John's concern to maintain a consistent connection with his
model is seen by the fact that almost every other passage which
describes the beast contains allusions to Daniel, from his first
introduction in 11.7 to his final capture and punishment in 19.20.[53]
The more extensive development of the beast pericope in 17.7-16a is
especially interesting, for it reveals a shift from the Harlot-Babylon
traditions of Isaiah, Jeremiah and Ezekiel to the eschatological enemy
of Daniel, and *then back again*.

A. Introduction of Harlot-Babylon:　17.1-6 (uses Isa., Jer., Ezek.)
B. Description of the beast and its horns:　17.7-16a (uses Daniel)[54]
A'. Description of Harlot-Babylon:　17.16b–19.4 (uses Isa., Jer., Ezek.)

John adopts one OT model to describe *personal* eschatological
opponents and another to characterize the *corporate* evil kingdom.
Whereas in the former he relies exclusively on Daniel, in the latter he
purposely seeks out OT Babylon oracles and reapplies them to the new
'Babylon'. An analysis of these Babylon traditions, which constitute
the largest and final category within the theme of judgment, can now
be given.

52. Beale (*Daniel*, pp. 237, 260-62) acknowledges both Rev. 13.7a and 17.14
as ironic parody, though in the latter case he underestimates the role of 11.7; 13.7a.
The flow of inspiration appears to be Dan. 7.21 → Rev. 13.7a, 11.7 → Rev. 17.14;
not Dan. 7.21 → Rev. 17.14 → (11.7, 13.7a).

53. For a more detailed discussion of Daniel in Rev. 13 and 17, see Beale,
Daniel, pp. 229-67, who presents other possible allusions; also Ernst, *Gegenspieler*,
pp. 132, 159-60, 182.

54. Beale correctly recognizes Daniel as the *Vorbild* for this section, but he overlooks the distinction between the harlot and beast themes and John's shift of OT
traditions when he suggests Daniel as the *Vorbild* for the *whole chapter* (*Daniel*,
pp. 265-67).

d. *Old Testament Oracles against the Nations*
The sounding of the seventh trumpet in Rev. 11.15 heralds the fulfilment of a prophetic mystery (10.7) which is revealed as the universal establishment of God's kingdom. The transformation of the 'kingdom of the *world*' into the 'kingdom of the Lord and of his Christ' necessarily involves the judgment and removal of all earthly opposition, in particular the recalcitrant nations who rage against the divine sovereign and his anointed viceroy (cf. Rev. 11.15-18a with Ps. 2). An eschatological agenda is then unveiled in 11.18 which exhibits a twofold program of judgment and salvation, wrath and reward.

> The nations raged, but thy wrath came,
> And the time for the dead to be judged,
> For rewarding the servants...
> For destroying the destroyers of the earth.

A visionary interlude follows (12.1–14.5) in which Rev. 12.1-17 describes the spiritual origin and background of the conflict, and 13.1-18 and 14.1-5 introduce the two opposing war leaders (the Beast and the Lamb) and their followers. The prelude to the final outpouring of wrath then comes in 14.6-13 with a series of last warnings and exhortations. The stage is now set for the seven bowl judgments (15.1–16.21), 'which are the last, for with them the wrath of God is ended' (15.16). The culmination of God's wrath with the seventh bowl is formally indicated in Rev. 16.17 with the exclamation, 'It is finished!'[55]

The worldly empire which is the focus of God's wrath is spiritually designated 'Babylon' and represents not only Rome, but the network of nations and provinces under her control or influence. John's presentation of Babylon and her judgment comes in three stages:

1. Rev. 14.8-11	Preliminary warnings
2. Rev. 16.1-21	Fall of Babylon
3. Rev. 17.1–19.4	Character and judgment of Babylon

---

55. John's use of ὀργή and θυμός in connection with God's wrath appears to have significance for the movement and structure of the book. Apart from 6.16-17, which I have already argued is a proleptic summary of the Day of the Lord, the motif of God's wrath is limited to events subsequent to the seventh trumpet (11.15), and is never mentioned in relation to the seal and trumpet judgments.

In each of these stages, the development of John's picture of Babylon is consciously dependent on and limited to OT oracles against the nations, and primarily those against Babylon and Tyre.[56]

Revelation	Referent	OT Referent	Source
11.18-19 (19.2b)	'Babylon'	Babylon	Jer. 51.25
14.8a (18.2)	'Babylon'	Babylon	Isa. 21.9
14.8b (18.3a)	'Babylon'	Babylon	Jer. 51.7
14.10a (16.19)	wicked of 'Babylon'	Nations (incl. Babylon)	Jer. 25.15; cf. Ps. 75.9; Isa. 51.17
14.10b-11a (19.3b)	wicked of 'Babylon'	Edom	Isa. 34.10
16.19 (14.10a)	'Babylon'	Nations (incl. Babylon)	Jer. 25.15
17.1b	'Babylon'	Babylon	Jer. 51.13
17.2a (18.3b, 9b)	'Babylon'	Harlot-Tyre	Isa. 23.17
17.2b	'Babylon'	Babylon	Jer. 51.7
17.4b	'Babylon'	Babylon	Jer. 51.7
17.5a	'Babylon'	Babylon	Dan. 4.30
17.16	'Babylon'	Harlot-Jerusalem	Ezek. 23.29, 25; cf. 16.39
18.2a (14.8a)	'Babylon'	Babylon	Isa. 21.9
18.2b	'Babylon'	Babylon	Isa. 13.21; 34.11-14; Jer. 50.39; 51.37
18.3a (14.8b)	'Babylon'	Babylon	Jer. 51.7; cf. 25.15
18.3b (17.2a; 18.9b)	'Babylon'	Harlot-Tyre	Isa. 23.17
18.3c	'Babylon'	Tyre	Ezek. 27.33
18.4a	'Babylon'	Babylon	Jer. 51.45
18.5a	'Babylon'	Babylon	Jer. 51.9
18.6a	'Babylon'	Babylon	Jer. 50.29 (cf. v. 15)
18.7b	'Babylon'	Babylon	Isa. 47.8
18.8a	'Babylon'	Babylon	Isa. 47.9a
18.9b (17.2a; 18.3b)	'Babylon'	Harlot-Tyre	Isa. 23.17
18.9-14	'Babylon'	Tyre	Ezek. 26.16-21; 27.6-22 (*passim*)
18.17b	'Babylon'	Tyre	Ezek. 27.29
18.18b	'Babylon'	Tyre	Ezek. 27.32
18.19	'Babylon'	Tyre	Ezek. 27.30-31

56. In spite of the abundance of current prophecies against Rome, such as are found in the Sibylline Oracles, John preferred to base his own prophetic doom song on OT models. Cf. H. Fuchs, *Der geistige Widerstand gegen Rom in der antiken Welt* (Berlin, 2nd edn, 1964), p. 61, who does think John borrows other contemporary anti-Roman traditions, but his examples do not go beyond interesting parallels, which might be expected in oracular contexts in general, and against Rome in particular.

Revelation	Referent	OT Referent	Source
18.21ab	'Babylon'	Babylon	Jer. 51.63-64
18.21c	'Babylon'	Tyre	Ezek. 26.21b
18.22a	'Babylon'	Tyre	Ezek. 26.13
18.22c, 23ab	'Babylon'	Nations (incl. Babylon)	Jer. 25.10 (cf. 7.34; 16.9; 33.11)
18.23c	'Babylon'	Harlot-Tyre	Isa. 23.8
19.2b	'Babylon'	Babylon	Jer. 51.25
19.3b	'Babylon'	Edom	Isa. 34.10

1. *Rev. 14.8-11*. Like some of his prophetic forerunners, John is called to 'prophesy about (ἐπί) many peoples and nations and tongues and kings' (10.11).[57] Along with a call for repentance (14.6-7) comes a warning stressing the certainty of Babylon's judgment and the judgment of those who continue to associate with her, that is, those who refuse to 'come out of her' (14.8-11; 18.4a). The appropriation of the prophetic perfect in 14.8, 'fallen, fallen is Babylon', emphasizes the immutable decree of God and anticipates its actual fulfilment in 16.19 (not 18.2). The relationship of this warning pericope to the subsequent judgment of Babylon is strengthened by the fact that each of the four OT texts adapted in 14.8-11 reappears in the later stages of John's Babylon oracle.

2. *Rev. 16.1-21*. The actual judgment of Babylon begins and ends with the seven bowl plagues. But the plagues themselves are nowhere based on OT oracles against the nations. These are of course dominated by Exodus plague traditions, as has already been noted. John only actually mentions Babylon in Rev. 16.19 in connection with the effects of the seventh bowl, and here again turns back to the OT model of prophecies against Babylon.

3. *Rev. 17.1–19.4*. We come finally to the most extensive development of the Babylon theme. Before discussing the use of OT traditions in this section, it is necessary to determine how it relates structurally and thematically to the surrounding context. Since the fall of Babylon takes place already in 16.19, it appears that Rev. 17.1–18.24 serves as

---

57. Perhaps ἐπί should be translated as 'against' here. προφητεῦσαι ἐπί commonly translates על הנבא or אל הנבא in OT oracles against nations: e.g. Jer. 25.13, 30; 26.11-12; Ezek. 4.7. Cf. A.T. Robertson, *A Grammar of the Greek New Testament* (Nashville, 1934), p. 605. In addition, the contents of the scroll in Ezekiel (2.9-10), on whom John depends here, are 'words of lamentation and mourning and woe'.

a parenthetical expansion to describe and explain the Babylon theme in more detail.[58] Two factors strengthen this conclusion:

1. Chapters 17 and 18 present no new action or progress subsequent to the bowl series. John's schedule of eschatological events moves from the preparation for Armageddon to the battle itself (16.12-16 → 19.11-21).[59]
2. Chapters 17 and 18 contain a motley blend of present, prophetic perfect and future verbs still anticipating the destruction of Babylon, which is never narrated as such in any subsequent passage.

Therefore, after we identify Revelation 17–18 as a unit which belongs chronologically before 16.19, we are left with 19.1-10, of which vv. 1-4 are a hymn of thanksgiving for Babylon's judgment, looking back to 16.19. While vv. 5-10 contain a hymn of anticipation looking forward to the marriage of the Lamb in Rev. 21.1ff.

Although the spiritual association of Rome with Babylon was already widely asserted by the end of the first century CE, no other author develops the Babylon image to the extent that John does.[60] Rather than being an atomistic collection of texts, his application of

58. So also Beckwith, *Apocalypse*, p. 670; Caird, *Revelation*, pp. 104, 211; Schüssler Fiorenza, *Revelation*, pp. 66 (n. 153), 72. Two factors may have influenced the separation of chs. 17–18: (1) unwillingness to interrupt the flow of the bowl judgments; (2) a desire to punctuate the harlot section because it serves as the anti-image of the bride in 21.9–22.5 (cf. 17.1 with 21.9). Cf. C.H. Giblin, 'Structural and Thematic Correlation in the Theology of Revelation 16–22', *Bib* 55 (1974), pp. 487-504.

59. Even after one makes allowances for the apocalyptic nature of the book, John's method of structural and thematic parallelism, and his predilection for parenthetical expressions and digressions (e.g. 7; 10.1–11.14; 17–18) causes difficulty for those seeking to discern a logical outline. The reader of Revelation can only expect telic progression, not episodic succession.

60. Cf. *Sib. Or.* 5.143, 159; *4 Ezra* 3.2, 28-31; 11–12; *2 Bar.* 11.1; 67.7?; 1 Pet. 5.13. All of these documents are usually dated after 70 CE. It is natural to expect that the outcome of the Jewish war of 66–70 CE was determinative for this typological transfer. The anti-Roman prophecy of *Sib. Or.* 3.350-380 (c. 30 BCE) does not employ the 'Babylon' figure, though neither do *Sib. Or.* 4.103-151 (c. 80 CE) and *T. Moses* 6.8-9 (chs. 6–7 are a later addition—first century CE). The use of this cryptic name in 1 Peter is especially significant, for it shows that Rome could be understood pejoratively as 'Babylon' and still be a God-appointed authority to be obeyed and prayed for (5.13; 2.13-17).

OT judgment oracles to Rome is thematically determined and emphasizes two factors in the current socio-political situation. The first relates to Rome's *political and religious* domination, and the second to its *economic* monopoly. In order to accentuate these two factors, John adopts two separate OT models: Babylon and Tyre.

1. *Babylon* is the symbol of a proud, idolatrous empire which flaunts its power at the expense of others and scoffs at the thought of its own downfall or judgment. Five Babylon oracles occur in the OT: Isaiah 13–14; 21.1-10; 47.1-15; Jer. 25.12-38 (including Judah and other nations); and Jeremiah 50–51. Together these passages prophesy God's judgment for sins of pride, idolatry, self-sufficiency, and injustice towards God's people. In setting forth his own 'burden of Babylon', John borrows traditions from *every one* of these oracles, though the foundational text is Jeremiah 50–51, which is the most extensive of the five Babylon oracles.[61] He has already prepared for this presentation of Babylon's judgment in the eschatological index of Rev. 11.18, where an allusion to Jer. 51.25, 'to destroy those who corrupt the earth', forms an *inclusio* with Rev. 19.2b, where thanksgiving is given for the judgment of the harlot 'who corrupted the earth'.

2. *Tyre*, on the other hand, is a symbol of international trafficking, opulent wealth and commercial hegemony. John's addition of the merchant theme in Revelation 18 is not simply a more literary or poetical method of describing Rome's judgment. Rome's economic control affected significantly the everyday lives and status of John's readers, and thus Revelation 18 is only a fuller development of socio-economic issues already expressed in earlier passages (Rev. 2.9; 3.17; 6.6; 13.16-17; cf. 18.4, 11).[62] Only two extended Tyre

---

61. A similar method appears to be adopted in *Sib. Or.* 5.169-174, though on a much smaller scale. This oracle against Rome (= Babylon—143, 159), possibly contemporary with Revelation, borrows several motifs from the prophecy against Babylon in Isa. 47. This text is discussed in more detail by Fuchs, *Der geistige Widerstand*, p. 67.

62. Asia was one of the three richest provinces (Tacitus, *Hist.* 2.6; 3.8; *Sib. Or.* 5.286-327), and just as Rome's granaries relied on Egypt's corn, so also her luxuries were to a large extent dependent on the trade and tribute of Asia (cf. Tacitus, *Ann.* 3.53-54). The economic relationship between Rome and Asia is almost a

2. *John and the Influence of the Old Testament*

oracles occur in the OT: Isa. 23.1-18 and Ezekiel 26–29. And John uses them both, though the longer Ezekiel passage is dominant.[63] The image of Rome as a 'harlot' may also have been originally suggested by the Tyre prophecies; for the first mention of the harlot in Rev. 17.2a corresponds to the first application of a Tyre oracle, in which the harlot image also appears.

An overall summary of John's use of OT oracles against the nations reinforces the supposition that he does not randomly select OT passages, but consciously appropriates specific themes and models germane to the subjects which he wishes to treat. Four passages in Revelation either allude to or discuss the corporate image of Rome as Babylon: 11.18-19; 14.8-11; 16.19; and 17.1–19.4. Of the 34 clear OT allusions (including repetitions) used in these sections, 21 stem from Babylon oracles, 11 from Tyre oracles, 2 from an Edom oracle (Isa. 34.10 2×), and one from a Harlot-Jerusalem oracle. If John is merely illustrating his prophecies with OT language and imagery, why does he not borrow *any* traditions or phrases from the numerous extended oracles against Egypt (e.g. Isa. 19–20; Jer. 46; Ezek. 29–32), or various prophecies against Moab, Philistia, Ammon, and other nations? Yet every Babylon oracle and every extended Tyre oracle is exploited. Such a thematic scheme would seem to indicate premeditated authorial motive.

4. *Eschatological Salvation*

a. *OT Salvation Oracles in Anticipation*

Revelation	Promise/Blessing	Source
1.6a; 5.10; 20.6	kings and priests of God	Exod. 19.6 (cf. 1 Pet. 2.9)
2.17	(saints) will receive a new name	Isa. 65.15; 62.2
2.26b	(saints) will receive authority over the nations	Ps. 2.8b

standard theme of oracular and apocalyptic prophecies against Rome, sometimes emphasizing Rome's exploitation of the province and its temporary poverty (*Sib. Or.* 3.350-80; cf. 4.145; 8.68-72); at other times chastising Asia's prosperity as a partner in the Roman cartel (*4 Ezra* 15.46–16.1; *Sib. Or.* 4.145-48). The latter situation seems to reflect the circumstances of Revelation.

63. Short oracles against Tyre are also found in Amos 1.9-10 and Joel 3.4-8.

2.27	(saints) shall rule with a rod of iron	Ps. 2.9
3.9b	enemies shall bow before them	Isa. 60.14
7.14b	wash robes in the blood of the Lamb	Exod. 19.10, 14 (Gen. 49.11)
7.16	shall no longer hunger or thirst, sun shall not strike them	Isa. 49.10a
7.17a	the lamb will be their shepherd and will guide them to springs of water	Isa. 49.10b
7.17b (21.4a)	God will wipe every tear from their eyes	Isa. 25.8b
19.7-8	bride clothed by God/righteous deeds	Isa. 61.10

With the smoke of Babylon's conflagration dissipating in the background, John's vision of judgment retreats to make way for the final vision of salvation. The expectation of this future consummation and renewal is kept alive in earlier parts of the book by John's strategic placement of eschatological 'reminders', the majority of which are based on OT salvation oracles.[64] Thus, the manifestation of divine renewal and reward outlined in Rev. 21.1–22.5 was already presupposed in the promises of chs. 2–3, projected in the eschatological index of 11.15-18, and anticipated in the hymnic pericopes of 7.9-17, 15.2-4 and 19.5-10. These promises serve as a preview to the main presentation and development of salvation oracles in Revelation 21–22.

b. *Oracles of Renewal and Presence (21.1-8)*

Revelation	Tradition	Source
21.1	a new heaven and a new earth	Isa. 65.17
21.2b	city prepared as a bride adorned	Isa. 61.10
21.3	tabernacle of God with men, they will be his people, he will be their God	Ezek. 37.27
21.4a (7.17b)	God will wipe every tear from their eyes	Isa. 25.8b
21.4b	no longer any death	Isa. 25.8a
21.4c	no more mourning or crying	Isa. 65.19b

64. Almost all the examples listed retain future verbs.

21.4d	former things passed away	Isa. 65.16c; Isa. 43.18
21.5a	behold, I make all things new	Isa. 43.19a (cf. 2 Cor. 5.17)
21.6b; 22.17	to the thirsty I will give water without price	Isa. 55.1
21.7	I will be his God and he will be my son	2 Sam. 7.14

The primary focus of Rev. 21.1-8 involves the announcement and introduction of the New Jerusalem. The structural arrangement and purpose of this section is revealed by the use of γέγοναν ('they are finished') in 21.6a. This divine exclamation formally sets off this unit as the fulfilment of the promises of salvation, as the same phrase in 16.17 (γέγονεν, 'it is finished') formally indicated the completion of God's wrath. The events of Rev. 21.1-8 conclude the acts of God begun with the sealed scroll in ch. 5, and there is now no more work for him to do in history—only in eternity with his people.[65]

The central theme of this section is summarized in the divine proclamation of 21.5, 'Behold, I make all things new' (cf. Isa. 43.19). John's addition of πάντα to the Isaiah text emphasizes the magnitude of his concept of renewal, which transcends any particular theological idea such as the new creation, the renewal of paradise, and so forth. Rather, John subsumes under the general theme of renewal a variety of important traditions, each of which evokes some aspect of the relationship between God and humanity. So we encounter motifs of creation and paradise, as well as of covenant theology,[66] the tabernacle and temple, and Zion-Jerusalem. John blends all these traditions

65. To style this section a *prologue*, as do Schüssler Fiorenza and Rissi, seems inconsistent with John's emphasis on finality and consummation (*Revelation*, p. 52; M. Rissi, *The Future of the World* [London, 1972], pp. 54-55). Since 21.9–22.5 forms a sort of 'appendix', the category of prologue does not adequately express the relationship between 21.1-8 and 21.9–22.5. In the former passage, all progress and movement has come to an end, as 21.6 makes clear, the emphasis being on *omega* and *end*. It is perhaps best to view the two sections as *summary* and *expansion*.

66. Rissi (*Future*, p. 57) assumes that the covenant formula of Rev. 21.3 is based on Lev. 26.11-12, but Ezek. 37.27 (itself probably a reapplication of the Sinai covenant formula) is closer in language and context; cf. Schüssler Fiorenza, *Priester für Gott* (Münster, 1972), p. 351. However, in 2 Cor. 6.16 Paul apparently conflates the two passages! The dynastic oracle of 2 Sam. 7.14 is applied corporately to those who will reign together with Christ—*the root of David* (Rev. 2.26-27; 3.21; 5.10; 20.4-6; 22.5). Cf. 2 Cor. 6.18; Gal. 4.6-7; 4QFlor.

together into a theology of 'presence', in which the restoration of communion between God and humanity, inaugurated by the Christ-event, reaches the final stage: when God himself σκηνώσει μετ' αὐτῶν.[67] The importance of this climactic event is shown by the fact that God himself makes the announcement, and is reinforced by the constant repetition of the presence motif in the final vision (21.3-4, 7, 11, 22-23; 22.3-4).

Thus with the events of Rev. 21.1-8 all progress and movement have come to an end; all divine action is consummated, creation is renewed, paradise is re-established, and all that remains is for God and his people to enjoy the eternal sabbath in the Holy City. The one task remaining for John is to provide a more detailed description of the New Jerusalem which was introduced in 21.1-8.[68] This is accomplished in a parenthetical expansion (21.9–22.5) which forms an antithetic parallel to the Babylon appendix of 17.1–18.24. Accordingly, this section has been called the *Jerusalem appendix*.

John's contrast of the harlot and the bride in these two sections encompasses both structural and thematic similarities:[69]

1. *Rev. 17.1*	*Rev. 21.9*
καὶ ἦλθεν εἷς ἐκ τῶν ἑπτὰ ἀγγέλων	καὶ ἦλθεν εἷς ἐκ τῶν ἑπτὰ ἀγγέλων
τῶν ἐχόντων τὰς ἑπτὰ φιάλας καὶ	τῶν ἐχόντων τὰς ἑπτὰ φιάλας... καὶ
ἐλάλησεν μετ' ἐμοῦ λέγων δεῦρο,	ἐλάλησεν μετ' ἐμοῦ λέγων δεῦρο,
δείξω σοι τὸ κρίμα τῆς πόρνης	δείξω σοι τὴν νύμφην
2. *Rev. 17.3a*	*Rev. 21.10a*
καὶ ἀπήνεγκέν με εἰς	καὶ ἀπήνεγκέν με ἐν πνεύματι
ἔρημον ἐν πνεύματι	ἐπὶ ὄρος μέγα καὶ ὑψηλόν

67. Even though σκηνή (= משכן) is used here as a metonym for the *Shekinah* presence, John's understanding of it still retains some of its cultic associations. Cf. Rev. 15.5 and σκηνόω in 7.15; also Jn 1.14. Schüssler Fiorenza comments, 'Steht das neue Jerusalem nicht als das Zentrum des eschatologischen Gottesvolkes, sondern als die heilige Stadt, die als Tempelort Ort der Anwesenheit Gottes bei seinem Volke' (*Priester*, p. 350).

68. The entire parenthetical description of 21.9–22.5 would fit logically after 21.2. Note καταβαίνουσιν in both 21.2, 10, and the bride motif in both 21.2 and 21.9. So also M. Wilcox, 'Tradition and Redaction of Rev. 21.9–22.5', in *L'Apocalypse johannique et l'apocalyptique dans le Nouveau Testament* (ed. J. Lambrecht; BETL, 53; Louvain, 1980), p. 205.

69. The first two of the following parallels are mentioned by numerous commentators. See esp. Schüssler Fiorenza, *Revelation*, p. 66 n. 153; and Wilcox, 'Tradition', p. 205.

3. Harlot-Babylon associated with the Beast (Rev. 17.3b)
   Bride-New Jerusalem associated with the Lamb (Rev. 21.9b)
4. Contrast of clothing and jewels (17.3; 18.16 // 19.7; 21.11, 18-21):

Harlot-Babylon	*Bride-New Jerusalem*
clothed in purple and scarlet,	clothed in fine linen, built of gold,
decked with gold and jewels and	radiance as a jewel, gates of pearls,
pearls, holding a golden cup.	foundations of precious stones.

5. Name tradition:

Rev. 17.5	*Rev. 21.2, 10*
Babylon the Great	New Jerusalem

6. City's relationship with the kings of the earth:

Rev. 17.18 (17.15; 18.9)	*Rev. 21.24-26 (1.5)*
Babylon: the great city which rules	New Jerusalem: kings of the earth bring
over the kings of the earth	their glory into it.

Although there is no formal eulogy to the New Jerusalem corresponding to the doom song of Rev. 18.1-24, John greatly expands the description of the Holy City and its glory. This description can be divided into two parts: (1) Architectural traditions in Rev. 21.9-21, (2) the temple-city in Rev. 21.22–22.5. And in both of these sections virtually every allusion is based on OT prophecies relating to eschatological Jerusalem and its future glory, sanctity and exalted position: Ezekiel 40–48; Isa. 52.1; 54.11-12; Isaiah 60; Zechariah 14.

c. *New Jerusalem Oracles: 1. Architectural Traditions (21.9-21)*

Revelation	*Tradition*	*Source*
21.10	Holy City shown on a mountain	Ezek. 40.2 (cf. 40.4; 43.5)
21.11a	presence of God's glory	Ezek. 43.2-5
21.12a	wall of the city	Ezek. 40.5
21.12b	twelve gates for twelve tribes	Ezek. 48.30-35
21.13	compass points of the gates	Ezek. 42.15-20; 48.30-34
21.15	measuring the city wall and gates	Ezek. 40.3-16
21.16	the city foursquare	Ezek. 41.4; 45.2; 48.16, 20
21.17	measuring the city wall	Ezek. 41.5; 40.5
21.18, 19a, 21b	wall, foundations, gates, and street of precious jewels, pearls and gold	Isa. 54.11-12; Tob. 13.16-18a

Following the visionary introduction and revelation of the city's glorious position on a mountain (Rev. 21.9-11), vv. 12-14 outline the structural components of the city: wall, gates and foundations.[70] Next, vv. 15-17 relate the measurements of the city and its walls. In both of these sections, John draws exclusively on motifs from Ezekiel's vision of the eschatological temple (Ezek. 40–48),[71] which served as a model for other authors and visionaries as well.[72] Because John presents the

70. All of 21.10-14 is a compound sentence, as Mounce observes (*Revelation*, p. 377). N[26] mistakenly puts a full stop at the end of v. 11, where a colon should be used. The ὄρος of v. 10 is not merely the vantage point of the vision, but the intended locus of the city, as in Ezek. 40.2; 43.12. Contrast the provenance of Harlot-Babylon in 17.3 (ἔρημος). Cf. Mount Zion in Rev. 14.1; Caird, *Revelation*, pp. 269-70.

71. Vanhoye, 'L'utilisation du livre d'Ezéchiel', p. 476 (*appendice*) provides a list of 'certaine' allusions for 21.9-22 in substantial agreement with my own. The table given by J. Lust is less complete ('The Order of the Final Events in Revelation and in Ezekiel', in Lambrecht [ed.], *L'Apocalypse johannique*, p. 180 n. 5).

72. See the *New Jerusalem Apocalypse* found at Qumran, and, to a lesser degree, the Qumran *Temple Scroll* and the Mishnah tractate *Middoth*, each of which, like John, borrows from, adapts or omits from Ezekiel's plan according to the author's own particular concerns. Ezekiel is never slavishly followed as a divine blueprint, but serves rather as a prophetic basis for cultic reform and temple renewal. The *New Jerusalem Apocalypse* appears to have been a popular work at Qumran, since at least five different caves (1, 2, 4, 5, 11) have yielded portions of it. A useful description, with text and translation, can be found in K. Beyer, *Die aramäischen Texte aus die Toten Meer* (Göttingen, 1984), pp. 214-22. Similarities between Rev. 21.9-21 and this work are to be expected in view of their common usage of Ezek. 40–48, which provided the basic substructure for eschatological city planning, including architectural and cultic traditions and conventional formulae, e.g. ואעלני // καὶ ἀπήνεγκέν με (Rev. 21.10/Ezek. 40.2 *passim*); אחז יאני // καὶ ἔδειξέν με (Rev. 21.10; 22.1 // cf. Ezek. 40.4); ומשה // καὶ ἐμέτρησεν... (Rev. 21.16-17 // Ezek. 40.5 *passim*).

Yet several parallels are independent of Ezekiel: (1) Both Revelation and the Qumran texts are apocalyptic visions of a *heavenly* Jerusalem. (2) Whereas Ezek. 48.16, 35 outlines a realistic perimeter for the city walls of 5.8 miles (using the long cubit—40.5; 43.13), the wall in the *New Jerusalem* text extends 34.6 miles around, and that of Revelation 5454.4 miles! (using a Greek stadium of 200 yards). Admittedly, 35 miles is still within the realms of possibility (cf. the Great Wall of China at c. 1500 miles), and John's wall is symbolic hyperbole, but both deliberately extend Ezekiel's conservative plan. Similar exaggeration can be found in *Sib. Or.* 5.250-52; *Cant. R.* 7.5, 3; *b. B. Bat.* 75b. Cf. *1 En.* 90.36; J. Licht, 'An Ideal Town Plan from Qumran—The Description of the New Jerusalem', *IEJ* 29 (1979), pp. 45-59. (3) Both works include a description of the building materials of the city, which Ezekiel omits.

I cannot find any justification for Milik's statement that 'L'énorme Ville

entire city as the dwelling of God, he is not concerned to distinguish between city and temple descriptions, and he deliberately transfers Ezekiel's temple imagery to the Holy City itself.

Finally, Rev. 21.18-21 specify the building materials employed, and here John shifts from Ezekiel to the New Jerusalem prophecy of Isa. 54.11-12. Such a transition here is to be expected, both because Ezekiel is completely uninterested in building materials and because Isa. 54.11-12 is the only OT passage which adorns the New Jerusalem with precious materials. Even before John, this particular Isaian tradition had been influential in other descriptions of the future glorified Jerusalem, such as that of Tob. 13.16-18a and the *New Jerusalem* text at Qumran.[73]

The purpose behind John's incorporation of the precious building materials theme is considered by most commentators to be an attempt to describe the splendour of the city as a reflection of the glory of God (21.11). But John's goal may have been more specific than that.

Sainte du chapitre 21 est ceinte d'un rempart à douze portes, exactement comme celle des manuscrits de Qumran et non pas comme la petite ville d'Ézéchiel' (*DJD*, III, p. 186). All three plans have 12 gates in the outer city wall, 3 on each side.

73. Tob. 13.16-17 (S): 'And the *gates* of Jerusalem will be built with sapphire and emeralds, and all your *walls* with precious stones; the towers of Jerusalem will be built with gold, and their battlements with pure gold; the *streets* of Jerusalem will be paved with ruby and stones of Ophir'. In *New Jerusalem* 2.6-7 the streets are paved with marble and jasper, and 5.21 mentions a gate of sapphire. Milik and others mention Isa. 54.11-12 in connection with this text, but the influence appears to be indirect (*DJD*, III, p. 186). In Isaiah the foundations are of sapphire, not the gates. Instead, it seems that the *NJ* apocalypse has incorporated the tradition of Tobit, of which 5 MSS (4 Aram., 1 Heb.; Schürer III.1, pp. 224-25) have been found at Qumran. Both Tobit and *NJ* have the gates made of sapphire, whereas Isa. 54.12 has *carbuncles*; and both include the motif of the streets paved with precious stones, not included in Isaiah. The author of the 11QT also goes beyond Ezekiel by stipulating the type and source/quality of building materials to be used (col. 3.1-14), though no gem tradition is evident. Perhaps this is to be explained in relation to the crucial and controversial passage in col. 29.8-10 which suggests that the temple and city described in 11QT is temporary, until the appearance of the eschatological sanctuary which God himself, and not men, will create (cf. Y. Yadin, *The Temple Scroll* (Jerusalem, 1984), I, pp. 140-44, 182ff.; J. Maier, *The Temple Scroll* [Sheffield, 1985], p. 86). The tradition of a New Jerusalem adorned with precious stones is associated with the city which *God himself* will establish, as first outlined in Isa. 54.11-12 ('I will set...lay...make'), and reflected in Rev. 21 and the *NJ* document (cf. *4 Ezra* 10.54). Tobit is ambiguous on this point.

His association of costly materials with the Holy City may be another way of extending temple imagery to the city as a whole.[74]

c. *New Jerusalem Oracles: 2. The Temple-City (21.22–22.5)*

Revelation	Tradition	Source
21.23	city needs no sun or moon glory of God illuminates it	Isa. 60.19; 60.1-2
21.24a	nations walk by its light	Isa. 60.3a
21.24b	kings bring their glory into it	Isa. 60.3b; 5b-9, 11-13, 16
21.25a	gates will never be shut	Isa. 60.11a
21.25b	shall be no night there	?Zech. 14.7a
21.26	glory and honour of nations brought into it	Isa. 60.11b (cf. 60.5)
21.27	the unclean will not enter it	Isa. 52.1c
22.1-2	river of life and tree of life	Ezek. 47.1-12
22.3a	no more curse	Zech. 14.11
22.5a	shall be no more night	?Zech. 14.7a
22.5b	Lord God will shine upon them	Isa. 60.1-2, 19 (cf. Num. 6.25)

This pericope continues the description of the city begun in 21.9, but John now moves to a new theme and a new OT model, which is best treated separately. Architectural features give way to a picture of life in the Holy City itself, and the nationalistic plan of Ezekiel is expanded with the universalistic program of Isaiah.[75] This final section likewise betrays John's procedure of blending together various OT passages dealing with the same topic. Each of the identifiable allusions, whether it be the dominant tradition of Isaiah 60 or a single phrase from Zechariah, comes from New Jerusalem prophecies.

The thematic unity of Rev. 21.22–22.5 is suggested by the consistent

74. Note 1 Chron. 28.2-9, which adds to the regular temple building materials (gold, silver, bronze, iron and wood) 'great quantities of onyx and stones for setting, antimony (פוּךְ—as in Isa. 54.11), colored stones, all sorts of precious stones and marble'. According to 2 Chron. 3.6-7, craftsmen adorned the temple with 'settings of precious stones... [and] lined the house with gold—its beams, its thresholds, its walls, and its doors'. And cf. John's presentation of the city as of pure gold with the temple descriptions in Josephus, *War* 5.5. 2-4, 6; *Ant.* 8.3.3; 11QT 31.8-9, 32.10, 36.11, 41.16-17; *Eupol.* 34.3-6, 12 (*OTP*, II, pp. 869-70), where gold is the dominant feature.

75. 'He prints over the image of the compact and clearly demarcated Ezekielian city another image, the comprehensive image of Isaiah' (R.J. McKelvey, *The New Temple* [London, 1969], p. 174).

2. *John and the Influence of the Old Testament* 99

use of Isaiah 60, and particularly the use of Isa. 60.19 as an *inclusio* in Rev. 21.23 and 22.5a.[76] The controlling idea behind most, if not all, of the passage, pertains to the absence of a physical temple and the corresponding extension of temple motifs to the city as a whole. Supporting evidence for this conclusion is strong:

1. *Rev. 21.22-23; 22.5* describe the Skekinah glory and its presence in the city rather than confinement to a physical temple (cf. 4.1-6).[77]
2. *Rev. 21.24-26* notes the relationship of the nations to the temple-city and the bringing of gifts, which are traditionally presented to the temple and its God (cf. 4.10).[78]

76. *Contra* Rissi (*Future*, pp. 53-54, 80-83), who sees in 22.1 the start of a new unit of thought, which he subsumes under *paradise* traditions. But the two main paradise elements of the river and tree(s) of life are still central features associated with Ezekiel's temple. John merely strengthens the prophet's own haggadic integration of *Urzeit* and *Endzeit* by adding ζωῆς. In addition John's modification of Ezek. 47.1 in Rev. 22.1 is dependent on 21.22, and 22.2 continues the 'nation' theme begun in 21.24.

77. 'δόξα is probably the זיו or brightness which went forth from the Shekinah or the glory (יקרא) of God' (Charles, *Revelation*, II, p. 172; cf. 206-207, 444 n. 1). Cf. Ezek. 43.1-5; 44.4; 48.35. In *Targ. Isa.* 60.2b שכינתיה interprets כבוד.

78. 'Because of thy temple at Jerusalem, kings bear gifts to thee' (Ps. 68.29). In regard to the temple, Josephus mentions 'tributes offered to God from every quarter of the world' (*War* 5.187; cf. *Ant.* 15.402). An especially interesting parallel to Rev. 21.26 is found in 2 Macc. 5.16, where the despoiling of the temple by Antiochus includes the removal of 'votive offerings which other kings had made to enhance the *glory and honor* of the place'. The concept of a universal eschatological pilgrimage of nations is a natural outgrowth of a prophetic nationalism which looked for a permanent restoration of the glories of the past (e.g. 1 Kgs 10.23-25) and combined common political customs with religious festival imagery. Zion-Jerusalem is the political and religious centre from which Yahweh or his anointed will rule the nations of the earth. This expectation is especially vibrant in Isaiah and the Psalms: Isa. 2.1-4; 11.10-12; 18.7; 60.1-16; 61.5-6; 66.12, 18, 23; Pss. 22.27-29; 47.7-9; 68.29; 72.9-11; 86.9; 102.21-22; 122.3-4; 138.4-5; cf. Zech. 14.9, 16-17; *1 En.* 90.30-33; 1QpPs 68.29-30. Yet after acknowledging the colourful and evocative nature of such a future scenario, one must recognize that John transforms various prophetic details and spatial expectations into spiritual realities. The events of Rev. 21–22 represent the final universal fulfilment of John's initial scene of divine worship (4.9, 11; cf. 5.12-13), where δόξα and τιμή lead the list of spiritual offerings, and which is proleptically illustrated by the worship of the international multitude of 7.9-12. Cf. McKelvey, *The New Temple*, pp. 173 (n. 3), 174-75; Schüssler Fiorenza, *Revelation*, p. 78 n. 18, who understands 'kings of the earth'

3. *Rev. 21.25* emphasizes the continuity of worship, which is not limited to a daylight service, but proceeds uninterrupted day and 'night' (cf. 4.8; 7.14-15).[79]
4. In *Rev. 21.27* the laws of purity associated with approaching God and entering the temple now apply to the entire city (cf. 7.14-15; 22.14-15).[80]
5. In *Rev. 22.1-2* the water and the tree of life, originally connected with Ezekiel's temple and city, are a central feature of John's temple-city.[81]

in Rev. 1.5 to denote *Christians* rather than literal earthly rulers.

79. '[they] serve him day and night in his temple' (Rev. 7.15a). In the Jerusalem temple service, the gates were closed after the evening sacrifice at dusk and opened again just before the morning sacrifice at dawn. Instead of a divine service dictated by the schedules and limitations of human beings and nature, worship in John's temple-city proceeds unbroken, ἡμέρας καὶ νυκτός (rather than לבקר—ולערב—τὸ πρωὶ καὶ τὸ ἑσπέρας, 1 Chron. 16.40; cf. 9.27). Cf. Schürer, II, pp. 286-87, 304-305; *m. Tam.*; Sir. 50.19; Ezek. 46.1-3; Acts 26.7; McKelvey, *The New Temple*, p. 166.

80. Adapting the cultic language of Isa. 52.1c. It is not clear whether ὁ ποιῶν βδέλυγμα καὶ ψεῦδος continues the cultic imagery or is simply ethical. βδέλυγμα = תועבה embraces various facets of ritual impurity and religious taboo, including unclean food, idolatry, witchcraft, etc.; and to 'practice abomination' (עשׂה תועבה) is a common OT idiom (*BDB*, p. 1072; 11QT 60.17-20; 62.16). As for ὁ ποιῶν... ψεῦδος (= שׁקר?), cf. Jer. 6.13; Prov. 11.18; 1QS 4; H. Braun, *Qumran und das Neue Testament* (Tübingen, 1966), I, p. 323. Possibly the angelic gatekeepers (Rev. 21.12) guard against such violators (cf. Philo, *Spec. Leg.* 1.156; Gen. 3.24).

81. 'The theme of the temple as bound up with the foundation of life occurs as [sic] Ps. 36.7-9 and frequently elsewhere (cf. Gen. 2.6-7; Zech. 14.8; Joel 3.18)' (W.J. Dumbrell, *The End of the Beginning: Revelation 21–22 and the Old Testament* [Homebush, 1985], p. 74 n. 36, cf. p. 58). Tacitus (*Hist.* 5.12) recounts a tradition of a perpetual spring within the temple area. The association of the tree of life with the temple or the New Jerusalem is found also in *1 En.* 25, *4 Ezra* 8.52, and *5 Ezra* 2.10-11. Paradise and the New Jerusalem are associated in Isa. 51.3, *2 Bar.* 4.1-6 and *T. Dan.* 5.12. E. Barnes observes that 'the connection between temple and garden is quite obvious to the eastern mind. A temple in the ancient east was not a building but a sacred enclosure round a (small) shrine... The Solomonic temple preserved the meaning of Eden, the garden-sanctuary, for its walls were adorned with figures of guardian Cherubim (cp. Gen. 3.24), palm trees and flowers (I Kg. 6.29)' ('Ezekiel's Denunciation of Tyre [Ezek. xxvi–xxviii]', *JTS* 35 [1934], pp. 51-52). On John's adaptation of Ezek. 47 in Rev. 22.1-2, see Vanhoye, 'L'utilisation du livre d'Ezéchiel', p. 470.

6.   Finally, *Rev. 22.3b-5* reveals the eternal priesthood which
     serves God in the temple-city (cf. 1.6; 5.10; 7.14-15; 20.6).[82]

The translocation of the throne of God and the Lamb from its
heavenly status in Revelation 4–5 to the New Jerusalem unites the
heavenly and earthly worshippers and inaugurates the universal authority of the kingdom of God (11.15-17). The final words of 22.5, 'they
shall reign forever and ever', heralds the fulfilment of the expectation
of 5.10, 'they shall reign on earth', and signals the realization of the
promises of 2.26-27 and 3.21 that those who overcome will reign
together with Christ (cf. 11.15; 20.4-6). The prophecies of salvation
are finally complete.

Summary

Having systematically examined the major OT traditions and texts
employed by John, it is now possible to draw together his use of
Scripture into an index of *thematic analogues.*

Revelation	Theme	Source(s)
1.10-19; 10.1-11	prophetic call narratives	**Ezek.** Isa., Dan.
1.13-17; 2–3;	Christological titles and	Isa., **Dan.**, **Pss**,
5.5-6; 19.11-16	descriptions	Gen., Zech., Jer.,
		Ezek.
4.1–5.2	throne-room theophanies	**Ezek.**, Isa., Dan.
6.12-17; 14.14-20;	Day of the Lord and holy war	Isa., **Joel**, Hos.
16.14; 19.11-21		
8–9; 16	serial judgments	**Exod.**, Joel
12–13; 17.6-16a	eschatological enemies	**Daniel**

82. Cf. the blessing of the priests in 1QSb 4 'May you be as an Angel of the
Presence in the Abode of Holiness... May you attend upon the service in the Temple
of the Kingdom' (G. Vermes, *The Dead Sea Scrolls in English* (London, 3rd edn,
1987), p. 237). Rissi and J. Comblin see no cultic allusion in these verses, but this
can hardly be doubted in light of Rev. 7.15 (*Future*, p. 83; 'La liturgie de la nouvelle
Jérusalem [Apoc. xxi,l–xxii,5]', *ETL* 29 [1953], pp. 25-26 n. 53). McKelvey
replies that 'The language and imagery of 22.4 [and 22.3!] clearly imply their priestly
office' (*The New Temple*, p. 174 n. 2). With regard to the phrase καὶ ὄψονται τὸ
πρόσωπον αὐτοῦ in 22.4a, Holtz remarks, 'Im Judentum hat sich die Wendung
"Gott schauen" als Bild für das Beteiligtsein an der Gegenwart Gottes im Tempel, in
der Synagoge und im Lehrhaus erhalten, also an Veranstaltungen, die kultisch oder
doch als Fortsetzungen des Kultus verstanden sind' (*Christologie*, p. 204). But it is
not exclusively a cultic idiom, and may derive from the royal court expression 'to see
the face of the king' (e.g. Est. 1.14); cf. *4 Ezra* 7.98.

| 14.8-10; 17.1-5, 16b–19.3 | oracles against the nations (Babylon and Tyre) | **Jer.**, **Isa.**, Ezek. |
| 7.14-17; 21.1– 22.5 | oracles of salvation (New Jerusalem) | **Isa.**, **Ezek.**, Zech. |

A discussion of the fuller implications of this thematic approach will be reserved for the final chapter. But several general observations can be made at this stage which will help to draw together the evidence of this chapter, and lay a foundation for future discussion.

Of first importance is the recognition that in the majority of cases the correspondence between an OT text and its application in Revelation goes beyond similarities in language and imagery, and extends also to the setting and purpose of the original biblical passage. Thus, when John wants to emphasize his own prophetic status and authority or illustrate his throne-room vision, he draws on the well-known experiences and examples of earlier prophets. And when he comes to describe the New Jerusalem, he builds on a biblical substructure of OT prophecies relating to the future glorified Jerusalem. Political oracles correspond to political oracles; prophecies of judgment to prophecies of judgment; and promises of salvation serve as the basis for promises of salvation. Furthermore, John employs corporate models for corporate subjects and individual models for individual subjects. Therefore we do not find Daniel being used in the portrayal of Harlot-Babylon, nor is Isaiah ever used to describe the eschatological enemy. All this challenges the common assumption that John is not consciously interpreting the OT, but simply using it as a language and image base.

Secondly, analysis of John's thematic application of Scripture suggests that his method transcends special authors and particular books. The prophet's strategy for employing OT texts appears to be determined more by the issue concerned than by its canonical source. We may rightly question, therefore, those theories of composition which suggest that John's visions were inspired by reading specific books or passages of the OT. For example, G.W. Buchanan supposes that John received the vision of Rev. 14.14-20 while reading Joel 3 and Daniel 7, and the vision of Revelation 17–18 while reading Jeremiah 50–51 and Ezekiel 26–27, and so on.[83] But this view does not account for the fact that often within a single visionary unit John brings together elements from a variety of books or isolated texts

83. 'The Word of God and the Apocalyptic Vision', *SBLASP* (1974), p. 190.

within a single OT book. *Special books do not appear to play as important a role as special themes.* Thus it misses the point to ask whether the book of Daniel, Ezekiel or Isaiah is more important to John. For it is not the book or author which dictates his choice of passages, but the topic.

These conclusions and others which will be drawn from John's thematic approach to the OT are of course based on a a general overview of all the clear OT allusions found in Revelation. The next stage of investigation, by means of which some of these ideas can be tested more precisely, involves a detailed evaluation of John's use of one OT book in particular. In the next section, therefore (Section II), we will turn our attention to the Isaiah allusions in Revelation, both those which have been generally accepted and those which have been proposed. The goal of this major portion of the study is twofold: first, to determine the strength of the evidence in favour of each allusion, and secondly, to explore the application and interpretation of each confirmed allusion. Following this, in the Conclusion (Chapter 8), we will then take up again the question of thematic analogues and see how John's use of Isaiah in particular relates to the categories and patterns laid out here in this chapter.

Part 2
JOHN AND THE PROPHET ISAIAH: ALLUSIONS AND APPLICATION

Chapter 3

ISAIAH IN REVELATION 1–3

Revelation 1.1a → *Isaiah 1.1*
J. Sweet notes that 'before the normal epistolary opening (Rev. 1.4ff.) comes a title reminiscent of OT prophetic books', and he gives Isa. 1.1 as an example.[1] The superscriptions of OT prophetic books exhibit a variety of formulae, with which one may compare Rev. 1.1.

'The revelation of' + divine revealer (= Jesus) + 'which'

1. 'The word(s) of' + divine revealer (= Yahweh) + 'which came unto' + prophet (Hosea; Joel; Micah; Zephaniah; cf. Lk 3.2)
2. 'The words of' + prophet + 'which he saw' (Amos)
3. 'The words of' + prophet (Jeremiah)
4. 'The vision of' + prophet + 'which he saw' (Isaiah)
5. 'The vision(s) of + prophet (Obadiah; Iddo in 2 Chron. 9.29)
6. 'The oracle which' + prophet + 'saw' (Habakkuk; cf. Malachi)

John's superscription comes closest to example one, though he uses ἀποκάλυψις instead of λόγος and substitutes Jesus for Yahweh as the divine revealer.[2] The intentional addition of a formal title before the epistolary introduction and the structural similarities between this title and OT superscriptions makes it likely that John is here influenced by OT models, though not exclusively by Isaiah. A consciousness of

1. *Revelation* (London, 1979), p. 57; similarly D'Aragon, *JBC*, p. 471.
2. Ἰησοῦ Χριστοῦ is a subjective genitive, as Beckwith shows (*Apocalypse*, p. 418); *contra* J.M. Ford (*Revelation* [Garden City, 1975], p. 373), whose unique source theory leads her to take it as objective. The fact that John calls his prophecy 'The revelation of *Jesus Christ*', and places himself at the end of the revelatory chain, tends to support the authorial authenticity of this section. The natural tendency of a disciple or editor would be to put ἀποκάλυψις Ἰωάννου, as indeed some early MSS do. See further Kraft, *Offenbarung*, pp. 17-18; Charles, *Revelation*, I, pp. 4–6. Schüssler Fiorenza points out the affinity between the title ἀποκάλυψις Ἰησοῦ Χριστοῦ and Pauline tradition (esp. Gal. 1.12), and suggests that John is consciously building on these earlier formulations (*Revelation*, pp. 150-51).

prophetic antecedents is confirmed by the close connection between Rev. 1.1-3 and 22.6, and by the presence of other prophetic expressions in Rev. 1.1-3, such as 'the word of God' (v. 2), 'the words of this prophecy' (v. 3), and the prophetic idiom of 'seeing words' (v. 2).[3] A Christian application of OT prophetic prologues to emphasize an individual's prophetic authority and succession is already found in Lk 3.1-2.

Revelation 1.1-3 → Isaiah 56.1-2
In the introduction to his commentary, A. Pohl suggests this possible connection: 'In 1.1-3 are found, for example, four words that also stand together in Isa. 56.1-2...could this be intentional on John's part?'[4]

While the four words mentioned—*revelation, blessed, keep* and *near*—do indeed appear in both texts, there is very little similarity in their context and application. An appeal to close proximity has little force in Revelation, where several different OT texts may underlie a single line. Three verses is indeed too large a verbal territory to expect a conscious connection between four isolated words. This appears to be simply a case of coincidence. At any rate, Pohl does not further mention or elaborate this proposal in his discussion of Rev. 1.1-3, and no other commentator makes reference to it.

Revelation 1.4b; 3.1; 4.5; 5.6 → Isaiah 11.2
Four times in the first few chapters of Revelation John refers to the 'seven spirits'. Attempts to understand this enigmatic phrase and appears to be background have led to a variety of interpretations, of which two are more prominent.

1.   Many scholars find the prehistory of the concept in Babylonian planetary speculation and/or Zoroastrian theology, which exercised an early influence on the development of Jewish angelology (e.g. Ezek. 9.1-11; Tob. 12.15). Consequently, the 'seven spirits' in Revelation simply refer to the seven 'angels of the presence' or archangels, a common Jewish concept which John appears to acknowledge in Rev. 8.2.[5]

---

3.   As in example 2 above (Amos); cf. Lindblom, *Prophecy*, pp. 121-22.
4.   *Offenbarung*, I, p. 31 n. 29.
5.   So E. Schweizer, *TDNT*, VI, p. 450; G.H. Dix, 'The Seven Archangels and the Seven Spirits', *JTS* 28 (1927), pp. 233-50; A. Yarbro Collins, *The Apocalypse* (NTM, 22; Dublin and Wilmington, DE, 1979), p. 7; Charles,

2.   Others hold that the phrase cannot refer to angelic beings and denotes the one Holy Spirit of God, whose sevenfold character is either a numerical symbol of completeness or an expression of its distributive activity. According to this view, one need look no further than the OT for the source of John's imagery; in particular Isa. 11.2 and Zechariah 4.[6]

The appeal to Zechariah 4 is natural in view of its obvious influence in Rev. 4.5 and 5.6, but the relevance of Isa. 11.2 is problematic. And imprecision among commentators has only added to the confusion. The heart of the problem lies in claims made about the translation and interpretative history of the Isaiah text. The association of the seven spirits with Isa. 11.2 is commonly based on the assumption that, while the MT only lists six qualities, the LXX and later Jewish and Christian interpreters include seven.[7]

Revelation, I, pp. 11-12 (though he considers this idea an interpolation); Mounce, *Revelation*, pp. 69-70, 136; Holtz, *Christologie*, pp. 138-40; G.R. Beasley-Murray, *The Book of Revelation* (NCB; London, 1974), p. 55, *contra* F.F. Bruce, who says that John is rarely 'in bondage to the religio-historical roots of his symbolism' ('The Spirit in the Apocalypse', in *Christ and Spirit in the New Testament* [ed. B. Lindars and S.S. Smalley; Cambridge, 1974], p. 336).

The understanding of angels as spirits is common at Qumran and not unknown in Christian circles (e.g. Heb. 1.7, 14; Hermas, *Mand.* 11.9). The exegetical base for this view probably derives from OT passages such as Num. 16.22, 27.16, and Ps. 104.4, as C. Newsom notes (*Songs of the Sabbath Sacrifice: A Critical Edition* [HSS, 27; Atlanta, 1985], p. 25). See her discussion of angelology, esp. p. 34. However, John never clearly designates angels as πνεύματα. In Revelation πνεῦμα designates (1) *Holy Spirit*: 2.7 (etc. 7×); 14.13; 22.17; (?1.10; 4.2; 19.10; 21.10); (2) *life spirit*: 11.11; 13.15; 22.6; (3) *evil spirits*: 16.13-14; 18.2.

6.   So Hemer, *Letters*, p. 142; Beckwith, *Apocalypse*, pp. 424-27; Bruce, 'The Spirit', p. 336; Prigent, *L'Apocalypse de Saint Jean* (CNT, 14; Paris, 1981), pp. 16-17; Sweet, *Revelation*, p. 65; Kraft, *Offenbarung*, p. 32; Pohl, *Offenbarung*, pp. 68-69. Prigent outlines the major arguments for this view (p. 17). The main objection to the angel view involves Rev. 1.4 and the question of whether an angel would be placed between the Father and Son in what appears to be a quasi-trinitarian doxology. But in the light of passages such as Lk 9.26, 1 Tim. 5.21, and even Rev. 3.5, where angels are closely connected with the Godhead, such opposition loses much of its force. Compare also Rev. 1.4b, ἃ ἐνώπιον τοῦ θρόνου αὐτοῦ, with 8.2, οἳ ἐνώπιον τοῦ θεοῦ—as distinct from the rest of the angels who stand κύκλῳ τοῦ θρόνου (7.11). Cf. Mounce, *Revelation*, p. 69.

7.   Assumed by Prigent, Ford, Mounce, Hemer and Bruce. Others who connect Rev. 1.4 etc. with Isa. 11.2 without mentioning the LXX specifically are Caird, Kraft

(Isa. 11.2) *MT*	*LXX*	*Targ. Isa.*
ונחה עליו	καὶ ἀναπαύσεται ἐπ' αὐτὸν	ותשרי עלוהי
רוח יהוה	πνεῦμα τοῦ θεοῦ,	רוח מן קדם יהוה
רוח חכמה ובינה	πνεῦμα σοφίας καὶ συνέσεως,	רוח חכמה וסכלתנו
רוח עצה וגבורה	πνεῦμα βουλῆς καὶ ἰσχύος,	רוח מילך וגבורא
רוח דעת ויראת יהוה	πνεῦμα γνώσεως καὶ εὐσεβείας	רוח מדע ודחלתא דיהוה
והריחו ביראת יהוה	ἐμπλήσει αὐτὸν πνεῦμα φόβου θεοῦ	ויקרביניה לדחלתיה יהוה

Each of these texts has an introductory clause, three couplets of two spiritual gifts, and a final clause. Which is the seventh quality? Bruce and Mounce give εὐσεβείας, but this is not an addition to the Hebrew list. It is merely an interpretative substitute for ירא יהוה as others have noted.[8] Hemer and Kissane opt for πνεῦμα φόβου θεοῦ in LXX 11.3a, but this is governed by a new verb and is clearly the translator's attempt at dealing with the awkward Hebrew verb in 3a, and the tautology of 2b and 3a.[9]

Admittedly, someone looking for seven spiritual manifestations could appeal to the LXX more easily than to the MT or Targum, but such a procedure is not attested until later Christian apologists.[10] Jewish exegetical traditions consistently interpret Isa. 11.2 of the

and Farrer. Holtz is one of the few commentators to emphasize that the texts, translations and Jewish traditions only attest six gifts (*Christologie*, p. 139 and n. 3).

8. Wildberger, *Jesaja*, I, p. 450; C.H. Dodd, *The Bible and the Greeks* (London, 1925), p. 77; Hatch–Redpath, II, p. 580; cf. Prov. 1.7; 4 Macc. 16.14.

9. Hemer, *Letters*, p. 261 n. 57; E.J. Kissane, *The Book of Isaiah* (Dublin, 1941), I, p. 142.

10. Justin (*Dial.* 86) is the earliest apologist to quote all of Isa. 11.2 with reference to the Messiah. Yet even though he lists seven gifts from the LXX, he nowhere emphasizes the number seven, and is merely interested in showing that Christ had all the gifts listed, whereas great kings and prophets had only one or two. The appeal of earlier commentators to Justin's *Cohort. ad Graecos* 32 no longer carries any weight since it is now widely acknowledged as spurious. For a more detailed account of the influence of Isa. 11.2 in early Christianity see K. Schlütz, *Isaias 11,2 (die sieben Gaben des hl. Geistes) in den ersten vier christlichen Jahrhunderten* (ATA, 11.4.9; Aschendorff, 1932); and M.A. Chevalier, *L'esprit et le Messie dans le Bas-Judaïsme et le Nouveau Testament* (Paris, 1958).

Messiah, who is endowed with six qualities rather than seven.[11]

Whether one accepts the seven spirits as the Holy Spirit or throne-angels, there is no need to look beyond Zechariah 4 for the immediate source of John's imagery, and in particular the use of the number seven with spirits. As others have noted, Rev. 1.4 is not primary and presupposes 4.5 and 5.6 where Zechariah is unquestionably in mind.[12]

Revelation 1.5a → Isaiah 55.4

Revelation	Isa. 55.4	
ὁ μάρτυς ὁ πιστός	הן עד לאומים	ἰδοὺ μαρτύριον ἐν ἔθνεσι
ὁ πρωτότοκος τῶν νεκρῶν καὶ	נתתיו נגיד	δέδωκα αὐτόν, ἄρχοντα καὶ
ὁ ἄρχων τῶν βασιλέων τῆς γῆς	ומצוה לאמים	προστάσσοντα ἔθνεσιν

Ps. 89.38, 28 (LXX 88.38, 28)

...ועד בשחק נאמן	ὁ μάρτυς ἐν οὐρανῷ πιστός...
אף אני בכור אתנהו	κἀγὼ πρωτότοκον θήσομαι αὐτόν,
עליון למלכי ארץ	ὑψηλὸν παρὰ τοῖς βασιλεῦσιν τῆς γῆς.

As part of an elaboration of the initial epistolary greeting, ὁ μάρτυς ὁ πιστός forms the first of a set of three christological titles, each of which appear to derive from a messianic application of OT texts. There is little disagreement among commentators that the designation *faithful witness* is based on a messianic interpretation of Ps. 89.38.[13]

11. *Num. R.* 13.11 'How do we know it of...the Messiah? Because it is written, and *the spirit of the Lord shall rest upon him; the spirit of wisdom and understanding*, this makes two; *The spirit of counsel and might* makes four; *The spirit of knowledge and of the fear of the Lord* makes six'; similarly *Gen. R.* 2.4.97; *Ruth R.* 7.2; *b. Sanh.* 93b. The oft-quoted example of *1 En.* 61.11 indeed mentions seven spiritual virtues, but these are seven blessings rendered by heavenly worshippers to the 'Lord of the spirits' and are not associated with the 'Elect One'. Besides this, only one of the virtues (*wisdom*) parallels the Isaiah list. Rather, the earliest Jewish and Christian messianic interpretations of Isa. 11.2 emphasize the fact of the Messiah's spiritual endowment and his qualities, but appear unconcerned with setting forth a quota of spiritual gifts: *Pss. Sol.* 17.37; *1 En.* 49.3; cf. 51.3; 1QSb 5.24-25; *T. Levi* 18.7; *T. Jud.* 24.2-3; Jn 1.32; Matt. 3.16; *Gos. Heb.* 2; cf. 4QpIsaᵃ 8–10; 1 Pet. 4.14.

12. So Hemer, Sweet and Beasley-Murray.

13. So Kraft, Schüssler Fiorenza, Charles, Schlatter, Brütsch, Lohmeyer, Sweet, Farrer, Prigent and Trudinger. A few only mention Ps. 89 in connection with

Even though the phrase belongs to common forensic terminology, and perhaps more convincing dictional parallels are available,[14] the almost certain dependence of the remaining two titles in Rev. 1.5 on Ps. 89.28 makes it likely that all three are the result of a single christological exegesis of this dynastic Psalm.[15]

While recognizing that John uses the language of Psalm 89, some scholars see a secondary influence of Isa. 55.4 in particular,[16] or of Second Isaiah's theology of *witness* in general (esp. 43.9-10; 44.8-9; 55.4).[17]

Schüssler Fiorenza's attempt to draw together Ps. 88.28, 38 LXX and Isa. 55.4 LXX by means of a *Stichwort* argument is open to difficulties.[18] There is no good reason for supposing that John here shifts from his tendency to work from the Hebrew tradition.[19] If the LXX is assumed there are no straightforward connections: μάρτυς versus μαρτύριον, ὑψηλός versus ἄρχων and βασιλεύς versus ἔθνος. Similarly Kraft's remark that μάρτυς in Rev. 1.5a 'geht unmittelbar auf Jes. 43,10 zurück' cannot be proved and is somewhat inconsistent

the last two titles, e.g. Ford, Beckwith, Pohl and Mounce—and Swete only with the last.

14. Prov. 14.5, 25; Jer. 42.5; cf. Isa. 8.2. W.H. Brownlee may be correct in suggesting Jer. 42.5 as the source for the similar, but expanded, title in Rev. 3.14 ('Messianic Motifs of Qumran and the New Testament', *NTS* 3 [1956–57], p. 208). H. Braun apparently misreads Brownlee's discussion, for he assumes that Brownlee connects Jer. 42.5 with Rev. 1.5 rather than 3.14 (*Qumran und das Neue Testament*, I, p. 307).

15. For messianic interpretation of Ps. 89 in Jewish circles, see Fishbane, *Biblical Interpretation*, pp. 466-67, 495. Traces of Christian exegesis can be found already in Acts 13.22b (which conflates Ps. 89.21a with 1 Sam. 13.14 and Isa. 44.28); ?Heb. 11.26 (Ps. 89.50-51). Note also *1 Clem.* 18.1; Irenaeus, *Dem.* 75; *b. Sanh.* 97a, 99a. The threefold unit may be taken from a pre-existing hymn or more likely, a kerygmatic formula emphasizing the death, resurrection and enthronement of Christ; cf. Satake, *Gemeindeordnung*, pp. 113-14; Prigent, *L'Apocalypse*, p. 17 n. 13; Kraft, *Offenbarung*, p. 26.

16. Schüssler Fiorenza, *Priester*, pp. 199-200, Ford, *Revelation*, p. 380, and Swete, *Apocalypse*, p. 7, all mention Isa. 55.4 in place of Ps. 89.38.

17. Kraft, *Offenbarung*, p. 26; Comblin, *Christ*, pp. 146-60; Brownlee, 'Messianic Motifs', p. 208. Cf. A.A. Trites, *The New Testament Concept of Witness* (Cambridge, 1977), p. 159.

18. Schüssler Fiorenza, *Priester*, pp. 199-200, cf. 164-66.

19. 'The text as found in Revelation... shows little affinity with any of the Greek OT versions' (Trudinger, 'Text', p. 45; cf. p. 95); Charles, *Revelation*, I, p. 14.

with his later statement that the 'ursprüngliche Quelle' for this phrase is Ps. 89.[20]

While John certainly is familiar with catchword methods and adopts them elsewhere, there is insufficient textual basis for concluding that he has done so here. Psalm 89 satisfactorily accounts for all the elements and there is no compelling evidence which points beyond it. Whether or not Isa. 55.4 and 43.10 and similar 'witness' texts from Second Isaiah lie behind John's concept of witness is a more fundamental question and takes us beyond Rev. 1.5 to the overall use of μάρτυς and μαρτυρία in Revelation.

Revelation 1.5c → Isaiah 40.2

A few commentators have suggested that the expression λύσαντι ἡμᾶς ἐκ τῶν ἁμαρτιῶν ἡμῶν ἐν τῷ αἵματι αὐτοῦ in Rev. 1.5c has its background in Isa. 40.2.[21] If so, it would have to be based on the LXX, λέλυται αὐτῆς ἡ ἁμαρτία, rather than the very different MT נרצה עונה. Others have suggested Ps. 129.8 LXX: καὶ αὐτὸς λυτρώσεται τὸν Ἰσραὴλ ἐκ πασῶν τῶν ἀνομιῶν αὐτοῦ.[22]

But the use of λύω in the sense of *to pardon* or *release from* is common enough, and is even found with ἁμαρτία outside biblical sources.[23] It is therefore doubtful whether any specific OT text is in view.[24] In any case, the phrase appears to be part of a standing liturgical formula which John has adapted.[25]

20. *Offenbarung*, pp. 26, 32.
21. Swete, *Apocalypse*, p. cxli; Vos, *Synoptic Traditions*, p. 40 n. 63; Trudinger, 'Text', p. 179; B.M. Metzger, *A Textual Commentary on the Greek New Testament* (London, 1981), p. 729, though none of these authors provides any support or discussion whatsoever.
22. Pohl, *Offenbarung*, I, p. 72 n. 40.
23. Aristophanes, *Ranae* 691: λῦσαι τὰς πρότερον ἁμαρτίας; cf. Sophocles *Philoctetes* 1224. P. von der Osten-Sacken states that, 'Der Ausdruck λύειν ἐκ τῶν ἁμαρτιῶν hat im NT, jedoch auch in LXX keine Parallele' ('"Christologie, Taufe, Homologie"—Ein Beitrag zu Apc John 1,5f.', *ZNW* 58 (1967), p. 259, cf. n. 19). But even if the exact wording is absent, the concept is present (cf. Mk 10.45; Col. 1.14; Eph. 1.7; 1 Pet. 1.18-19; and again Ps. 129.8 LXX).
24. Beasley-Murray suggests that this phrase belongs with 1.6a and shares in its Exodus typology (*Revelation*, p. 57).
25. Both von der Osten-Sacken and Schüssler Fiorenza argue for an original baptismal setting, but in view of John's emphasis on corporate rather than individual experience (which the latter also acknowledges), a eucharistic background may be

Revelation 1.6a; 5.10a; 20.6b → Isaiah 61.6a

Rev. 1.6a	*5.10a*	*20.6b*
καὶ ἐποίησεν ἡμᾶς	καὶ ἐποίησας αὐτοὺς	ἀλλ' ἔσονται
βασιλείαν, ἱερεῖς	τῷ θεῷ ἡμῶν	ἱερεῖς τοῦ θεοῦ
τῷ θεῷ καὶ πατρὶ αὐτοῦ	βασιλείαν καὶ ἱερεῖς	καὶ τοῦ χριστοῦ

Exod. 19.6a		*Isa. 61.6a*	
ואתם תהיו	ὑμεῖς δὲ ἔσεσθέ μοι	ואתם כהני יהוה	ὑμεῖς δὲ ἱερεῖς κυρίου
ממלכת כהנים	βασίλειον ἱεράτευμα	תקראו משרתי	κληθήσεσθε, λειτουργοὶ
וגוי קדוש	καὶ ἔθνος ἅγιον	אלהינו יאמר לכם	θεοῦ

The unique imagery of this Exodus passage, in which individual political and religious prerogatives are promised to the nation as a whole, made it appealing to a variety of later hierophants.[26] And there is little debate that it is the primary inspiration for John as well—at least in Rev. 1.6a and 5.10a.[27] The case of Rev. 20.6 is different and requires more detailed treatment. Both Schüssler Fiorenza and J.H. Elliot discuss in detail the use of Exod. 19.6 in Revelation and suggest that a similar tradition in Isa. 61.6a has been taken up in Rev. 20.6b.[28]

The differences between Rev. 20.6 and 1.6/5.10 are succinctly presented by Elliot:[29]

just as likely ('Redemption as Liberation: Apoc. 1.5f. and 5.9f', *CBQ* 36 [1974], pp. 220-32).

26. Jewish and Christian interpretation of Exod. 19.6 can be found in *Jub.* 16.18; 33.20; 2 Macc. 2.17; Philo, *Sobr.* 66; *Abr.* 56; 1 Pet 2.5, 9; and in a Greek fragment (67c) of *T. Levi* 11.4-6. Cf. Schüssler Fiorenza, *Priester*, pp. 90-101; and J.H. Elliott, *The Elect and the Holy* (NovTSup, 12; Leiden, 1966), pp. 63-107, who includes a discussion of the LXX, targums and rabbinic literature.

27. Kraft is the only commentator to imply that John had Isa. 61.6 in view as well as Exod. 19.6 when he penned Rev. 1.6 and 5.10, but this is merely assumed and not argued (*Offenbarung*, p. 33).

28. Schüssler Fiorenza, *Priester*, pp. 78-116; Elliott, *The Elect and the Holy*, pp. 50-128. Most other commentators either simply list Isa. 61.6 as an interesting parallel (e.g. Pohl, Charles, Beckwith, Brütsch); or do not mention it at all (e.g. Caird, Prigent, Lohmeyer, Sweet, Swete, Beasley-Murray).

29. Elliott, *The Elect and the Holy*, pp. 114-15. He accepts the textual reading βασιλεύουσιν in 5.10 over the future βασιλεύσουσιν. This verse almost certainly anticipates at least 22.5, if not also 20.6, and the future is preferred by other commentators. But even those who accept the present tense either understand it proleptically, or in an inaugurated sense. Cf. Schüssler Fiorenza, *Priester*, pp. 73-75; Sweet, *Revelation*, pp. 130-31.

1.   It is not hymnic.
2.   It lacks βασιλεία [though the kingdom motif may be implied in the accompanying phrase 'καὶ βασιλεύσουσιν μετ' αὐτοῦ'].
3.   The context concerns martyrs, not Jesus' redemptive work.
4.   The promise is for a limited group (martyrs) rather than the church as a whole.
5.   It is presented as a future expectation instead of a present reality.

On the basis of these and other considerations, Elliot and Schüssler Fiorenza postulate that, instead of Exod. 19.6, John here takes up the eschatological promise of Isa. 61.6.[30] In order properly to evaluate this claim, it is necessary to examine both the linguistic-textual and theological-contextual arguments for such a connection.

Linguistic-Textual Evidence. Schüssler Fiorenza states that both passages (Isa. 61.6 and Rev. 20.6) agree

> with respect to the nominal character of the priest title, as is shown in the genitive construction, as well as the promissory nature of the passage, expressed by the future verb.[31]

None of these arguments compellingly excludes Exod. 19.6 from consideration, for it contains the same title (כהנים), and is likewise a promise with a future verb. Furthermore, the genitive construction in 20.6a (τοῦ θεοῦ) does not express any different relationship between ἱερεῖς and θεός than does the dative case in 1.6a and 5.10a (τῷ θεῷ). In these last two passages the combination of βασιλεία and ἱερεῖς limits *theologically* the grammatical options. John does not want to say a 'kingdom *of* God', but a 'kingdom *to/for* God'. The omission of βασιλεία in 20.6 frees him to adopt the more natural genitive construction with ἱερεῖς.[32] Finally, Rev. 20.6a uses θεοῦ where

---

30.   *Priester*, pp. 336-38; *The Elect and the Holy*, p. 116. Trudinger ('Text', p. 180) lists Isa. 61.6 with Rev. 20.6 but does not discuss it, as does also C.G. Ozanne, 'The Influence of the Text and Language of the Old Testament on the Book of Revelation' (PhD thesis, University of Manchester, 1964), p. 85.

31.   *Priester*, p. 336.

32.   Though it could also be argued that the dative in 1.6 and 5.10 reflects the ל of Exod. 19.6, and the genitive of 20.6 the construct כהני of Isa. 61.6.

Isa. 61.6a has יהוה/κυρίου. Thus the only unique correspondence between Rev. 20.6a and Isa. 61.6 is the use of the genitive.

Theological–Contextual Evidence. The main weakness in Elliot's evaluation arises from discussing Rev. 1.6, 5.10 and 20.6 in isolation from Revelation's overall theology of *kingdom* and *priesthood.* He implies that John does not develop the concept of believers as priests, and concludes that the primary significance of Exod. 19.6 for John 'lay in the term "kingdom" and the royal status of the believing community'.[33] Therefore, he argues, since John does not use βασιλεία in 20.6, Exod. 19.6 is probably not in view.

This sort of exegetical dissection of theological kernels is certainly valid in many documents and even parts of Revelation, but it is questionable in those parts of Revelation where an OT tradition or text is concerned. John's use of Scripture exhibits a clear pattern of conscious repetition which often involves a base text and the recapitulation of its various units or key words.[34] Exod. 19.6 is clearly the base text which John adopted in the heavenly vision in 5.10, and it is the same text he repeats and emphasizes in the epistolary introduction (1.6) which was probably added after 5.10 and 20.6 were written. Having laid this scriptural foundation, is it likely that subsequent allusions to the church as a kingdom or priests are based on a different OT model?

In Rev. 1.9 the 'kingdom in Jesus' refers to the present kingdom established by Christ's saving work and clearly relates to 1.6 and 5.10 (= Exod. 19.6), although the priests motif is not here included.[35] And in 7.14-15 the idea of believers as priests is developed in the same context of the redemptive work of Christ, though here not even ἱερεῖς is used.[36] John develops one thread of the tradition here,

33. *The Elect and the Holy,* p. 112.

34. See ch. 2 above (p. 70) where from c. 150 clear OT allusions come c. 72 recapitulations. E.g. Rev. 2.26-27 gives Ps. 2.8-9, of which portions are repeated in 12.5 and 19.15. Similarly 7.17b with 21.4a; 11.7b with 13.7a; 11.18c with 19.2; 21.23 with 22.5; etc.

35. This kingdom in Jesus is not equivalent to the kingdom of God, but representative of it, as the beast's kingdom (16.10; 17.17-18) is representative of the 'kingdom of the world' (11.15). This evil kingdom stands in political and religious opposition to God and needs to 'become' a part of his rule (11.15; cf. 12.10).

36. In Rev. 7.15 priestly privilege and function is the result (διὰ τοῦτο) of Christ's redemptive work (7.14), no different than in 1.5-6 and 5.9-10. Rev. 7.15 in

another there, knowing that his readers have already been provided with the scriptural background.

In view of this, the omission of βασιλεία in 20.6 is hardly significant, for the presence of ἱερεῖς alone, together with the verb βασιλεύω, is enough to connect it in the reader's mind with 1.6 and 5.10 (= Exod. 19.6). While Isa. 61.6 may have been familiar to John and possibly provided further prophetic force to the promise in Exodus, there is little justification for it displacing Exod. 19.6 as the base text in Rev. 20.6.

Revelation 1.11a → Isaiah 30.8

In his commentary, E. Lohmeyer assumes that John here takes his language and sense from Isa. 30.8, γράψον... εἰς βιβλίον. He concludes from this that βιβλίον in Rev. 1.11 designates a parchment codex and not a papyrus roll and suggests that John is placing his prophetic book on a par with the Jewish Scriptures: 'für den Juden ist Pergament das traditionelle Schreibmaterial, auf dem vor allem heilige Schriften geschrieben werden'.[37] Kraft rightly criticizes this conclusion, though he is prepared to retain an allusion to Isa. 30.8, 'The reference to Isa. 30.8 is correct. The author undoubtedly views his book as the word of God, though not as Holy Scripture. But there is no basis for thinking of anything other than a scroll here.'[38]

But it is doubtful whether any conscious dependence on Isa. 30.8 by John can be maintained,[39] and it is almost impossible to expect such a connection to be recognized by his readers. Commands to 'write into a book' are not an uncommon feature of apocalyptic commission scenes.[40]

---

turn anticipates 21.22–22.5 (cf. esp. λατρεύω in 7.15 and 22.3), where the community of believers as priests relates closely to the absence of a temple. All who come into the city are privileged to enter God's immediate presence. The city is his temple—the people are his priests.

37. *Die Offenbarung des Johannes* (HNT, 16; Tübingen, 2nd edn, 1953), p. 16.

38. *Offenbarung*, pp. 43-44.

39. The syntactical correspondence of the two texts is not straightforward; with reference to the Hebrew, it involves pairing the verb of the initial clause with the noun of a second parallel clause. The LXX, as is common, leaves out the second parallel verb.

40. Hermas, *Vis.* 2.4.2-3; 5.5, 7; cf. *Barn.* 12.9; Rev. 10.4.

Revelation 1.16b; 2.12, 16; 19.15a, 21 → Isaiah 11.4b; 49.2

In the initial commission scene of Rev. 1.10-20, one of the more striking visionary attributes of Christ is the sword which proceeds from his mouth: ἐκ τοῦ στόματος αὐτοῦ ῥομφαία δίστομος ὀξεῖα ἐκπορευομένη (1.16b). This image, with minor variations, recurs in Rev. 2.12, 16 and 19.15, 21.[41] The source of the sword–mouth motif is generally attributed to a combination of Isa. 11.4b and 49.2.[42] The initial development of this idea appears to have been in connection with the parousia pericope of Rev. 19.11-21. If so, then John has expanded the motif into the letters series (2.12, 16) and the introductory Christophany (1.16). Whether or not this evolution is accepted, it is ch. 19 which provides the best evidence for evaluating the traditions underlying the sword motif, and this will be our starting point.

John's presentation of the messianic warrior and judge in 19.11-21 incorporates a variety of eschatologically understood OT texts, including an allusion to Isa. 11.4a in 19.11b and Isa. 11.4b in 19.15a.

Rev. 19.11b/15a	*Isa. 11.4ab*	
καὶ ἐν δικαιοσύνῃ κρίνει...	...בצדק ושפט	ἀλλὰ κρινεῖ ταπεινῷ κρίσιν...
καὶ ἐκ τοῦ στόματος αὐτοῦ	והכה ארץ בשבט	καὶ πατάξει γῆν τῷ λόγῳ
ἐκπορεύεται ῥομφαία ὀξεῖα,	פיו	τοῦ στόματι αὐτοῦ
ἵνα ἐν αὐτῇ πατάξῃ τὰ ἔθνη		

As is customary in Revelation, close textual correspondence is limited to a few words here and there. In order properly to assess John's use of Scripture, it is often necessary to compare individual units of tradition. Thus the main text of interest (Isa. 11.4bα) may be broken down into five parts.

        a. agent—He (Messiah)
        b. action—will smite
        c. sphere—the earth
        d. instrument—with the rod
        e. genitive phrase—of his mouth

41. 2.12 lacks ἐκ τοῦ στόματος and 2.16 leaves out δίστομος ὀξεῖα, but this is traceable to stylistic considerations. They both refer to the same image and clearly presuppose 1.16b. The differences between 19.15a and 21 should be similarly understood. In 19.15a the MSS vary as to the inclusion of δίστομος; but the weight of evidence favours its omission.

42. Isa. 11.4b/49.2—Swete, Kraft, Charles, Lohmeyer, and Ford; Isa. 49.2/ 11.4—Rissi, Holtz, and Hemer; Isa. 49.2 alone—Caird and Pohl; Isa. 49.2/Ps. 149.6/Isa. 11.4b—Ozanne.

The specific application of Isa. 11.4 to the Messiah in his capacity as the eschatological judge was apparently already widespread in Jewish circles, for it appears in a variety of texts of differing theological backgrounds. The assimilation of this concept to Jesus as Messiah would have been natural and it appears to have been taken over with little variation. A comparison of Rev. 19.15, 21 with these similar traditions will help to illuminate various details of John's usage.

Text	Agent	Action	Sphere	Instrument	Genitive Phrase
Pss. Sol. 17.24, 35	Lord Messiah	destroy (24) smite (35)	nations (24) earth (35)	word	of his mouth
4QpIsa[a] 8–10	Root of David	judge	peoples	sword	—
1QSb5 24a	Prince	smite	peoples?	might	of your mouth
1QSb5 24b	Prince	devastate	earth	rod	—
1QSb5 24-25	Prince	slay	wicked	breath	of your lips
2 Thess. 2.8	Lord Jesus	slay	the wicked one	breath	of his mouth
4 Ezra 13.9-11, 37-38	(God's) Son	destroy (38)	nations (37)	fire (= law v. 38)	from his mouth, lips, tongue
1 Enoch 62.2	Chosen one	slay	wicked	word (= sword v. 12?)	of his mouth
Rev. 19.15, 21	(Messiah)	smite	nations	sword	of his mouth

It will be seen that none of these examples corresponds exactly to the Isaian text in every unit of the tradition. But for the most part, the variations are minor and the visibility of the prophetic testimony is not left in doubt. As for John's modifications, these are limited to the categories of *sphere* and *instrument*.[43]

1. *Sphere*. For the original object of נכה/πατάσσω (ארץ/γῆ), John

---

43. But note the change of verbs (action) between 19.15 (πατάσσω) and 19.21 (ἀποκτείνω); the latter as in 1QSb 5.24-25; 2 Thess. 2.8, and *1 En.* 62.2. Cf. also Rev. 2.16.

substitutes the more specific τὰ ἔθνη. While such a change could easily be explained as an interpretation of the ambiguous *earth* in Isa. 11.4b (e.g. *4 Ezra*),[44] an examination of the immediate context in Rev. 19 suggests that the addition of τὰ ἔθνη in fact arises from a conflation of Isa. 11 and Ps. 2.8-9 in Rev. 19.15a: ἵνα ἐν αὐτῇ πατάξῃ τὰ ἔθνη, καὶ αὐτὸς ποιμανεῖ αὐτοὺς ἐν ῥάβδῳ σιδηρᾷ. In Ps. 2.9, αὐτούς refers back to the גוים/ἔθνη of 2.8.

A similar concatenation of Ps. 2.9 and Isa. 11.4 in *Pss. Sol.* 17.24 results in exactly the same interchange of spheres, so that the ἔθνη of Ps. 2.8 stands in the place of γῆ of Isa. 11.4b. This is more than just conflation or substitution; it is an interpretation of γῆ, as is evident from *Pss. Sol.* 17.35, where Isa. 11.4 is again quoted, but this time with γῆ. Thus, for both John and the author of *Pss. Sol.* 17, a messianic understanding of Psalm 2 and Isaiah 11 meant not only that the two texts could be synthesized, but that each could be used to augment and elucidate the other.[45]

2. *Instrument*: A more difficult issue concerns the sword motif itself, which John adopts in place of the שבט/ῥάβδος of Isa. 11.4b.[46] Determining a possible scriptural antecedent for this idea is complicated by the variation with which he expressed it. There is no way of accounting for the complete phrase ῥομφαία δίστομος ὀξεῖα in 1.16 and 2.12 on the basis of a single OT model, and it is not likely

---

44. Contextual problems surrounding ארץ in Isa. 11.4b also open it naturally to reinterpretation. Because of the positive use of ארץ in the previous line (11.4a) and the supposition that רשע in 11.4bβ expects a similar parallel, almost all commentators emend ארץ to עריץ (cf. Wildberger, *Jesaja*, I, p. 438). *Targum Isaiah* removes the difficulty by omitting the first ארץ and adding חייבי (*guilty of*) before the second occurrence in 11.4b. Cf. πατάξαι τὴν γῆν in Rev. 11.6, where γῆ has a negative sense.

45. *Pss. Sol.* 17.37; 18.7 also use Isa. 11.2. Despite the close correspondence between this work and Revelation in texts and method, there is no need to posit literary dependence. Besides the fact that the order of *Pss. Sol.* 17.24 (Ps. 2 → Isa. 11) is the opposite of Rev. 19 (Isa. 11 → Ps. 2), the former presupposes רעם in Ps. 2.9 where John assumes רעה (= ποιμαίνω); cf. Ozanne, *Influence*, pp. 89-90. For a detailed discussion of the use of Isa. 11 and Ps. 2 in early Christianity, see Chevalier, *L'esprit et le Messie*.

46. LXX λόγος (α´ σ´ θ´ have ῥάβδος) is an interpretation of שבט not out of keeping with Isaiah's original intention. For the idea of a 'rod of the *mouth*' and the parallel of פבט // רוח already assumes a figurative meaning of שבט, such as '*powerful word*' (cf. Hos. 6.5).

that John resorts to various texts for individual adjectives.[47] In 19.15, if the textual omission of δίστομος is accepted, the ῥομφαία ὀξεῖα may have been influenced by Isa. 49.2, with δίστομος added elsewhere on John's own initiative. On the other hand, the simple form of the tradition in 2.16 and 19.21 with ῥομφαία alone may well have been original with both adjectives secondary elaborations.

John's preference for the sword image over the rod is no doubt determined in part by his desire to represent Christ as the bearer of universal judicial authority, in contrast to earthly rulers, whose executive power is often symbolized by the sword (Rev. 6.3-4; 13.10; 20.4; Rom. 13.4).[48] It is also a more appropriate weapon for the conquering messianic king in the eschatological battle.

The context of Isa. 11.4 of a messianic ruler who acts as Yahweh's agent of judgment, as well as the common metaphor of human and divine speech as a sharp instrument makes, 'sword of his mouth' a not unexpected substitute or parallel for 'rod of his mouth'.[49] If this

47. The nearest parallels are Isa. 49.2 חרב חדה/μάχαιραν ὀξεῖαν; Ps. 149.6 חרב פיפיות/ῥομφαία δίστομοι; cf. Judg. 3.16; Prov. 5.4; Sir. 21.3; Heb. 4.12. Ozanne's suggestion that 'from Isa. 49.2 (John) derived... ῥομφαία ὀξεῖα, and from Ps. 149.6 (ῥομφαία) δίστομος' is most unlikely ('Influence', p. 90).

48. Some suggest that John specifically has in mind the *ius gladii* (*law of the sword*), which represented 'the right to try and punish capital crimes, delegated by the emperor to individual provincial governors' (*OLD*, p. 765); Ford, *Revelation*, pp. 397-98; Hemer, *Letters*, p. 97; Acts 12.2; Rev. 2.13; 1 Pet. 2.13-14. But cf. Caird, *Revelation*, pp. 37-38 and n. 1. In 1QpHab 6 Rome's power is characterized by the sword.

49. Cf. 4QpIsaᵃ and *1 En.* 62 in the chart above. John even uses sword in parallel with rod in 19.15, where ῥομφαία ὀξεῖα // ῥάβδῳ σιδηρᾷ and πατάξῃ // ποιμανεῖ. The verbal parallel is based on the assumption that John either mistakenly or purposely assigns to ποιμαίνω the rare negative meaning of רעה (rather than רעע) in Ps. 2.9: 'to devastate' or 'to break'; Charles, *Revelation*, I, pp. 75-76.

God's judgment is often associated with the figure of a sword: Isa. 27.1; 34.5-6; 66.16; Ezek. 21.1-17; *Jub.* 9.15; *Sib. Or.* 3.672-73; 689-90; *1 En.* 62.12; Wis. 18.15-16; 1QH 6.29; 1QM 15.1-3; 19.10-11. The War Scroll passages are of particular interest because like Revelation they concern the final eschatological conflict and include (a) Preparation for battle (Rev. 16.12); (b) The gathering of earthly kings with the Roman emperor (Rev. 16.13-16; 19.19); (c) The association of the wicked forces with Satan (Rev. 16.13-14; 20.1-3, 7-10); (d) The defeat of the assembled nations by the Sword-of-God (written as one word—בחרבאל) (Rev. 19.17-21).

The analogy of the tongue/speech with a sword is commonplace in biblical lit.

change was influenced by any particular OT text other than Isa. 11.4, then the most likely candidate would be Isa. 49.2, not only because it contains the sword–mouth image, but because it concerns the *Servant*, making it liable to messianic speculation. But such a connection is only probable, not provable, and is secondary to the dominant inspiration of Isa. 11.4.[50]

Finally, a few words may be said concerning the purpose and meaning of the sword motif in Revelation. Whereas Rev. 1.16 and 2.12 merely reveal the possession of the sword by Christ, 2.16 and 19.15, 21 describe its purpose and particular sphere of operation. The Christophany of Revelation 1 sets forth Christ's judicial authority and prepares the way for its application—to the community in ch. 2, and to the rebellious nations in ch. 19. But it is doubtful whether the threat of judgment in 2.16 contemplates a separate manifestation from the appearance of Christ in Revelation 19. The rewards of the letters are eschatological and it is likely that some or all of the threatened judgments are likewise reserved for the parousia (11.18; 22.12).[51]

In Rev. 2.16 the threat itself is not against the entire church but against those who hold the Nicolaitan and 'Balaam' errors (ἔρχομαί σοι...πολεμήσω μετ' αὐτῶν). It is the church's duty to root out evil and hold fast in the short time remaining—it is Christ's task to pass sentence on heretics who practice idolatry and fornication at the final judgment (cf. 2.14-15 with 21.8).[52]

In any case, the principal application of the sword image is reserved for the appearance of the messianic judge in Revelation 19. While the objects of his wrath include the beast, false prophet, dragon, and all the nations gathered in opposition to him, the sword-judgment itself is directed only against the nations in general and not the war leaders.[53]

---

and in ancient culture in general: Isa. 49.2; Wis. 18.15-16; Pss. 57.5; 59.8; Hos. 6.5; Eph. 6.17; Heb. 4.12; 1QH 5.10-15; *Ahikar* 100; *Ps.-Phoc.* 124. Further parallels and discussion in L. Dürr, *Die Wertung des göttlichen Wortes im alten Testament und im antiken Orient* (Leipzig, 1938).

50. Yarbro Collins (*The Apocalypse*, p. 135), and Prigent, (*L'Apocalypse*, p. 30 n. 47) believe that John borrows from Wis. 18.15-16 in Rev. 19. It is a close parallel in language and thought, though not in context.

51. *Contra* Rissi, *Future*, p. 22.

52. A similar threat to apostates is laid out in CD 1.17; 3.11; 7.13; 8.1; 19.10, 13, where those who break the covenant will be judged by the sword when the Messiah appears.

53. The condemnation of the ungodly nations is an important theme for John and

All commentators are agreed that the sword which proceeds from Christ's mouth is symbolic of his verbal power and more specifically emphasizes the judicial authority which he wields as God's agent of judgment.[54] This accords well with the function of the imagery in both Isa. 11.4 and 49.2.

Revelation 1.17b; 2.8; 22.13 → Isaiah 44.6; 48.12; 41.4

The descriptive title (ἐγώ εἰμι) ὁ πρῶτος καὶ ὁ ἔσχατος occurs three times in Revelation: twice as a self-designation of the exalted Christ (1.17b; 22.13), and once as part of a messenger formula introducing Christ's proclamation to the church at Smyrna (2.8). It is unanimously agreed among commentators that the phrase has its source in the divine self-predication found in Isa. 44.6, 48.12 and 41.4, and that John did not adopt the LXX version, but works directly from the Hebrew—אני ראשון ואני אחרון.[55]

More problematic is the relationship of this title to two similar divine appellatives which appear in Revelation: τὸ ἄλφα καὶ τὸ ὦ (1.8; 21.6; 22.13), and ἡ ἀρχὴ καὶ τὸ τέλος (21.6; 22.13). While it appears that John uses these other two titles interchangeably, and can equally apply them to God or to Christ, their religio-historical backgrounds are nonetheless distinct.[56]

its fulfilment is anticipated in Rev. 2.26-27 (break them); 17.14 (conquer them); 19.15 (smite, break them); 19.21 (kill them). Cf. 6.15-17; 11.18; 16.14.

54. An interesting exception is S. Bartina, '"Una espada salía de la boca de su vestido". (Apc. 1,16; 2,16; 19,15.21)', *EstBib* 20 (1961), pp. 207-17. He understands the sword literally and says passages such as Isa. 49.2, Heb. 4.12, etc. are 'falsos paralelos bíblicos'. He thinks by στόμα John really means περιστόμιον, and refers to nomadic traditions still current in Palestine, in which the sword is carried in the upper portion ('mouth') of the garment.

55. Marconcini says that the short phrase 'non presenta una forte base letteraria in favore del T.M.', but still considers John's use of ὁ ἔσχατος as evidence for use of the Hebrew over the Greek tradition ('L'utilizzazione', p. 120). Though ἔσχατος is the usual equivalent of אחרון, the LXX avoids this in all three passages by various unique circumlocutions, probably for theological reasons; cf. Holtz, *Christologie*, pp. 82 (and n. 3), 83. Trudinger ('Text', p. 52) suggests that it is useless to argue which Isaiah text (41.4; 44.6; 48.12) was determinative, for they each present the same idea with minor variations. But it should be pointed out that only Isa. 44.6 invites a double application to God and to Christ by employing two introductory divine titles, 'Thus says the Lord...and *his Redeemer*'. Most commentators prefer Isa. 44.6, and for convenience I shall use this text as representative of all three.

56. W.C. van Unnik, *Het Godspredikaat 'Het Begin en het Einde' bij Flavius*

The designation of God as 'the beginning and the end' is widely attested in ancient cultures and specifically in the period encompassing Revelation.[57] Both Josephus and Philo borrow it from pagan philosophical tradition and apply it to the Jewish God for apologetic reasons.[58] It is extremely likely that John was likewise familiar with the concept and appropriated it as an extra-biblical testimony to the divine title of Isaiah.[59]

The origin of the *Alpha and Omega* title, however, which is unique to Revelation, cannot be determined with any degree of certainty. Various proposals have been offered:

1. W.J.P. Boyd regards it as originating from John himself, being a 'brilliant translation of the Hebrew logion found in Isaiah 44.6'.[60]
2. A. Farrer rejects the idea that Α–Ω is merely a paraphrase of Isa. 44.6, and takes it in connection with the copula (εἰμί) as an expression of the Greek trigrammaton ΙΑΩ.[61]

Josephus en in de Openbaring van Johannes (Amsterdam, 1976), p. 74 (cf. the review of J.C.H. Lebram in *NedTTs* 31 [1977], pp. 164-66). Van Unnik's work deals mainly with the 'beginning and end' phrase, but also gives a detailed treatment of the other two parallel titles of Revelation.

57. Van Unnik, *Het Godspredikaat*, pp. 13-26; 36-71.

58. The tradition was current in two forms: a threefold designation—e.g. Plato, *Leg.* 4.715E (θεὸς... ἀρχήν τε καὶ τελευτὴν καὶ μέσα τῶν ὄντων ἁπάντων ἔχων) found also in Josephus, *Apion* 2.190; and a twofold formula as in *Ant.* 8.280 (θεὸν... ἀρχή καὶ τέλος τῶν ἁπάντων); similarly Philo, *Plant.* 93. The use of this phrase in the *Bhagavad-gītā* shows the extent of its popularity as a description of the divine being, 'I am the beginning, the middle, and the end of all contingent beings' (10.20; cf. also v. 32; 11.16, 19); R.C. Zaehner, *The Bhagavad-gītā* (Oxford, 1969), p. 79. The date of this passage is no later than the 1st–2nd cent. CE, and many scholars would date it much earlier.

59. For other examples of John's dependence on Hellenistic traditions, see van Unnik, *Het Godspredikaat*, p. 75 and n. 204.

60. 'I am Alpha and Omega (Rev. 1, 8; 21, 6; 22, 13)', *SE*, II (= TU 87) (1964), p. 526 (quoted from Mounce, *Revelation*, p. 73).

61. *Rebirth*, pp. 263-65; 282-83. Farrer goes on to 'find' this formula hidden in many other phrases throughout Revelation. The discussion in his later commentary is more subdued, but he still clings to his theory (*The Revelation of St John the Divine* [Oxford, 1964], p. 63). For criticism, see Kraft, *Offenbarung*, p. 36, and Holtz, *Christologie*, p. 149 n. 3.

3.   J. Roloff finds its background in Gnostic speculation on numbers and letters, already strong in the second century CE.[62]
4.   G.R. Beasley-Murray and others suggest a possible relationship to the enigmatic *rotas-sator* word square, in which a–o seems to have some theological significance.[63]
5.   The majority of commentators lean towards the theory that John's use of A–Ω stems from alphabet speculation in Hellenistic Judaism as an equivalent of ת–א.[64]

Thus while the designation *the First and Last* is based on Isa. 44.6, and *the Beginning and End* is adopted from current religious vocabulary, the source of the *the Alpha and Omega* title must be left open, though it seems likely that it is not original with John.

Whereas the latter two titles are used both of God and Christ, Revelation applies the first only to Christ: in a speech to John in Rev. 1.17; in 2.8 introducing the speech to the church at Smyrna; and in 22.13 directed to both John and the churches. The significance of the title in these three passages can be presented in more detail.

a. *Revelation 1.17b-18a.* μὴ φοβοῦ· ἐγώ εἰμι ὁ πρῶτος καὶ ὁ ἔσχατος καὶ ὁ ζῶν. These are the first words of Christ to John in the climax of the prophetic commission scene of 1.10-20. In this context, they act as a *Präsentationsformel* which serves to identify the one speaking (1.10-11), and relates the auditions of 1.17-20 with the visionary description of 1.12-16.[65] John has thus adapted the Isaian

62.   *Offenbarung*, p. 36. Note esp. the theories of the Gnostic teacher Marcus, who taught in Asia Minor (Irenaeus, *adv. Haer.* 1.14-16).

63.   *Revelation*, pp. 59-63. Examples of this word-puzzle have been found from as early as 79 CE in Pompeii. Seemingly patterned on the *Pater Noster*, it has been ascribed by some to Latin-speaking Jews, and by others to Christian circles. For discussion and bibliographical material, see D. Fishwick, 'On the Origin of the Rotas-Sator Square', *HTR* 57 (1964), pp. 39-53. He leaves out the important article by F. Dornsieff, 'Das Rotas Opera Quadrat', *ZNW* 36 (1937), pp. 222-38.

64.   Brütsch, *Offenbarung*, III, p. 32; E. Lohse, *Die Offenbarung des Johannes* (HNT, 16; Göttingen, 1960), p. 16; Ford, *Revelation*, p. 379; Swete, *Apocalypse*, p. 10; G. Kittel, *TDNT*, I, pp. 1-3; D'Aragon, *JBC*, p. 472. But the uncertain dating of the material leads Kraft and Roloff to reject this view (*Offenbarung*, p. 36). See further F. Dornsieff, *Das Alphabet in Mystik und Magie* (Leipzig, 1922), pp. 122-25.

65.   This is according to Bultmann's classification of ἐγώ εἰμι formulae, applied

phrase for his own purpose, since in Isa. 44.6 it serves as a *Qualifikationsformel* following the identification of the speaker as Yahweh.[66]

Furthermore, John has here expanded the twofold title into a tripartite formula by the addition of καὶ ὁ ζῶν. This threefold designation of Christ encompassing past, present and future aspects of being is therefore parallel to the self-predication of God in Rev. 1.8, which is made up of a twofold title elucidated by a threefold formula of being.[67]

The first words of Christ (1.17-18) are thus placed in conscious relation to the first words of God (1.8), and together with 22.13 play an integral role in the authoritative framework of the book. Hartman is undoubtedly correct in concluding that the self-predication of 1.8 is an accreditation statement which lends divine authority to John's *words of prophecy*.[68] The same judgment can be applied to 1.17-18. This double authorization is merely an outworking of the dualistic revelatory scheme already given in Rev. 1.1-2.

Rev. 1.1	*Rev. 1.2*	*Rev. 1.17-18/1.8*
Revelation of Jesus Christ	→ Testimony of Jesus Christ	→ ἐγώ εἰμι formula—Christ
which God gave him	→ Word of God	→ ἐγώ εἰμι formula—God

In what way, then, is Christ here the *First and the Last*? What is the basis of his authority? Among commentators, two views appear most prominent. One group understands the designation as an expression of Christ's eternity, which underlies his authority as the Lord of all history.[69] The other group connects the title with the event of Christ's

---

to Revelation by L. Hartman, 'Form and Message. A Preliminary Discussion of "Partial Texts" in Rev. 1–3 and 22,6ff.', in Lambrecht (ed.), *L'Apocalypse johannique*, pp. 138-40. Aune calls this a 'self-disclosure oracle' (*Prophecy*, p. 281).

66. Noted also by Bultmann (in Hartman, 'Form and Message', p. 139).

67. The use of Α–Ω may be understood to include all that lies between them as well, thus making the connection with a threefold formula more natural. A relationship between the Α–Ω title and the 'is, was, coming' phrase is accepted by many commentators (e.g. Beckwith, Swete, Farrer, Holtz, Mounce, Prigent, Roloff and Lohmeyer). For a more detailed discussion of the threefold phrase, see van Unnik, 'A Formula Describing Prophecy', *NTS* 9 (1962–63), pp. 86-94. Cf. Heb. 13.8.

68. 'Form and Message', pp. 139-40. He also notes a similar example in *Apoc. Abr.* 9.

69. E.g. Charles, Holtz, Prigent, Lohmeyer, Beasley-Murray and Mounce.

resurrection and subsequent enthronement, which authenticated his past existence, confirmed his divine authority, and established him as God's agent of salvation and judgment.[70]

The first view is based on the assumption that all three double titles, whether applied to God or Christ, have exactly the same force.[71] Yet this overlooks the fact that *first and last* is reserved for Christ alone. Not only is it associated with the resurrection explicitly in two of its three uses (1.17-18; 2.8), but John relates Christ's 'firstness' specifically to the resurrection when in 1.5 he calls him the 'firstborn from the dead'. In addition, he repeatedly gives evidence that Christ's victory over death is the basis of his authority over the church and the world.[72] It appears then that the second view best accords with the immediate context and John's overall perspective.

b. *Revelation 2.8.* τάδε λέγει ὁ πρῶτος καὶ ὁ ἔσχατος, ὅς ἐγένετο νεκρὸς καὶ ἔζησεν. It is surely significant that John here does not merely take over the first and last designation from 1.17, but retains its connection with the resurrection. Christ's power over life and death, his authority over the first and last phases of human existence serves here a paraenetic function, which is directed to the circumstances of the Smyrnean church. In the face of persecution and possible death, they are to gain strength from Christ's example and take comfort in his authority to bestow the crown of life and deliver them from the second death (2.10-11).

c. *Revelation 22.13.* ἐγὼ...ὁ πρῶτος καὶ ὁ ἔσχατος. This final application reinforces the premise that *first and last* is fundamentally a title of authority. It stands here in connection with the role of Christ as the eschatological judge, whose judgment encompasses both wrath and reward (2.2, 19; 3.1-2, 8, 15; 11.18; 14.13; 20.12-13). The basis for his authority is not included in this passage, but there can be little

---

70. E.g. Kraft, Sweet and D'Aragon; Prigent (*L'Apocalypse*, p. 31 n. 52) rejects Kraft's position.

71. Criticized by van Unnik, *Het Godspredikaat*, p. 6. 'Nu is het algemeen gebruikelijk om de drie termen gezamenlijk te behandelen en eenvoudig als varianten te beschouwen. Maar toch is er alle aanleiding om ze afzonderlijk te bezien'.

72. Rev. 1.5—firstborn of the dead → ruler of the kings of the earth; 1.18; 2.2, 10-11—resurrection → authority over death and Hades: 3.21—because Christ has conquered, he has authority in relation to the Church: 5.5—because Christ has conquered, he has authority to open the scroll. Cf. Col. 2.18.

doubt that, as in 1.17-18 and 2.8, it is related to Christ's victory over death (cf. 2.26-27 with 5.5-7). The collocation of all three titles in Rev. 22.13 does not necessarily justify their being homogenized into a single theological kernel. Whereas God is *beginning and end* in relation to creation (4.11; 21.6), Christ is *first and last* in relation to the church. Where Christ shares in God's role as Creator, he is called ἀρχή, and not πρῶτος or even πρωτότοκος (3.14; cf. Col. 1.15).

Revelation 1.19 → Isaiah 48.6

Swete, Trudinger, Kraft and van Unnik all mention the parallel between the phrase ἃ μέλλει γενέσθαι in Rev. 1.19 and the LXX of Isa. 48.6, where ἃ μέλλει γίνεσθαι translates נצרות (*secret things*) in the MT.[73] However, none of these authors goes on to discuss this connection. If indeed John borrowed the phrase directly from the LXX, the textual question of γενέσθαι versus γίνεσθαι would weigh in favour of the latter, although some LXX MSS witness to the former reading. But the probability of dependence on Isaiah here is made unlikely by traditions which lay closer to hand.

The phrase ἃ μέλλει γενέσθαι may simply be a variation of ἃ δεῖ γενέσθαι which John uses repeatedly (1.1; 4.1; 22.6), and which can be attributed with some confidence to another OT source (Dan. 2.28).[74] Compare especially Rev. 1.19 with 4.1: ἃ μέλλει γενέσθαι μετὰ ταῦτα / ἃ δεῖ γενέσθαι μετὰ ταῦτα.

In addition, van Unnik argues that the phrase is a standard feature of a tripartite formula associated with prophetic revelation, and that it is common in various forms and orders in pagan as well as Christian literature.[75] But even if John is in touch with this tradition for the threefold formula as a whole, the influence of the Daniel formula on the last member is not thereby ruled out. In any case, there is little necessity or basis for bringing Isa. 48.6 into the discussion.

73. Swete, *Apocalypse*, p. cxlii, Trudinger, 'Text', p. 180; Kraft, *Offenbarung*, p. 49; van Unnik, 'A Formula Describing Prophecy', p. 87.

74. The similarities between the two phrases gave rise to conflation (i.e. δεῖ μέλλει) in some MSS at 1.19, as J.S. Schmid observes (*Studien zur Geschichte des griechischen Apokalypse–Textes* [Munich, 1955], II, p. 98). Cf. Beale, *The Use of Daniel*, p. 168.

75. Van Unnik, 'A Formula Describing Prophecy', pp. 86-94.

Revelation 2.17; 3.12 → Isaiah 62.2; 65.15

In the overcomer speech of the Pergamene letter Christ promises τῷ νικῶντι δώσω αὐτῷ τοῦ μάννα τοῦ κεκρυμμένου καὶ δώσω αὐτῷ ψῆφον λευκήν, καὶ ἐπὶ τὴν ψῆφον ὄνομα καινὸν γεγραμμένον ὃ οὐδεὶς οἶδεν εἰ μὴ ὁ λαμβάνων. There is little difficulty in discerning the background and purpose of the heavenly manna promise, which is an appropriate spiritual compensation for those who have refused the earthly sustenance of food sacrificed to idols (2.14). It is the second reward—the white stone engraved with a new and secret name—which poses many questions for the interpreter. That John has combined in this phrase elements from various backgrounds can hardly be doubted. There is no OT or early Christian parallel to the motif of the white stone and it is generally acknowledged that he adapts it from common tradition, whether judicial, magical or otherwise.[76]

The promise of ὄνομα καινόν, however, is taken by some commentators to be inspired by Isa. 62.2, where a שם חדש (LXX ὄνομα... καινόν) is the eschatological reward to be given by Yahweh to afflicted Jerusalem.[77] Instead of *forsaken* (עזובה), the city will be called *my delight is in her* (חפצי בה); and instead of *desolate* (שממה), the land will be named *married* (בעולה). In the program of renewal set out by Third Isaiah, this renaming of city and land is completed by the renaming of God's faithful people in 65.15b: 'and he will call his servants by a different name'.[78]

The question naturally arises as to whether the *new name* of Rev. 2.17 is the victor's own name or is to be identified with the promise of Christ's *new name* in 3.12. The answer is not likely to be found by grouping all of the book's 'naming' texts together and seeking a collective interpretation.[79] Despite the similar terminology, it seems

76. Hemer outlines the various theories (*Letters*, pp. 96-105).

77. So Comblin, Hemer, Ozanne, Prigent and Kraft.

78. MT שם אחר, but LXX has ὄνομα καινόν. Some commentators accept the LXX reading over the MT (e.g. Whybray, Westermann). The omission of this line from 1QIsaᵃ may mean no more than that the scribe's exemplar was faulty or illegible at this point. His haphazard attempt at completing the sense does not seem to suggest an intentional omission on theological grounds, as J.R. Rosenbloom theorizes (*The Dead Sea Isaiah Scroll* [Grand Rapids, 1970], p. 67).

79. As do Caird, Roloff and Prigent, tying in 2.17 and 3.12 with the names of the warrior Messiah of 19.12, 13, 16 and/or the divine names on the foreheads of the saints in 14.1 and 22.4.

3. *Isaiah in Revelation 1–3*

best to see 2.17 and 3.12 as separate promises, each with a different focus and aim.[80] The context of 2.17, in which *each* conqueror receives a stone with a personal name known only to *each* recipient, implies individual believer's names. The fact that no one knows the name except the victor himself is quite different from 3.12, where all receive the same name of Christ. And if Rev. 19.12 may be connected with 3.12, the secret name of Christ is said to be known only to himself.

It is more likely that the believer's new name is an intentional analogy to the new name of Christ in 19.12. As Christ conquered and received a new name known only to himself, so too his fellow conquerors (2.26-27; 19.14)—who follow him wherever he goes (14.4), and share in his reign (5.10, 20.6, 22.5)—receive new names known only to themselves.[81] The operative word is καινός, and the conquerors' reception of *new names* is commensurate with their future existence in the *new heavens*, the *new earth* and the *New Jerusalem*.[82]

If, then, the promise of a *new name* is related to John's overall scenario of renewal, there is good ground for maintaining a connection with Isa. 62.2, and especially 65.15, because of the latter's proximity to the renewal prophecy of 65.16-20, which John elsewhere uses extensively (21.1-4).[83]

Therefore, the purpose of the *new name* on the white stone has nothing to do with endowing the recipient with magical protection or spiritual power over their enemies.[84] This is a promise for the

80. Along with Kraft, *Offenbarung*, pp. 66-67, 83; Beckwith, *Apocalypse*, p. 462-63; Mounce, *Revelation*, p. 100; Hemer, *Letters*, pp. 102, 105; Ozanne, 'Influence', p. 155; and Pohl, *Offenbarung*, I, p. 130. *Contra* H. Haarbeck, *et al.*, who think that 'the new name would not be that of the bearer, but of the one giving authority to the bearer' (*NIDNTT*, II, p. 674).

81. The concept of a spiritual victory followed by a new name is closely paralleled in Phil. 2.9-10, where, as in Rev. 19.12, 16 the name ascribed to the exalted Christ is *Lord*. Kraft (*Offenbarung*, p. 83) also emphasizes this connection. Cf. also Gen. 32.24-28 (where Jacob 'prevails' and receives a new name); *Pr. Jos.* 6–9; Philo, *Mut. Num.* 81–87; Homer, *Iliad* 1.403-404.

82. 'Wie am Anfang alles bei Namen gerufen wurde (1 Mo 1.5.8) und damit seine Stellung, Berufung und sein Geschick empfing, so auch in der Erneuerung aller Dinge' (Pohl, *Offenbarung*, I, p. 130).

83. Farrer also prefers Isa. 65.15 (*Revelation*, p. 81).

84. Those who regard the white stone as an amulet and the secret name as a magical formula include W. Bousset (*Die Offenbarung Johannis* [Göttingen, 6th

eschaton, and what need is there for protection in the New Jerusalem, where all dwell in the presence of God (21.3-4)? Moreover, for this present life John offers no formula of immunity from the sword or captivity (13.10), and the only safeguard against spiritual evil is steadfast faithfulness to Christ.

Revelation 3.7b, 12a → Isaiah 22.22-23

Revelation	Isaiah	
ὁ ἔχων τὴν κλεῖν Δαυίδ,	תתחי מפתח בית דוד	καὶ δώσω τὴν δόξαν Δαυίδ
ὁ ἀνοίγων καὶ οὐδεὶς κλείσει	על שכמו ופתח ואין	αὐτῷ, καὶ ἄρξει, καὶ οὐκ
καὶ κλείων καὶ οὐδεὶς ἀνοίγει...	סגר וסגר ואין	ἔσται ὁ ἀντιλέγων. καὶ
ποιήσω αὐτὸν στῦλον	פתח ותקעתיו יתד	στήσω αὐτὸν ἄρχοντα ἐν
ἐν τῷ ναῷ τοῦ θεοῦ μου	במקום נאמן והיה	τόπῳ πιστῷ, καὶ ἔσται
	לכסא כבוד	εἰς θρόνον δόξης τοῦ
	לבית אביו	οἴκου τοῦ πατρὸς αὐτοῦ.

This descriptive phrase forms part of an extended christological title introducing the letter to the church at Philadelphia. The connection with Isa. 22.22 is obvious, and, as has already been noted above, the contextual visibility of this allusion is more well-defined than others in Revelation.[85]

The original oracle in Isaiah concerned the promotion of Eliakim to the position of major-domo in the palace of king Hezekiah. The *key of the house of David* promised to him by Yahweh serves as a symbol of

edn, 1906], p. 215); Roloff, *Offenbarung*, p. 55; and D'Aragon, *JBC*, pp. 473-74. This view, while at first compelling, does not really fit the context: (a) it does not accord with the eschatological nature of the reward; (b) the secret name is not a divine name, but the victor's own; (c) ψῆφος is an uncommon conductor in magical praxis, as are stones in general. LS (*s.v.* ψῆφος) lists one case of a ψῆφος inscribed with a formula, and J. Naveh and S. Shaked add a Nabataean incantation on a 'large pebble'; but precious and semi-precious metals and stones are preferred (*Amulets and Magic Bowls* [Jerusalem, 1985], pp. 13-14). The non-magical use of stones inscribed with personal names is also known; see F. Rosenthal, 'Nabataean and Related Inscriptions', in H.D. Colt (ed.), *Excavations at Nessana* (London, 1962), I, pp. 198-210.

85. Most commentators accept it as a rendering of the Hebrew (e.g. Trudinger, Ozanne, Marconcini, Charles and Holtz). Only Kraft (*Offenbarung*, p. 80) maintains a Greek source (*Sinaiticus*). For discussion of the Greek versions of this passage, see R.R. Ottley, *The Book of Isaiah according to the Septuagint* (Cambridge, 2nd edn, 1909 [1906]), II, pp. 211-12.

his great authority, which extends not only over the royal household, but without to the entire city (Jerusalem) and nation (Judah) as well (Isa. 22.21).[86] Although a messianic application of this prophecy is unattested in early Jewish literature, several factors open it naturally to such speculation, particularly to Christian interpreters.[87]

1. In v. 20 Eliakim is called 'my servant' by Yahweh.
2. In v. 22 the promise is connected with the 'house of David' (cf. Rev. 5.5; 22.16).
3. The relationship of authority between the king and his chosen steward offers a ready analogy to the association between God and the Messiah.[88]

That John understands the passage messianically is therefore not surprising, and its appropriateness to the circumstances of the Philadelphian church lay precisely in what it asserts about the Messiah's authority. As the royal steward exercised complete control over the palace and governed access to the king's presence, so Christ holds the power of admission or exclusion from God's kingdom.[89]

86. For more detailed discussion see R. Martin-Achard, 'L'oracle contre Shebna et le pouvoir des clefs, Es. 22,15-25', *TZ* 24 (1968), pp. 241-54.

87. *Targ. Isa.* 22.20-25 is a possible exception, though the dating is of course problematic. Verse 22a reads, 'And I will put the key of the sanctuary and the government of the house of David into his hand'. Significantly the Targum strengthens the idea of political authority and adds to it the motif of cultic authority (cf. v. 24), thereby investing the figure of Eliakim with both royal and priestly power. See further B. Chilton, *The Glory of Israel* (JSOTSup, 23; Sheffield, 1983), pp. 19, 24, 131 n. 21. The messianic flavour of even the MT is recognized by O. Kaiser (*Isaiah 13–39* [OTL; London, 1974], pp. 156-57); and esp. G. von Rad, *Old Testament Theology* (Edinburgh, 1965), II, pp. 48-49, 373, 'The almost Messianic full powers of the unworthy Shebna pass over, solemnly received, to Eliakim. Yet he too will fail. Thus, the office of "the key of David" remained unprovided for until finally it could be laid down at the feet of Christ (Rev. III.7).'

88. Especially suggestive are the references to the steward's role 'in his father's house' (22.23, 24; cf. 15). John presents God as the Father of Jesus in Rev. 1.6; 2.28; 3.5, 21; and 14.1. A striking parallel is found in Heb. 3.1-6, where the writer develops the theme of Jesus as the faithful steward appointed over God's house. Perhaps the comparison there between Moses and Christ was originally suggested by similarities between Num. 12.7 LXX (Moses) and Isa. 22.20-24 (LXX), messianically understood.

89. 'Even as I have received power from my Father' (Rev. 2.28); cf. 2.7; 3.5, 12; Mt. 28.18; Eph. 1.22.

Even though the Philadelphian Christians may be shut out and rejected by the 'synagogue of Satan', Christ has set before them 'an open door, which no one is able to shut' (3.8).

This 'open door' is hardly a reference to missionary opportunity, for the purpose of the letter is wholly devoted to comforting the community in its struggles and promising rewards for its faithfulness.[90] The open door is rather to be connected with the eschatological promise of 3.12 and the overcomer's entrance into the New Jerusalem.[91] Those who 'enter the city by the gates' (22.14) can do so only by means of him who controls the 'key of David' (3.7).[92]

If we accept the suggestion of Kraft, the influence of Isaiah 22 extends also to the eschatological promise of the Philadelphian letter in Rev. 3.12. He notes the similarity between the peg promise in Isa. 22.23 and the pillar promise in the overcomer blessing of 3.12.[93]

90. *Contra* Charles, Swete and Caird (*Revelation*, pp. 51-52): 'So here Christ has opened a door in front of the Philadelphia Christians, by giving them an opportunity for the conversion of the Jews, with every expectation of success'. This interpretation is rejected by a few older, and the majority of recent, commentators, including Beckwith, Lohmeyer, Mounce, Sweet, Roloff, Kraft and Prigent. Cf. Hemer (*Letters*, pp. 162-63, 174-75), who does not consider the two views mutually exclusive; likewise Kiddle–Ross, *Revelation*, pp. 50-51.

91. Both Kraft and Prigent think the phrase 'I have set before you an open door' is adapted from Isa. 45.1b (*Offenbarung*, p. 81; *L'Apocalypse*, p. 69). This is possible, though the language of Isa. 22.22 could alone account for it.

92. The concept of the keys as symbolic of Christ's authority is further supported by 1.18, so that 1.18 and 3.7 are complementary rather than identical (cf. 9.1-2; 20.1-3). The former emphasizes his power over the sphere of death, the latter his authority over the sphere of eternal life; cf. Holtz, *Christologie*, pp. 86-88; *Odes Sol.* 42.15-17. Many scholars see Isa. 22 as also lying behind the presentation of the 'keys of the kingdom' by Christ to Peter in Mt. 16.19 (cf. 23.13; 25.10). There it is used to illustrate ecclesiastical authority, in contrast to the eschatological and messianic application of John. For further discussion see Martin-Achard, L'oracle', pp. 251-54. The possibility of an intentional contrast to the Roman god Janus, whose symbol is a key, is interesting and may be worth further study. For this idea see C. de Ambrogio, *L'Apocalisse* (Turin, 1964), I, p. 52; and R. Schilling, *Rites, Cultes, Dieux de Rome* (Paris, 1979), pp. 220-62, esp. 224-25, 260-61.

93. Kraft, *Offenbarung*, p. 82. He makes the interesting observation that several Greek MSS (B Q Orig) read στήλω instead of στήσω in the LXX of Isa. 22.23. But it seems almost certain that John is using the Hebrew for vv. 22-23, and if there is any influence from the Greek translations, the LXX here is the least likely candidate.

Rev. 3.12a	Isa. 22.23
I will make him	I will fasten him
A pillar in	(as) a peg in...
the temple of my God	his father's house

The common image of a peg as a symbol of stability, the promise-form, and the fact that John has already used the previous verse of Isaiah (22.22) in the same letter, all support the conclusion that Isaiah's peg metaphor is unlikely to be an accidental parallel to John's pillar metaphor.[94]

The point of the pillar promise here is not that the overcomers will 'support' God's temple, but that they will be firmly fixed in it, stable, immovable from God's presence, as is clear from the accompanying phrase, καὶ ἔξω οὐ μὴ ἐξέλθῃ ἔτι.[95]

Revelation 3.9b → Isaiah 60.14; 49.23

Revelation	Isa. 60.14	
ποιήσω αὐτοὺς ἵνα ἥξουσιν	...והלכו אליך	καὶ πορεύσονται πρὸς σὲ
καὶ προσκυνήσουσιν	על כפות רגליך	...καὶ παροξυνάντων σε[96]
ἐνώπιον τῶν ποδῶν σου	והשתחוו	
καὶ γνῶσιν ὅτι ἐγώ...		

Isa. 49.23	
אפים ארץ ישתחוו לך	ἐπὶ πρόσωπον τῆς γῆς προσκυνήσουσί σοι
ועפר רגליך ילחכו	καὶ τὸν χοῦν τῶν ποδῶν σου λείξουσιν·
...וידעת כי אני	καὶ γνώσῃ ὅτι ἐγώ...

Christ's words of encouragement to the struggling but faithful church at Philadelphia shift in focus from the privileged status of the community (3.7-8; Isa. 22), to the future recognition of that status by its enemies (3.9). And again the authority of the message is heightened by means of a prophetic testimony from Isaiah. Not only does the conflict between the church and local synagogue involve disputes about spiritual

94. The metaphorical use of στύλος is a natural Greek analogue to the Semitic use of יתד in a figurative sense. Compare Ezra 9.8, 'To give us a secure hold [lit. 'tent-peg'] within his holy place'; Isa. 33.20; 54.2; Zech. 10.4; b. Giṭ. 17a. Cf. also Gen. R. 43, where Abraham, Isaac and Jacob are called the 'three great pegs', with Gal. 2.9, where James, Peter and John are called the 'pillars' of the church.

95. Farrer comments, 'To compensate for exclusion from the place of honour in the synagogue Christ promises them a place (as pillars) in God's temple' (*Revelation*, p. 80).

96. α´σ´θ´: καὶ προσκυνήσουσιν ἐπὶ τὰ ἴχνη τῶν ποδῶν σου.

legitimacy and the possession of divine favour, but it is no doubt aggravated by the political sanction enjoyed by Judaism, in contrast to the social and political discrimination endured by the Christian community. To emphasize that the present disadvantage is only temporary, John takes up an image employed by Second and Third Isaiah to illustrate the future reversal of the circumstances of the faithful remnant vis-à-vis their oppressors.

Isa. 45.14	*Isa. 49.23*	*Isa. 60.14*
Thus says the Lord: 'The wealth of Egypt and the merchandise of Ethiopia, and all the Sabeans... shall come over to you... they shall come over in chains and bow down to you... saying: "God is with you only"'.	Kings shall be your foster fathers, and their queens your nursing mothers. With their faces to the ground they shall bow down to you, and lick the dust of your feet. Then you will know that I am the Lord.	The sons of those who oppressed you shall come bending low to you; and all who despised you shall bow down at your feet; they shall call you the City of the Lord.

From the point of view of both diction and context, it is fairly obvious that John has in mind particularly Isa. 60.14, and this accords well with his later prominent use of Isaiah 60 in Rev. 21.22–22.5.[97] But there is some evidence to suggest that he has conflated Isa. 60.14 and 49.23, using a phrase from the latter as a bridge to the next allusion to Isa. 43.4 in 3.9c.

Isa. 60.14 πορεύσονται... καὶ προσκυνήσουσιν ἐπὶ τὰ ἴχνη τῶν ποδῶν σου (α´σ´θ´)
Rev. 3.9bc ἥξουσιν καὶ προσκυνήσουσιν ἐνώπιον τῶν ποδῶν σου
καὶ γνῶσιν ὅτι ἐγὼ ἠγάπησά σε
Isa. 49.23 ...τῶν ποδῶν σου
...καὶ γνώσῃ ὅτι ἐγὼ...
Isa. 43.4 ...κἀγώ σε ἠγάπησα

While this may seem somewhat of a complicated procedure to us, it obviously did not appear so to early scribes, translators and commen-

97. So also Charles, Ozanne, Pohl, Mounce, Beasley-Murray, Schüssler Fiorenza and Roloff. Lohmeyer, Caird and Müller cite all three Isaiah texts in general, and Kraft, for some unexplained reason, singles out Isa. 45.14 (*Offenbarung*, p. 82). Hemer rightly notes the many parallels between the Philadelphian letter and the New Jerusalem vision of Rev. 21–22 (*Letters*, pp. 161, 266 n. 33). Of the seven churches, Philadelphia appears to come the closest to the ideals of the future Holy City, and may be upheld as a sort of earthly model of the New Jerusalem.

tators, who assimilated John's γνῶσιν to Isaiah's γνώση.[98] And a comparison of Isa. 43.4 with the three Isaiah texts laid out above (esp. 45.14) shows that they all convey the same eschatological idea and serve a similar paraenetic purpose. It may be then that we are dealing here with another thematic collection of texts from which John has drawn various motifs to apply to the 'faithful remnant' of God's people at Philadelphia.

From a modern perspective, the application of Isa. 60.14, 49.23 and 43.4 to the church's Jewish opponents—effectively placing them in the role of Gentile oppressors—is an ironic reversal of the original OT prophecy. But such a judgment fails to take into account the self-identity of the early Christian community and its pre-understanding of the Scriptures. According to this *Vorverständnis*, the OT prophets directed their promises not to an ethnic group ('who say they are Jews and are not', Rev. 3.9a), but to a community of faith drawn together from 'every tribe and tongue and people and nation' through the redemptive work of Christ' (5.9-10). The continuity of election allowed John to draw a line from the oppressed community of Isaiah to the struggling saints in Philadelphia, thereby appropriating the former's promises for the present conflict.[99]

Exactly what the circumstances and timing of the fulfilment of this prophecy will be is left unspecified. The context of Isaiah and the letter, as well as the hint of coercion (ποιήσω αὐτούς), suggest that John has in mind an eschatological rather than a historical setting.[100] In any case, there is probably no thought here of a conversion of the church's opponents.[101]

---

98. ℵ 61 69 1094 (2351) *pc sah arm*[4] *Prim. Tyc.* A similar conflation of Isa. 60.14 and 49.23 is found in 1QM 12.14-15 = 19.6-7; J. van der Ploeg, *Le rouleau de la guerre* (Leiden, 1959), pp. 148-49.

99. Eusebius, in his commentary on Isaiah, interprets 60.14 in the context of those who blaspheme and trouble the church (GCS, IX, p. 376, II, 6-18).

100. 'Whether this promise was understood by the readers to refer to the immediate earthly future, or more probably, to the last times, the choice of this scripture was related to their present rejection' (Hemer, *Letters*, pp. 163-64); cf. Pohl, *Offenbarung*, I, p. 147; Roloff, *Offenbarung*, p. 61; Schüssler Fiorenza, *Revelation*, p. 105.

101. *Contra* Swete, *Apocalypse*, p. 55; Caird, *Revelation*, p. 52. Cf. n. 90 above, and Mounce, *Revelation*, pp. 118-19; Beasley-Murray, *Revelation*, p. 101.

Revelation 3.9c → Isaiah 43.4

> Revelation   Isaiah
> ὅτι ἐγὼ ἠγάπησά σε   ואני אהבתיך κἀγώ σε ἠγάπησα

The identification of such a short text involving a single common verb with any specific OT archetype must always carry some doubt.[102] However, if we add to the affinity in diction a similarity in application, and take into account the previous discussion of Rev. 3.9b, which likewise applies to the church an election motif from Isaiah, the weight of evidence favours the supposition of a conscious allusion.[103]

While the verbal basis of comparison is too scant to give a certain judgment about the textual tradition behind the allusion,[104] various suggestions have been advanced by commentators as to the significance of the aorist ἠγάπησα.

Both S. Thompson and G. Mussies assume an underlying Hebrew perfect tense, but the former gives it a present sense and the latter 'perfective value'.[105] Mussies appears to be closer to the mark with 'I have loved you', for the present sense ('I love you') does not take into account the eschatological nature of the promise. Holtz probably has the right idea when he says that while at present their persecutors oppose them, in the *eschaton* 'they' (i.e. the opponents) will be made to recognize that already in that period of earthly persecution the church was loved by Christ.[106] It will help to look at the original context of Isaiah more closely and compare John's usage.

Isa. 43.1-7 is an oracle of salvation and comfort intended to encourage the struggling band of exiles and remind them of their divine

---

102. Thus Lohmeyer, Kraft and Roloff do not even mention any connection, while Prigent, Beckwith and Trudinger only suggest it as a *possible* allusion.

103. Those who recognize the allusion include Schüssler Fiorenza, Holtz, Mussies, Thompson, Vos, Rissi, Ozanne, Swete, Charles, Caird, Hemer, Sweet, and Pohl.

104. The word order favors MT, but Schüssler Fiorenza argues that as in Rev. 1.5 (τῷ ἀγαπῶντι ἡμᾶς), the aorist form of ἀγαπάω followed by the acc. reflects baptismal tradition. On this basis, she accepts an LXX *Vorlage*, but it is not clear why her thesis necessitates such a textual preference (*Priester*, pp. 213-14; 'Redemption as Liberation', pp. 224-25).

105. Thompson, *The Apocalypse and Semitic Syntax*, p. 40, who apparently follows N. Turner, *A Grammar of New Testament Greek*. IV. *Style* (Edinburgh, 1976), p. 155; Mussies, *Morphology*, p. 338.

106. Holtz, *Christologie*, p. 62; so also Beckwith, *Apocalypse*, p. 482.

calling. In particular, 43.4 speaks of the surpassing worth of the people of Israel over other peoples.[107] As C. Westermann has put it, 'A tiny, miserable, and insignificant band of uprooted men and women are assured that they—precisely they—are the people to whom God has turned in love'.[108]

For John, to whom the church constituted the *true Israel*, these promises provided a fitting encouragement to the struggling Philadelphian church. The conflicts between church and local synagogue may have included rival claims of divine election ('who *claim* to be Jews' 3.9), supported perhaps by these very testimonies of Isaiah. To a church with little power (3.8), holding on with the fingertips of faith, weary from fighting off threats to its own spiritual identity, John brings assurance of their calling as God's true chosen people.

Thus the divine utterance 'I have loved you' is primarily a statement of *election* rather than *affection*.[109] Even if John contemplates in ἠγάπησα a specific christological act of love, such as Christ's death and resurrection, it is this event which is the founding act of election for the Church (5.9-10), as was the Exodus for Israel.[110]\

Revelation 3.14a → Isaiah 65.16
In the messenger formula which introduces the final prophetic letter to the Laodicean church Jesus is designated as ὁ ἀμήν, ὁ μάρτυς ὁ πιστὸς καὶ ἀληθινός. This use of *amēn* as a divine title is unique to

107. K. Maalstad, 'Einige Erwägungen zu Jes. XLIII 4', *VT* 16 (1966), p. 514.
108. *Isaiah 40–66* (London, 1969), p. 118.
109. The association of divine love with election goes back to Deuteronomistic theology. Note the parallel of בחר and אהב (LXX—ἐκλέγω and ἀγαπάω) in Deut. 4.37; 10.15; Pss. 47.5 (46.5); 78.68 (77.68); Isa. 41.8; cf. *4 Ezra* 3.13-14; 5.27. E.M. Good calls it the 'love of election' (*IDB*, III, p. 168), and Westermann recognizes it as a special emphasis in Isa. 43.1-7 (*Isaiah 40–66*, p. 118). Cf. Cremer, *BTL*, p. 773; *TDNT*, IV, pp. 163, 168; Swete, *Revelation*, p. 103; D'Aragon, *JBC*, p. 474.
110. Pohl thinks that the promise is not that all Jews will bow down and recognize the 'true' messianic community at the Judgment, since the term 'synagogue of Satan' does not automatically write off all Jews, or even necessarily all Jews in that synagogue. Rather it is directed against a specific group from (ἐκ) the Philadelphian synagogue who reject and oppose the local Christian community. 'Die Glieder der Synagoge sind nicht abgeschrieben, so wenig Petrus abgeschrieben war, als der Herr zu ihm sagte: "Gehe hinter mich, Satan!" (Mt. 16,23)' (*Offenbarung*, I, p. 147).

Revelation.[111] In view of its brevity, and currency as a liturgical response, it is somewhat surprising to find that the majority of commentators have little difficulty in accepting Isa. 65.16 as the inspiration behind this special use of *amēn*.[112]

The connection is suggested by the fact that the Isaiah passage likewise employs the Hebrew אָמֵן in an atypical manner as part of a divine epithet: אֱלֹהֵי אָמֵן = *God of Amēn*. This involves vocalizing the Hebrew word as an adverb אָמֵן, as found in the MT and some Greek versions (e.g. σ΄), rather than the nouns אֹמֶן or אֱמֶן (*faithfulness*), presupposed by the LXX (τὸν θεὸν τὸν ἀληθινόν).[113] The probability that John knew and adapted this OT text is enhanced by the fact that he elsewhere borrows from both the preceding and following verses of Isaiah 65, as well as from the last part of Isa. 65.16 itself.[114]

What does it mean for John that Jesus is the *Amēn*, and what significance does this christological designation have for the Laodicean letter

111. The nearest parallel is 2 Cor. 1.20: ἐν αὐτῷ τὸ ναί... δι αὐτοῦ τὸ ἀμήν. As Taylor notes, it is but a short step from here to calling Christ 'the Amen' (*The Names of Jesus*, p. 168). Note the parallel use of ναί and ἀμήν in Rev. 1.7; 22.20; cf. 14.3. K. Berger argues for a close connection between ναί and ἀμήν in revelatory contexts (*Die Amen–Worte Jesu* [BZNW, 39; Berlin, 1970], pp. 7 [n. 11], 9, 63). While there is certainly evidence for this, there is no justification for calling Rev. 3.14 a 'ναί-Wort' (p. 63); it is not even an ἀμήν-*Wort*, but an ἀμήν-*Prädikat*. For John's use of ἀμήν in general (9×), see K.P. Jörns, *Das hymnische Evangelium* (SNT, 5; Gütersloh, 1971), pp. 85-89.

112. Accepted by Lohmeyer, Sweet, Ozanne, Roloff, Brütsch, Prigent, Preston–Hanson, Kiddle–Ross, Pohl, Holtz, Rissi, Schlier, Bietenhard, Berger, Brownlee, and Betz; with some reservation by Hemer, Mounce, Charles, Taylor and Hempel; rejected only by Swete, Silberman and Trudinger.

113. A completely different understanding of the *Amēn*-title and its origin is advanced by L.H. Silberman, 'Farewell to O AMHN. A Note on Rev. 3, 14', *JBL* 82 (1963), pp. 213-15, who is followed with minor variations by Trudinger, 'Text', pp. 145-47; 'Observations', pp. 87-88; and 'O AMHN (Rev. III.14), and the Case for a Semitic Original of the Apocalypse', *NovT* 14 (1972), pp. 277-79. A similar view was proposed earlier by J.A. Montgomery, 'The Education of the Seer of the Apocalypse', *JBL* 45 (1926), pp. 72-73. Silbermann sees all three titles in Rev. 3.14 as the product of *wisdom* speculation inspired by various texts from Proverbs. See the criticism of Prigent, *L'Apocalypse*, pp. 74-75; and Holtz, *Christologie*, p. 142.

114. Isa. 65.15 in Rev. 3.12; 65.17 in 21.1; and 65.16c in 21.4d; cf. Sweet, *Revelation*, p. 107.

as a whole? At least three suggestions may be offered, none of which necessarily excludes the others.

1. If the inspiration of Isa. 65.16 is accepted, John's use of ὁ ἀμήν would quality as another example of an OT divine title transferred to Jesus, thus further underscoring John's high Christology.[115]
2. Many commentators understand it in connection with the following title, ὁ μάρτυς ὁ πιστὸς καὶ ἀληθινός, and regard this phrase as simply an expansion and explanation of the preceding *Amēn*-title.[116] According to this view then the two titles are complementary and together emphasize the authenticity of Christ's character and testimony (cf. 22.6).[117]
3. The use of ὁ ἀμήν as an *introduction* to the words of Jesus to the church may in part be influenced by the unique use of ἀμήν in the teaching of Jesus.[118] In contrast to the conventional use of *amēn* as a liturgical response or concluding affirmation, Jesus 'uses *amen* to introduce His own words. His *amen* does not corroborate what He said just before, but solemnly and authoritatively opens some new declarations of His'.[119] It may then be no accident that John connects ὁ ἀμήν

115. 'The divine name of Isa. 65.16 is here applied to Christ' (Rissi, *Future*, p. 92 n. 17). So also Holtz, Lohmeyer, Comblin, Roloff and Beasley-Murray.

116. Charles, *Revelation*, I, p. 94; Berger, *Amēn-Worte*, pp. 150, 109; Schüssler Fiorenza, *Priester*, p. 245; Comblin, *Le Christ*, p. 137; Taylor, *The Names of Jesus*, p. 168; H. Schlier, *TDNT*, I, p. 337; Bietenhard, *NIDNTT*, I, p. 99; O. Betz, 'Donnersöhne, Menschenfischer und der Davidische Messias', *RevQ* 3 (1961–62), p. 57; W.H. Brownlee, 'Messianic Motifs', p. 208; Beasley-Murray, *Revelation*, p. 104; and Ford, *Revelation*, p. 418.

117. 'Christ as the Amen, therefore, is the perfect revelation of the truth' (Brownlee, 'Messianic Motifs', p. 208). Brownlee and Betz ('Donnersöhne', p. 57) think the two titles originally involved a play on words in Hebrew—הָאָמֵן עֵד־ הָאָמֵן. This is possible, though it would have little significance for the Greek readers. A further problem with this theory is that if the title ὁ μάρτυς ὁ πιστός (Rev. 1.5) is correctly derived from Ps. 89.38, or even, with Brownlee, from Jer. 42.5, נאמן and אמת are used rather than אמן.

118. So Swete, *Apocalypse*, p. 59; Taylor, *The Names of Jesus*, p. 168; and L. Gillet, 'Amen', *ExpTim* 56 (1944–45), pp. 134-36.

119. Gillet, 'Amen', p. 135.

directly with τάδε λέγει, producing a messenger formula similar to the introductory *amēn* formula of the Gospels:[120]

τάδε λέγει ὁ ἀμήν... (Rev.)

ἀμὴν λέγω ὑμῖν... (Gospels)

The use of this messenger formula introducing a word of Jesus to the Laodicean church would thus provide an extra reminder of Christ's authority before the strong criticisms and warnings of the letter.

---

120.   Note the use of 'thus says' with an *amēn*-formula in *T. Abr.* 8.5-7. For a comparison of the *amēn*-formula with prophetic messenger formulae, see V. Hasler, *Amen: Redaktionsgeschichtliche Untersuchung zur Einführungs-formel der Herren-worte 'Wahrlich ich sage euch'* (Zürich, 1969), pp. 174-80; Berger, *Amen-Worte*, p. 106 n. 101.

Chapter 4

ISAIAH IN REVELATION 4–7

Revelation 4.4 → Isaiah 24.23
A unique and enigmatic element in John's throne-room vision (Rev.
4–5) is the description of the 24 elders seated around the throne (4.4).
Various aspects of this image have long intrigued commentators and
raised a host of questions.[1] Where does the idea of elders in the presence of God come from? Are they celestial beings or glorified human
beings? What is the significance of the number 24? Only the first
question will be directly addressed in this study.[2]

One OT passage which speaks of Yahweh in the presence of elders
is found in Isa. 24.23.

> Then the moon will be confounded,
> and the sun ashamed,
> for the Lord of hosts will reign
> on Mount Zion and in Jerusalem
> and before his elders he will
> manifest his glory

On the basis of the conceptual parallel between Revelation and
Isaiah involving a court of elders in the presence of God, a significant
number of commentators are prepared to accept a conscious connection.[3] While Feuillet emphasizes that it is impossible to prove that

1. The two most extensive treatments are J. Michl, *Die 24 Ältesten in der
Apokalypse des Hl. Johannes* (Munich, 1938), and A. Feuillet, 'Les vingt-quatre
vieillards de l'Apocalypse', *RB* 65 (1958), pp. 5-32.
2. For a recent helpful study dealing with these issues, see L. Hurtado,
'Revelation 4–5 in the Light of Jewish Apocalyptic Analogies', *JSNT* 25 (1985),
pp. 105-24.
3. So Kraft, Halver, Bornkamm, (*TDNT*, VI, p. 656), Lohmeyer, Marconcini,
Bietenhard and Satake; with more hesitation: Michl, Feuillet, Kiddle–Ross,
R.H. Preston and A.T. Hanson (*The Revelation of Saint John the Divine* (London,
1949) and Schlatter.

John had this Isaiah text in mind, he gives three reasons for a probable link:[4]

1. Both texts refer to an eschatological group in God's presence, who are witnesses of his triumph.
2. Both texts refer to this group as *elders*.
3. Both texts refer to the appearance of Yahweh to the elders on Sinai.

Feuillet's reference to Sinai, which is not specifically mentioned in either Isaiah 24 or Revelation 4, is influenced by the observation that behind both texts probably lies another OT passage, which likewise speaks of a group of elders in the presence of God: Exod. 24.9-10.[5]

> Then Moses... and seventy of the elders of Israel went up, and they saw the God of Israel; and there was under his feet as it were a pavement of sapphire stone, like the very heaven for clearness.

The context in this Exodus passage of divine theophany and the attendant description of the throne-room floor (cf. Rev. 4.6) comes closer to the setting of Revelation 4 than does the more eschatological scenario of Isaiah 24. John's dependence on other theophany traditions in Revelation 4–5 further increases the possibility of influence.

But while this alternative makes the case for Isa. 24.23 even more uncertain, it does not necessarily rule it out altogether. Even if Exodus 24 was primarily in mind, Isa. 24.23 may have played a supporting role, by means of which the earthly elders of Exodus 24 were given a more permanent celestial capacity, and through which further eschatological motifs could be drawn into the basic theophany tradition.

---

4.   Feuillet, 'Les vingt-quatre vieillards', pp. 13-14; H. Bietenhard also emphasizes the similarities between Rev. 4 and Isa. 24 (*Die himmlische Welt im Urchristentum und Spätjudentum* [WUNT, 2; Tübingen, 1951], pp. 58-59).

5.   That the Isaiah passage is influenced by Sinai traditions (Exod. 24.1, 9-11, 16-18) is recognized by many OT commentators: e.g. Wildberger, Clements, Gray, Kaiser and Kissane. This dependence confirms the view that the *elders* (זקנים) of Isa. 24.23 are either representatives of Israel or of all the nations. Even the *Targum* recognizes this when it adds *of the people* to *elders* (סבי עמיה). This strengthens the growing consensus that the elders of Revelation are not angels. In fact, with the possible exception of *2 En.* 4.1 (see *OTP*, I, p. 110 n. 4a), angels are never called *elders*, not even in the *Angelic Liturgy* found at Qumran, where over 25 different titles of angels are used, but never זקן; cf. Newsom, *Songs*, pp. 23-28; Hurtado, 'Revelation 4–5', p. 113.

If we take into account that the manifestation of the divine glory and the enthronement of the Lamb in Revelation 4 and 5 are cosmic preludes to the establishment of the divine presence in the New Jerusalem (Rev. 21–22), two further parallels between Isa. 24.23 and Revelation may be added to Feuillet's list:

4. Both depict the eschatological reign of God on Mt Zion and in the New Jerusalem (cf. Rev. 14.1 with 21.10).
5. Both emphasize the presence of God's glory and its effect on the sun and moon (Isa. 24.23a; Rev. 21.3, 11, 23; 22.5).[6]

Now while it is recognized that in Revelation 21–22 other OT texts play a primary role in the formulation of these traditions (e.g. Ezek. 40–48; Isa. 60), it has been argued above that John's method consistently involves the collection of texts around a central theme. Thus the numerous key words of Isa. 24.23, *glory—reign of Yahweh— Jerusalem—Mt Zion—sun and moon—kings of the earth* (24.21), certainly render it an attractive thematic analogue for John's eschatological scenario.[7] Thus the possibility that Isa. 24.23, as well as Exod. 24.9-10, has influenced John's presentation of the elders in 4.4 seems very likely.[8]

Revelation 4.8 → Isaiah 6.2a, 3a

καὶ τὰ τέσσαρα ζῷα,		
ἕν καθ᾽ ἕν αὐτῶν	שׁשׁ כנפים שׁשׁ	ἕξ πτέρυγες τῷ ἑνὶ
ἔχων ἀνὰ πτέρυγας ἕξ,	כנפים לאחד	καὶ ἕξ πτέρυγὲς τῷ ἑνί
...λέγοντες	ואמר...	ἔλεγον

6. Kaiser (*Isaiah 13–39*, p. 195) comments on 24.23, 'The splendour of [God's] light, manifesting his presence, his *kābōd*...shines so bright that not only the holy city but the whole earth is lit by it and the light of the sun and the moon grows pale and is superfluous (cf. Isa. 60.19; Zech. 14.7 and Rev. 21.23; 22.5)'. Cf. G.B. Gray, *A Critical and Exegetical Commentary on the Book of Isaiah: I– XXXIX* (Edinburgh, 1912), I, p. 423.

7. Evidence of early Christian interpretation of Isa. 24.21-23 can be found in *Asc. Isa.* 4.14-16 (*OTP*, II, p. 162 n. *p*), where it is applied to events surrounding the parousia. M. Knibb's suggestion that the phrase quoted in *Asc. Isa.* 4.15 'the sun will be ashamed' (from Isa. 24.23a) is a gloss is unnecessary. He fails to see that the events and terminology of *Asc. Isa.* 4.14-16 correspond closely to the eschatological agenda of Isa. 24.21-23.

8. Both Feuillet and Hurtado accept a double reference here ('Les vingt-quatre vieillards', p. 14; 'Revelation 4–5', p. 113). Schlatter's suggestion that John combines here Isa. 24.23 and 3.14 is unlikely (*Das alte Testament*, p. 15).

ἅγιος ἅγιος ἅγιος κύριος   קָדוֹשׁ קָדוֹשׁ קָדוֹשׁ   "Αγιος ἅγιος ἅγιος κύριος
ὁ θεὸς ὁ παντοκάτωρ,   יהוה צבאות   σαβαωθ,
ὁ ἦν καὶ ὁ ὢν καὶ ὁ ἐρχόμενος   מלא-כל הארץ   πλήρης πᾶσα ἡ γῆ τῆς
                                 כבודו   δόξης αὐτοῦ

Up to this point in Revelation 4, John's portrait of the heavenly temple and its occupants (4.2-7) has been patterned almost exclusively on the throne-room vision of Ezekiel 1. Beginning in 4.6b, the description of the four living creatures continues on the Ezekiel model in depicting their eyes (Rev. 4.6b // Ezek. 1.18) and *faces* (Rev. 4.7 // Ezek. 1.10). But when John comes to describe their *wings* (4.8a), he adopts the six-wing tradition of Isa. 6.2 rather than the four wings of Ezek. 1.6-12.[9] An outline of Rev. 4.8 reveals the transitions more clearly:

And the four living creatures	*Ezek. 1.15*
each of them with six wings,[10]	*Isa. 6.2a*
are full of eyes all around and within,	*Ezek. 1.18*
... they never cease to sing, Holy, holy, holy	*Isa. 6.3a*
is the Lord God Almighty.	

The transition from Ezekiel to Isaiah coincides with a shift from the physical description of the living creatures to a presentation of their function (4.8b-9). Whereas in Ezekiel the duties of the Cherubim are limited to the movement and activity of the divine throne chariot and have no function of worship or praise, the Seraphim of Isaiah 6 serve as close attendants who lead in worship.[11] Thus while John is willing to take over various physical attributes of Ezekiel's living creatures (= Cherubim, Ezek. 10.2-22), their role as *Merkabah* attendants is abandoned in favour of the worshiping Seraphim of Isaiah.[12]

    9.   Such is the preference in almost all other descriptions of throne-room figures: e.g. *Lad. Jac.* 2.15; *Quest. Ezra* 29; *2 En.* 16.7; 19.6; 21.1; *Apost. Const.* 8.12.27; *Apoc. Elijah* 5.2. The only use of a four-wing motif occurs in *1 En.* 40.2, but here the author apparently takes up the two Cherubim tradition associated with the ark of the covenant (Exod. 25.18-22), rather than the four Cherubim of Ezekiel.
    10.   John retains the distributive emphasis of the original by adding ἀνά in addition to ἕν καθ'. We might translate 'each one of them having six wings apiece'.
    11.   This distinction is also found in the Gnostic *Orig. World* 105.
    12.   *Contra* Ozanne, 'Influence', p. 97. The conflation of Seraphim and Cherubim with regard to both physical description and duties is not unknown in later traditions. One can find references to chariot Seraphim (*T. Isaac* 6.24; *2 En.* 16.7); six-winged Cherubim who sing the trisagion (?*2 En.* 19.6; 21.1; *Quest. Ezra* 29; *Apost. Const.* 7.35.3; 8.12.27; *T. Adam* 4.8); Cherubim and Seraphim who are six-winged and many-eyed (*2 En.* 21.1 text uncertain). Cf. *y. Ber.* 2C; *Lev. R.* 27.2. *Apoc. Paul* 14

Thus, using Isa. 6.3a as a base text, in Rev. 4.8b John next describes the activity of the living creatures in the heavenly throne-room, where they 'never cease to sing, "Holy, holy, holy, is the Lord God Almighty"'. In Isaiah 6 the thrice-holy, otherwise known as the *trisagion*, forms part of a short hymn of acclamation sung by the Seraphim and addressed to Yahweh, who is seated on his throne in the temple.[13] While it is unanimously recognized that Isa. 6.3 lies behind Rev. 4.8b, there is some question as to whether it involves direct influence, or perhaps is mediated to John by means of other literary or liturgical traditions. K.P. Jörns suggests the possible agency of apocalyptic texts such as *1 En.* 39.12 and *2 En.* 21.1,[14] while Prigent builds a more extensive argument on the supposition that John adapts the *trisagion* from current Jewish liturgical models.[15] But the evidence for such dependence is problematic, particularly in the area of dating, and these suggestions ultimately remain inconclusive. In addition, John's use of Isaiah's vision in other parts of Revelation transcends liturgical applications and reveals his interest in it as a visionary, rather than a

appears to define the living creatures of Revelation as Cherubim.

13. Mainly on the basis of 1QIsaᵃ 6.3, which attests only a double-*qadosh*, N. Walker postulates that the triple form of Isaiah was not original and represents a later conflation of a single- and double-holy ('The Origin of the "Thrice-Holy"', *NTS* 5 [1958–59], pp. 132-33). This hypothesis has been justly called into question by B.M. Leiser, 'The Trisagion of Isaiah's Vision', *NTS* 6 (1959–60), pp. 261-63. To the discussion of Leiser, we might add the testimony of 4QIsaᶠ, which apparently attests the triple form, F.J. Morrow, 'The Text of Isaiah at Qumran' (PhD dissertation, Catholic University of America, 1973). Morrow concludes that 1QIsaᵃ is aberrant even by Qumran standards, and this judgment is supported in the present case by Rosenbloom, 'The MS tendency to reject repeated words and phrases is seen in. . . 6/3 where one קדוש is missing' (*The Dead Sea Isaiah Scroll*, p. 13).

14. *Das hymnische Evangelium*, pp. 24-25; The presence of the *trisagion* in a variety of other documents suggests that it was widely diffused by at least the end of the second century CE. In addition to *1 En.* 39.12 and *2 En.* 21.1(5), add *T. Ab.* 20.12; *T. Adam* 1.4, 4.8; *Lad. Jac.* 7.15-20; *4 Bar.* 9.3; *Ques. Ezra* 29; *1 Clem.* 34.6; *Apost. Const.* 7.35.3, 8.12.27; *Pass. Perp.* 12.2.

15. Prigent, *L'Apocalypse*, pp. 87-89; similarly Mounce, *Revelation*, p. 139; Sweet, *Revelation*, p. 120. Prigent makes much of the Jewish *Qeduscha* liturgy, though the earliest attestation is late second-century. The appeal to *1 Clem.* 34.6 as evidence for the use of the *trisagion* in early Christian (eucharistic) liturgy has been convincingly overturned by W.C. van Unnik, '1 Clement 34 and the "Sanctus"', *VC* 5 (1951), pp. 204-48. His detailed exegesis reveals that the setting is eschatological paraenetic rather than liturgical. Cf. G. Kretschmar, *TRE*, I, p. 244.

liturgical, model (1.10-18; 15.8). A more productive pursuit is to evaluate the purpose of this Isaiah passage within the context of Revelation 4 and the book as a whole.

An examination of the original setting in Isaiah, when compared with Rev. 4.8 and the use of Isaiah 6 in Rev. 15.8, offers evidence that the elements of Isaiah 6 which appear in Revelation 4—and especially the thrice-holy—play an important role in the movement of John's plot, and are not simply added as ornamental colour or liturgical filler.

In Isaiah 6 the *trisagion* serves to express a *moral* contrast between Yahweh and the Prophet. The immediate response of Isaiah to the revelation of God's holiness is a realization of personal unholiness, accompanied by an expectation of divine judgment: 'Woe is me! For I am lost' (6.5).[16] The outward manifestation of God's holiness is represented by his glory (כבוד) and heightened by theophanic symbols such as shaking and smoke (6.3b-4).[17]

This presentation of God's holiness and its consequence for sinful humanity is taken up by John and serves as part of the theological substructure for his own proclamation of divine judgment. But rather than woe for the prophet himself, God's holiness brings the threat of woe and wrath to an evil society and those in the churches who 'share in its sins' (18.4). More specifically, the revelation of God's holiness in Rev. 4.8 forms the basis for the revelation of his wrath in Revelation 15. Several factors bear out this conclusion:

1. The use of Isaiah 6 in both Rev. 4.8 and 15.8:

Rev. 4.8, 15.8a	*Isa. 6.3-4*
Holy, holy, holy is the Lord God Almighty,	Holy, holy, holy is the Lord of hosts
Who was and is and is to come.	The whole earth is full of his glory.
And the temple was filled with smoke from the glory of God and from his power	and the foundations of the threshold shook... and the house (= temple, v. 1) was filled with smoke

---

16. Isaiah's use of טמא (2×) in 6.5 brings out the contrast with קדוש. Unclean lips, like unclean hands, heart, etc. are symbolic of moral impurity (cf. 6.7; *IDB*, I, p. 644).

17. 'Ist so Jahve Zebaot als קָדוֹשׁ seiner innersten Natur nach bezeichnet, so enthält seine "Herrlichkeit" (כְּבוֹדוֹ) die Erscheinungsseite seines Wesens' (Procksch, quoted by Wildberger, *Jesaja*, I, p. 249).

2. In Rev. 15.7 it is one of the living creatures who sang the *trisagion* which acts as the agent of God in handing over the bowls of wrath to the seven angels.[18]

3. John's consciousness of a relationship between God's holiness and his judgment is expressed in two passages adjacent to 15.7-8:

> For thou alone art holy... for thy judgments have been revealed (15.4).
> Just art thou in these thy judgments thou who art and wast, O Holy One (16.5).

4. The divine name ὁ θεὸς ὁ παντοκράτωρ and the triple-title ὁ ἦν καὶ ὁ ὢν καὶ ὁ ἐρχόμενος associated with the *trisagion* in 4.8 are especially prominent in connection with God's wrath (16.7; 18.8; 19.15; 11.17-18). And John's expectation of God as ὁ ἐρχόμενος in 4.8 is fulfilled in his coming for judgment, as is clear by the omission of this element of the threefold title in 16.5 and 11.17-18.[19]

All these factors reinforce the assumption that the use of Isaiah 6 in Revelation 4 is structurally and thematically connected with the presence of motifs from Isaiah 6 in Revelation 15. In this we get a small glimpse of the care with which John selects and arranges his source material. Thus, the revelation of God's holiness in the emphatic strains of the *trisagion* is more than simply a statement of being—it is a basis for action. The *Holy One* is also the *Coming One* (ὁ ἐρχόμενος), and the action contemplated is fulfilled in the judgments of Revelation 15–16.[20]

For John, the practical outworking of God's holiness for humanity is contained in his commandments, and the genuine 'saint' in Revelation is one who not only holds faith in Jesus, but also keeps God's commandments.[21] The moral demands of a holy God as expressed in his commandments are specifically laid out by John and repeated frequently throughout the course of the book. He stresses in particular five

18. A connection between Rev. 4 and 15 is also seen by the fact that the latter resumes the focus on God and his activity (as opposed to the Lamb) begun in Rev. 4. Thus, for the first time since ch. 4, a hymn to God forms a prelude to his action (15.3-4).

19. Noted also by G. Delling, 'Zum gottesdienstlichen Stil der Johannes-apokalypse', *NovT* 3 (1959), pp. 126-27.

20. Bietenhard also notes the eschatological function of Rev. 4 and remarks, 'die Thronvision steht am Anfang der Endgerichte' (*Die himmlische Welt*, p. 580). This use of the *trisagion* also accords well with its application in *1 Clem.* 34 (see above n. 15).

21. Rev. 12.17; 14.12, using ἐντολή. John never uses νόμος.

commandments which are rendered negatively as corresponding sins.

Immorality	Falsehood
πορνεύω—2.14, 20; 17.2; 18.3, 9	ψεύδομαι—3.9
πορνεία—2.21; 9.21; 14.8; 17.2,	ψεῦδος—14.5; 21.27; 22.15
4; 18.3; 19.2	ψευδής—2.2; 21.8
πόρνος—21.8; 22.15	ψευδοπροφήτης—16.13;
πόρνη—17.1, 5, 15, 16; 19.2	19.20; 20.10

Murder	Idolatry	Sorcery
ἀποκτείνω (= φονεύω)	εἰδωλόθυτος—2.14, 20	φαρμακία—9.21;
—2.13; 6.11; 11.7;	εἴδωλον—9.20	18.23
13.10, 15	εἰδωλολάτρης—21.8,	φαρμακός—21.8;
σφάζω—6.9; 18.24	22.15	22.15
φονεύς—21.8; 22.15		φάρμακον—9.21
φόνος—9.21		

The subsequent extension of God's holiness to the New Jerusalem—the *Holy* City (21.2, 10; 22.19)—necessitates a ban on anything unholy (21.27), which in 22.15 encompasses the very five categories of sin outlined above: 'outside are the...sorcerers and fornicators and murderers and idolators, and every one who loves and practices falsehood'.[22]

A final word on John's use of Isaiah 6 concerns his omission of the phrase which accompanies the *trisagion* in Isa. 6.3b: 'The whole earth is full of his glory'.[23] In place of this John substitutes the threefold title 'who was and is and is to come'. The passing over of this complementary phrase of Isaiah cannot be attributed to John's lack of interest in the theme of God's glory, for he accentuates this very idea in Rev. 21.11, 23-26.

It is more likely that John understood Isa. 6.3b as an eschatological promise rather than a theological statement.[24] A world in need of seal,

22. John's emphasis on holiness is revealed in other ways as well: (a) his preference for οἱ ἅγιοι as a title for believers (14×); (b) the frequent use of white clothing as a symbol for moral purity or holiness (3.4-5, 18; 4.4; 6.11; 7.9, 13, 14; 16.15; 19.8, 14); (c) the final exhortation to holiness in 22.11.

23. This omission further supports the contention that John is not simply presenting a liturgical formula, for this phrase is an inseparable part of the liturgical tradition; van Unnik, '1 Clement 34 and the "Sanctus"', p. 226.

24. A similar interpretation appears to lie behind 1QM 12.11, which anticipates an eschatological fulfilment of Isa. 6.3b, 'fill thy earth/land with glory'. Here the manifestation of God's glory follows his judgment with the sword (12.11; cf. Rev. 19) and is related to the concept of a New Jerusalem (12.12-15; cf. Rev. 21–22).

trumpet, and bowl judgments can hardly be said to be full of God's glory. Thus a passage preparing for judgment (Rev. 4.8-11) is not the appropriate place or time for such a positive concept.[25] For John the heavenly temple can be full of God's glory now (Rev. 15.8 // Isa. 6.1, 4), but the universal manifestation of his glory on earth must wait for the removal of all that is unholy preparatory to his enthronement in the New Jerusalem.[26] As the Apocalyptist of *4 Ezra* notes: 'This present world is not the end; the full glory does not abide in it' (7.112).

Revelation 5.1 → Isaiah 29.11

Less than a handful of commentators suggest that the motif of the sealed book of Rev. 5.1 (βιβλίον...κατεσφραγισμένον) has been influenced by or partially modelled on Isa. 29.11, 'and the vision of all this has become to you like the words of a book that is sealed' (הספר החתום—βιβλίου...ἐσφραγισμένου).[27] But the connection is tenuous. The dictional basis for such a literary relationship consists of two words, the first of which (βιβλίον) in fact goes back to Ezek. 2.9, which serves as the main inspiration for Rev. 5.1. The picture of a *sealed* book is certainly not unique, for sealed books, letters, registers, rolls, etc., were part of everyday life in ancient society, and the image lent itself naturally to metaphorical application in various types of literary contexts, not limited to apocalyptic.[28]

There are also no strong contextual similarities between the two texts. Whereas in Revelation the seven-sealed scroll is a vehicle for the presentation of God's judgment, in Isaiah the sealed book is simply a

25. For a discussion of the temporal and theological relationship between 4.8 and 4.9-11, see Jörns, *Das hymnische Evangelium*, p. 29-31; Mussies, *Morphology*, pp. 342-46.

26. Wildberger notes in connection with Isa. 6.3 that even in liturgical texts the appearance of God's glory is placed in the perspective of the future (cf. Pss. 57.6, 12; 72.19; Num. 14.21; Isa. 40.5) and states, 'Das entspricht der Erwartung, dass das Königtum Jahwes, das nach den "ThronbesteigungsPsalmen" bereits ein gegenwärtiges ist, in der Heilszukunft voll in Erscheinung treten wird, Jes 52.7 24.23' (*Jesaja*, I, p. 250).

27. Kraft, *Offenbarung*, p. 103; Vos, *Synoptic Traditions*, p. 40 n. 63; Ozanne, 'Influence', p. 162; Beale, *Daniel*, pp. 201-202. The last suggests that both Isa. 29.11 and Dan. 12.4, 9 have been utilized here 'because of the almost identical wording and the common idea of a sealed book which conceals divine revelation from man and is associated with judgment'.

28. *IDB*, IV, pp. 254-59 (esp. A4). Cf. *1 En.* 89.71; *Odes Sol.* 23.5-9.

metaphor for spiritual lethargy and blindness. There, the content of the book is beyond the purpose of the metaphor—indeed there is no content, whether judgment or otherwise.[29] If another prophetic text besides Ezek. 2.9 has influenced this passage in Rev. 5.1, then the most likely candidate would be Dan. 12.4, 9, which John uses elsewhere (Rev. 22.10; ?10.4),

Revelation 5.5b; 22.16b → Isaiah 11.10

Rev. 5.5b	*Isaiah*
ἡ ῥίζα Δαυίδ	שׁרֶשׁ ישׁי ἡ ῥίζα τοῦ Ιεσσαι

Rev. 22.16b
ἐγώ εἰμι ἡ ῥίζα καὶ τὸ γένος Δαυίδ

Twice in Revelation Christ is called the *Root of David*, once by one of the 24 elders in 5.5b, and once as a self-designation of the exalted Jesus in 22.16b. The source of this messianic title is generally recognized to be Isaiah 11, with most commentators opting for Isa. 11.10 rather than 11.1.[30] A comparison of Isa. 11.1 and 10 shows that such a distinction is justified.[31]

Isa. 11.1	*Isa. 11.10*
There shall come forth a shoot from the stump of Jesse, and a branch (נצר) shall grow out of his roots (שׁרֶשׁ)	In that day the root (שׁרֶשׁ) of Jesse shall stand as an ensign to the peoples...

29. *Contra* Beale, *Daniel*, p. 201.

30. So Lohmeyer, Kraft, Prigent, Pohl, Roloff, Holtz, Schüssler Fiorenza and Maurer. Charles, Rissi and Ford mention both passages without distinction; and Mounce only gives Isa. 11.1. However, J. Carmignac, E. Cothenet and H. Lignée seem convinced that Jer. 23.5 and 33.15 lie behind Rev. 5.5b (*Les textes de Qumran traduits et annotés* (Paris, 1961, 1963), II, p. 287 n. 6).

31. Of course, the messianic application of Isaiah's Davidic shoot prophecy in general, whether based on 11.1 or 11.10, was already current in Jewish and Christian circles well before its appearance in Revelation (e.g. Sir. 47.22c; Rom. 15.12; *T. Jud.* 24.5; 4QpIsaᵃ 8–10; *4 Ezra* 12.32a; cf. *Targ. Isa.* 11.1; *LAB* 62.9). The messianic title צמח דויד (*shoot of David*) used in 4QPBless 1.4 and 4QFlor 1.11 is a variation of the tradition inspired by Jer. 23.5; 33.15, rather than Isa. 11; G. Vermes, *Scripture and Tradition in Judaism: Haggadic Studies* (SPB, 4; Leiden, 1961), p. 53 n. 4; A.S. van der Woude, *Die messianischen Vorstellungen der Gemeinde von Qumran* (Assen, 1957), p. 172; Carmignac, *et al.*, *Les textes*, II, pp. 283 n. 25, 287 n. 6. M. Philonenko thinks the prophecies of Jer. 23.5 and Isa. 11.1 are brought together in *T. Jud.* 24.4, 5 (*La Bible Ecrits intertestamentaires* (ed. A. Dupont-Sommer and M. Philonenko; Paris, 1987), pp. 873-74.

As C. Maurer has observed,[32] *of his roots* (מֹשָׁרָשָׁיו) in Isa. 11.1 is a genitive of apposition (i.e. the root which = Jesse), while in v. 10 *root of Jesse* (שֹׁרֶשׁ יִשַׁי) is a genitive of source (i.e. the root which proceeds from Jesse). In the first passage the promised deliverer is the *shoot* from the root while in the second he is the *root* itself. And whereas the first passage is a nationalistic prophecy which concerns a successor to the royal house of David and which forms part of a larger unit (10.33–11.5), the second is probably a later addition which recasts the earlier prophecy with more messianic and universalistic overtones.[33] Thus the *root of Jesse* in Isa. 11.10 is already on its way to becoming a messianic title and would lend itself more naturally to appropriation than the more complex parallel sentences in 11.1.[34]

The substitution of David for Jesse is the next stage in the transformation of Isaiah's prophecy, and this was probably facilitated by interpretational assimilation with other messanically understood texts (e.g. 2 Sam. 7.14; Jer. 23.5; 33.15).[35] This way not only was the messianic focus of the title sharpened, but its relationship to the dynastic covenant was also heightened. The prophecy no longer concerns the root of Jesse, the father of David, but the root of David, God's anointed king and dynastic father.

John's use of ῥίζα deserves some explanation. Is it to be understood in its natural meaning of *root*, or is its semantic value extended to cover that which springs from the root: the *shoot*? Particularly in connection with the expanded title in Rev. 22.16b, ἡ ῥίζα καὶ τὸ γένος Δαυίδ, several commentators have accepted the first definition and have understood John to mean that Christ is both 'root and shoot' of David.[36] That is, Christ is not only descended from David in a

---

32. *TDNT*, VI, p. 986, followed by Kraft, Prigent and Rissi.

33. Wildberger discusses these points more fully (*Jesaja*, I, pp. 439, 442, 458-59).

34. Paul adapts Isa. 11.10 in Rom. 15.12 (ἔσται ἡ ῥίζα τοῦ Ιεσσαί). Sir. 47.22c (καὶ τῷ Δαυιδ ἐξ αὐτοῦ ῥίζαν) may likewise reflect this verse if ῥίζα stands for an original שֹׁרֶשׁ (cf. 40.15) and is not assimilated to the LXX of Isa. 11.1b.

35. Found already in the pesher on Isa. 11.1 in 4QpIsaᵃ 8–10, 17: '[its interpretation concerns the shoot of] David who will arise at the e[nd of days'. (*DJD*, V, p. 14); and in *4 Ezra* 12.32a 'This is the Messiah...who will arise from the posterity of David' (*OTP*, I, p. 550; cf. 4QFlor.).

36. Swete, *Apocalypse*, p. 309; Lohmeyer, *Offenbarung*, p. 181; Caird, *Revelation*, p. 286; Brütsch, *Offenbarung*, I, p. 253; Ozanne, 'Influence', p. 162.

physical sense (γένος), but he is also the divine source (ῥίζα) from whom David himself derived his existence and call. In this way, Christ is both Lord and Son of David.

But such an interpretation, apart from being well beyond John's theological purpose, is contextually unsuitable. Both שׁרשׁ (Isa. 11.10) and its standard LXX equivalent ῥίζα can have the figurative sense of *offspring* or *shoot*, and this secondary sense (*shoot*) is clearly to be preferred in Revelation.[37] This means that in 22.16b τὸ γένος is merely a synonym of ῥίζα, so that the title should read: 'I am the shoot, *even* the offspring of David'.[38] Further justification for this lexical choice can be adduced by evaluating John's use of this designation.

The first appearance of the title in Rev. 5.5 comes in response to the angelic query in 5.2: 'who is worthy to open the scroll and break its seals?' The answer comes in 5.5b: 'the Lion of the tribe of Judah, the Root of David... can open the scroll and its seven seals'. And what is here only indirectly attributed to a figure which John from now on calls the Lamb, is expressly claimed by Jesus himself in the last 'I am' title of Rev. 22.16b. In both places the *Root of David* title is linked with other well-known Jewish messianic *testimonia*, and serves to identify Jesus as the fulfilment of traditional messianic expectations.[39]

Among these messianically understood OT passages John appears to give a high priority or at least visibility to Davidic promises. Christ is not only from the tribe of Judah and the family of David (5.5; cf. 7.5a with 14.1), but he also holds the *key of David* (3.7 // Isa. 22.22). And because Yahweh's covenant with David (2 Sam. 7.14; Ps. 89.4) has

37. '*srs* "root", in the figurative sense "offspring", [is] attested in Ugaritic, Phoenician... Aramaic, and biblical Hebrew (Is. 11,1 14,29 Hos. 9,16 Ps. 52,7 Prov. 12,3)' (T. Penar, *Northwest Semitic Philology and the Hebrew Fragments of Ben Sira* [Rome, 1975], p. 5). For ῥίζα as *shoot* see BAGD, p. 736, LS, p. 1570. Both Isa. 11.10 (שׁרשׁ) and Paul's application of it in Rom. 15.12 (ῥίζα) assume the meaning *shoot*, as does also *Targ. Isa.* 11.10.

38. Taking καί then as epexegetical. See further Holtz, *Christologie*, pp. 151-52; Maurer, *TDNT*, VI, pp. 986, 989; Prigent, *L'Apocalypse*, p. 357. Kraft, Roloff, Comblin, Rissi, Kiddle–Ross and Beckwith come to the same conclusion.

39. *Lion of tribe of Judah* (Gen. 49.9); *bright morning star* (Num. 24.17). The merging of the messianic prophecies of the Lion from Judah and Davidic shoot is found also in *4 Ezra* 12.31-32. 4QpBless also brings together Gen. 49 and the Davidic shoot motif, though the latter derives from Jer. 23.5 and 33.15 rather than Isa. 11.

found its fulfilment in Jesus, John can call him the 'ruler of the kings of the earth' (Rev. 1.5 // Ps. 89.28).[40] Therefore, the title *Root of David* functions not only as a messianic identification, but emphasizes Christ's royal authority as the legitimate Davidic heir.[41] Its presence in a vision of Christ's enthronement and reception of authority (Rev. 5) is not incidental but provides a foundation for later statements concerning Christ's *kingship, kingdom* and *rule* (11.15; 17.14; 19.16; 20.4, 6; 1.5).[42]

Revelation 5.6 (et passim) → *Isaiah 53.7*
Immediately following the elder's announcement concerning the *Lion of Judah* and the *Root of David* in Rev. 5.5, John beholds near the throne not a lion but a lamb: καὶ εἶδον...ἀρνίον ἑστηκὸς ὡς ἐσφαγμένον ἔχων κέρατα ἑπτὰ καὶ ὀφθαλμοὺς ἑπτά (5.6). In this way we are introduced to the christological title which dominates the rest of the book, being used 28 times of the exalted Jesus.[43] A great deal of discussion has surrounded the use of this prominent designation, and a variety of views are held as to its origin, one of which supposes a relationship to Isa. 53.7. In order to deal adequately with the vast amount of material it will be best to treat separately questions of lexical background and source.
Lexical Background. Ἀρνίον is the diminutive of ἀρήν (sheep, lamb), but by NT times it no longer carried a diminutive sense *little*

40. Note also Ps. 89.38 applied to Christ in Rev. 1.5, and 2 Sam. 7.14 used in 21.7.
41. Therefore, even though this title is ascribed to the exalted Christ, it presupposes Christ κατὰ σάρκα (Rom. 1.3 ἐκ σπέρματος Δαυίδ). What John and Paul state simply, the Gospels present in the form of 'genealogical apologetic' (e.g. Mt. 1.1: Ἰησοῦ Χριστοῦ υἱοῦ Δαυίδ; cf. Lk 3.23-38).
42. R. Bauckham argues convincingly that both titles in Rev. 5.5 also evoke holy war traditions and serve to introduce the Lamb as a military leader whose example of victory through faithful suffering and martyrdom is the model set before the struggling churches. In this capacity he guides the tribes of 'Israel' into battle (7.3-8), and leads them to victory against the beast and his forces (7.9-17; 14.1-5); *Climax of Prophecy: Studies on the Book of Revelation* (Edinburgh: T. & T. Clark, 1993), pp. 213-15.
43. Both Swete (*Apocalypse*, p. 78), and Charles (*Revelation*, I, p. 141) mistakenly give 29 references to the glorified Jesus, but ἀρνίον in 13.11 refers to the false prophet.

lamb, and was practically a synonym of ἀμνός.[44] But even while recognizing that linguistically the word means *lamb*, several commentators insist that the accompanying description and functions of John's lamb demands a more potent rendering such as *ram*. Since the main force of the 'ram' thesis hangs on contextual rather than lexical issues it will be dealt with in the following discussion of source.

Another theory relating to ἀρνίον presupposes an Aramaic background in which טליא could mean not only *lamb*, but also *boy* (παῖς) and *servant* (δοῦλος). Therefore, it is suggested, John clearly has in mind Isaiah 53 and identifies Christ not only with the 'lamb that is led to the slaughter', but with the *Servant* of Isaiah 53 as well. This is the application to Revelation of a theory which first appeared in connection with the 'lamb of God' phrase in Jn 1.29.[45]

But whatever merits this view may have in explaining the origin of the difficult verse in the Gospel, there is little to commend its adoption in Revelation.[46] John nowhere connects τοῦ θεοῦ with ἀρνίον and in his very broad and highly developed presentation of Christ there is no clear trace of 'Servant' Christology. Rather, δοῦλος in Revelation (14×) and specifically δοῦλος τοῦ θεοῦ stands for God's people in

---

44. BAGD, p. 106; *TDNT*, I, pp. 341; Prigent, *L'Apocalypse*, p. 97. In Jn 21.15-16, the only other NT passage where ἀρνίον appears, it is used in parallel with πρόβατον. Cf. P. Whale, 'The Lamb of John: Some Myths about the Vocabulary of the Johannine Literature', *JBL* 106 (1987), pp. 289-95. Pohl remarks that John himself uses other diminutives with no special force, e.g. βιβλίον in Rev. 5 and θηρίον in Rev. 13 (*Offenbarung*, I, p. 176 n. 184). But βιβλίον is not diminutive, and θηρίον, like ἀρνίον, had lost any diminutive emphasis generally by the first century CE, as Mussies points out (*Morphology*, pp. 108-109).

45. Applied to Jn 1.29 by C.J. Ball, 'Had the Fourth Gospel an Aramaic Archetype?', *ExpTim* 21 (1909–10), pp. 91-93, and taken up more fully by C.F. Burney, *The Aramaic Origin of the Fourth Gospel* (Oxford, 1922), pp. 104-108. It was transferred to Revelation by Lohmeyer (*Offenbarung*, pp. 54-55), but almost all other commentators deny any relevance for the use of ἀρνίον in Revelation. See the more extensive arguments in Kraft, *Offenbarung*, pp. 109-10; Schüssler Fiorenza, *Revelation*, p. 95; Holtz, *Christologie*, pp. 42-43.

46. Neither Ball nor Burney ever mentions the use of 'lamb' in Revelation, and even proponents of an Aramaic original for Revelation (e.g. R.B.Y. Scott, C.C. Torrey) do not take up the theory. For discussion of the *talja* thesis in relation to John's Gospel, see C.H. Dodd, *The Interpretation of the Fourth Gospel* (Cambridge, 1968), pp. 235-38; and C.K. Barrett, 'The Lamb of God', *NTS* 1 (1954–55), pp. 210-18.

general (e.g. 7.3; 22.3) or specific groups or individuals who serve God in some special capacity (e.g. prophets, 10.7; John, 11.1; Moses, 15.3).

Source Theories. Various traditions and combinations of traditions have been adduced in an attempt to discover the origin of John's *Lamb* figure.[47] These can be presented with their advocates as follows:

1. *The lamb of Isa. 53.7*: Swete, Charles, Lohmeyer, Sickenberger, Wikenhauser, Kraft, Preston–Hanson, Sweet
2. *The paschal lamb*: Schüssler Fiorenza, Pohl, Roloff, Holtz
3. *The apocalyptic warrior lamb/ram*: Mounce, Ford
4. *The daily sacrifice lamb (tāmîd)*: Beckwith
5. *The astrological ram* (constellation): Boll, Hadorn (1/3)
6. *Isaiah 53 and paschal lamb*: Comblin, Vanni, Hadorn (2/3)
7. *Paschal lamb and warrior ram*: Beasley-Murray, Casey, Prigent

Among the single options (1–5), only 1–3 have any significant support from internal and external evidence. Of these three views the least support can be mustered for the use of Isa. 53.7. A connection is usually assumed on the basis of the similarity between ἀρνίον...ὡς ἐσφαγμένον of Rev. 5.6 and ὡς πρόβατον ἐπὶ σφαγὴν of Isa. 53.7 (LXX).[48] A further implication may be squeezed from ἑστηκὸς ('standing', 5.6) by relating it to the exaltation of the Servant after suffering in Isa. 53.10b-12.[49]

But these potential links can be explained otherwise. Furthermore, if John here is primarily dependent on a Servant Christology, one would expect to find further traces of it in his many descriptions of

47. Caird's comment (*Revelation*, p. 74), 'we need not waste time searching through the Old Testament and other Jewish literature to find the meaning of this symbol', is unacceptable. In a writer so heavily indebted to previous tradition, and the OT in particular, this is always a necessary task for the interpreter of Revelation. Such a routine is especially warranted in the present case since c. 12 out of 15 Christological designations used by John come directly from the OT.

48. Cf. Jer. 11.19 ὡς ἀρνίον...ἀγόμενον τοῦ θύεσθαι.

49. 'Il faut reconnaître avec J. Comblin [*Le Christ*, p. 24] qu' Es. 53 est l'une des rares prophéties de l'AT qui offrent une base possible à l'exploitation du binôme mort–résurrection et à son application au Christ. Mais rien dans l'Apocalypse ne vient souligner cette possible correspondence' (Prigent, *L'Apocalypse*, pp. 97-98). For a discussion of Isa. 53.11 (esp. in 1QIsaᵃ) as signifying the 'resurrection' of the Servant, see W.H. Brownlee, *The Meaning of the Qumran Scrolls for the Bible* (New York, 1964), pp. 226-33.

Christ. Yet in a book saturated with OT allusions, of which Isaiah forms one of the main sources, there is no clear allusion to any of the so-called Servant Songs.[50] If Isa. 53.7 were the only available parallel for the figure of a 'slain lamb', then perhaps the supposition of a relationship between John's picture and Isaiah would warrant more confidence. As it is, however, there are numerous indications that John is inspired by a paschal Christology rather than a Servant Christology.[51]

The understanding of Christ as the paschal lamb who 'purchases' redemption for an elect multitude is in harmony with John's overall interest in Exodus typology. The accompanying explication of the slain lamb in Rev. 5.9-10 contains implicit paschal imagery as well as an explicit reference to Exod. 19.6.[52] In Rev. 15.2-3 John plainly connects the redemption of the Lamb with the Red Sea deliverance. And further metaphors of redemption as 'purchase' or 'freedom' through the agency of Christ's blood appear in 1.5-6 and 12.11 (cf.

50. Except possibly Isa. 49.2 in Rev. 1.16 par (see above pp. 117-22). An indirect allusion to Isa. 53.9 in Rev. 14.5 is probable, but the primary text is clearly Zeph. 3.13 (see below pp. 191-92). From very little evidence, Comblin constructs an elaborate presentation of John's debt to Isa. 53 and the Servant motif (*Le Christ*, pp. 17-47).

51. It would be difficult to imagine that John was unaware of or unsympathetic to a Servant Christology. Among first century Christian writers, the messianic application of Isa. 53 is found explicitly in Matthew (8.17, cf. 12.18-21; 27.57-66), Luke–Acts (22.37; cf. 24.26; Acts 8.32; cf. 3.18; 17.2-3), 1 Peter (2.22-25) and *1 Clement* (16.1-14). More implicit allusions may lie behind Rom. 4.25; Phil. 2.7-9; Mk 1.11 par. John's own preference for a paschal Christology may in part have been influenced by his paraenetic purpose, since a Servant Christology appears to have functioned predominately as an apologetic Christology (but cf. 1 Peter and *1 Clement*). An example of the paraenetic use of paschal imagery is found in 1 Cor. 5.6-8. For the Christian use of Isa. 53 in general, see H.W. Wolff, *Jesaja 53 im Urchristentum* (Berlin, 2nd edn, 1950).

52. Paschal and Exodus traditions in Rev. 5 and elsewhere are discussed more fully in Casey, 'Exodus Typology', esp. pp. 143-52; Schüssler Fiorenza, *Revelation*, pp. 96-97; Prigent, *Apocalypse et Liturgie*, pp. 73-76; and M.H. Shepherd, *The Paschal Liturgy*, pp. 77-97. There are also striking similarities between Rev. 5.9-12 and the Jewish Passover haggadah found in *m. Pes.*, 10.5-6. That such a Passover liturgy was known and used by some early Christians, and particularly in one of the churches of Revelation (Sardis), finds later confirmation in Melito's work *Peri Pascha*, in which Christ is compared to the paschal lamb. In this homily, which actually quotes from Revelation, clear use of the Jewish Passover haggadah is found in ch. 68; S.G. Hall, 'Melito in the Light of the Passover Haggadah', *JTS* NS 22 (1971), pp. 29-46.

14.3-4; 7.14).[53] The use of passover imagery to explain the death of Christ is found already in Paul, 'For Christ, our paschal lamb, has been sacrificed' (1 Cor. 5.7), and also plays a part in Johannine passion traditions.[54]

If, therefore, John's lamb is modeled on paschal imagery, what is to be made of the remaining theory (3), which holds that John's lamb springs from apocalyptic tradition and functions as a warrior-ram?[55] How does one explain the description of the lamb with seven horns who subsequently acts in a capacity as judge? Is it accidental that John sets a *lamb* against a *beast* in a manner typical of earlier apocalypses?[56] One cannot help but think that he is fully aware of the ambiguity which the lamb with seven horns evoked and that he has exploited it for just this reason.

Nonetheless, while this idea may be present, it does not appear to have been determinative for John's choice of the lamb image, for the warrior motifs have in fact been chosen as a deliberate contrast to the slain lamb in order to effect a radical transformation of apocalyptic messianic expectations. The contradictory association of the slain lamb with the titles and description of the warrior Messiah is actually a

53. The remark of Schüssler Fiorenza (*Revelation*, p. 95) 'The Lamb of Rev. has no sacrificial aspects or expiatory functions' may warn us not to automatically read into John's language and images a Pauline view of atonement; but it cannot stand in view of John's overall Christology. She recognizes the difficulty of Rev. 7.14, but fails to add 1.5-6; 'to him who... has freed us from our sins by his blood'. While the latter passage is obviously not a Lamb text, it is implicitly connected to 5.9-10 by the recapitulation of Exod. 19.6.

54. Cf. Conzelmann, *1 Corinthians*, pp. 98-99, who calls the Passover Christology a 'stock tradition'; E. Lohse, *Märtyrer und Gottesknecht* (Göttingen, 1963), pp. 141-46. For the Gospel of John, note esp. 19.36 and G. Reim, *Studien zum Alttestamentlichen Hintergrund des Johannesevangeliums* (Cambridge, 1974), pp. 51-54: "Wir finden im Johannesevangelium eine schon in der Tradition vorgegebene Anschauung, die in Jesus das Passahlamm sieht' (p. 52).

55. Ford, *Revelation*, pp. 86, 88-91; Beasley-Murray, *Revelation*, pp. 124-26; and Prigent, *L'Apocalypse*, p. 98, provide the main evidence for this view.

56. Dan. 7–8; *1 En.* 89–90. Lohmeyer's statement that *lamb* was already a messianic designation in Judaism cannot be maintained on the basis of *1 Enoch*'s animal imagery (*Offenbarung*, p. 54). The appeal of others to *T. Jos.* 19 is fraught with difficulty since the passage shows clear signs of Christian interpolation based on Revelation itself. And the presentation of Moses as a lamb in *Targ. Yer. Exod.* 1.15 is no less debated. For discussion see Schüssler Fiorenza, *Revelation*, p. 95 and the literature cited there.

potent reinterpretation of holy war tradition, and at the same time a deliberate overturning of apocalyptic militarism. As Bauckham has noted, 'By placing the image of the sacrificial victim alongside those of the military conqueror, John forges a new symbol of *conquest* by sacrificial death'.[57]

Revelation 6.12-17 → Isaiah 50.3; 34.4; 2.19, 10 (21)
The opening of the sixth seal in Rev. 6.12-17 sets into motion a series of cosmic catastrophes which culminates in an eschatological confrontation between God and the Lamb on one side and earthly sinners on the other. The collocation of OT Day of the Lord traditions in this passage and its proleptic relationship to the later parousia vision of 19.11-21 have already been discussed in some detail. A closer examination of the Isaiah allusions in these verses can now be made.

(1) *Rev. 6.12*   *Isa. 50.3*

καὶ σεισμὸς μέγας ἐγένετο
καὶ ὁ ἥλιος ἐγένετο μέλας   אלביש שמם קדרות καὶ ἐνδύσω τὸν
                                                   οὐρανὸν σκότος
ὡς σάκκος τρίχινος   וש אשם καὶ θήσω ὡς σάκκον
καὶ ἡ σελήνη ὅλη ἐγένετο ὡς αἷμα   כסותם τὸ περιβόλαιον αὐτοῦ

Besides this proposal for the use of Isa. 50.3, other less convincing Isaiah connections have been suggested for this verse which may be discussed first. Caird (*Revelation*, p. 89) finds the inspiration for the eschatological earthquake (σεισμὸς μέγας) in Isa. 2.19, a passage which John uses a few verses later in 6.15-16. But in the absence of any dictional connection, the frequency with which the earthquake motif recurs in contexts of judgment and theophany makes it impossible to confirm a link in this case.[58] The following image of the

57. *Climax of Prophecy*, p. 215; Sweet, *Revelation*, pp. 124-26. For additional material on the use of lamb symbolism in early Christianity, see F. Nikolasch, *Das Lamm als Christussymbol in den Schriften der Väter* (Vienna, 1963). I have not been able to include P.A. Harlé, 'L'Agneau de l'Apocalypse et le Nouveau Testament', *ETR* 31 (1956), pp. 26-35. F. Rousseau revives the almost forgotten view of Vischer that the Lamb passages of Revelation originally formed a separate work. In his view Rev. 4–11 and 15–22, which he calls '*L'Apocalypse de l'Agneau*' comprises an original Jewish document with Christian redaction (*L'Apocalypse et le milieu prophétique du Nouveau Testament: Structure et préhistoire du texte* (Paris, 1971).

58. R.J. Bauckham outlines and compares the use of this concept in the OT, apocalyptic literature and the Book of Revelation ('The Eschatological Earthquake in

darkening of the sun is sometimes associated with Isa. 13.10 rather than the more likely Joel 3.4, from which John also derives the next figure of the moon as blood.[59] This leads us back to main question concerning the origin of the sackcloth simile (ὡς σάκκος τρίχινος) which John adds to the sun motif. Certain differences between the two passages are evident. In Revelation it is the sun rather than the heaven which is darkened, and John modifies σάκκος with τρίχινος, a feature lacking in Isa. 50.3. Furthermore, the context of Isaiah 50 has no connection with the Day of the Lord, in contrast with the other OT passages which underlie this section of Revelation (6.12-17). Yet on the other hand, Isa. 50.3 is the only place where celestial darkness is compared to a sackcloth. Of course it is not unlikely that ὡς σάκκος may have been a common idiom employed in colour similes, of which one application could be the description of certain cosmological phenomena (e.g. lunar and solar eclipses, dark clouds, and the like). Even so, one cannot completely rule out the possibility that John has borrowed his language from Isa. 50.3.[60]

(2) *Rev. 6.13*   *Isa. 34.4*
καὶ οἱ ἀστέρες τοῦ οὐρανοῦ   ונמקו כל צבא השמים   καὶ πάντα τὰ ἄστρα
ἔπεσαν εἰς τὴν γῆν,   וכל צבאם יבול...   πεσεῖται...
ὡς συκῆ βάλλει τοὺς ὀλύνθους   כנבלת מתאנה   ὡς πίπτει φύλλα
αὐτῆς ὑπὸ ἀνέμου μεγάλου   ἀπὸ συκῆς
σειομένη

the Apocalypse of John', *NovT* 19 [1977], pp. 224-33). Caird suggests further that the prophecy of judgment against the heavenly hosts and earthly kings in Isa. 24.21 lies behind the program of Rev. 6.12-16. This is likewise impossible to demonstrate. See H.W. Günther, *Der Nah- und Enderwartungshorizont in der Apokalypse des heiligen Johannes* (Würzburg, 1980), p. 201, who discusses the difficulties of this proposal.

59. While it appears evident that John is acquainted with and adapts a scheme of eschatological events similar to that of the synoptic apocalypse, this does not justify the assimilation of his OT basis to synoptic parallels (e.g. Mk 13.24; Mt 24.29). See above, Chapter 2 n. 43. For a discussion of John's use of synoptic traditions here see Vos, *Synoptic Traditions*, pp. 117-20.

60. Compare our idiom 'black as coal' with *1 Clem.* 8.3, 'blacker than sackcloth'; cf. Sir. 25.17 (LXX). The combination of σάκκος and τρίχινος is not uncommon (MM, p. 567; LS, p. 1825). Those who accept a connection with Isa. 50.3 include Lohmeyer, Marconcini, Ozanne, Vos, Günther and Vögtle.

Both here and in the synoptic apocalypse, the traditional triad of sun, moon and stars in cosmic upheaval depends on Isa. 34.4 for the description of its third member. The formation of the first clause above may be the result of a conflation of the parallel Hebrew phrases, bringing together *heaven* (השמים) and *fall* (יבול), as is found in the reading of 1QIsaᵃ (וכול צבא השמים יבולו). John then adds εἰς τὴν γῆν to prepare for the fig analogy.

In the second clause he retains the primary image of the stars falling to earth as fruit from a fig tree, but adapts and expands it, transforming the kernels of the old prophecy into a vivid new picture. The two building blocks which are taken over are συκῆ (= תאנה) and ὀλύνθους (= נבלה). All else is amplification. While the first parallel is evident, the second needs further explanation. Because of misunderstanding surrounding the meaning of נבלה in Isa. 34.4b, few, if any, commentators have recognized that John's ὀλύνθους corresponds to Isaiah's נבלה.[61] נבלה is not to be analysed as a feminine participle from נבל (*to fade*), but rather as a noun found in Mishnaic Hebrew and attested in several cognate languages as a term for an inferior variety of fig.[62]

(3) *Rev. 6.14a*   *Isa. 34.4aβ*
καὶ ὁ οὐρανὸς ἀπεχωρίσθη   ונגלו כספר השמים   καὶ ἑλιγήσεται ὁ οὐρανὸς
ὡς βιβλίον ἑλισσόμενον   ὡς βιβλίον

Apart from the addition of ἀπεχωρίσθη, John leaves his prophetic model relatively intact here. The rolling up of the heavens is not one of the cosmic signs included in the synoptic apocalypse, even though other parts of Isa. 34.4 were utilized. Nevertheless it appears in earlier apocalyptic tradition in *Sib. Or.* 3.81-82, in a list of cosmic events leading up to the judgment of God.[63] As A. Vögtle observes,

---

61. Thus even Marconcini, who is specifically comparing the MT with Revelation, says wrongly that John 'sostituisce le foglie...con fichi immaturi' ('L'utilizzazione', p. 131).

62. So Jastrow (*TD*, p. 870), who identifies Aram. נבלא (used in *Targ. Isa.* 34.4) with Heb. נובלה). G.R. Driver notes, 'the feminine *nōbelet* "fading" (!) cannot qualify the masculine *'āleh* "leaf"; it is a different word, namely the Mishn. Hebr. *nōbelet* and Aram. *niblâ* "fig(s) falling unripened from the tree", as the Pesh.'s *paqô'â* "immature fig; wild fig"... shows' (Isaiah I–XXXIX: Textual and Linguistic Problems', *JSS* 13 [1968], p. 54). Cf. KB and C. Brokelmann, *Lexicon Syriacum* (Halle, 2nd edn, 1928), p. 590.

63. οὐρανόν εἵλιξη, καθάπερ βιβλίον εἰλεῖται. It is also found in later

John carefully rearranges Isa. 34.4 in order to maintain the traditional order of sun–moon–stars, and works in 34.4aβ after it.[64]

The addition of the heavens motif to the conventional apocalyptic series may be more than simply the inclusion of another cosmic sign. For one whose vision of God came by means of 'a door opened in heaven' (4.1-2), the 'rolling up of the heaven' would completely remove the barrier between God's throne and the earth, and usher in the eschatological confrontation between God, the Lamb and the sinful world.[65] The view once reserved for the apocalyptist or the Christian martyr (Acts 7.55-56) now becomes a universal revelation of the divine Judge and his agent.

Thus the rolling up of the heaven leads to the visible manifestation of God and the Lamb and prepares for the following scenario of human beings seeking to hide 'from the face of him who is seated on the throne and from the wrath of the Lamb' (6.16).

(4) *Rev. 6.15b, 16b*	*Isa. 2.19, 10 (21)*	
ἔκρυψαν ἑαυτοὺς εἰς	ובאו במער ות צרים	εἰσενέγκαντες εἰς
τὰ σπήλαια		τὰ σπήλαια
καὶ εἰς τὰς πέτρας	ובמחלות עפר	καὶ εἰς τὰς σχισμὰς
τῶν ὀρέων...		τῶν πετρῶν
κρύψατε ἡμᾶς ἀπὸ	הטמן...מפנ	...κρύπτεσθε...ἀπὸ
προσώπου τοῦ		προσώπου τοῦ
καθημένου ἐπὶ τοῦ θρόνου	פחד יהוה	φόβου κυρίου
καὶ ἀπὸ τῆς ὀργῆς τοῦ ἀρνίον	ומהדר נאו	καὶ ἀπὸ τῆς δόξης
		τῆς ἰσχύος αὐτοῦ

The gradual buildup of cosmic events followed by the appearance of the divine Judge (6.12-14) reaches its intended climax with the response of godless humanity to the impending fury of God's wrath (6.15-17). For the description of the physical terror of humankind at the divine presence John turns to another Day of the Lord tradition in

sources (e.g. *Gos. Thom.* 111; *Sib. Or.* 8.233, 413; cf. *NTApoc.*, II, p. 671 n. 2).

64. *Das Neue Testament und die Zukunft des Kosmos* (Düsseldorf, 1970), p. 73.

65. The opening of the heavens as a prelude to the epiphany of God in judgment is well illustrated by Isa. 64.1-2: 'O that thou wouldst rend the heavens and come down, that the mountains might quake at thy presence... to make thy name known to thy adversaries, and that the nations might tremble at thy presence!' (cf. Ps. 18.9); Vögtle and Günther similarly accord this significance to the rolling up of the heaven (*Zukunft*, p. 73; *Der Nah- und Enderwartungshorizont*, p. 203). Cf. also Rev. 6.14 with 19.11; 20.11; 1.7; *2 En.* 31.1-2.

Isaiah 2.[66] The primary text appears to be Isa. 2.19, but with κρύπτω (= טמן) conflated from 2.10. The substitution of τῶν ὀρέων in line 2 is probably influenced by the following use of Hos. 10.8 in Rev. 6.16a.[67] Although a relationship between the first two lines in Rev. 6.15b and Isaiah 2 is accepted by all commentators, very few have gone on to recognize that John continues the allusion in lines 3-5 (6.16b).[68] In line 3 'to hide from the face of/presence of' reproduces a common idiom used especially with verbs of hiding, fleeing and escaping.[69] In line 4 he merely replaces the יהוה/κύριος of Isaiah with his own characteristic circumlocution for God. Line 5 requires a more detailed analysis.

Whereas in Isaiah both prepositional phrases (ἀπό + genitive) refer to Yahweh, John replaces the object of the second preposition (*glory*) with *wrath* and refers the phrase to the Lamb. No specific word for *wrath* or *anger* occurs in the Isaiah passage, although the פחד יהוה in line 4 (Isa. 2.19b) may have evoked the idea of *wrath*.[70] Be that as it may, the more important question is how, in the light of John's use of Isa. 2.19, the Lamb came to be paralleled with God as the agent of wrath. It would be easy to conclude that John's alteration of line 5 is simply his own substitution and redaction, which depends on the Isaiah *Vorlage* only for diction and not for theological substance. But another possibility exists.

One of the earliest features of Pauline eschatology was the assimilation of the prophetic Day of the Lord to the Day of Christ.[71] This association made it possible for early Christian teachers to develop the theme of the parousia in accordance with specific OT texts which

---

66. Used also in *Sib. Or.* 3.607 ἐν σχισμαῖς πετρῶν κατακρύψαντες δἰ ὄνειδος.

67. So also Holtz, *Christologie*, p. 161; and Ozanne, 'Influence', p. 102.

68. Only Holtz, Ozanne and Vögtle explicitly refer to it.

69. BDB, p. 818 n. 6.

70. The פחד יהוה in Isa. 2.10, 19, 21 is a subjective genitive which refers to the terror or fearful consequences that Yahweh's presence will bring upon sinners. Cf. J. Becker, *Gottesfurcht im Alten Testament* (AnBib, 25; Rome, 1965), pp. 7-8, 48. Both Holtz and Ozanne suggest that John's ὀργή may be a *translation* of פחד; but if there is any connection, *interpretation* would be a better description (*Christologie*, p. 161; 'Influence', p. 102).

71. 1 Thess. 5.2; 2 Thess. 2.1-2; 1 Cor. 1.8; 5.5; 2 Cor. 1.14; Phil. 1.6, 10; 2.16.

prophesied or described the Day of the Lord.[72] It would thus be natural to expect that the functions, characteristics and terminology originally associated with Yahweh and the Day of the Lord would be transferred to Jesus and the parousia event. This is exactly the kind of procedure which we find applied in 2 Thess. 1.9, where the very Isaiah text in question (2.19) is employed to describe the Day of Christ.[73]

2 Thess. 1.9b

ἀπὸ προσώπου τοῦ κυρίου καὶ
ἀπὸ τῆς δόξης τῆς ἰσχύος αὐτοῦ

Isa. 2.19 (LXX)

ἀπὸ προσώπου τοῦ φόβου κυρίου καὶ
ἀπὸ τῆς δόξης τῆς ἰχύος αὐτοῦ

Here κύριος refers to Jesus, so that both clauses of Isaiah, and probably the whole passage (2.6-22), were understood of Christ. John, however, takes a more mediating position. He retains the OT term 'Day of God' (16.14), rather than 'Day of Christ', and prefers to associate the κύριος of Isa. 2.19 with the Lord God instead of Christ, as is his custom generally.[74] Instead, John takes advantage of the *parallelismus membrorum* of his Isaiah model to introduce Christ (the Lamb) into the second parallel clause (καὶ ἀπὸ τῆς δόξης τῆς ἰσχύος αὐτοῦ). Perhaps this was facilitated by an interpretation of δόξα in accordance with the view that Christ was the manifestation of God's *glory*.[75]

Having analyzed the individual Isaiah allusions in Rev. 6.12-17, it is now necessary to discuss their function in the pericope as a whole along with the other primary OT allusions to Joel 3.4 and Hos. 10.8. While many commentators recognize that John consciously borrows

72. That the themes of judgment and the parousia were a basic feature of early Christian catechesis and even evangelistic preaching is evidenced in numerous texts: e.g. Acts 17.31; 24.25; Heb. 6.1-2; 1 Thess. 4.13–5.11; 2 Thess. 1.5–2.12.

73. Recognized by Tertullian (*Adv. Marc.* 5.16.3): 'His very expression, *from the face of the Lord and from the glory of his power*, in which he uses Isaiah's words'.

74. John's view of the Day of the Lord is balanced between divine participation and messianic agency, similar to Acts 17.31, 'He has fixed a day on which he [God] will judge the world... by a man whom he has appointed'.

75. Note in this regard Jn 12.41, where Isaiah is said to have seen *Christ's* glory in his vision of the Lord (Isa. 6.1-13); cf. Jn 1.14; 17.5, 22; Heb. 1.3 ὅς ὢν ἀπαύγασμα τῆς δόξης... αὐτοῦ; 1 Cor. 2.8; Jas 2.1 (*Lord of Glory*); Lk 9.26 (of Christ coming for judgment 'in the glory of the Father'); Mk 13.26 par.; and *4 Ezra* 7.42. Only Holtz mentions the possibility of this interpretation of δόξα (*Christologie*, p. 162).

Day of the Lord traditions in this section,[76] there is a wide variety of opinion as to the exact significance of the imagery.

Some take the signs in the sun, moon and stars as symbolic of the judgment of the celestial powers and rulers.[77] Others accord them the same role as in the synoptic apocalypse: that of signs of the imminent end of the world.[78] A few commentators even engage in figurative or even allegorical interpretations.[79] Günther argues at length that the cosmic events of Rev. 6.12-17 constitute the actual breaking up and removal of the physical universe in order to make way for the new heavens and earth.[80] None of these views, however, adequately takes into account either John's premeditated choice of Day of the Lord texts in 6.12-17 or his special eschatological agenda and its relation to the structure of the book as a whole.

The major issue concerns whether these pictures of cosmic upheaval are intended to announce actual spatial realities or whether they are merely conceptual hyperbole. Any theory which holds that Rev. 6.12-17 signals the actual destruction of the cosmos ignores the role of the millennium in John's construct. The events of the sixth seal are a preview and summary of the final outpouring of wrath in Rev. 16.17-21, which leads into the appearance of the messianic Judge in 19.11-21.[81] These are all pre-millennial events. It is not until Rev. 20.11 that John announces (in passing) the removal of the heaven and earth— *after* the millennium.

Neither is Rev. 6.12-17 simply a list of traditional signs heralding the end of the age, as in the synoptic apocalypse. These signs are not for the benefit of the disciples or the church, but for the godless world.[82]

---

76. E.g. Lohmeyer, Sweet, Roloff, Pohl, Beasley-Murray, Prigent, Kraft, Günther and Vögtle.

77. Sweet, Caird and Preston–Hanson.

78. Pohl, Swete, Beasley-Murray and Beckwith.

79. D'Aragon thinks the cosmic disturbances are symbolic of social upheavals (*JBC*, II, p. 477). Pohl finds in the mountains, hills and islands symbols of political and economic pride (*Offenbarung*, I, p. 210).

80. *Der Nah- und Enderwartungshorizont*, pp. 201-204. *Contra* Vögtle, *Zukunft*, p. 75.

81. The structural and thematic relationships are discussed in detail above pp. 78-80.

82. 'Seine Vision nicht die Auflösung des Kosmos verkünden, sondern in prophetisch- apokalyptischer Bildsprache die Gewalt und Unabwendbarkeit des göttlichen Gerichtszornes für die feinde Gottes und Christi verkünden will. Ihre

While it is true that the sixth seal comes in answer to the prayers of the martyrs in the fifth seal, 'How long before thou wilt judge and avenge our blood?', the cosmic events which follow are presented as omens which announce to the ungodly the day of God's judgment.[83] This parallels closely the setting and purpose of the model text in Isaiah 2.

More specifically, the cosmic signs are set in the context of holy war imagery and anticipate the final eschatological battle of Rev. 16.12-16 → 19.11-21. Each of the OT passages which John adopts in 6.12-17 derives from the Day of the Lord contexts in which the concept of holy war is present. This is explicit in Joel 3, Isaiah 2 and Isaiah 34, and can be implied from Hosea 10, as H.W. Wolff has noted.[84] In connection with the Day of the Lord theme, A.J. Everson remarks:

> It is clear that the Day of Yahweh concept is used by the prophetic writers primarily in connection with the realities of war—the memories of war or the anticipation of new occasions of war. The Day of Yahweh is a concept that is used to interpret momentous events of war.[85]

John's own presentation of the Day of the Lord in Revelation 6 consciously begins on the foundation of these OT precedents, and by means of this tradition the prophet appears to anticipate his own vision of the final eschatological battle. It is against this background that the

---

Erwähnung ist in der gerichtsvision 6,12–16 gar nicht zu erwarten, da diese nur das Endschicksal der ungläubigen Menschheit ins Auge fasst (Vögtle, *Zukunft*, p. 75).

83. Such signs were culturally relevant even to those unacquainted with biblical or apocalyptic tradition. Note, for example, the preoccupation with similar omens in Tacitus: earthquake (*Ann.* 12.43); sun darkened (*Ann.* 14.12); moon losing its light (*Ann.* 1.28); falling stars (*Ann.* 15.47). Seneca, in *Nat. Quaest.* 7.2, remarks, 'the usual collection of stars which distinguishes the immense firmament does not attract people's attention, but when something is changed from the ordinary the eyes of all are on the sky. The sun does not have a spectator unless it is in eclipse, no one watches the moon if it is not in eclipse, but then cities cry out and each person makes a din in accordance with inane superstition.'

84. 'Wie einst Jahwe im heiligen Krieg gegen die sich sammelnden (Ri 6 33), d.h. zum Kampf antretenden Völker für Israel einschritt, so schreitet er am neuen "Tage Jahwes" (der Terminus fehlt bei Hosea; vgl. Am 5.18-20 Jes 2.12) gegen sein Volk ein' (*Dodekapropheton.* I. *Hosea* [BKAT, 14; Neukirchen, 1961], p. 239). For a discussion of these OT passages and the relationship between the Day of the Lord and the concept of holy war see G. von Rad. 'The Origin of the Concept of the Day of Yahweh', *JSS* 4 (1959), pp. 97-108.

85. 'The Days of Yahweh', *JBL* 93 (1974), p. 336.

changes in the natural order should be seen. Instead of being indicators of the final dissolution of the cosmos, these signs are traditional prophetic announcements of theophany and symbolic preludes to holy war. They signal not merely the parousia (as in the Synoptics), but the decisive intervention of God in the final battle between the armies of heaven led by the messianic war-leader, and the wicked earthly forces led by the Beast (19.11, 14, 19).[86]

Revelation 7.2a → Isaiah 41.2, 25

In Rev. 7.2 an angel appears 'from the rising of the sun (ἀπὸ ἀνατολῆς ἡλίου) in order to seal the servants of God. Kraft believes that this phrase evokes more than just geographical orientation and sees behind it the influence of Isa. 41.25 and Mal. 3.20.[87] According to him the motif of arising from the east alludes to a comparison between the angel and Christ, based on a messianic understanding of Isa. 41.25, 'I have stirred up one... from the rising of the sun', combined with the 'sun of righteousness' prophecy of Mal. 4.2 (MT 3.20).

Although a messianic interpretation of ἀνατολή is attested in early Christian circles,[88] there is nothing in the context of Revelation 7 to suggest that such a procedure is in view here. Likewise, the context of Isa. 41.25 is completely unrelated to the purpose of Rev. 7.2-3. Since John uses the exact same phrase in 16.12 to denote simply a geographical direction—East (cf. also 21.13)—there is little reason to think he intends a further hidden meaning in the earlier passage. *Why* the angel comes from the east is another matter, which most commentators relate to traditional expectations surrounding the appearance of God or the Messiah.[89]

---

86. Roloff (*Offenbarung*, p. 85) is one of the few to connect the events of 6.12-17 with the parousia of 19.11-21, though he does not emphasize the holy war theme. Kraft correctly emphasizes John's use of OT tradition in this passage (*Offenbarung*, pp. 120-21).

87. *Offenbarung*, p. 125; cf. also the margin of N[26]. Holtzmann earlier cited Isa. 41.2 (Charles, *Revelation*, I, p. 204).

88. E.g. Lk 1.78, based on the LXX of Jer. 23.5; Zech. 3.8; 6.12; Num. 24.17; cf. *TDNT*, I, pp. 351-53.

89. Most cite Ezek. 43.2-4, *Sib. Or.* 3.652; *1 En.* 61.1; Gen. 2.8; Mt. 2.1; Ign. *Rom.* 2.2; Herm. *Vis.* 1.2.1, 3. Swete says, 'from the writer's point of view the East is the direction of Palestine... and it was fitting that the angel who is to seal the tribes of Israel should appear from that quarter' (*Apocalypse*, p. 96).

Revelation 7.14b → Isaiah 1.18b

John's vision of a great multitude in white robes (7.9-17) culminates in a revelatory dialogue in which the identity of the heavenly throng is revealed by one of the 24 Elders:

οὗτοί εἰσιν οἱ ἐρχόμενοι ἐκ τῆς θλίψεως τῆς μεγάλης
καὶ ἔπλυναν τὰς στολὰς αὐτῶν
καὶ ἐλεύκαναν αὐτὰς ἐν τῷ αἵματι τοῦ ἀρνίου

Various proposals have been offered as to the possible OT background to the striking metaphor of *washing robes in blood* in the latter part of Rev. 7.14. Of these, three are more important: Exod. 19.10, 14, Gen. 49.11, and Isa. 1.18.

Primary consideration must be given to the Exodus passage because the whole context of Rev. 7.14-17 (as well as 7.9-10, cf. 15.2-3) flows in a steady pattern of Exodus imagery. The innumerable multitude of those who have 'come out of (ἐκ) the great tribulation' recalls the Exodus of the host of Israel from Egypt and their own liberation from tribulation (θλίψις—Exod. 4.31 LXX). The subsequent motifs of God tabernacling among them (7.15), provision of food and water (7.16a, 17b), protection from the elements (7.16b), guidance (7.17a) and divine comfort and assurance (7.17c) all continue the Exodus imagery.[90]

The washing of robes figure fits in perfectly with this thematic progression and parallels closely Exod. 19.10, 14, where the Israelites are told to purify themselves and wash their garments before approaching Yahweh at Sinai. It is no accident, then, that John follows the purification ritual of 7.14 with a proclamation of access to the presence of God in 7.15a. This correspondence in context is reinforced by close dictional conformity:

Rev. 7.14ba   *Exod. 19.14*
καὶ ἔπλυναν τὰς στολὰς αὐτῶν   ויכבסו שמלתם   καὶ ἔπλυναν τὰ ἱμάτια

If, as it appears, John has utilized the context and language of Exodus 19 for the washing motif in general and the phrase in 7.14bα in particular, what is to be made of the parallel clause κ α ὶ

90. Discussed more fully by Casey, 'Exodus Typology', pp. 153-54; 176-77; 182-84. J.A. Draper completely ignores the more general Exodus imagery in pursuit of his thesis ('The Heavenly Feast of Tabernacles: Rev. 7.1-17', *JSNT* 19 [1983], pp. 133-47). As Prigent observes, it is unlikely that a specific feast is here in view (*L'Apocalypse*, pp. 124, 127).

ἐλεύκαναν αὐτὰς ἐν τῷ αἵματι τοῦ ἀρνίου in 7.14bβ? It may be that a catchword association based on *washing* and *robe* led John to conflate Gen. 49.11 with the primary text from Exodus. The Genesis passage, which forms part of the patriarchal blessing on Judah, reads: πλυνεῖ ἐν οἴνῳ τὴν στολὴν αὐτοῦ καὶ ἐν αἵματι σταφυλῆς τὴν περιβολὴν αὐτοῦ (LXX).

While this connection provides a possible basis for explaining the metaphor of washing garments *in blood* (substituting τοῦ ἀρνίου for σταφυλῆς),[91] it faces a difficulty in that the Genesis text is contextually dissimilar. Since John has already used a portion of the Judah blessing messianically (Rev. 5.5), it would seem odd that he would then turn around and apply it to the corporate messianic community. Furthermore, the washing in the blood of the grape in Gen. 49.11 is not a purification rite, but rather symbolizes the bounteous agricultural blessings of Judah.

Whatever one may decide as to the influence of Genesis 49 here, it does not explain the use of ἐλεύκαναν, for which some refer to Isa. 1.18b: 'Though your sins are like scarlet, they shall be white as snow' (ὡς χιόνα λευκανῶ).[92] If it were simply a matter of correspondence between verbs, this view could easily be dismissed. But the similar theme of cleansing from sin increases the likelihood of an allusion, though it does not confirm it.[93] The use of λευκαίνω with the whitening of clothes is not unique (Mk 9.3), and may simply have been drawn into the circle of cleansing imagery by common association with πλύνω and στολή. Or, possibly, the idea derives from an interpretation of Dan. 11.35 and 12.10, where the righteous martyrs 'purify themselves and make themselves white'.[94] At any rate, one must conclude that Exodus 19 is primarily in view, though it is

91. For the phrase 'blood of the grape', cf. Sir. 39.26, 50.15.

92. An early Christian use of this passage to explain the atoning value of Christ's blood is found in *1 Clem.* 8.4, cf. 7.4.

93. For a discussion of the atonement theology behind this imagery see G. Delling, *Der Kreuzestod Jesu in der urchristlichen Verkündigung* (Göttingen, 1972), pp. 112-14; *contra* Schüssler Fiorenza, *Priester*, pp. 219-21. Cf. also Holtz, *Christologie*, pp. 74-75; and Prigent, *L'Apocalypse*, p. 126. A. Feuillet ties in Rev. 7.14 more specifically with the paschal imagery of 5.9 ('"L'exode" de Jésus et le déroulement du mystère rédempteur d'après S. Luc et S. Jean', *RevThom* 77 [1977], pp. 181-206).

94. So Bauckham, *Climax of Prophecy*, p. 227.

possible that secondary influence from Gen. 49.11 and Isa. 1.18 is present.[95]

Revelation 7.15b → Isaiah 4.5-6

A few commentators have noted the similarity of theme between Rev. 7.15b and Isa. 4.5-6 and have suggested a possible influence, though none affirms a clear literary connection.[96] Perhaps Rev. 7.16b should also be taken into account when comparing the two passages.

Rev. 7.15b, 16b	*Isa. 4.5-6*
And he who is seated on the throne will spread his tent over them... the sun shall not strike them, nor any scorching heat.	Then the Lord will create over the whole site of Mount Zion and over her assemblies a cloud by day, and smoke and the shining of a flaming fire by night; for over all the glory there will be a canopy and a pavilion. It will be for a shade by day from the heat, and for a refuge and a shelter from the storm and rain.

There is no question of literary dependence, for both lines in Revelation are based on other sources. The origin of Rev. 7.15b can be found by first reverting John's circumlocution for God (ὁ καθήμενος ἐπὶ τοῦ θρόνου) back to θεός, giving καὶ θεός σκηνώσει ἐπ' αὐτούς. This phrase then parallels and anticipates Rev. 21.3, καὶ [ὁ θεός] σκηνώσει μετ' αὐτῶν. They are both variations of a single tradition which probably goes back to Ezek. 37.27.[97] As for Rev. 7.16b, we shall see in the next section that it is clearly adapted from Isa. 49.10.

Therefore, the recognition of these primary texts and the corresponding absence of any clear dictional connections with Isa. 4.5-6

---

95. The views of various commentators are: (1) Exod. 19 and Gen. 49: Swete, Lohmeyer, Prigent, Mounce (Exod. 19 only); (2) Exod. 19 and Isa. 1: Holtz, Schüssler Fiorenza; (3) Gen. 49 alone: Trudinger, Ozanne, Kraft.

96. Ford, Beasley-Murray and Swete.

97. With possibly some influence from Zech. 2.10 (MT 2.14). The covenant formula שכנתי בתוכם/בתוך derives from priestly circles: Exod. 25.8, 29.45-46; Num. 35.34; 1 Kgs 6.13. The variation of this promise in Ezek. 37.27 uses the noun משכן rather than שכן, but is the only example where the preposition על is used (עליהם), corresponding to John's ἐπί. The use of ἐπί in Rev. 7.15, rather than μετά (21.3), prepares for the image of protection from the elements in the following verse (7.16b).

makes it impossible to verify an allusion of this passage. On the other hand, the presence of strong thematic similarities between the Isaiah passage and Rev. 7.13-17 means one cannot rule out altogether the possibility that John was influenced by this OT text. Yet although the images and context of the eschatological prophecy in Isa. 4.2-6 offer a close parallel to John's presentation (note esp. the holy and saved remnant in vv. 2-3), a major theological distinction remains. In Isa. 4.5-6 the manifestation of God's presence is still indirect and symbolized by the fire and cloud, while John emphasizes the immediate presence of the divine glory in the New Jerusalem (Rev. 7.15; 21.3; 22.3-5).

Revelation 7.16-17 → Isaiah 49.10, 25.8b

Revelation	Isaiah	
οὐ πεινάσουσιν ἔτι	לא ירעבו	οὐ πεινάσουσιν
οὐδὲ διψήσουσιν ἔτι	ולא יצמאו	οὐδὲ διψήσουσιν,
οὐδὲ μὴ πέσῃ ἐπ' αὐτοὺς	ולא יכם	οὐδὲ πατάξει αὐτοὺς
ὁ ἥλιος	שרב	καύσων
οὐδὲ πᾶν καῦμα,	ושמש	οὐδὲ ὁ ἥλιος,
ὅτι τὸ ἀρνίον	כי מרחמם	ἀλλὰ ὁ ἐλεῶν αὐτοὺς
τὸ ἀνὰ μέσον τοῦ θρόνου		
ποιμανεῖ αὐτοὺς	ינהגם	παρακαλέσει
καὶ ὁδηγήσει αὐτοὺς	ועל מבועי מים	καὶ διὰ πηγῶν ὑδάτων
ἐπὶ ζωῆς πηγὰς ὑδάτων	ינהלם	ἄξει αὐτούς
καὶ ἐξαλείψει ὁ θεὸς	ומחה אדני יהוה	καὶ πάλιν ἀφεῖλεν ὁ θεὸς
πᾶν δάκρυον	דמעה	πᾶν δάκρυον
ἐκ τῶν ὀφθαλμῶν αὐτῶν	מעל כל פנים	ἀπὸ παντὸς προσώπου

Even a cursory comparison of the parallel texts above reveals the depth of John's dependence here. As the longest and most faithful illustration of his usage of the OT, this passage was presented earlier as an example of quotation in Revelation. Despite several points of correspondence between Revelation and the LXX, a comparison of this unit as a whole favours the supposition that John has here utilized a Semitic rather than a Greek source.[98] Some commentators have suggested that John has modified the base text of Isa. 49.10 in 7.16-17a in accordance with kindred statements found elsewhere in the OT. The main proposals are these:

---

98. The same conclusion is reached by other commentators: e.g. Trudinger, Marconcini, Schlatter, Vos, Ozanne, Charles and Thompson.

1.   Ps. 22(23).1-3, providing ποιμαίνω and ὁδηγέω in Rev. 7.17ab.[99]
2.   Jer. 2.13, for the association of 'living' with springs of water.[100]
3.   Ezek. 34.23, for the idea of the messianic shepherd feeding his flock.[101]

Even though each of these passages is close in thought and vocabulary to the statements expressed in Rev. 7.16-17, it must remain questionable whether John had any of them specifically in mind. ποιμαίνω and ὁδηγέω in Rev. 7.17ab can still be accounted for on the basis of Isa. 49.10c, making the appeal to Psalm 23 unnecessary.[102] The modification of Isaiah's 'springs of water' with ζωῆς is hardly unique enough to be pinned down to an otherwise unrelated OT text.[103] And in the case of Ezek. 34.23, there are simply no dictional connections to substantiate dependence.

Although John makes various characteristic modifications to his OT model it is important to recognize with Trudinger that he nevertheless retains 'all the elements contained in the OT passage'.[104] As has already been suggested above, it would seem best to conclude that John has purposely chosen Isa. 49.10 and 25.8 as foundation texts and left them recognizable in order to emphasize their prophetic origin and thereby enhance their paraenetic force.

99.   So Lohmeyer, Swete, Kiddle–Ross, Ozanne, Caird, Kraft, Pohl, Casey, Ford and Thompson.
100.   Or Jer. 17.13? Charles, Ozanne and Caird.
101.   Swete, Caird, Casey, Kraft and Ford.
102.   ποιμαίνω translates נהג in Ps. 48.15 (47.15) and ὁδηγέω is an acceptable translation of נהל. LXX equivalents should of course be a guide rather than a rule. Holtz also questions the influence of Ps. 23 in Rev. 7.17ab (*Christologie*, p. 199 n. 3).
103.   The motif of *living water* or *water of life* is found in Cant. 4.15; Zech. 14.8; 1QH 8.7, 8, 14, 16; Jn 4.10, 14; 7.38; *Odes. Sol.* 6.18; cf. 2 Macc. 7.36. If John has derived the living water theme from Johannine tradition, he has reinterpreted it. Whereas in the Gospel the gift of living water is offered as a present reality, in Revelation it is strictly an eschatological promise reserved for those who share in the New Jerusalem (21.6; 22.1, 17); Holtz, *Christologie*, pp. 199-201.
104.   Trudinger, 'Text', p. 66. The insertion of πᾶν in 7.17c, besides being almost required by the terse Hebrew of Isa. 25.8 (cf. LXX), is typical of John before neuter nouns (cf. 7.16; 21.27; 22.3), Trudinger, 'Texte', p. 68; Ozanne, 'Influence', p. 106.

The relationship of this section to the rest of the book is clear enough. There can hardly be any doubt that Rev. 7.14-17 is a proleptic glimpse of the overcomers' future inheritance. Besides the use of future verbs, nearly every facet of this pericope anticipates the eschatological conditions of the New Jerusalem.[105] Just as Rev. 6.12-17 was a premonitory summary of the fate awaiting the wicked, so 7.14-17 is a paraenetic preview of the destiny of the righteous. The two units stands in antithetic parallel and combine to form an eschatological overture anticipating both final judgment and salvation.[106]

The selection of Isa. 49.10 is particularly apposite and evokes a plurality of images. As part of Second Isaiah's *New Exodus* theme, Isa. 49.10 concerns the return of God's elect from the Babylonian captivity and their restoration to Zion. Amidst the uncertainties of abandoning the known for the unknown and the difficulties which lay along the path, this verse in Isaiah promises divine provision, protection and guidance using imagery which recalls the earlier wilderness experience of Israel. John's readers too have chosen to forsake the tangible comforts and security of the latest 'Babylon' and have set their sights in faith on the as yet unseen glory of the New Jerusalem.

But whereas in Isa. 49.10 the imagery pertains to God's provision and protection while in transition, John gives the whole scene a future orientation which is reinforced by the subtle addition of ἔτι. Like the manna promise of 2.17 he transforms the wilderness motifs of feeding, watering and protection from the elements (7.16) into eschatological gifts reserved for those who make it to the 'promised land'.[107] John has no interest in the easy return language of Second Isaiah. For this

---

105. Rev. 7.15a // 22.3-4; 7.15b // 21.3; 7.16-17ab // 21.6, 22.1; 7.17c // 21.4. So also Swete, Kiddle–Ross, Vos, Caird, Schüssler Fiorenza, Holtz, U.B. Müller (*Die Offenbarung des Johannes* [ÖTK, 19: Gütersloh, 1984]); and G. Bornkamm, 'Die Komposition der apokalyptischen Visionen in der Offenbarung Johannis', *ZNW* 36 (1937), pp. 132-49.

106. Brütsch, *Offenbarung*, I, p. 339; Bornkamm, 'Die Komposition', p. 148.

107. The paraenetic use of eschatological rewards for the persecuted is closely paralleled in the beatitudes of Mt. 5.1-12 and Lk 6.20-23.

Blessed are those who hunger and thirst. . . for they shall be filled.	They shall hunger no more, neither thirst anymore. . .
Blessed are those who mourn for they shall be comforted.	and God will wipe away every tear from their eyes.

Cf. K. Koch, *The Growth of the Biblical Tradition* (London, 1969), pp. 6-8.

struggling band of Christians no mountains will be leveled and no roads will be smoothed. The catalogue of divine comforts is only for those who have experienced the great tribulation and persevered.

There are some who would extend the influence of Isaiah 49 to other parts of Revelation 7. Both Ford and Kraft explain the 12 tribes and their sealing (7.4-8) on the basis of the Servant's task in Isa. 49.6:

> It is too light a thing that you should be my servant
> to raise up the tribes of Jacob
> and to restore the preserved of Israel;
> I will give you as a light to the nations,
> that my salvation may reach to the end of the earth.[108]

According to this view, the *preserved of Israel* correspond to the 144,000, sealed from each tribe, who later appear with the Messiah on Mount Zion (14.1-5). Building on this suggestion one might attempt to discover a more deep-rooted *remnant* theology behind John's development. Assuming a blend of Exodus and restoration imagery, the church is portrayed as the *holy remnant*, the *true Israel*, the spiritual fulfilment of those prophecies which promise the eschatological re-establishment of the 12 tribes.[109] Led by the Lamb (7.17; 14.4), as Israel was led by Moses, the faithful remnant forsake 'Babylon', and after a difficult journey, patterned after the Red Sea and wilderness experiences (15.2-5; 12.14), enter the Holy City, the New Jerusalem, through gates especially named for them (21.2, 12-13; cf. Isa. 49.18). Thus the reassembly of the 12 tribes in Revelation 7 culminates in their restoration in ch. 21.

But however attractive this construct may be for drawing together various related traditions in Revelation, the connections remain

---

108. Kraft, *Offenbarung*, p. 131; Ford, *Revelation*, pp. 120, 126-28. It is interesting to note also that Isa. 49.6 juxtaposes tribes of Israel with the nations, as does Rev. 7.4-8 and 9-17.

109. Ezek. 47.13-14; 48.23-35; Isa. 63.17. The hope for the restoration of the 12 tribes develops further in the intertestamental period and following, and becomes the task of the Messiah: Sir. 36.11; 48.10; *4 Ezra* 13.39; *2 Bar.* 77.17-19; cf. Acts 26.6-7. The understanding of the church as spiritual Israel is pretty well taken for granted by early Christians. For example, the Church is called the *Israel of God* (Gal. 6.11; Rom. 9.6-8), God's λαός (Rom. 9.25-26; 2 Cor. 6.16; Acts 15.14; 1 Pet. 2.9-10; Rev. 18.4; 21.3; *1 Clem.* 64.1; *2 Clem.* 2.1-3; *Barn.* 5.7; 7.5) and *the twelve tribes* (Jas 1.1 cf. διασπορά here with the LXX of Isa. 49.6; Mt. 19.28 // Lk 22.30; *T. Abr.* 13.6. Particularly interesting is Herm. *Sim.* 9.17.1-4, where 12 tribes stand for the nations who receive a seal (i.e. baptism); cf. *Barn.* 8.3.

obscure, and difficulties remain. Not least is a rival explanation of the 144,000 which understands them against the background of holy war mythology. Here, the 12,000 mustered from each tribe represent the church *militant*, who stand along with their war leader—the Lamb— in opposition to the Beast and his followers.[110] In view of the uncertainty, the influence of Isa. 49.6 must be left open.

The final use of Isa. 25.8 in 7.17c brings the salvation oracle to a close and turns the focus back to the activity of God who will comfort those who come out of the great tribulation. As such it looks forward to the union of human beings and God in the New Jerusalem (Rev. 21–22), where Isa. 25.8 is repeated and even expanded with further allusions (21.4). A more detailed discussion of Isa. 25.8 will be undertaken in the treatment of that passage.[111]

110. Although the two views are not necessarily mutually exclusive; cf. Bauckham, *Climax of Prophecy*, pp. 215-19; and cf. Rev. 13.1-8, 16-17 with 14.1-5; 19.14-15.

111. Pohl's conjecture (*Offenbarung*, p. 226) that Isa. 49.10 and 25.8 may have been brought together through the *stichwort* עין, which can mean both *eye* and *spring* is rather dubious, particularly since Isa. 49.10 uses מבוע rather than עין.

Chapter 5

ISAIAH IN REVELATION 8–13

Revelation 8.5 → Isaiah 6.6
Only Charles and Schlatter accept this connection, citing Isa. 6.6 as the source for the *altar* (θυσιαστήριον), and the fire taken from it.[1] But there is no need to seek beyond Ezek. 10.2 for the imagery and setting of Rev. 8.5. The only aspect missing in Ezekiel 10 is explicit mention of the altar, but this is a basic feature of temple furnishing which needs no special source to account for its presence. John has just used θυσιαστήριον in 8.3 in relation to the prayers of the saints in a manner similar to standard cultic practice.[2] Furthermore, the agent in Revelation and Ezekiel is an angel, whereas in Isaiah it is one of the Seraphim which correspond to John's living creatures. Other parallels with Ezekiel 10 include the idea of *filling, fire* (versus simply *coals* in Isaiah), and the unique motif of casting fire to the earth as a symbolic prelude to divine judgment.

Revelation 11.2b → Isaiah 63.18
Isa. 63.18 is only one of many passages which speak of the trampling of the holy city or sanctuary by Israel's enemies. It is not even the closest parallel to Revelation 11, for Isa. 63.18 has *adversaries* instead of *nations*, and *sanctuary* rather than *holy city*. This idea is found also in Zech. 12.3 (LXX); *Pss. Sol.* 7.2; 17.22; 1 Macc. 3.45, 51; 4.60; 3 Macc. 2.18; Dan. 8.10, 13; Lk. 21.24; cf. Ps. 79.1. If a specific source is to be sought, Dan. 8.10-14 (cf. Lk 21.24, which is based on Daniel) offers more by way of correspondence in language and context than

1. Charles, *Revelation*, I, p. 229; Schlatter, 'Das alte Testament', p. 27.
2. Schürer, II, pp. 305-306; cf. Lev. 16.12-13; Ps. 141.2; Lk 1.10; Rev. 5.8, and K. Nielsen, *Incense in Ancient Israel* (VTSup, 38; Leiden, 1986), p. 87.

Isa. 63.18, especially since both Daniel 8 and Revelation 11 limit the trampling to a set period of time.[3]

Revelation 11.8b → Isaiah 1.10

In Rev. 11.8, the two witnesses are said to lie slain in the 'great city which is allegorically called Sodom and Egypt, where their Lord was crucified'. A few scholars, who identify the 'great city' as Jerusalem, mainly on the strength of the final clause, also list Isa. 1.10 as the precedent for the spiritual attribution of 'Sodom' to Jerusalem.[4] But this connection loses some of its force if it is accepted with most commentators that the city is not literally Jerusalem, but Rome, or the *universal city* as a symbol of corrupt humanity in general.[5] It appears more likely that the application of the epithet *Sodom* to this evil metropolis comes directly from the author's consideration of the proverbial city of Genesis and its fate.[6]

Revelation 11.9b → Isaiah 53.9 LXX

Kraft (*Offenbarung*, p. 159) proposes that the idea of the two witnesses who are refused burial has been influenced by Isa. 53.9 LXX and Ezekiel 37. Whereas the MT has 'they make his grave with the

---

3.   Only Marconcini ('L'utilizzazione', pp. 125, 134) accepts the use of Isa. 63.18 here unquestioningly, and even argues for the MT over the LXX! Kraft and Ozanne offer it as a partial parallel (*Offenbarung*, pp. 153-54; 'Influence', p. 171). The former argues in favor of the major influence of Zech. 12.2-3 LXX, *contra* Ozanne.

4.   Charles regards it as an echo (*Revelation*, I, p. lxxxi), while Marconcini ('L'utilizzazione', p. 133) goes so far as to suppose that John has replaced the *Gomorrah* of Isa. 1.10 with *Egypt*! The argument of Alford (followed by Mounce, *Revelation*, p. 226), that Isa. 1.10 refers to the people rather than to the city, is certainly wrong. The city is clearly implied, as was recognized by the author of the *Ascension of Isaiah* (3.10), where one of the accusations against the Prophet is that 'he has called Jerusalem Sodom'. Cf. *Targ. Isa.* where the meturgeman has removed the ambiguity to avoid possible insult to the city. Other uses of Sodom as a type are found in Isa. 3.9; Jer. 23.14; Ezek. 16.46-56; Lam. 4.6; Amos 4.11; Zeph. 2.9, Wis. 19.13-21 ties Sodom and Egypt together as types of godlessness and oppression.

5.   So Mounce, Swete, Kiddle–Ross, Kraft, Caird, Wellhausen, Munck, D'Aragon and Comblin; *contra* Charles, Beckwith and Wikenhauser; cf. Müller, *Offenbarung*, pp. 213-14.

6.   Note possible allusions to Sodom's destruction (Gen. 19.28) in Rev. 14.11; 19.3b.

wicked', the LXX reads 'I will give the wicked for (ἀντί) his burial'. Besides being highly improbable, this proposal is unnecessary.[7]

Revelation 12.1-6 → Isaiah 7.14; 26.17-27; 66.7-8
The interpretation of Revelation 12 has always been seen as one of the key issues in the understanding of the book as a whole. The object of an ever increasing mass of articles, books and appendices, this chapter has been submitted to an endless variety of approaches.[8] In the process virtually no historical, mythological, structural or linguistic stone has been left unturned in the attempt to illuminate the background and purpose of its symbols.

The major issue on which commentators differ concerns the sources of John's imagery and the extent of his own contribution. Two prevailing schools of thought have emerged. Some hold that—apart from minor redaction and additions—the bulk of the chapter, including its main characters and development, derives from a source(s) which John (or an editor) has taken over.[9] The basic features of this source are usually identified as belonging to a popular pagan myth involving a cosmic struggle between a woman, her child, and an adversary. Several versions of this myth circulated in the ancient world.[10] Other commentators however, while allowing various degrees of mythological influence, uphold the unity of the chapter and argue that most, if

7.   A much closer parallel is found in Ps. 79.1-4, which forms the inspiration for the interesting passage in 4QTanh I, 1–4: '...thy sanctuary, and shall dispute with the kingdoms over the blood of...Jerusalem, and shall see the bodies of Thy priests...and none to bury them' (Vermes, *The Dead Sea Scrolls*, p. 302).

8.   Bibliographical surveys of the interpretation of Rev. 12 are provided by P. Prigent, *Apocalypse 12: Histoire de l'exegese* (BGBE, 2; Tübingen, 1959), and A. Feuillet, 'Le Messie et sa Mère d'après le chapître xii de l'Apocalypse', *RB* 66 (1959), pp. 55-86. More recent treatments by these authors and others include: H. Gollinger, *Das 'Grosse Zeichen' von Apokalypse 12* (SBM, 11; Würzburg, 1971); Yarbro Collins, *Combat Myth*, pp. 57-156; Prigent, *L'Apocalypse*, pp. 176-82; R. Bergmeier, 'Altes und Neues zur "Sonnenfrau am Himmel (Apk 12)", Religionsgeschichtliche und quellenkritische Beobachtungen zu Apk 12,1-17', *ZNW* 73 (1982), pp. 97-108; A. Feuillet, 'La femme vêtue du soleil (Ap 12) et la glorification de l'Epouse du Cantique des Cantiques (6, 10). Réflexions sur le progrès dans l'interprétation de l'Apocalypse et du Cantique des Cantiques', *NovVet* 59 (1984), pp. 36-67.

9.   So Charles (following the influential source-critical study of Gunkel), Yarbro Collins, Bergmeier and Holtz, among others.

10.   Charles, *Revelation*, I, pp. 310-14; Yarbro Collins, *Combat Myth*, pp. 59-83.

not all, of the imagery and story line can be explained on the basis of OT allusions and Christian tradition.[11]

As is often the case in Revelation, both views have a certain amount of support from the evidence. On the one hand, there are striking similarities between the narrative in Revelation 12 and the so-called 'combat myth', a form of which was known in Asia Minor.[12] In addition, the chapter's structural and theological progression appears somewhat incongruous with John's style. On the other hand, John's method elsewhere almost always involves the use of OT traditions, and it would be hard to believe that in this all-important chapter he completely abandons his favourite source for an unassimilated pagan model. One solution proposes that John has taken over an earlier Jewish adaptation of the myth which already contained a messianic outlook and biblical language.[13] This is not unlikely.

In the end it seems best to conclude with Roloff that Revelation 12 reflects a combination of pagan myth, OT prophecy and Christian tradition.[14] Having taken over the basic framework of a well-known legend (whether from a source or oral tradition), John has filled the symbols with new meaning and given it a new context.[15] It appears

11. Comblin, Prigent, Feuillet, Kraft, Ford and Sweet (*Revelation*, p. 194), whose comment is representative of this position—that although John may use myth, the 'dominant imagery is biblical'.

12. Beckwith, *Apocalypse*, p. 615; Yarbro Collins, *Combat Myth*, pp. 70-71, 245-61. The latter argues for the dominant influence of the Leto–Apollo–Python myth, while Beckwith and other commentators suggest that John has adopted the basic pattern of a widely diffused legend with no specific connection to mythical personalities.

13. Charles, Kraft, Beckwith, Holtz and Yarbro Collins.

14. *Offenbarung*, p. 124. There is certainly no need or justification for presenting the myth theory and the OT theory as mutually exclusive. A certain amount of polarization has ensued from scholars emphasizing the one and ignoring the other. Thus Bergmeier ('Altes und Neues'), while reaffirming the need to recognize the mythical background and its importance for understanding the text, almost completely overlooks any possible OT influence. On the other side, M. McNamara, following Feuillet, completely dismisses any mythical dependence, 'Since it is psychologically unlikely that the author is passing in ch. 12 from biblical to pagan parallels, the context calls on us to interpret the entire chapter... in the light of the OT and Jewish traditions', *The New Testament and the Palestinian Targum*, p. 223. Cf. more recently Prigent, *L'Apocalypse*, p. 180.

15. Jewish and Christian assimilation and reapplication of popular legends is obviously not unique. Similar adaptations can be found in Isa. 14.12-15; Ezek. 28.11-19; Tobit; Herm. *Vis.* 4.1.2-10 (which develops a common superstition of

that this transformation is accomplished primarily by emphasizing those parts of the myth which correspond closely to OT prophecy as seen through the eyes of Jewish-Christian messianism, and then filling out this outline with further strategic allusions to the Scriptures. Apart from the Isaiah texts in question and the hymnic section (12.10-12), which will be discussed separately, clear allusions to the OT are found in Rev. 12.5 (Ps. 2.9), 12.14b (Dan. 7.25) and 12.9, 17 (Gen. 3).[16] Probable allusions occur in 12.3b (Dan. 7.7, 24), 12.4a (Dan. 8.10) and 12.14a (Exod. 19.4). How many of these allusions are to be attributed to John's hand and which were already part of his source(s) is in most cases impossible to determine.[17] The Isaiah allusions which have been proposed are: 7.14, 26.17–27.1 and 66.7-9. Keeping in mind the basic source-critical background given above, it is now possible to treat these proposals in more detail.

(1) *Rev. 12.1-2, 5*   *Isa. 7.14*

σημεῖον μέγα ὤφθη...	יתן אדני הוא לכם אות	δώσει κύριος αὐτὸς ὑμῖν σημεῖον
γυνὴ...ἐν γαστρὶ ἔχουσα	הנה העלמה הרה	ἰδοὺ ἡ παρθένος ἐν γαστρὶ ἕξει
καὶ ἔτεκεν υἱὸν ἄρσεν	וילדת בן	καὶ τέξεται υἱόν

At first glance the linguistic basis for accepting an allusion to Isa. 7.14 seems substantial, and it is thus not surprising that many commentators have accepted a conscious connection.[18] Assuming that this view

---

dragons which commanded roads and killed travelers), to name only a few.

16. The connection with Gen. 3 is especially evocative, extending to parallels in *characters* (woman, serpent, seed), and *context* (pain in childbirth and the origin of hostility towards the saints). C. Hauret goes so far as to call Rev. 12 a *midrash* on Gen. 3.15 ('Eve transfigurée. De la Genèse à l'Apocalypse', *RHPR* 59 [1979], pp. 327-39). M. Morgen points out similarities between John's method and the Targums ('Apocalypse 12, un targum de l'Ancien Testament', *Foi Vie* 80 [1981], pp. 63-74). Cf. the discussion above, Chapter 2 n. 5.

17. 'Whatever reminiscences of the OT may be found in this passage, it is not possible to determine whether these are the colouring given to the myth by the apocalyptist, or by its transmission through Hebrew tradition', (Beckwith, *Apocalypse*, p. 614). However, Ps. 2.9 in Rev. 12.5 is likely to be John's contribution since this Psalm generally and v. 9 in particular is employed elsewhere throughout Revelation. Note especially the prominence of Ps. 2 in the passage leading into ch. 12 (Rev. 11.15-18).

18. Charles, Kraft, Comblin, Feuillet, Roloff, Sweet, Lohmeyer, A.T. Kassing (*Die Kirche und Maria: Ihr Verhältnis im 12. Kapitel der Apokalypse* [Düsseldorf,

were correct, one of the more notable points to be observed is that John's version reflects the Hebrew עלמה (young woman) rather than the LXX παρθένος (virgin), a difference exploited predominantly by later Christian apologists. But a closer examination of this proposal raises a host of difficulties:

1. John's use of σημεῖον (*sign*) is not limited to the woman, but is applied similarly to the dragon (12.3), and the seven bowl angels (15.1). The word has more of an apocalyptic flavour to it and seems better understood in the company of such passages as Mt. 24.24, 30; Lk 21.11 etc.

2. The *Woman* in Revelation 12 appears to function mainly as a corporate image. This would bring it more in line with those OT passages which depict Zion as a woman or mother in travail, in contrast to the individual birth promise of Isaiah 7.[19]

3. Another integral feature of John's birth scene is the pain and torment of the mother; an idea entirely absent from the Immanuel prophecy. But not only do the Zion-woman traditions emphasize the motif of birth pangs, they also can account for the conventional birth language: ἐν γαρτρὶ ἔχειν and ἔτεκεν υἱόν/ἄρσεν.

4. Some scholars retain the allusion to Isa. 7.14 simply because it alone of the proposed Isaian birth texts can account for the use of υἱός in 12.5. But a more likely source for this designation is Ps. 2.7 where God declares: 'You are my *son*, today I have *begotten* you'. In Rev. 12.5, a clear allusion to Ps. 2.9 follows directly on from the birth of the son.[20] This will be developed in more detail below.

5. There is little evidence that the Immanuel prophecy of Isaiah 7 was widely employed in early Christian circles as a

1958]) and R.D. Aus ('The Relevance of Isaiah 66.7 to Revelation 12 and 2 Thessalonians 1', *ZNW* 67 [1976], pp. 252-68); *contra* Prigent.

19. It is widely acknowledged that the woman clothed with the sun, moon and stars is the anti-image of another collective figure in Rev. 17—the Harlot-Babylon—and symbolizes Mother-Zion, the persecuted messianic community, or some similar idea. Even Catholic interpreters have generally come to accept this conclusion and accord to Mary only a secondary allusion; Kassing, *Die Kirch und Maria*, pp. 29-75.

20. This connection seems to be confirmed by John's use of Ps. 2 in the letter to the church in Thyatira (2.18-29), which opens with the title Son of God (Ps. 2.7) and closes with promise of authority over the nations (Ps. 2.8-9).

messianic testimony. Apart from Mt. 1.23, and possibly Lk. 1.31, it does not figure in any early Christian literature including the Apostolic Fathers, and only seems to come to the fore with the second-century apologists.[21]

Finally, as one can see from the parallel texts above, a certain amount of ellipsis between three separate verses of Revelation (12.1, 2, 5) is necessary to bring out the similarities. While it is perhaps not possible to rule out the influence of Isa. 7.14 completely, the language and thought of John's birth narrative is better explained by other texts.

(2) *Rev. 12.2, 4b*   *Isa. 26.17*

(γυνὴ) ἐν γαστρὶ ἔχουσα,	הרה תקריב ללדת	ἡ ὠδίνουσα ἐγγίζει τοῦ
καὶ κράζει	תחיל תזעק בחבליה	τεκεῖν καὶ ἐπὶ τῇ
καὶ βασανιζομένη τεκεῖν...		ὠδῖνι αὐτῆς ἐκέκραξεν
τῆς μελλούσης τεκεῖν		

Following a description of the woman as the queen of heaven in Rev. 12.1 (cf. 17.1-6; 18.7), John goes on in 12.2 to reveal not only that the woman is pregnant, but that she is in an advanced stage of labour. The imminence of the birth is restated in 12.4b in more precise language: she is 'about to bring forth' (τῆς μελλούσης τεκεῖν). Most of the words or phrases used to describe the woman's condition are part of the typical vocabulary which one would expect to find in any birth narrative. But whereas one or more of these expressions is found in a number of biblical passages, the particular combination of ideas chosen by John comes strikingly close to the birth metaphor related in Isa. 26.17. When compared with the MT, the various components of Rev. 12.2, 4b admit the following parallels.

1. ἐν γαστρὶ ἔχειν is a stock periphrasis for the Hebrew הרה.
2. κράζω commonly translates זעק.
3. ὠδίνω is the standard equivalent of the verb חול, although it could also here be a verbal rendering of the noun חבל.[22]
4. τεκεῖν is the standard translation of the infinitive ללדת.

---

21. An explanation for this late start is perhaps to be found in the fact that Isa. 7 was not understood messianically in Jewish circles. There is some evidence that early Jewish interpreters regarded the Immanuel prophecy as fulfilled in Hezekiah. See B.M. Nolan, *The Royal Son of God* (Göttingen, 1979), pp. 67, 206-208.

22. חבל and חול → חיל (noun) are similar in meaning, and are often translated by the same Greek word in the LXX (ὠδίν). Cf. Jer. 22.23 where the two nouns are used synonymously.

5.   μέλλω with the infinitive τεκεῖν in Rev. 12.4b is an acceptable equivalent for the periphrastic בקריב ללדת.[23]

6.   The inspiration for the remaining term βασανίζω (*torment*)
is less certain, though it is not impossible as a rendering of
חול, which has a wide semantic range.[24] This correspondence
would allow ὠδίνω above (3) to be more certainly connected
with חבל.

Thus between the two passages, every verbal unit has a possible
parallel. To this can be added similarities in context. The most significant aspect which Revelation 12 shares with Isaiah 26 is the
application of the birth metaphor corporately to the elect, though with
one major difference. In Isaiah the birth language serves as a simile of
frustration and unfulfilment experienced by the community and
expressed to God. The nation has suffered the pains and agony
necessary for new birth without realizing the goal. The expectation of
salvation for itself (v. 18) and judgment on its enemies (v. 21)
remains frustrated. They went through the motions but only 'brought
forth wind'. In Revelation however, the goal is achieved and the
tension is resolved. The hopes and struggles of the salvation
community have been rewarded with the advent of the male child—
the messianic agent of judgment and salvation.

It is important to recognize that, in contrast to Revelation 12, Isaiah
26 does not contemplate a physical birth or appearance of a messianic
deliverer, but looks for the direct intervention of God. If John has
borrowed from Isaiah 26—and we must conclude that this is
extremely likely—it provided him with the language and context to
explain the condition of the woman (pregnant), the intensity of her
labour (full of pain and anguish), and the nearness of the birth
(imminent), but *not the birth itself*. It appears he only uses Isaiah 26

---

23. Cf. Gen. 12.11 where the *hifil* of קרב followed by the infinitive has the sense
of 'about to' (as the RSV recognizes).

24. According to BAGD, p. 134, βασανίζω can be used figuratively for any
severe mental or physical distress or torment, and the noun βάσανος is even used of
birth pangs. Over 30 different verbs are used to translate חול in the LXX, several of
which contain the idea of anguish and distress, e.g. ὀδυνάω, πονέω, φοβέω,
χειμάζω. The RSV translates βασανίζω in Rev. 12.2 with 'anguish' and Vermes
gives the same translation to חול in 1QH 3.8 (*Dead Sea Scrolls*, p. 171).

to illustrate the situation of the community in a state of anxiety and expectation and turns to a parallel text to bring about a resolution of the birth metaphor.[25]

(3) *Rev. 12.5-6*

καὶ ἔτεκεν υἱὸν ἄρσεν
καὶ ἡ γυνὴ ἔφυγεν εἰς τὴν ἔρημον

Isa. 66.7-8

והמליטה זכר   ἐξέφυγεν καὶ ἔτεκεν ἄρσεν

The contrast between Isa. 26.17 and 66.7-8 could not be greater. In the one Zion endures the pains of labour without giving birth; in the other she gives birth without even experiencing labour.

> Before she was in labour she gave birth
> before her pain came upon her
> she was delivered of a son...
> for as soon as Zion was in labour
> she brought forth her sons (66.7, 8b).

The influence of Isa. 66.7-8 in Rev. 12.5-6 is accepted by a wide variety of scholars,[26] who support this connection on the basis of:

1. Thematic similarities: A birth metaphor involving a collective mother (= Zion), and other considerations.
2. Dictional parallels: καὶ ἔτεκεν...ἄρσεν, and φεύγω.

Taking the second category first, the main item of interest is the double description υἱὸν ἄρσεν. Grammarians are divided over whether this combination is another example of John's habit of solecism. Instead of seeing ἄρσεν as a neuter adjective qualifying a masculine noun, some treat it as a second descriptive noun in apposition to υἱόν: i.e. 'she brought forth a son (υἱόν), a male child

---

25. Other similarities between Rev. 12 and Isa. 26.17–27.1 have been noticed: the hiding of the people for a short period in 26.20 (cf. Rev. 12.14), and the slaying of the dragon and serpent (LXX) by God in 27.1. While Rissi, Ford, Sweet and Kassing accept a connection in the case of 27.1, there is not enough evidence to make a certain judgment. John's use of ὄφις (serpent) is probably drawn from Gen. 3, and the dragon image is more likely to have originated from the source which he adapts. In addition, the dragon in Rev. 12 is not slain, he only suffers a reduction of authority.

26. Bousset, Torrey, Brownlee, Feuillet, Ford, Vos, Holtz, Kraft, Court, Sweet, Aus, Prigent and Roloff.

(ἄρσεν)'.[27] This conclusion would seem to be justified by Rev. 12.13 where the masculine ἄρσενα is used substantively. At any rate, the awkwardness of the double object is probably not occasioned by the presence of ἄρσεν, but by υἱόν. The reader is led to expect a birth announcement as a conclusion to the birth narrative begun in 12.2. The common and expected idiom would be ἔτεκεν υἱόν, less likely ἔτεκεν ἄρσεν, and unlikely, though not impossible, ἔτεκεν υἱόν ἄρσενα.[28] It would seem much easier to account for υἱός as a secondary addition rather than ἄρσεν. As has been argued above, the use of υἱός here is probably occasioned by the immediately following quotation of Ps. 2.9.

Rev. 12.5 appears to betray a synthesis of two layers of tradition—a primary source which simply provided the birth formula, and a secondary redaction on the basis of Ps. 2.7-9, which assigned the birth messianic significance.

1.   καὶ ἔτεκεν...ἄρσεν...(Isa. 66.7)
2.   υἱὸν...ὃς μέλλει ποιμαίνειν πάντα τὰ ἔθνη
           ἐν ῥάβδῳ σιδηρᾷ (Ps. 2.7, 9)

The relationship between υἱόν and the phrase from Ps. 2.9 is demonstrated by the use of the *masculine* relative ὅς, and is further supported by the previous collocation of the term *Son* (Ps. 2.7) and Ps. 2.8-9 in the Thyatiran letter.

As for the origin of the birth formula καὶ ἔτεκεν ἄρσεν, there is no one overwhelming factor which confirms dependence on Isa. 66.7,

27. MG, IV, p. 153; cf. II, p. 161; III, p. 315; BDF, 136.3; Charles, *Revelation*, I, p. 320.

28. τίκτειν ἄρσεν is used in LXX Exod. 1.16; 2.2; Isa. 66.7; Jer. 37.6; Lev. 12.2, 7; Jer. 20.15; cf. 1QH 3.9. The combination υἱὸς ἄρσην is unusual, though not unknown: Tob. 6.12 (S); CPR 28.12 (110 CE) τῶν δὲ ἀρρένων υἱῶν (MM, p. 79); PSI 9.1039.36 (LS, p. 1847). But in each of these examples ἄρσην is masculine and adjectival, with υἱός understood in the more general sense of *child*. No parallel has been found for the juxtaposition of υἱός with the neuter ἄρσεν as in Rev. 12.5, although Jer. 20.15 זכר בן has been suggested as a possible Hebrew precedent. But apart from the fact that זכר here is more naturally taken as an adjective, there is little in the context to warrant a connection with Rev. 12 (cf. Swete, *Apocalypse*, pp. 150-51). It is true that the earliest textual witnesses (P[47] א) read masc. ἄρσενα, but these MSS are considered inferior to those which contain the *lectio difficilior* (A C).

but the cumulative evidence favours such a connection.[29]
Not only does the collective image of Zion giving birth suit the corporate nature of the pregnant woman in Revelation 12, but the ambiguity of the metaphor in Isa. 66.7-8 allows for *both* an individual birth (the Messiah), and a collective birth (the salvation community).[30]

She was delivered of a *son* (Isa. 66.7b)
She brought forth a son, a male child (Rev. 12.5)

She brought forth her *sons* (Isa. 66.8b)
the woman [and]... the rest of her offspring (Rev. 12.17)

And in both passages the birth serves as a reference point for the eschatological inauguration of both judgment and salvation—salvation for the persecuted community (Isa. 66.5, 10-14a; Rev. 12.6, 10-11, 14-17), and judgment on its enemies, the nations (Isa. 66.6, 14b-18; Rev. 12.5, 7-9).[31]

29. Aus ('The Relevance of Isaiah 66.7', p. 255) thinks the use of φεύγω in both Rev. 12.6 and Isa. 66.7 makes the use of Isa. 66.7 in 12.5 certain. This does not seem to me a compelling argument. In the first place, the motif of flight is only found in the LXX, which gives (wrongly) a double translation of Hebrew מלט. Secondly, John uses φεύγω whereas the LXX has ἐκφεύγω. Granted, there is little difference in meaning between the simplex and compound forms. But this is just the point—why would he change it? Finally, a more fundamental difference is that in Isa. 66.7 LXX the woman flees and gives birth while in Rev. 12 she gives birth and then flees (cf. Ottley, *Isaiah*, II, p. 384).

30. An individual messianic interpretation of Isa. 66.7 can be found in both Jewish and Christian sources: *Targ. Isa.* 66.7; *Gen. R.* 85; *Lev. R.* 14.9; Justin *Dial.* 85.8-10; Iren. *Dem.* 54. 1QH 3.9 also appears to allude to 66.7, but it is debated whether an individual or collective sense is in view. For further discussion see Aus, 'The Relevance of Isaiah 66.7', pp. 256-63; cf. *TDOT*, IV, p. 347.

31. Isa. 66 appears to have become almost a standard proof text to illustrate eschatological judgment and was taken over early by Christian interpreters and applied to the parousia and judgment: 2 Thess. 1 (66.4-5, 15); Mk 9.48 (66.24); *2 Clem.* 7.6, 17.4-5 (66.18, 24); cf. CD 2.5 (66.15). John also appears to use 66.5 in connection with the bowl judgments in 16.1, 17. Aus discusses the use of this text in 2 Thess. in more detail ('The Relevance of Isaiah 66.7', pp. 264-68). For Rev. 12 and its relation to the inauguration of judgment and salvation see A. Vögtle, 'Mythos und Botschaft in Apokalypse 12', in G. Jeremias, H.-W. Kuhn and H. Stegemann (eds.), *Tradition und Glaube: Das frühe Christentum in seiner Umwelt*. Festgabe K.G. Kuhn (FS K. Kuhn; Göttingen, 1971), pp. 395-415.

Revelation 12.9 (9.1; 8.10-11) → *Isaiah 14.12-15*

Revelation	*Isaiah*
And the great dragon was thrown down... he was thrown down to the earth, and his angels were thrown down with him (12.9).	How you are fallen from Heaven, O Day Star, son of Dawn... you said in your heart, 'I will ascend to heaven; above the stars of God I will set my throne on high'...
I saw a star fallen from heaven to earth (9.1)	But you are brought down to Sheol, to the depths of the Pit.

A great star fell from heaven (8.10).

Isa. 14.5-20 contains the well-known taunt song against the king of Babylon, which forms part of a larger Babylon oracle covering Isa. 13.1–14.23. In vv. 12-15, the prophet draws on a current version of an ancient Canaanite myth to contrast the vainglorious ambitions of the Babylonian ruler with his subsequent downfall and death.[32] The principal description of the king as a *great star* who sought to set himself above the *stars of God* provided fertile ground for later speculation and reapplication in Jewish and Christian circles, when the association between stars and angels became a part of popular fancy. It is along these lines that commentators have supposed various points of contact between John's story of the dragon in Revelation 12 and the so-called Lucifer myth of Isaiah 14.

Rev. 12.7-9 relates that a war in heaven between Michael and his angels and the dragon and his angels resulted in the defeat of the latter and their ejection from heaven. It is the view of several commentators that the motif of the dragon's expulsion from heaven is based in part or whole on an interpretation of Isa. 14.12.[33] Since there is little evidence of any literary relationship, the basis for such a connection rests to a great extent on the history of interpretation of the Isaiah text and the dating of certain developments in Jewish and Christian angelology. An equally important factor in the discussion is the context and purpose of the dragon image in Revelation 12. When taken

---

32. For a discussion of the mythological background, see Wildberger, *Jesaja*, II, pp. 550-56, and the literature cited on p. 531.

33. Kraft, Roloff, Yarbro Collins, *Combat Myth*, p. 82; K.L. Schmidt, 'Lucifer als gefallene Engelmacht', *TZ* 7 (1951), pp. 161-79; and T.H. Gaster, *IDB*, IV, p. 227.

together, an evaluation of these elements casts even more doubt on an already tenuous connection.

To begin with, the spiritual interpretation of Isa. 14.12 with reference to a fall of Satan is only first attested certainly with Origen.[34] While such an exegesis is also contained in *2 En.* 29.3-5 and *Adam and Eve* 12–16, neither of these works can be positively dated before 100 CE.[35] To be sure, early Jewish interpretation and reapplication of Isaiah 14 can be found in many places, but it is never referred to Satan. Rabbinic testimony from at least the time of Johanan b. Zakkai († c. 80 CE) interprets the passage uniformly of Nebuchadnezzar.[36]

Earlier examples of reapplication in the Apocrypha and Pseudepigrapha likewise retain a historical understanding of Isa. 14.12-15 but contemporize it by applying it to current rulers who fit the proud king model or evil personages generally.[37] In view of the broad

34. Origin brought together texts from Job 41, Ezek. 28 and Isa. 14 and referred them to Satan's fall on account of pride; J.B. Russell, *Satan: The Early Christian Tradition* (Ithica, NY, 1981), pp. 130-31 n. 59. Contrary to the opinion of some, 1 Tim. 3.6, which warns against allowing a recent convert to become a bishop, 'or he may be puffed up with conceit and fall into the condemnation of the devil', does not probably refer to Satan's fall through pride. The 'condemnation of the devil' is better taken as a subjective genitive which alludes to Satan's classic role as accuser. This is supported by the synonymous parallelism with 3.7 and comparison with 2 Tim. 2.26.

35. Cf. Schürer, III.2, pp. 748-49, 759; *OTP*, I, pp. 94-95; II, p. 252; Russell, *Satan*, pp. 130-31 n. 59; and the important discussion of R. van den Broeck, *The Myth of the Phoenix according to Classical and Early Christian Traditions* (Leiden, 1972), pp. 287-93. Cf. also the late demonology of the *Testament of Solomon*, esp. 6.1-7.

36. *B. Hag.* 13a; *b. Hul.* 89a; *b. Pes.* 94ab; *Exod. R.* 8.2; 15.6; 21.3; *Lev. R.* 18.2; *Num. R.* 9.24; 20.1; *Midr. Ps.* 14.2. The comment of Ibn Ezra reflects the common acceptance of this interpretation, 'There is at least no doubt, that this verse refers to Nebuchadnezzar', *The Commentary of Ibn Ezra on Isaiah* (ed. M. Friedländer; London, 1873), I, p. 72. There are likewise no hints of anything but a historical interpretation of Isa. 14 in the LXX and Targum.

37. Isa. 14 is used as a model to describe Antiochus Epiphanes in Dan. 8.9-12, 11.36, and 2 Macc. 9.1-12; more generally of evil kings in *1 En.* 46.5-7; and of the enemies of the righteous in Wis. 4.18-19; 5.3-5; G.W.E. Nicklesburg, *Resurrection, Immortality and Eternal Life in Intertestamental Judaism* (Cambridge, 1972), pp. 15, 69-70, 75, 79-80; J.A. Goldstein, *II Maccabees* (AB, 41A; Garden City, 1983), pp. 353-55, 359; P. Skehan, 'Isaias and the Teaching of the Book of Wisdom', *CBQ* 2 (1940), p. 296. The connection of Dan. 7.8, 20, 25 with Isa.

diffusion of the historical interpretation of Isaiah 14 in early Judaism one would more naturally expect John to apply it to the beast rather than to Satan.[38]

Further difficulties arise when we consider the context of Revelation 12. To read into the description of the 'fall' of the dragon and his angels a Miltonian view of a primordial heavenly power-play is grossly anachronistic and misleading. In the first place, John gives no hint that the fall is the result of angelic ambitions and pride. Instead, Satan is cast in his typical role as the heavenly adversary—complete with explicit courtroom imagery.[39] Secondly, the heavenly battle and 'fall' is not presented as an event of the remote past but is understood as a direct consequence of the appearance and work of the Messiah.[40] And finally, Satan is not cast here into the pit, as in Isaiah 14 (this does not come until Rev. 20.1-3), but is simply expelled to the earth, his former privileged access to the divine throne-room being terminated. Thus the 'fall' of Satan here does not signify a change of character, but only a change of authority and sphere of operation.

It would seem unlikely, then, that John here (or his source) has utilized the myth of Isaiah 14 to describe the downfall of the dragon. The same conclusions can be drawn for Rev. 9.1, where the angel is most likely to be understood as a minion of Satan.[41] And this brings us

14.12-15 by M.E. Stone is less convincing (*OTP*, I, p. 568). The oracle against Capernaum in Mt. 11.23 and Lk. 10.15 has also been connected with Isa. 14.11, 13, 15, but may simply reflect a common metaphor; cf. Obad. 3-4 (influenced by Isa. 14?); *Sib. Or.* 3.360-61; 5.72; 8.101; *T. Mos.* 10.9; *T. Levi* 18.3.

38. As does *Gr. Apoc. Ezra* 4.29-32. *Apoc. Elij.* 4.7-15 uses Isa. 14 in reference to the Antichrist, but also compares him to a devil (4.12).

39. Especially Satan as ὁ κατήγωρ in 12.10b. Further use of legal terminology in this passage is discussed by Trites, *Witness*, p. 170-71. A. Wikenhauser summarizes, 'Nach dem AT und dem jüdischen Glauben zur Zeit Christi ist Satan kein gefallener Engel, sondern gehört zum göttlichen Hofstaat und hat dort die Funktion eines himmlischen "Staatsanwaltes", der die Menschen vor Gott verklagt', *Offenbarung*, p. 79. In addition to 1 Tim. 3.6 cited above (n. 34), Satan's role as adversary probably also lies behind such NT texts as Lk 22.31, 1 Pet. 5.8 and Jude 9, where Michael also figures prominently.

40. Rev. 12.10-11; 1.18; cf. Lk 10.18; Jn 12.31; Heb. 2.14-15; 1 Jn 3.8; Mk 3.22-27 par.; *T. Dan.* 5.10-11; *Asc. Isa.* 5.16; 7.12; Wikenhauser, *Offenbarung*, pp. 96-97; H.A. Kelly, 'The Devil in the Desert', *CBQ* 26 (1964), pp. 208-209; Bietenhard, *NIDNTT*, III, p. 470.

41. Especially if this angel is to be identified with the one named in 9.11. Those who recognize in 9.1 an evil angel include, Caird, Günther, Yarbro Collins, Ford,

to the remaining passage for which the influence of Isa. 14.12 has been suggested—Rev. 8.10.

The third angel blew his trumpet, and a great star fell from heaven, blazing like a torch, and it fell on a third of the rivers and on the fountains of water.

It was Caird who first put forth this proposal and saw in the falling star a symbol of 'Babylon' (= Rome).[42] While this view has the advantage of being nearer to the type of historical reapplication that Isaiah 14 enjoyed, it is extremely difficult to find an allusion to Babylon behind the imagery. Since the judgment of Babylon does not come until after Revelation 11, one would have to hold that 'Babylon' here is in some way employed in judging creation, which, if not impossible, remains a rather unlikely proposition. The tendency to invoke Isaiah 14 every time a text says 'a star fell from heaven' is mistaken, and ignores the fact that such a phrase was common parlance in ancient cosmology, apocalyptic imagery and metaphorical speech.

Revelation 12.12a → Isaiah 44.23; 49.13
These two Isaiah passages (44.23; 49.13) are frequently cited as parallels to John's summons to joy (*Jubelruf*) in Rev. 12.12a: διὰ τοῦτο εὐφραίνεσθε, [οἱ] οὐρανοί, although few commentators are prepared to suggest direct literary influence.[43] Very little can be added to this opinion and these Isaiah texts thus must remain merely close parallels. Apart from the fact that the basis for comparison is limited to two words, similar hymnic formulas consisting of calls to praise in the imperative are found elsewhere in the OT and in early Jewish literature (e.g. Deut. 32.43 LXX; Ps. 96.11 (95.11); 1 Chron. 16.31 LXX; cf. Pr. Azar. 36).[44]

Beasley-Murray, Roloff and Sweet. Only Kraft identifies him with Satan. The divine use of evil agents for the purposes of judgment is common: e.g. 1 Kgs 22.19-22; *1 En.* 53.5; CD 2.6; 8.2 (cf. 1QS 4.12); 1 Cor. 5.5; 1 Tim. 1.20; 3.6.

42. *Revelation*, p. 17; followed by Ford, Sweet and Marconcini.

43. But cf. Charles, *Revelation*, I, p. lxxix; Mussies, *Morphology*, p. 84; Kraft, *Offenbarung*, p. 169; and Ozanne, 'Influence', p. 120. Charles points out that the use of the plural οὐρανοί in 12.12 (otherwise only singular 49×) probably indicates the use of a source here.

44. The reading of Deut. 32.43 LXX (*heavens* versus MT *nations*) is supported by 4QDeut 8. Kraft and Prigent make special note of the similarity in context between Rev. 12.12a and Ps. 96.11 (95.11) (*Offenbarung*, p. 169; *L'Apocalypse*, p. 194).

The remaining proposals for the use of Isaiah in Revelation 12 and 13 (12.14 → 40.13; 13.8 → 53.7; 13.16 → 44.5) likewise do not rise above the level of parallels. The eagle wing tradition in Rev. 12.14 comes closer to Exod. 19.4, and Revelation 13 is dominated almost completely by allusions to Daniel.[45]

See further on the hymnic development and background Jörns, *Das hymnische Evangelium*, pp. 116, 140-41; cf. Trites, *Witness*, p. 172.

45. On Isa. 44.5 and 53.7 in Rev. 13, see V. Cruz, *The Mark of the Beast: A Study of ΧΑΡΑΓΜΑ in the Apocalypse* (Amsterdam, 1973), pp. 18, 74.

Chapter 6

ISAIAH IN REVELATION 14–19

Revelation 14.5a → Isaiah 53.9

Revelation	*Isaiah*	
καὶ ἐν τῷ στόματι	ולא מרמה	οὐδὲ εὑρέθη δόλος
αὐτῶν οὐχ εὑρέθη ψεῦδος	בפיו	ἐν τῷ στόματι αὐτοῦ
	Zeph. 3.13b	
	ולא ימצא בפיהם	καὶ οὐ μὴ εὑρεθῇ
	לשון תרמית	ἐν τῷ στόματι αὐτῶν
		γλῶσσα δολία

Rev. 14.5 concludes the description of the 144,000 who appear on Mount Zion with the Lamb (14.1-5). In hearing the phrase 'no lie was found in their mouth', the modern interpreter naturally is reminded of a similar quality attributed to the Servant in Isa. 53.9. This has led some commentators to the premature conclusion that John has specifically adapted this text in his portrayal of the holy remnant in 14.5.[1] But it appears almost certain that he had in mind a less familiar passage in Zeph. 3.13b which says of the remnant of Israel, 'They shall do no wrong and utter no lies, nor shall there be found in their mouth a deceitful tongue'.[2] Supporting evidence for this connection is substantial, extending to similarities in both context and language.

The setting of the salvation oracle contained in Zeph. 3.9-20 provides several analogies with Rev. 14.1-5, including the presence of the Lord in the midst of his holy remnant (3.13, 15, 17; Rev. 14.1), the mention of Mount Zion (3.11, 14, 16; Rev. 14.1), and the association of loud singing with salvation (3.17-18; Rev. 14.2-3). And whereas Isa. 53.9 only involves the speech of a single individual (αὐτοῦ), Rev.

1. Including Swete, Ford, Sweet, Bauckham, and especially Caird, *Revelation*, pp. 180-81.
2. Accepted by Charles, Lohmeyer, Wikenhauser, Kraft, Mounce, Trudinger and Ozanne. Kraft provides the most extensive discussion (*Offenbarung*, p. 190).

14.5 follows Zeph. 3.13 in depicting the truthful character of the salvation community collectively (αὐτῶν).

Finally, although John's use of ψεῦδος instead of לשון תרמית/γλῶσσα δολία may be his own adaptation (for he commonly uses ψεῦδος and its cognates), a possible antecedent may be found in Zeph. 3.13a ולא ידברו כזב ('and they shall speak no lie'), a phrase leading directly into the clause which John borrows.[3]

However, a primary allusion to Zephaniah 3 does not necessarily rule out an allusion to Isa. 53.9 altogether. In fact, the context of Rev. 14.1-5 supports the supposition that the corporate application of Zephaniah 3 is part of a larger evocation of shared characteristics between the Lamb and the 144,000, which *presupposes* an individual application of Isa. 53.9 to Christ.

In the description of the multitude standing on Mt Zion (14.1-5), John combines holy war and sacrificial imagery in accordance with his program of victory through suffering and martyrdom. The supreme example has been set by the Lamb (5.5-6), and those who wish to be fellow-conquerors must 'follow the Lamb wherever he goes' (14.4). Not only this, but they must share his qualifications to be perfect sacrifices to God (cf. 6.9).[4] No deceit was found in his mouth, and no lie shall be found in their mouths.

Thus, by exploiting not only the similarity in language between Isa. 53.9 and Zeph. 3.13, but also the referential distinction between an individual and corporate subject, John sets out before the community a divine precedent for their partnership of innocence with the Lamb.[5]

Revelation 14.9c-20a; 19.13a, 15c → Isaiah 63.1-6
The justification for treating these two discontinuous passages of Revelation jointly derives from more than just the possibility that they make use of the same OT text. A more fundamental structural and thematic relationship exists between the units of 14.14-20 and 19.11-21.

---

3. Ozanne, 'Influence', p. 122. כזב is translated both with ψεῦδος and ψευδής in the LXX.

4. John's development of holy war and sacrificial concepts in 14.1-5 is discussed in detail by Bauckham (*Climax of Prophecy*, pp. 229-32), whose comments have significantly influenced my own discussion.

5. Therefore, even though Caird and Bauckham incorrectly attribute Isa. 53.9 to the 144,000, they rightly perceive the martyrs as the corporate analogue of the suffering Servant, Jesus.

Together with 6.12-17 they describe the same eschatological event—the parousia—from various perspectives and in increasing detail.[6] The general sketch of the Day of the Lord in 6.12-17 is given sharper focus in the harvest metaphors of 14.14-20, which in turn anticipates the ultimate intervention of the messianic judge in 19.11-21. In each of these sections the final encounter between evil people and a holy God is conceived in terms of a military conflict and developed to a large extent according to biblical traditions of the Day of Yahweh and holy war.

In the pericope of harvest and judgment in 14.14-20, John has woven together elements from the OT prophets, Jewish apocalyptic and early Christian tradition, and arranged this material into two interdependent units: 14.14-16 and 14.17-20. While there is virtual unanimity among commentators that the grape harvest in 14.17-20 concerns the judgment of the wicked, there is as yet no consensus as to the significance of the unspecified harvest in 14.14-16.[7] It has been variously understood as a general harvest of the righteous and wicked together, a harvest of the righteous alone, or simply a doublet of the following harvest of the wicked. A decision on this issue is not crucial to our discussion, since John's use of Isaiah involves mainly the second account of the grape harvest. However, I favour the view that both units are parallel images of judgment.[8]

What is important to recognize is that the activity of reaping and gathering in 14.14-19a does not constitute the judgment itself, but is preparatory to the act of judgment illustrated by the winepress metaphor of 14.19b-20. The harvest, the gathering, and the casting of the ripe clusters into the winepress are preliminary stages leading to the formal ceremony of judgment. The introductory tasks can be

6.   So also Charles, Beckwith, Ford, Wikenhauser, Müller and Yarbro Collins (*Combat Myth*, p. 37 and n. 123).

7.   It may be implied from the use of θερισμός and ξηραίνω that a *grain* harvest is here in view. This would accord with John's use of Joel 4.13a where קָצִיר, which especially denotes the grain harvest, is used.

8.   With the first a general overview, and the second providing a more detailed development. This procedure would accord well with John's frequent use of doublets in a relationship of summary and expansion (e.g. 14.8-11 // chs. 17–18; 19.7-9 // 21.2, 9-21; 21.1-8 // 21.9–22.5). And it is also in harmony with the singular focus on the judgment of the nations in Joel 4.13, which underlies *both* units of the pericope.

performed by angels. The judgment itself is performed only by the messianic Warrior (19.15).

Therefore, it would seem necessary to view all of 14.14-20 as a linear development of eschatological traditions leading to a preconceived climax. It is this climax of judgment which is the goal of the pericope from the beginning.

This is not to say that the prophet here is simply informing the church about the fate of its enemies. John is addressing those tempted to exchange the future glory of the New Jerusalem for the present glory of 'Babylon', and the worship of God for the worship of the beast, whether by enticement or pressure. Some have already made the break (Rev. 3.4), others have opted for a more syncretistic approach (2.14-15, 20-22), and others are dangerously near the edge (2.24-25; 3.2-3; cf. 18.4).

Consequently, we must not assume that in John's mind there was a clear division between those harvested for salvation and those harvested for judgment. His concern is that when the 'harvest' does occur there may be some within the range of his prophetic authority who will be gathered out and judged with the beast and his followers. Such an understanding of the paraenetic significance of the harvest pericope fits well with the series of final warnings and exhortations which lead up to it (14.6-13).

a. *Revelation 14.19c-20a*. Having set out the logical development and contextual framework of this section (14.14-20), it is now possible to examine the scriptural sub-structure on which it is based. The main item of interest is of course the use of Isaiah, but it will be helpful to outline the other traditions employed in this unit.

1. The harvest pericope opens with a visionary description of a figure like a son of man having a golden crown and seated on a cloud (14.14). This picture is unquestionably based on Daniel 7.13-14, either directly or filtered through synoptic traditions.[9] The kingly crown

---

9. Schüssler Fiorenza (*Revelation*, p. 103) sees here the influence of Mk 13.26-27 par. The major difference between Revelation and the Gospels in this regard is that in the latter the angels are the agents of the eschatological harvest, while in the former the son of man figure himself does the reaping. John apparently follows a variant, perhaps earlier and less developed Jewish messianic tradition, such as is attested in *Apoc. Abr.* 31.1 and *2 Bar.* 72.2; cf. *Did.* 10.5; 16.6-8.

bears out the relationship of this section with 19.11-21, and anticipates the formal announcement of Christ as king of kings in 19.16 (cf. 17.14; 19.12). The identification of this figure with the Messiah seems confirmed by the use of Daniel 7, since it is unlikely that John would apply this traditional text to an angel.[10]

2. The form and much of the language of the angelic commands to reap and gather is drawn from Joel 3.13a (MT 4.13a), 'Send forth the sickle, for the harvest is ripe'.

Rev. 14.15b	*Rev. 14.18c*
Send your sickle and reap	*Send your* sharp *sickle*
for the hour to reap has come,	and gather the clusters
for the harvest of the earth *is ripe*	of the vine of the earth,
	for her grapes *are fully ripe*

In both verses John has expanded Joel's bicolon with an additional stich. The middle stich of 14.15b is probably taken from Jer. 51.33c, where the future judgment of Babylon is compared to a threshing-floor when it is trodden, and the prophet states, 'the time of her harvest will come'.

3. The completion of the gathering of the grapes in 14.19ab leads directly into the winepress metaphor in 14.19c-20a. It is natural to assume that since Joel 4.13 serves as the backbone of John's redaction from vv. 15-18 that the winepress metaphor of vv. 19-20 simply continues this dependence. This is undoubtedly so, but there is more to it than that. It appears that John has here brought together two texts, Joel 4.13 and Isa. 63.3, both of which use the trampling of a winepress as a figure for judgment.

---

10. *Contra* Yarbro Collins, *Combat Myth*, p. 37. The eschatological appearance of the Son of Man or the Messiah on a cloud or with the clouds is never understood of an angel: Mk 13.26-27; 14.62; Mt. 24.30; 26.64; Lk. 21.27; Acts 1.9; *4 Ezra* 13.1-3; *Did.* 16.8; *Sib. Or.* 2.240-44; and most significantly Rev. 1.7. The objection that a Christian writer would hardly have an angel give orders to Christ is misplaced, and ignores the fact that the angel is simply an intermediary who delivers the message from the temple, i.e. from God himself, the Lord of the harvest (Mt. 9.38). Cf. D'Aragon, *JBC*, II, p. 485.

And he cast it into the great winepress of the wrath of God and the winepress was trodden ...and blood came out of the winepress (Rev. 14.19c-20a).	Come, tread ye, for the winepress is full, the vats overflow (Joel 4.13b). I have trodden the winepress alone...and trampled them in my wrath; their lifeblood is sprinkled upon my garments (Isa. 63.3).

Both OT passages concern the day of God's judgment against his enemies and both present this judgment in terms of holy war (Joel 4.9-16; Isa. 63.1-6).[11] A comparison of individual motifs shows that Joel alone cannot completely account for all the elements in John's description.

Rev. 14.19c-20a	Joel 4.13	Isa. 63.2-3
winepress	winepress	winepress
wrath	—	wrath
trampling	trampling	trampling
blood	—	blood

The probability that the additional features of *wrath* and *blood* are traceable to a relationship with Isaiah 63 is increased by their recurrence in Rev. 19.13-15, where the inspiration of Isaiah 63 is virtually certain.[12]

As has been noted above, the goal of the harvest pericope (14.14-20) is the trampling of the winepress. Everything from the first reaping to the casting in of the grapes is part of the introductory drama. It is appropriate then that Isaiah 63 only comes into play after the harvest language and in connection with the formal act of judgment itself, since the ideas of harvest, reaping and gathering are not found there.

The agent of trampling who will administer God's wrath is for now veiled in the passive ἐπατήθη, awaiting fuller revelation in 19.13, 15. It is not until this parousia vision that the implications of the winepress judgment in 14.19c-20 are finally developed.

11. Taking up again the theme of 6.12-17. The use of these underlying holy war texts shows a stronger connection between 14.14-20 and the combat settings of 6.12-17 and 19.11-21 than is at first evident on the surface, where only 14.20 implies a military conflict.

12. Commentators who accept the use of Isa. 63 in 14.19-20 include Bousset, Charles, Caird, Ozanne, Kraft, Yarbro Collins, Schüssler Fiorenza, Roloff, Müller and Günther.

b. *Revelation 19.13, 15*

Rev. 19.13, 15	*Isa. 63.2-3*
He is clad in a garment dipped in blood... and he himself will tread the winepress of the wine of wrath of the anger of God almighty.	Why is thy apparel red, and thy garments like his that treads in the winepress? I have trodden the winepress alone, and from the peoples no one was with me; I trod them in my anger, and trampled them in my wrath; their lifeblood is sprinkled upon my garments, and I have stained all my raiment.

Isa. 63.1-6 depicts Yahweh as a warrior returning victorious from battle, drenched in the blood of his enemies. The conquered foe is designated as Edom, but this is probably a collective cipher for God's eschatological enemies in general. The occasion for the conflict is two-fold, encompassing both vindication and salvation (63.1), vengeance and redemption (63.4).

There is little disagreement among commentators that this passage has inspired John's description of the messianic Warrior dressed in a blood-stained robe and treading the winepress of judgment.[13] Besides these two dominant features, two lesser parallels not generally noticed by interpreters may be added.

1.   The use of both wrath and anger in Isa. 63.3, 6 and Rev. 19.15 (אף, חמה // θυμός, ὀργή).
2.   An emphasis on the singular activity of the agent of judgment, expressed by the emphatic 'I' and 'I alone' of Isa. 63.1, 3 and the double αὐτός in Rev. 19.15.[14]

In Rev. 19.13 the figure of Christ wearing a bloodstained robe has occasioned some debate among commentators. With whose blood is the robe stained? Christ's own, or that of his enemies, or perhaps that of the martyrs'?[15] When one takes into consideration the interrelationship

13. So Bousset, Swete, Lohmeyer, Beckwith, Preston–Hanson, Ford, Caird, Ozanne, Kraft, Schüssler Fiorenza, Wikenhauser, Mounce, Holtz, Yarbro Collins, Prigent, Günther, Müller, Beasley-Murray and Roloff.

14. Ford, *Revelation*, p. 321 is the only one to mention this possible parallel. Although in Rev. 19 Christ is accompanied by heavenly armies, they play no role in the execution of judgment. Cf. 2 Thess. 1.6-10; *4 Ezra* 13.3-11; 32-38; *Num. R.* 11.7 (commenting on Isa. 63.3a): 'He fights by his name alone and requires no aid'.

15. Rissi, *Future*, pp. 23-24, argues strongly for identification with Christ's blood, and similar proponents are listed by Brütsch, *Offenbarung*, II, p. 301. The

between Rev. 14.19-20 and 19.13, 15 and their mutual association with Isaiah 63, there can hardly be any doubt that the blood of Christ's enemies is intended. The messianic Warrior tramples his enemies in the winepress of God's wrath and their blood flows out 'up to the horse's bridle' (14.20; 19.15). The natural result for the treader is a blood-stained robe which becomes a symbol of victory (19.13). This metaphor of judgment follows exactly the scenario of Isaiah 63.[16]

Those who object to this interpretation make much of the fact that Christ appears in a blood stained robe *before* the winepress judgment even takes place. But such an approach suffers from over-literalism. Presenting events in their logical sequence is not a major concern of John's, either here or elsewhere in the book.[17]

It should not be surprising that John has here transferred the imagery of Isaiah 63, where God is the agent, to Christ, since it is characteristic of him and early Christian writers in general to assimilate Day of the Lord and judgment texts to the Messiah as God's agent.

interpretation of the blood as that of the martyrs has been suggested by Caird, *Revelation*, pp. 192-93, 242-44.

16. Those who maintain the 'Christ's blood' view necessarily play down the influence of Isa. 63 in Rev. 19.13 and elicit support by emphasizing the preferred reading βεβαμμένον (*dipped, dyed*) over the slightly weaker attested variants based on ῥαντίζω (*sprinkle*). There is little agreement among textual critics and commentators on this problem. Hort believed that ῥεραμμένον was original and best explained the rest of the variants (followed by Swete, *Apocalypse*, p. 252). Others take the opposite view and consider ῥαντίζω a scribal harmonization to Isa. 63.3 (cf. Metzger, *Textual Commentary*, pp. 763-64). Kraft, on the other hand, thinks the reading closest to Isa. 63.3 should be accepted and takes βεβαμμένον as a deliberate scribal alteration to make the blood Christ's (*Offenbarung*, p. 249). Prigent accepts both βεβαμμένον and the direct use of Isa. 63.3 on the basis of a somewhat convoluted argument related to *Targ. Gen.* 49.11 (*L'Apocalypse*, pp. 294-95). Despite all the attention devoted to this dilemma, no one seems to have noticed that βάπτω is not itself inappropriate for describing the scene portrayed in Isa. 63.1-6. Difficulties are created only when one wishes to connect John's description specifically with Isa. 63.3a 'Their lifeblood is *sprinkled* upon my garments'. A robe dyed, as it were, in blood, is implied in 63.1a חמוץ בגדים; 63.2a אדם ללבושך, and 63.3cβ 'I have stained all my raiment'. And although βάπτειν usually has the meanings to *dip* or to *dye*, it does occur in connection with *blood* in the sense of stain or *sprinkle*: J.A. Scott, 'The Meaning of the Verb βάπτω, βαπτίζω', *ClassJ* 16 (1921–21), pp. 53-54. The absence of ἐν in 19.13 would seem to favour such a rendering.

17. Holtz, *Christologie*, p. 172; Müller, *Offenbarung*, p. 327.

Nevertheless, John's messianic interpretation of Isa. 63.1-6 may be the result of a more complex exegetical procedure, whereby a non-messianic text has been reinterpreted in the light of a messianic text which contains similar ideas or terminology.

A possible catalyst for this modification is found in Gen. 49.11b, where it is prophesied of Judah, 'he washes his garments in wine and his vesture in the blood of grapes'. John has already used Gen. 49.9 messianically in Rev. 5.5, and it is significant that the context of 19.11-15 is dominated by similar testimonies traditionally associated with the Davidic Messiah (Isa. 11, Ps. 2).[18] The shared language and imagery between Genesis 49 and Isaiah 63 consisting of a figure whose *garments* are soaked in 'blood' offers a ready basis for comparison.

That this kind of thematic assimilation could and did take place in Palestinian messianism is confirmed by the Palestinian Targum to Gen. 49.11, where the warrior Messiah is described in terms borrowed from Isaiah 63.

> How beautiful is King Messiah who is to arise
> from among those of the house of Judah!
> He girds his loins and goes out to wage war on those
> that hate him, and slays kings with their rulers,
> making the mountains red with the blood of their slain
> and making the hills white with the fat of their warriors
> and his vestments are soaked in blood.
> He is like a presser of grapes.[19]

The similarity between the Targum interpretation and Revelation 19 was first pointed out by Schlatter and was more fully explored later by P. Grelot, and to a lesser extent M. McNamara.[20] But whether or not this Targum interpretation pre-dates 100 CE, as Grelot and McNamara believe, is difficult to prove. Still, the close affinities between the Targum and Revelation warrant the consideration that John may here be influenced by current Jewish exegesis.

18. Gen. 49.11b may also lie behind Rev. 7.14.

19. Translation by M. McNamara, *Palestinian Targum*, p. 232. For the dating of haggadic additions in the Palestinian Targum, see Schürer, I, pp. 104-105.

20. P. Grelot, 'L'exégèse messianique d'Isaïe LXIII,1–6', *RB* 70 (1963), pp. 371-80; M. McNamara, *Palestinian Targum*, p. 232. Prigent tries to confirm John's dependence on the Targum by arguing for a textual link on the basis of βάπτω (*L'Apocalypse*, pp. 294-95).

Revelation 15.8 → Isaiah 6.1c, 4b

Revelation	*Isaiah*	
καὶ ἐγεμίσθη ὁ ναὸς καπνοῦ	ושוליו מלאים את	καὶ πλήρης ὁ οἶκος
ἐκ τῆς δόξης τοῦ θεοῦ	ההיכל	τῆς δόξης αὐτοῦ... καὶ
καὶ ἐκ τῆς δυνάμεως αὐτοῦ	והבית ימלא עשן	ὁ οἶκος ἐπλήσθη καπνοῦ

With regard to the cultic imagery of Rev. 15.8, most commentators are content to see a more general OT background related to theophany texts such as Exod. 40.34-35; 1 Kgs 8.10-11; 2 Chron. 5.14, 7.1-2; Isa. 6.4; Ezek. 10.3-4; 43.5; 44.4.[21] Only a handful suggest a more definite connection with Isa. 6.4.[22] A comparison of Isaiah 6 with the other passages listed above provides fairly convincing evidence that John does indeed make specific use of Isaiah 6 here.

1. In all the OT only Isa. 6.4b speaks of *smoke* (καπνός) filling the temple, while the other texts use *glory* or *cloud*.

2. John's passive construction with ἐγεμίσθη conforms exactly to Isaiah's ימלא (*niphal*), whereas the other passages (except Ezek. 10.4) all use מלא in an active syntax.

3. Only Isaiah 6 contains the exact term *temple* (היכל = John's ναός) in relation to the filling, while other texts adopt *house* (בית = οἶκος). Isaiah also uses בית in 6.4b, but it refers back to the היכל of 6.1. It appears, then, that John has conflated the two 'filling' phrases in 6.1c and 6.4b.[23]

In addition to this evidence from vocabulary and structure, there is good reason to suppose that the use of Isa. 6.1, 4 in Rev. 15.8 forms a thematic link with the use of Isa. 6.2-3 in Rev. 4.8. The significance of this relationship and the purpose of both allusions in the overall context of Revelation is discussed above (pp. 143-49).

---

21. So Swete, Beckwith, Lohmeyer, Caird, Kraft, Ford, Prigent and Müller. Exod. 40.35 (or 2 Chron. 7.2) may have inspired the second half of Rev. 15.8 (cf. 15.5).

22. Charles, Schlatter, Kiddle–Ross, Ozanne and Trudinger.

23. Both the LXX and Targum interpret the *skirt* (שול) in 6.1c as the 'glory' of God. John explains the smoke as symbolic of both God's glory (δόξα) and power (δύναμις). While the relationship between *smoke* and *glory* is implied in Isa. 6, the connection between *smoke* and *power* may have been inspired by the secondary meaning of the verb עשן 'to be wrathful', in relation to the expression of God's anger (Deut. 29.20; Pss. 74.1; 80.5).

Revelation 16.1a, 17b → Isaiah 66.6a

Revelation	Isaiah	
καὶ ἤκουσα μεγάλης	קול מהיכל	φωνὴ ἐκ ναοῦ, φωνὴ
φωνῆς ἐκ τοῦ ναοῦ...		
καὶ ἐξῆλθεν φωνὴ μεγάλη	קול יהוה מֹשֵלם	κυρίου ἀνταποδιδόντος
ἐκ τοῦ ναοῦ ἀπὸ τοῦ θρόνου	גמול לאיביו	ἀνταπόδοσιν τοῖς
		ἀντικειμένοις

The influence of Isaiah here seems likely, though the possibility that
the 'voice from the temple' is simply a natural apocalyptic development growing out of the heavenly temple setting leaves the question
uncertain.[24] The context in Isaiah of Yahweh 'rendering recompense
to his enemies' fits well with the inauguration of divine judgment in
Revelation 16. It is also important to note that John uses the following
verse of Isaiah (66.7) in ch. 12. Perhaps ἀπὸ τοῦ θρόνου in 16.17 is
an oblique periphrasis of Isaiah's φωνὴ κυρίου.

Revelation 16.12 → Isaiah 11.15-16

Revelation	Isaiah
The sixth angel poured his bowl on the great river Euphrates, and its water was dried up, to prepare the way for the kings from the east.	And the Lord... will wave his hand over the River with his scorching wind, and smite it into seven channels that men may cross dryshod.

In Isa. 11.11-16 the return of the remnant of Israel from dispersion is
explicitly compared with the Exodus from Egypt. In particular, the
Red Sea deliverance becomes the model and inspiration for describing
the divine removal of a new barrier between captivity and freedom:
the Euphrates river. The same miracle of deliverance is given a more
eschatological setting in Zech. 10.10-11 and *4 Ezra* 13.39-47. In each
case the purpose of the supernatural event relates to the return of
God's holy remnant, and only in Zechariah does God specifically dry
up the water.

These traditions are significantly different from the presentation
which John gives. In Revelation 16 the drying up of the Ephrates does
not provide a road for salvation but for judgment. The suggestion of
some that John here intentionally reverses the goal of the miracle
tradition seems somewhat forced. Neither are there any compelling

24. Only Kraft, Holtz and Ozanne posit a direct connection. Cf. also the similar
vocabulary and context of Jer. 25.30-31.

dictional connections between Revelation 16 and Isaiah 11.[25]

A more fitting biblical model is found in Joshua 3–5 where the waters of the Jordan river are held back so that the Israelite forces can engage in conquest. Echoes of the subsequent fall of Jericho appear to lie behind the collapse of the cities of the nations in Rev. 16.19. The transfer of this tradition to the Euphrates river does not require a biblical source, for in John's day the river was well recognized as a natural boundary between Parthia and Rome, and a major obstacle in the movement of large armies.[26]

Revelation 16.16 → Isaiah 14.13

In Rev. 16.13-14 three demonic spirits are sent out as agents of the evil triad to gather together the kings of the whole world for the final battle. After the somewhat disruptive interjection of 16.15, the assembly point for these kings and their armies is revealed: 'And they assembled them at the place which is called in Hebrew Armageddon' (16.16). Numerous theories have arisen in the attempt to explain the source and significance of the transliterated Hebrew place name Ἁρμαγεδών.

One such hypothesis, proposed by F. Hommel in 1890 and taken up by a few more recent commentators, sees Ἁρμαγεδών as a corruption of הר מוֹעֵד in Isa. 14.13.[27] Har Moʻed is the 'Mount of Assembly', the sacred mountain of the north where the gods convened, according to the Canaanite myth which lies behind Isa. 14.12-15. It is to this

---

25. Beasley-Murray, *Revelation*, p. 244; Roloff, *Offenbarung*, p. 163. Only Ozanne ('Influence', p. 179) and Marconcini ('L'utilizzazione', p. 126) uphold a direct connection with Isa. 11.15-16. Other commentators relate it more generally to the Red Sea event and subsequent typological development, of which Isa. 11 stands as the prime example. Cf. Jer. 51.36.

26. Tacitus, *Hist.* 5.9; *Ann.* 15.17. That a successful fording of the Euphrates was a prime military concern is well illustrated in *Ann.* 6.37, where Tacitus states that the Parthians sought a good omen of crossing through the sacrificial offering of a horse to the river. Rivers were respected as ancient and natural defenses and any significant drop in water level was considered a prodigy (*Hist.* 4.26; cf. Josh. 5.1). Some commentators suggest that John may have had in mind Cyrus's conquest of Babylon, facilitated by diverting the Euphrates (Herodotus 1.191); see Swete, *Apocalypse*, p. 205, and esp. W.H. Shea, 'The Location and Significance of Armageddon in Rev. 16.16', *AUSS* 18 (1980), pp. 157-62.

27. *NKZ* 1 (1890), pp. 407-408, cited by Brütsch, *Offenbarung*, pp. 215-17, along with other proposals. Other commentators who accept this theory or lean towards it include C.C. Torrey ('Armageddon [Apoc 16, 16]', *HTR* 31 [1938], pp. 237-48), Ford, Kraft and Roloff.

holy height that the haughty king of Babylon presumes to exalt himself. As the 'demonic counterpart of Mt Zion (Rev. 14.1)', Har Mo'ed would be a fitting site for the *gathering* of the arrogant earthly kings.[28]

The phonetic dissimilarity between מוֹעֵד and μαγεδών is explained on the basis of a common occurrence whereby the Hebrew letter ע (ayin) is represented by a Greek γ (gamma), thus producing μωγέδ. According to this theory, then, John originally wrote 'Αρ-μωγέδ, which in the earliest stages of scribal transmission became assimilated to the more familiar ('Αρ-)μαγεδών.

While this theory has an initial attractiveness, it is much more natural, both philologically and contextually, to associate μαγεδών with the biblical Megiddo, the proverbial site of many ancient battles.[29] Admittedly, the textual variants for 'Αρμαγεδών are quite diverse, but there is nothing to suggest that any other word besides Μαγεδδώ = Megiddo was ever in view. The form attested by the best witnesses (Αρ)μαγεδών is used to translate מְגִדּוֹ in Judg. 1.27 (LXX A), 2 Chron. 35.22, and some MSS of Jos. *Ant.* 8.151.[30] In comparison with this straightforward transliteration, the consonantal and vocalic changes necessary to make מועד into μαγεδών are too great to seriously challenge the majority view.[31]

The argument from context is on no better grounds. Isa. 14.12-15 has nothing to do with armies or battles, and the mountain mentioned serves only as a metaphor to illustrate the arrogant attitude of an earthly king. It is not in any way associated with judgment. As

28. Ford, *Revelation*, p. 274.

29. So the majority of commentators: Charles, Beckwith, Swete, Lohmeyer, Jeremias (with reservation), Ozanne, D'Aragon, Wikenhauser, Beasley-Murray, Sweet, Prigent, Müller and Shea. Why the ancient city of Megiddo, located in a plain, is associated by John with a mountain has not yet been satisfactorily explained. The most likely theory supposes here the conflation of two traditions: (1) Megiddo as a strategic military site and location of many battles (2); Ezek. 38–39, where the eschatological battle takes place on the 'mountains of Israel' (Müller, *Offenbarung*, p. 282); cf. Isa. 13.2-6; 14.25.

30. Hoskier, *Concerning the Text*, II, p. 433; Metzger, *Textual Commentary*, p. 757. μαγεδδών is found in Josh. 12.21(A) and some MSS of 2 Kgs 9.27. The Hebrew spelling מְגִדּוֹן is attested only in Zech. 12.11. On this form see Gesenius, *Hebrew Grammar*, §85v.

31. The problems and possibilities related to orthography and transliteration are discussed in detail by Jeremias, 'Har Magedon (Apc 16, 16)', *ZNW* 31 (1932), p. 77.

E. Powers has stated, 'All interpretations of the Hebrew expression, Armageddon, except the obvious one, 'mount of Megiddo', are too fanciful to be seriously considered'.[32]

Revelation 14–19 → Isaian Oracles against the Nations

The general structure and use of biblical traditions in Revelation 14–19 has already been discussed above in the thematic analysis of eschatological judgment. There it was seen that John develops his own prophecy of judgment against 'Babylon' in accordance with OT oracles against the nations. Those traditions which dominate are the Babylon oracle of Jeremiah 50–51 and the Tyre oracle of Ezekiel 26–27. In addition to these primary texts, he borrows motifs from shorter Babylon and Tyre oracles found in Isaiah. Together with an Edom oracle from Isaiah 34, these Isaiah texts can now be evaluated in more detail.[33]

1. *Revelation 14.8-11 Oracles Against the Nations: Introduction.* Rev. 14.6-13 forms a prelude to the bowl series judgment which contains final premonitory exhortations. In vv. 8-11 the fate of those who refuse to disassociate themselves from Babylon and the beast is taken up. The function of this section as an anticipatory warning and its relationship to the main Babylon prophecy of 16.19–19.4 is formally indicated by a literary technique peculiar to John: the repetition of base texts and motifs. Each of the OT texts adopted in 14.8-11 subsequently reappears in the Babylon prophecy of 16.19–19.5.[34] Probably by design, then, 14.8-11 serves as an epitome of Babylon's judgment, which begins with the fall of the city (14.8 // 16.19; 18.2), and concludes with the eternal consequences of its judgment, reflected in the fate of its clients (14.11 // 19.3, 20).

a. *Revelation 14.8a → Isaiah 21.9*

Revelation	*Isaiah*	
ἔπεσεν ἔπεσεν βαβυλών	נפלה נפלה בבל	πέπτωκεν [+ πέπτωκεν
		B V σ´] βαβυλών

32. Quoted by Ozanne, 'Influence', p. 180.

33. More detailed treatments of the use of Jeremiah and Ezekiel in this section of Revelation are found in Wolff, *Jeremia*, pp. 166-74; and Vanhoye, 'L'utilisation du livre d'Ezechiel', respectively.

34. Rev. 14.8a/Isa. 21.9/Rev. 18.2; Rev. 14.8b/Jer. 25.15; 51.7/Rev. 18.3a; Rev. 14.10a/Jer. 25.15; Isa. 51.17/Rev. 16.19; Rev. 14.11a/Isa. 34.10/Rev. 19.3b.

While the larger questions of form and background will be reserved for the main development of this allusion in 18.2, a brief explanation of its appearance and function in the present context will be appropriate here. The announcement of Babylon's fall as a realized event is both in Isaiah and Revelation a dramatic way of emphasizing the certainty of the divine decree which lies behind the prophet's message. This prophetic idiom is formally described as *perfectum propheticum*.[35]

Within the framework of 14.6-13, the fall of Babylon constitutes the second of three angelic announcements which serve as final warnings from heaven to those who dwell on the earth before the commencement of God's wrath. The prophetic certainty of Babylon's destruction may function here as both exhortation and encouragement—exhortation to those still under her influence (18.4), and encouragement to those waiting for her judgment (14.12; 18.6).

b. *Revelation 14.10a → Isaiah 51.17*

Revelation	Isaiah	
καὶ αὐτὸς πίεται ἐκ τοῦ	אשר שתית מיד	ἡ πιοῦσα τὸ ποτήριον
οἴνου τοῦ θυμοῦ τοῦ θεοῦ	יהוה את כוס חמתו	τοῦ θυμοῦ ἐκ χειρὸς κυρίου
τοῦ κεκερασμένου ἀκράτου	את קבעת כוס	τὸ ποτήριον γὰρ τῆς πτώσεως,
ἐν τῷ ποτηρίῳ τῆς ὀργῆς αὐτοῦ	התרעלה שתית מצית	τὸ κόνδυ τοῦ θυμοῦ ἐξέπιες

A shorter variation of the cup of wrath image is found in the description of the seventh bowl in 16.19 (cf. 15.7; 19.15). In Revelation the theme of the cup/wine of God's wrath is to be distinguished from the cup/wine of fornication associated with Babylon in 14.8, 17.2, ?4, and 18.3. The former is a metaphor of God's judgment on Babylon; the latter a figure describing Babylon's seductive influence over the nations. Both images are brought together in 18.6c, where a distinction between the cup which Babylon mixed and the cup which God will mix is explicit.

Because this figure of judgment appears in a variety of earlier texts,

---

35. Gesenius, 106n; John's use of the aorist (ἔπεσεν) rather than the perfect (πέπτωκεν) is proleptic, perhaps influenced by the Hebrew stative perfect. S. Thompson, *The Apocalypse and Semitic Syntax*, p. 122 n. 117. Mussies limits John's use of this idiom to 14.8 and regards 18.2 as contextually different. Such a distinction however is unlikely—both announcements serve a similar purpose.

mainly prophetic, there is some difficulty in attributing John's usage to a particular OT antecedent.[36] In any case, Isa. 51.17 seems less likely as the inspiration here than Jer. 25.15, as the following comparison shows.

Rev. 14.10a	Isa. 51.17	Jer. 25.15	Ps. 75.9(74.9)	Pss. Sol. 8.14
(will) drink	(has) drunk	(to) drink	(will) drink	(to) drink
wine	—	wine	wine	wine
of wrath	—	of wrath	—	—
of God	of Yahweh	(of Yahweh)	of Yahweh	God
mixed/poured	—	—	mixed/poured (LXX)	mixed/poured
unmixed	—	—	unmixed (LXX)	unmixed
cup of	cup of	cup of	cup	cup
anger	wrath	(wine)	—	—

Not only does Jer. 25.15 better account for the various elements, but the context of judgment against the nations culminating with Babylon (25.26) is more appropriate than Isa. 51.17, which concerns Jerusalem.[37] Furthermore, John also uses Jeremiah 25 (v. 10) in 18.22c-23ab, while Isaiah 51 is nowhere else attested.

c. *Revelation 14.10b-11ab; 19.3b → Isaiah 34.9-10a*

Revelation	Isaiah	
καὶ βασανισθήσεται ἐν	ונהפכו נחליה	καὶ στραφήσονται αὐτῆς
πυρὶ καὶ θείω... καὶ	לזפת	αἱ φάραγγες εἰς πίσσαν
ὁ καπνὸς τοῦ βασανισμοῦ	ועפרה לנפרית	καὶ ἡ γῆ αὐτῆς εἰς θεῖον,

36. Isa. 51.17, 22; Jer. 25.15-17, 27-28; 49.12; Ezek. 23.31-33; Ps. 60.3; Lam. 4.21; Zech. 12.2; Hab. 2.16; *2 Bar.* 13.8; *Sib. Or. Frag.* 3.39-40. In 1QpHab 11.14 the 'cup of the Lord's right hand' in Hab. 2.16 is interpreted as 'the cup of the wrath of God'. On the background and significance of this metaphor, see H.A. Brongers, 'Der Zornesbecher', *OTS* 15 (1969), pp. 177-92.

37. The dominance of Jer. 25.15 is also accepted by Swete, *Apocalypse*, p. 185; and Wolff, *Jeremia*, p. 174; *contra* Marconcini, 'L'utilizzazione', p. 132 (based on Isa. 51.17), and Ozanne, 'Influence', p. 123 (conflation of Isa. 51.17 and Jer. 25.15). The origin of the motifs 'mixed/poured' and 'unmixed' is generally attributed to Ps. 75.8(74.8), though this is complicated by the fact that the MT has almost the opposite sense of the LXX.

Revelation	Isaiah	
αὐτῶν εἰς αἰῶνας αἰώνων	והיתה ארצה לזפת	καὶ ἔσται αὐτῆς ἡ γῆ
ἀναβαίνει, καὶ οὐκ ἔχουσιν	בערה לילה	καιομένη ὡς πίσσα νυκτὸς
ἀνάπαυσιν ἡμέρας καὶ νυκτὸς	ויומם לא תכבה	καὶ ἡμέρας καὶ οὐ σβεσθήσεται εἰς
	לעולם	τὸν αἰῶνα
καὶ ὁ καπνὸς αὐτῆς ἀναβαίνει	יעלה	χρόνον, καὶ ἀναβήσεται
εἰς τοὺς αἰῶνας τῶν αἰώνων (19.3b)	עשנה	ὁ καπνὸς αὐτῆς ἄνω

Isa. 34.1-17 comprises an oracle of judgment which begins in terms of a universal and cosmic destruction (1-4) and then focuses specifically on Yahweh's desolation of Edom (5-17). John has already adapted 34.4 in Rev. 6.13-14 and is probably influenced by 34.11-14 in Rev. 18.2. In the present instance, possible dependence on Isa. 34 involves three units of tradition.

i. καὶ βασανισθήσεται ἐν πυρὶ καὶ θείῳ (Rev. 14.10b). The only verbal connection between Revelation and Isaiah in this line is 'brimstone'. A parallel for John's 'fire' may be sought in לזפת/πίσσα (*pitch*) or בערה (*burning*) which is rendered by πῦρ in Exod. 22.6 LXX, but such a procedure is somewhat artificial. The combination of 'fire and brimstone' was a traditional motif inspired by the example of Sodom and Gomorrah, whose destruction became the classic model of divine judgment.[38] It is impossible to determine whether John has inserted this tradition independently of Isaiah 34 or whether he has assimilated Isaiah's picture of judgment to the Sodom account.[39] Some ambiguity is inevitable since Isa. 34.9-10 is itself dependent on the Sodom model. In any case the image recurs repeatedly in connection with the description of the 'lake of fire' (19.20; 20.10, 14, 15; 21.8).

ii. καὶ ὁ καπνὸς τοῦ βασανισμοῦ αὐτῶν εἰς αἰῶνας αἰωνων ἀναβαίνει (Rev. 14.11a). Apart from the redactional addition of τοῦ βασανισμοῦ αὐτῶν in 14.11a, this phrase parallels Isa. 34.10b almost exactly. The reprise of this line in Rev. 19.3b with the feminine

---

38. Gen. 19.24-25; Deut. 29.22-24; Ps. 11.6; Ezek. 38.22; *3 Macc.* 2.5; 1QpHab 10.5; Lk 17.29.

39. The majority of commentators limit the influence to Gen. 19, but Charles, Ozanne and Ford accept also the inspiration of Isa. 34.9.

pronoun αὐτῆς follows the original even more closely.[40] Because this part of Isaiah 34 is based on the example of Sodom (Gen. 19.28b 'the smoke of the land went up as the smoke of a furnace'), a secondary allusion to the Sodom tradition on John's part is not unlikely.

iii. καὶ οὐκ ἔχουσιν ἀνάπαυσιν ἡμέρας καὶ νυκτός (Rev. 14.11b). By itself, this phrase does not have a strong basis in Isa. 34.10a 'night and day it shall not be quenched'. Even though both Isaiah 34 and Revelation 14 use 'day and night' in the context of judgment, this adverbial phrase is a common idiom, especially in Revelation. While the presence of neighbouring motifs from Isa. 34.9-10 in Rev. 14.10-11 increases the likelihood that this line forms part of an allusive cluster, it is difficult to reconcile this with Rev. 4.8, where exactly the same phrase forms an antithetic parallel to 14.10, contrasting two groups of worshipers. Thus this proposed allusion must remain doubtful.[41]

When we turn to evaluate the significance of John's application of Isaiah 34 in this passage, particularly in relation to the second phrase (ii above), two issues arise.

The first concerns the double application of Isa. 34.10b 'and the smoke...goes up forever and ever' in 14.10 and 19.3. In the former passage it refers to the eternal judgment of individuals and in the latter to the judgment of Babylon in general. What is the relationship between these two scenes? Does John have in mind two distinct events or is the torment in fire and brimstone simply an extension of God's judgment on Babylon? The difficulty may be resolved by seeing the images of *torment* and *ascending smoke* as the matrix of two inter-related aspects of judgment: corporate and individual.

Just as the eternal reward of the righteous is inseparably connected with the appearance of the New Jerusalem (3.12; 21.1–22.5, 14, 19), so the recompense of the wicked is inextricably bound up with the fate of Babylon.[42] The corporate aspect receives a clearer focus in the

---

40. A. Lancellotti explains the tense of ἀναβαίνει (present for future) in connection with יעלה in Isa. 34.10b (= *yiqtol* durative); *Sintassi ebraica*, pp. 68, 115. John's tendency to translate לעולם by εἰς αἰῶνας αἰώνων may also find support in Rev. 4.9-10 (Dan. 4.34; 12.7?), Trudinger, 'Text', pp. 63, 79.

41. Only Ozanne ('Influence', p. 125) and Trudinger ('Text', p. 79) suppose dependence on Isa. 34.10 in this case.

42. It is not by accident then that the announcement of individual judgment (14.9-

destruction of Babylon in Revelation 18, where the motifs of Babylon's *torment* and the *smoke of her burning* reappear (18.9-10, 15, 18). The individual element is highlighted in the image of the *lake of fire* (19.20; 20.10, 14, 15; 21.8). It is only natural, therefore, that the judgment of those associated with the city is described by analogy with the judgment of the city itself; they were inseparably connected in life and appropriately share the same fate in death, as was forewarned: 'Come out of her, my people, lest you take part in her sins, lest you share in her plagues' (18.4).[43]

The second question centres on John's choice of an oracle against Edom to illustrate God's judgment on Rome. We have seen that his use of Babylon as a metonym for Rome led to a conscious predilection for OT Babylon oracles. Could it be that the rabbinic association of Edom with Rome was likewise known to him? It is particularly striking that the Targum to the very text which John adopts (Isa. 34.9-10) reads, 'And the streams of Rome will be turned to pitch'. Tracing the development of this identification is problematic, however, both in terms of dating and motive.

According to rabbinic tradition, the earliest testimony to the use of Edom as a codename for Rome goes back to Rabbi Akiba in connection with the Bar-Kochba revolt (132–135 CE) and interpretation of Num. 24.17-18.[44] Evidence contemporary with Revelation has been adduced from *4 Ezra* 6.7-10 where Esau (= Rome?) represents 'the end of this age, and Jacob is the beginning of the age that follows', but

---

11) follows directly the announcement of corporate judgment (14.8). That they both drink of the same wine of God's wrath is suggested by the (emphatic) καὶ αὐτός ('he also') in 14.10.

43. 'The fate of the individual is depicted in terms of the fate of the city which has corrupted him' (Sweet, *Revelation*, p. 227). Caird goes a step further and refers 14.10-11 directly to the city and only by association to individual destiny (*Revelation*, p. 186). Kraft, by interpreting Babylon abstractly, makes no distinction at all between corporate and individual judgment: 'Babel ist somit hier weder ein historische, noch eine mythische Grösse; es meint weder das alte Babylon, noch Rom, es bezeichnet die Gefolgschaft des Tiers' (*Offenbarung*, pp. 193-94).

44. *Gen. R.* 65.21; C.H. Hunzinger, 'Babylon als Deckname für Rom und die Datierung des 1, Petrusbriefes', in *Gottes Wort und Gottes Land* (ed. H.G. Reventlow; Göttingen, 1965), pp. 69-72; M.D. Herr, *EncJud*, VI, col. 379; G.D. Cohen, 'Esau as Symbol in Early Medieval Thought', in *Jewish Medieval and Renaissance Studies* (ed. A. Altmann; Cambridge, 1967), pp. 19-48.

this may merely symbolize cycles of history in general rather than concrete political entities.[45]

Notwithstanding this uncertainty, it is fairly probable that the identification of Edom with Rome was known by the end of the first century, for the seeds of such a typological transfer, as in the case of Babylon = Rome, were present already in the OT, needing only the events of 70 CE to stimulate speculation.[46] The taking over and reapplication of past prophecies to explain the present and organize the future was both natural and necessary, in view of the absence of recognized contemporary prophets who could interpret such events and provide direction. So also John's application of Isaiah 34 (and Isa. 63.1-6?) to Rome, instead of being random, may reflect a current interpretational equation of Edom and Rome.

2. *Revelation 17–18 Oracles against the Nations: Primary Development.* The narration of the actual fall of Babylon takes place in conjunction with the seventh and final bowl in 16.19, but there it is only stated briefly and not described. Chapters 17 and 18 serve to fill this void, and this section has appropriately been titled the 'Babylon Appendix'.[47] An overall perspective of this visionary supplement is best gained by way of outline.

45. M. Knibb, *2 Esdras* (CBC; Cambridge, 1979), p. 147; Cohen, 'Esau as Symbol', p. 21; Huzinger, 'Babylon als Deckname', pp. 69-70.

46. Both Hunzinger and Cohen argue that the association of Edom with Rome grew out of the biblical antithesis between Jacob/Israel and Esau/Edom. In particular, Edom's complicity with historical Babylon in the destruction of Jerusalem and the prophetic reproaches which ensued could take on new meaning after the events of 70 CE. Ps. 137.7-9 names Edom as an accessory to Babylon's crimes (cf. *b. Git.* 57b; 58a), and Obadiah chastises Edom's pride and violent treatment of Jerusalem. But perhaps the most influential catalyst for the identification of Edom with Rome was the book of Lamentations. Nowhere are Babylon or the Chaldeans mentioned and only Edom comes under accusation (4.21-22). As a result, in the Tannaitic period the book came to be regarded as a prophetic lament over the Roman violation of Zion. A similar view may already be alluded to in Josephus, *Ant.* 10.78-79. As Cohen remarks, 'Scripture named Edom, and history pointed at Rome. By the most elementary syllogism, the two became one' ('Esau as Symbol', p. 25).

47. A. Yarbro Collins, 'Revelation 18: Taunt-Song or Dirge?', in Lambrecht (ed.), *L'Apocalypse johannique*, pp. 189, 191; *Combat Myth*, pp. 14-15. Phrases linking the fall with the description include 'God remembered great Babylon' (16.19 // 18.5), and the 'cup of wrath' motif (16.19 // 18.6).

a. *Revelation 17.2a; 18.3b, 9b → Isaiah 23.17b*

μεθ' ἧς ἐπόρνευσαν οἱ βασιλεῖς τῆς γῆς (Rev. 17.2a)
καὶ οἱ βασιλεῖς τῆς γῆς μετ' αὐτῆς ἐπόρνευσαν (Rev. 18.3b)
οἱ βασιλεῖς τῆς γῆς οἱ μετ' αὐτῆς πορνεύσαντες (Rev. 18.9a)

Isa. 23.17b

וזנתה את כל ממלכות   καὶ ἔσται ἐμπόριον πάσαις ταῖς
הארץ על פני האדמה   βασιλείαις τῆς οἰκουμένης

Isa. 23.1-17 relates the 'burden' of Tyre, whose commercial relationship with the nations is described in terms of a harlot and her lovers (23.15-18). It is appropriate then that John's first introduction of Harlot-Babylon incorporates this harlot text (Rev. 17.1-2). The adoption of a Tyre oracle no doubt anticipates the subsequent development of the merchant theme in Revelation 18, where the only other extended OT prophecy against Tyre (Ezek. 26–27) is employed.

John is evidently influenced by the Hebrew tradition here, even though he changes *kingdoms* to *kings* and omits the quantitative adjective *all*. πορνεύω is the expected rendering of זנה, which in Isa. 23.17 has a figurative sense of 'improper intercourse with foreign nations'.[48] As K.G. Kuhn has noted, the common prophetic association of harlotry with idolatry does not appear to be featured in the context of Isaiah 23.[49] But whereas John certainly places a strong emphasis on

48. BDB, p. 275.
49. *TDNT*, I, p. 515 n. 11; cf. Nah. 3.4; *contra* J.M. Court, *Myth and History in the Book of Revelation* (London, 1979), p. 140. Further support for this judg-

the socio-economic communion between Rome and the nations, idolatry cannot be excluded as one of the elements which in his mind made the relationship illicit.

What the prophet means when he says that the kings of the earth 'committed fornication' with Rome can be deduced from parallel passages (esp. Rev. 18.3, 15, 23-24). Translating this metaphor into possible historical references begins by understanding the complementary roles of the two parties involved: Rome as the harlot, and the kings/ nations as her suitors. The enticements of the one expose the weaknesses of the other. The services rendered in this case are described in 17.4, where Babylon's fornication includes all manner of abominations and impurities. Getting beneath this moral tag to the underlying prophetic critique of concrete social, political and religious circumstances involves both internal evaluation of John's polemic and external examination of contemporary Roman and anti-Roman propaganda.

At the very least John wishes to expose what he perceives as the nations' sycophantic relationship with Rome whereby all things Roman have been sought and accepted (including the Emperor cult);[50] their veneration of Rome's supposedly invincible power;[51] and their partnership in the inevitable corollaries of vast and irresponsible power and wealth: violence, social injustice and immorality.[52] It is only natural, therefore, that those cities of the nations and their kings who shared in Rome's glory are also pictured as sharing in her fall (16.19; 18.9). The essence of John's indictment is neatly summarized by the anonymous prophet of *4 Ezra* (15.46-49).

> And you, Asia, who share in the glamour of Babylon and the glory of her person—woe to you, miserable wretch! For you make yourself like her; you have decked out your daughters in harlotry to please and glory in your lovers, who have always lusted after you. You have imitated that hateful harlot in all her deeds and devices; therefore God says, 'I will send evils upon you, widowhood, poverty, famine, sword, and pestilence, to lay waste your houses and bring you to destruction and death'.

ment can be elicited from the LXX and Targum translations of 23.17, which both treat זנה as purely an economic metaphor.

50. Rev. 13; 14.9-11; 16.2; 19.20; *Asc. Isa.* 4.2-13; Tacitus, *Ann.* 4.55-56. A convenient listing of the many Imperial temples and shrines found in Asia Minor is given by S.R.F. Price, *Rituals and Power: The Roman Imperial Cult in Asia Minor* (Cambridge, 1984), pp. 249-74.

51. Rev. 13.3-4; 18.10, 18; Tacitus, *Ann.* 2.25; *b. Giṭ.* 56b.

52. Rev. 13.16; 17.6; 18.7, 24; Tacitus, *Ann.* 14.15; 1QpHab 2.12–4.13.

b. Revelation 18.2a → Revelation 21.9[53]

Chapter 18 forms a special unit in John's construct which is marked off from chs. 17 and 19 by the formula μετὰ ταῦτα (18.1; 19.1). A comparison with ch. 17 in particular reveals a fundamental shift from an apocalyptic format (17) to one dominated by prophetic forms and language (18).[54] Within the wider structural division of 17.1–19.4, ch. 18 serves as the primary illustration of the κρίμα of the great harlot announced in 17.2. The *fact* of Babylon's fall and its place in the chronological scheme of judgment has been proclaimed in 16.19. The *manner* of her fall and its relation to historical events is given in 17.16-17. Now finally in 18.1-24 the Babylon theme culminates with a carefully constructed account of the *consequences* of her judgment and the factors which led to it.

Although Rev. 18.1-24 begins as a vision report, the bulk of the chapter is essentially comprised of a series of angelic and divine auditions. The opening words of the divinely authorized angel ring out suddenly and forcefully (ἐν ἰσχυρᾷ φωνῇ): 'Fallen, fallen is Babylon the great!', and the reverberations of this dramatic announcement resonate throughout the remainder of the chapter.

The OT passage from which John borrows this statement (Isa. 21.1-10) likewise concerns the fall of Babylon, where, as in Revelation, the announcement is not delivered by the prophet himself, but issues from heaven.[55] Strict form-critical analysis traces the basic idiom ('fallen,

53. See the discussion of Rev. 14.8 (above) for the texts.
54. Elements typical of OT prophecy include (a) the prophetic perfect in 18.2 (2×); (b) the structure of prophetic threat followed by the reason (Begründung) in 18.2-3, 21-24 (following H.W. Wolff, 'Die Begründungen der prophetischen Heils- und Unheilssprüche', *ZAW* 52 [1934], pp. 1-22); (c) the prophetic symbolic act in 18.21; (d) several formulas or phrases typical of prophetic speech (though not necessarily exclusive to it), such as 'God remembering iniquity' (18.5b; cf. 16.19; Hos. 8.13; 9.9; Jer. 14.10); 'it shall be burned with fire' (in prophecies against cities: 18.8b; cf. 17.16; Jer. 51.58; 38.17); οὐ μὴ... ἔτι or οὐκέτι οὐ with a future verb or equivalent subjunctive of emphatic denial (18.21-23b, 14; Amos 8.14; Isa. 5.6; Ezekiel, *passim*). The interchange of tenses and persons of verbs which at first seems puzzling to the reader of Rev. 18 is also a feature of prophetic oracles against the nations. Note especially Jer. 50–51, which contains a mixture of past, present and future verbs, second and third person declarations, and includes direct exhortations to God's people (50.8; 51.6, 45; Rev. 18.4-5) and interjections of rejoicing (51.48; Rev. 18.20).
55. The adjective ἡ μεγάλη is probably inspired by Dan. 4.27 בבל רבתא = LXX, θ′ 4.30 βαβυλὼν ἡ μεγάλη.

fallen is...') to the individual funeral lament, which was taken up by the Israelite prophets and applied collectively to the downfall of a city, tribe or people, in advance of death.[56] Both in Isaiah and Revelation, very little, if any, of the original setting or purpose of lament is retained. Rather, the scene has been changed from a funeral setting to the war zone, and the function from mourning to proclamation. In essence, a new sub-genre emerges: the *victory* or *siege report*, which belongs with other customs of war such as the *call to battle* and the *retreat order*.[57]

In Isaiah and Revelation God's judgment on Babylon is accomplished through the agency of historical military forces who successfully besiege and overthrow the city (Isa. 21.2, 9; Rev. 17.16-18; 18). In Revelation 18, the prophetic announcement of Babylon's fall reveals beforehand the outcome of this eschatological conflict and sets the stage for the laments over the fallen city in 18.9-19.

c. *Revelation 18.2b → Isaiah 13.21; 34.11, 13b-14*

Revelation   *Isa. 13.21*

καὶ ἐγένετο κατοικητήριον   ורבצו שם ציים   καὶ ἀναπαύσονται
δαιμονίων   ἐκεῖ θηρία
καὶ φυλακὴ παντὸς πνεύματος   ומלאו בתיהם אחים   καὶ ἐμπλησθήσονται
ἀκαθάρτου
καὶ φυλακὴ παντὸς ὀρνέου   ושכנו שם בנות   αἱ οἰκίαι ἤχου, καὶ
ἀκαθάρτου
[καὶ φυλακὴ παντὸς θηρίου   יענה ושעירים   ἀναπαύσονται ἐκεῖ
ἀκαθάρτου]   σειρῆνες, καὶ
καὶ μεμισημένου   ירקדו שם   δαιμόνια
                                                                                     ἐκεῖ ὀρχήσονται

Isa. 34.11, 13b-14

וירשוה קאת   καὶ κατοικήσουσιν ἐν αὐτῇ ὄρνεα
וקפוד וינשוף וערב ישכנו בה...   καὶ ἐχῖνοι καὶ ἴβεις καὶ κόρακες...
והיתה נוה תנים חציר   καὶ ἔσται ἔπαυλις σειρήνων καὶ
לבנות יענה ופנשו   αὐλὴ στρουθῶν καὶ συναντήσουσι
ציים את איים ושעיר   δαιμόνια ὀνοκενταύροις καὶ βοήσονται

56. O. Eissfeldt, *The Old Testament: An Introduction* (Oxford, 1974), pp. 91-92; N.K. Gottwald, *Studies in the Book of Lamentations* (London, 1954), p. 35; Yarbro Collins, 'Revelation 18', pp. 192-93; Wildberger, *Jesaja*, II, p. 784.

57. W.E. March, 'Prophecy', in *Old Testament Form Criticism* (ed. J.H. Hayes; San Antonio, 1974), p. 169.

על רעהו יקרא אך שם הרגיעה   ἕτερος πρὸς τὸν ἕτερον ἐκεῖ ἀναπαύσονται
לילית ומצאה לה מנוה   ὀνοκένταυροι, εὗρον γὰρ αὐτοῖς
       ἀνάπαυσιν.

Although the majority of commentators recognize here an allusion to Isaiah 13 or 34 or both, it is far from certain to what extent John was directly influenced by either of these texts.[58] The issue is complicated by his paraphrasing style and the existence of parallel traditions which have led some to see in this passage simply the application of conventional images.[59] Therefore, before engaging in an analysis of the function of the desolation motif in the context of Rev. 18, a linguistic comparison with the proposed Isaiah texts is necessary.

1. The introductory phrase καὶ ἐγένετο κατοικητήριον (δαιμονίων) finds a close parallel in Isa. 34.13b נוה והיתה (תנים), but an even closer parallel is attested in Jer. 51.37a והיתה בבל...מעין (תנים).[60] In favour of the Jeremiah text are the direct reference to Babylon, the fact that מעון (or מעונה) is commonly translated by κατοικητήριον in the LXX, and John's use of a neighbouring text (Jer. 51.7) in 18.3.[61] Nevertheless, Jer. 51.37 does not contain any further possible links with Rev. 18.2, whereas Isa. 34.11-14 does, and John uses 34.10 of 'Babylon' elsewhere (14.11; 19.3). Since he uses both the oracle against Edom in Isaiah 34 and the one against Babylon in Jeremiah 50–51 in other places, and is evidently familiar with their context, it is not unlikely that both Isa. 34.13b and Jer. 51.37a provided inspiration for this idea.

2. The major point of comparison concerns the categories of desert-dwellers which John employs. His approach to the long lists of obscure animal names in Isaiah 13 and 34 is both economical and effective. The various types of animals are grouped into their general classes—beasts and birds—and

---

58. *Isa. 13.21*: Mounce, Lohmeyer, Ford, Kaiser; *Isa. 34.11-14*: Marconcini, Kiddle–Ross; *Isa. 13 and 34*: Schlatter, Charles, Swete, Caird, Kraft, Schmid, Metzger.

59. Beckwith, Wikenhauser, Prigent, Sweet and Müller.

60. תנים (jackals) is occasionally confused with תנין (serpent, dragon)—Ezek. 29.3; 32.2, and is translated by σειρήν in Job 30.29; Isa. 34.13b; 43.20. This is not however, the most likely source for John's δαιμονίων.

61. Wolff, *Jeremia*, p. 167.

παντός is added to each by way of compensation.[62] Although the beast clause is missing from some important manuscripts (א C 051 𝔐 vg, and omitted in KJV, ASV, RSV and others), it is much easier to account for its omission than its addition, and it should be retained.[63] John's δαιμονίων almost certainly corresponds to שעירים (LXX δαιμόνια) in Isa. 13.21; 34.14a, and πνεύματος ἀκαθάρτου is probably a parallel expansion, though it may be inspired by the legendary לילית of Isa. 34.14.[64]

In summary, apart from the introductory phrase (i), there is little which favours Isaiah 13 over Isaiah 34 or vice-versa. Each passage contains a reference to demons, and unclean birds and beasts, as in Revelation, while the parallel traditions of Jer. 50.39 and 51.37 lack the demon element. Since each of these texts (Isa. 13, 34, Jer. 50–51) either directly or indirectly (Isa. 34: Edom = Rome?) prophesies the destruction and desolation of Babylon, it seems best to conclude that their *cumulative* testimony to Babylon's fate provided both the inspiration and basic material for John's portrayal.

Within the wider framework of the Babylon appendix (Rev. 17–18), the description of 18.2 takes up and develops the theme of the harlot's judgment announced already in 17.1-3, where John sees

62. Of the birds, Isa. 13.21 and Jer. 50.39 list only the ostrich, while Isa. 34 gives the hawk, owl, raven, ostrich and kite. All of these are found in the list of unclean (שמא—ἀκάθαρτος) birds in Lev. 11.13-19 and Deut. 14.11-18. Of the beasts, the אי in Isa. 13.22; 34.14 and Jer. 50.39 is a species of desert animal no longer identifiable. So while the LXX of 13.21 translates the plural ציים with θηρία, this is not necessarily the source for John's θηρίον. The same word is translated by σειρήν in Isa. 34.14 and ἴνδαλμα in Jer. 50.39. The other wild beasts listed include the hyena, jackal and porcupine. None of these is specifically listed as unclean in Lev. 11.1-8, 26-27 or Deut. 14.3-8, but they would undoubtedly be considered as such by the general principles there given. They are all proverbially associated with desolate places.

63. It is found in MS A, some important miniscules, and a variety of lesser witnesses. Schmid (*Apokalypse-Textes*, II, pp. 143-46) argues for its inclusion, as does also Metzger (*Textual Commentary*, pp. 758-59).

64. The Targum also understands שעיר as a demon and לילית as a night demon; cf. Schlatter, 'Das alte Testament', p. 91. The association of demons with desolate places was commonplace: [Babylon] κατοικηθήσεται ὑπὸ δαιμονίων (Bar. 4.35); Mt. 12.43-45; cf. Lev. 16.10; Lk. 4.1-2; *4 Macc.* 18.8; *T. Sol.* 5.12; *IDB*, I, pp. 823-24; Wildberger, *Jesaja*, II, pp. 522-23.

Babylon in the *wilderness* (ἔρημος).⁶⁵ Like the Holy City on a mountain (21.10), the harlot in the desert is more than just a statement of visionary provenance. In accordance with John's OT model, it contains an implicit prophetic announcement concerning Babylon's destiny: '(Babylon) shall be...a wilderness dry and desert' (Jer. 50.12).⁶⁶ The principal role of the wilderness motif is one of contrast.⁶⁷ By juxtaposing Babylon's former glory with her latter desolation John emphasizes to his readers the power of God to bring upon her a sudden and complete reversal of fortunes. It is therefore not surprising to find that he invests the laments of her clients with an element of surprise and bewilderment: 'In one hour all this wealth has been laid waste' (ἐρημόω—18.17a; cf. 18.10, 19).

The inaugural prophecy of Rev. 18.2 also forms a sort of chiastic parallel with 18.21-23b, where the theme of desolation continues; but this time not what is present, but what is absent from the city is outlined. In 18.21 the announcement of the angel begins with the general statement that Babylon will no longer be found and moves to the specific characteristic signs of urban life which will cease to exist— those everyday sights and sounds which symbolize the life-pulse and existence of a city. The oracle thus ends as it began: Babylon is fallen, deserted and forgotten. As the haunt of every manner of unclean beast and spirit, it stands in stark contrast to the New Jerusalem—the Holy City through whose gates nothing unclean can enter (21.27).⁶⁸

65. Lohmeyer and Roloff also make this connection (*Offenbarung*, p. 141; *Offenbarung*, p. 175). Kraft finds dependence in 17.3 on Isa. 21.1 LXX ὅραμα τῆς ἐρήμου, but this seems doubtful (*Offenbarung*, p. 213). ἐγένετο, like ἔπεσεν before it, qualifies as a *prophetic perfect*.

66. Cf. Jer. 50.13; 51.41-43. The desolation motif is common in prophecies against cities and nations: *Edom* (and Egypt) (Joel 3.19; Mal. 1.3-4); *Nineveh* (Zeph. 2.13); *Judah* (Jer. 4.26-27; 9.10-12; 22.5-6); *Israel* (Hos. 2.3; Ezek. 6.14; Isa. 27.10; cf. 43.19-20); *Jerusalem* (Isa. 64.10-11; 1 Macc. 3.45). The association of wild animals with ruined cities is not just found in OT laments and prophecies of doom, but also occurs in ancient Near Eastern treaty curses and royal inscriptions (D.R. Hillers, *Treaty Curses and the Old Testament Prophets* [Rome, 1964], pp. 43-45, 88).

67. Müller, *Offenbarung*, p. 304.

68. Caird, *Revelation*, p. 223; Ford, *Revelation*, p. 301. A striking parallel to the judgment of Babylon in Rev. 17–18 is found in 4Q179, a lamentation over Jerusalem dated to c. 30 BCE. Similarities abound: God remembering iniquity (I, i.2; Rev. 18.5b); burning with fire (I, i.6; Rev. 18.9, 18); become a lair for wild beasts (I, i.9a; Rev. 18.2); become a wilderness (I, i.10-12; Rev. 17.3); sound of joy not

218   Isaiah and Prophetic Traditions in the Book of Revelation

d. Revelation 18.7b-8a → Isaiah 47.7-9

Revelation	Isaiah MT
ὅτι ἐν τῇ καρδίᾳ αὐτῆς λέγει	ותאמרי לעולם אהיה גבות עד...
ὅτι κάθημαι βασίλισσα	היושבת לבטח האמרה בלבבה
καὶ χήρα οὐκ εἰμὶ	אני ואפסי עוד לא אשב
καὶ πένθος οὐ μὴ ἴδω.	אלמנה ולא אדע שכול
διὰ τοῦτο ἐν μιᾷ ἡμέρᾳ	ותבאנה לך שתי אלה
ἥξουσιν αἱ πληγαὶ αὐτῆς,	רגע ביום אחד
θάνατος καὶ πένθος καὶ λιμός	שכול ואלמן

Isaiah LXX
καὶ εἶπας εἰς τὸν αἰῶνα ἔσομαι ἄρχουσα...
ἡ καθημένη πεποιθυῖα ἡ λέγουσα ἐν τῇ καρδίᾳ αὐτῆς
'Εγώ εἰμι, καὶ οὐκ ἔστιν ἑτέρα οὐ καθιῶ χήρα οὐδὲ
γνώσομαι ὀρφανείαν. νῦν δὲ ἥξει ἐξαίφνης ἐπὶ σὲ
τὰ δύο ταῦτα ἐν μιᾷ ἡμέρᾳ χηρεία· καὶ ἀτεκνία

John's adaptation of this Babylon oracle is one of the best examples of
his literary approach to the OT. In the process of rendering Isaiah's
poem suitable to a new context, a variety of changes can be observed,
including the interpretation and substitution of certain elements of the
base text. An analysis of these modifications, together with verbal and
structural parallels, reveals three constituent units of influence.

i. ὅτι ἐν τῇ καρδίᾳ αὐτῆς λέγει ὅτι κάθημαι βασίλισσα. Each of
the components which make up this sentence has an antecedent in the
(Hebrew) text of Isa. 47.7-8, though some rearrangement has taken
place. The introduction to the reported speech (ὅτι...ὅτι) is drawn
intact from 47.8b, but with a change from second person to third
person singular. When we come to the actual speech of personified
Babylon, however (κάθημαι βασίλισσα), a more complex procedure
is seen. κάθημαι is probably inspired by ישׁב in 47.8(2×), interpreted
in the light of 47.1, where Babylon's 'sitting' in a royal capacity is

heard in it (I, i.13; Rev. 18.22-23); lament for those clothed in purple, fine linen, silk
and ornaments of gold (I, ii.10-12; Rev. 18.16); description of Jerusalem as (a) a
hated woman (I, ii.3; Rev. 17.16); (b) a princess of the nations (ii.5; Rev. 18.7; cf.
17.15); (c) a woman stripped (ii.6-7; Rev. 17.16); (d) one whose inhabitants weep
and mourn (ii.8-10; Rev. 18.9-19). For text and discussion, see M.P. Horgan, 'A
Lament over Jerusalem (4Q179)', *JSS* 18 (1973), pp. 222-34. Like John, the author
of this lament builds on earlier biblical models. But whereas John uses mainly
Babylon and Tyre oracles, the author of 4Q179 borrows primarily from
Lamentations (as is fitting in a lament over Jerusalem).

implied (cf. 47.5). βασιλίσσα almost certainly corresponds to גברת in 47.7a. Both the context of Isaiah 47 and the semantic range of גברת support this.[69] In essence then what John has done is to take the *introduction* to one reported speech (47.8) and combine it with the *statement* of another (47.7). The motivation for this will become clearer in the next section.

ii. καὶ χήρα οὐκ εἰμὶ καὶ πένθος οὐ μὴ ἴδω. In these two coordinate clauses John retains the paratactic structure of his *Vorlage* (47.8c), but somewhat modifies the vocabulary. The change of verb in the first clause is probably to be understood in connection with the previous statement κάθημαι βασίλισσα. Because John is blending the elements of two separate reported speeches into one, and because these two speeches are contrasting (*I am...I am not*), a transposition of verbs was undertaken to gain a better overall literary effect. Since it appears that the second speech served as the basic framework for this amalgamation, a possible outline of the mental stages of development may be suggested:

> Because she says in her heart (that):
>> I am... and I shall not sit (as) a widow (Isa. 47.8bc).
>> *I am a *queen* and I shall not sit (as) a widow (47.7 + 8bc)
>> I sit (as) a queen and I am not a widow. (Rev. 18.7)[70]

As for the second clause καὶ πένθος οὐ μὴ ἴδω, the major question concerns the relationship of πένθος to שכול. Since πένθος generally denotes mourning associated with death and שכול means bereavement, the ideas are similar enough to suggest that John is interpreting rather

---

69. BDB (p. 150) generally gives גברת the meaning *mistress*, but in Isa. 47.5, 7 they render it *lady* or *queen*. The latter option is supported by the cognate גבירה (*queen, queen-mother*) which occurs in tandom with מלך in Jer. 29.2(36.2), where the LXX translates with βασίλισσα (cf. 1 Kgs 11.19). Further incentive for translating the word as *queen* could be gained from the context of Isa. 47, which speaks of Babylon's *throne* (47.1), and her exalted position over other kingdoms (47.5). Cf. also the Targum's rendering תקיפא. Trudinger and Ozanne explicitly make this connection ('Text', p. 136; 'Influence', p. 134). Gangemi comes to a similar conclusion, though in a somewhat roundabout manner ('L'utilizzazione', p. 121 n. 42). Kraft appears to overlook this evidence when he says 'die Benennung Babels als Königin hat im Alten Testament kein Vorbild' (*Offenbarung*, p. 231).

70. It is interesting to compare at this point textual assimilations to the OT model; 046 69 61 arm sah boh have a future verb καθιῶ (as in LXX); while Sahidic keeps 'sit' with 'widow' (ὅτι ἐγὼ μὴ καθιῶ οὖσα χήρα).

than substituting.[71] That πένθος corresponds to שכול (whether as interpretation or substitution) is confirmed by its repetition in the following judgment clause (iii).

The remaining variation of ἴδω (*see*) versus ארע (*know*) is not surprising, since both words are used figuratively in the sense of 'to experience'. In fact, in 1QIsa[a] 47.8, the exact same substitution is attested, so that the text reads אראה rather than MT אדה.[72]

iii. διὰ τοῦτο ἐν μιᾷ ἡμέρᾳ ἥξουσιν αἱ πληγαὶ αὐτῆς θάνατος καὶ πένθος καὶ λιμός (Rev. 18.8a). Very little need be said about this last section. Except for a change from singular to plural in the verb, the phrase 'In one day will come...' follows exactly Isa. 47.9a. In the final clause John expands the catalogue of judgments from two to three, retaining πένθος // שכול but replacing אלמן = χηρεία (expected as the parallel to χήρα in 18.7) with θάνατος (= *pestilence*) and λιμός (*famine*).[73] While these constitute the most significant changes of the model text which John has effected, it is important to recognize that they only occur at the point of transition where the influence of Isaiah 47 fades out and new traditions emerge.[74]

On the whole, then, despite minor adjustments, John retains a significant proportion of the vocabulary and structure of Isa. 47.7-9. This close correspondence in form is complemented by a faithful adherence to the context and function of Second Isaiah's prophecy. That portion of Isa. 47.1-15 which John appropriates (47.7-9) takes the form of a legal trial in which the words of Babylon serve as evidence against her.[75]

---

71. Trudinger regards πένθος as an interpretation of שכול ('Text', p. 137; cf. Gangemi, 'L'utilizzazione', p. 121); while Ozanne takes it as a substitution ('Influence', p. 134; cf. also Charles, *Revelation*, II, p. 100).

72. Ozanne also notes this, 'Influence', p. 134. Several manuscripts of Revelation (א C pc) actually read εἰδῶ (*know*) rather than ἴδω (*see*).

73. John's choice of judgments—pestilence, mourning, famine—and the following motif of burning with fire seem best explained against the background of Babylon's judgment by the armies of the beast and the dire consequences of siege warfare. Cf. 2 Kgs 25.1-3; Josephus, *Ant.* 10.131-32; *War* 5.512-21; 5.548-49; Rev. 6.8.

74. The reference to Babylon's sorcery in Rev. 18.23d may reflect Isa. 47.9, 12.

75. R. Martin-Achard, 'Esaïa 47 et la tradition prophétique sur Babylone', in J.A. Emerton (ed.), *Prophecy: Essays Presented to Georg Fohrer on his 65th Birthday* (Berlin, 1980), p. 91; cf. Trites, *Witness*, p. 172.

In Revelation 18, this lawsuit dialogue comprises the centrepiece of a wider judicial setting. The accusations of the plaintiff, 'as she glorified herself and played the wanton' (18.7a), are corroborated by the arrogant depositions of the defendant: 'a queen I sit, I am no widow, mourning I shall never see' (18.7b). The formal charges add up to political absolutism and blasphemous presumption.[76] The punishment corresponds to the crime, in accordance with the principle of *jus talionis* invoked by her accuser: 'render to her as she herself has rendered', 'give her a like measure' (Rev. 18.6a, 7a). The humiliation of her judgment is increased by the suddenness of destruction: 'in a single day' (18.8a, cf. 18.10, 17, 19). That such a mighty power can fall so quickly is testimony to the even greater power of her judge: 'for mighty is the Lord God who judges her' (18.8c). As she is led from the dock her clients prepare to lament the fate of their patron (Rev. 18.9-19).[77]

e. *Revelation 18.23c → Isaiah 23.8*

Revelation	Isaiah	
ὅτι οἱ ἔμποροι σου ἦσαν	אשר סחריה שרים	οἱ ἔμποροι αὐτῆς ἔνδοξοι,
οἱ μεγιστᾶνες τῆς γῆς	כנעניה נכבדי־ארץ	ἄρχοντες τῆς γῆς

There is little doubt that Isa. 23.8 lies behind this statement. By omitting the poetic expansion of the second parallel Hebrew clause (כנעניה נכבדי), and retaining ארץ with the first clause, a precise verbal archetype of John's phrase is obtained.[78] But the close correspondence

76. Westermann, *Isaiah 40–66*, p. 192. Rome's presumptuous pride is well reflected in the title she claimed for herself: *Aeternitas* (Sweet, *Revelation*, p. 278). Probably implicit in Babylon's declamation is her military supremacy and apparent immunity from the disastrous effects of war which leave her enemies without husbands and children (Martin-Achard, 'Esaïa 47', p. 94; Mounce, *Revelation*, p. 326). Cf. the monologue of the Laodicean church in 3.17.

77. A strikingly similar and probably contemporary use of Isa. 47.7-8 in anti-Roman propaganda appears in *Sib. Or.* 5.169-73, 444; both in oracles against 'Babylon' (= Rome), 'Alas, city of the Latin land, unclean in all things...as a widow you will sit by the banks, and the river Tiber will weep for you, its consort ...but you said, "I alone am, and no one will ravage me". But now God...will destroy you' (168-74); 'though thinking as a queen, you will come under the judgment of your adversaries' (444-45, *OTP* I, pp. 397, 493). For dating see Schürer III.1, 641-44.

78. ἔμπορος and μεγιστάν are the standard LXX equivalents of סחר and שר respectively. John has already used this Tyre oracle (23.17) at 17.2a and 18.3b, 9a.

in diction is not matched by a similarity in function. In Isaiah the phrase adds an element of irony to the mocking song. In Revelation it appears to serve as one of the grounds for Babylon's judgment. As such it forms the first of three causes for her destruction introduced by ὅτι clauses in Rev. 18.23-24.[79]

1. Rome's economic monopoly—affecting the whole earth (18.23c).
2. Rome's moral corruption of the nations (18.23d).
3. Rome's bloodguiltiness—against righteous and unrighteous alike (18.24).

The addition of Rev. 18.23c as a ground for judgment should be interpreted in the light of what John says elsewhere of the merchants.[80] It is clear that the issue of economic control and oppression was an important one for the prophet, for the lament of the merchants is by far the longest and most developed of the three (kings: 2 verses; mariners: 3 verses; merchants: 7 verses). From the list of commodities given in 18.12-13 it would seem that he has in mind especially those involved in the trade of luxury items (cf. v. 14). John does not mean simply anyone who made a living by trading, but those who obtained wealth and power by exploiting Roman society's Corinthian appetite, regardless of moral issues (Rev. 18.3c, 11, 15).

It is these merchant barons who have helped to clothe the harlot with purple and scarlet and provided her with gold, jewels and pearls (17.4). And when these wear out they are more than willing to perpetuate her decadent image by selling her more (18.11-12, 16). As an integral part of the empire's economic network, the merchants not only help to advertise Rome's prosperity, fostering an image which tempts Christian and non-Christian alike to pursue wealth (cf. 3.17; 1 Tim. 6.9-10; 17-19), but they serve to endorse and legitimate her social and religious excesses.

---

79. These concluding clauses (18.23-24) form a chiastic parallel with the introductory causes of 18.3. Yarbro Collins leaves v. 24 out of consideration and sees only two grounds for judgment here (23cd; *Combat Myth*, p. 19).

80. Charles overlooks this and regards 18.23c as meaningless as a ground for judgment (*Revelation*, II, p. 112). As Ozanne notes, the issue is not merely in their *being* μεγιστᾶνες, but in the methods by which they attained such status (*Influence*, p. 138). Kraft rightly observes that the verse should be interpreted through the economic reproach of Ezek. 27 (*Offenbarung*, p. 238).

The relationship of materialistic interdependence which existed between the merchants and Rome is brought out clearly in 18.11-14, where the former lament the loss of their market (vv. 11-13), and the latter—through a prophetic interjection—is deprived of her luxuries (v. 14). For these traders, commercial success in the Roman market brought not only personal wealth, but social status and political influence as well. As John says, Rome's merchants became 'the great men of the earth'.[81]

Revelation 19.11c → Isaiah 11.4a

Revelation	Isaiah	
καὶ ἐν δικαιοσύνη κρίνει	ושפט בצדק	ἀλλὰ κρινεῖ ταπεινῶ κρίσιν...
καὶ πολεμεῖ	דלים	τοὺς ταπεινοὺς τῆς γῆς

The introductory task associated with the messianic warrior of 19.11-21 is that 'with righteousness he judges and make war'. John here attributes to Christ one of the qualities ascribed to the 'shoot of Jesse' in Isa. 11.4a, 'with righteousness shall he judge the poor'. The allusion is strengthened by the following use of Isa. 11.4b in 19.15, 21, and by John's earlier application of this OT passage to Christ in 5.5 (and 22.16). The real question concerns not the validity of the allusion but the scope of its meaning in relation to its biblical antecedent.

The majority of commentators are content to understand κρίνω in a negative sense here and relate the task of *judging* to the destruction of Christ's enemies in 19.15-21.[82] According to this view the act of *judging* is complementary to that of *making war* and effects the same

---

81. John's association of ἔμποροι with μεγιστᾶνες is significant for Rev. 6.15, where the μεγιστᾶνες follow the βασιλεῖς in the list of those judged. It is probably more than coincidental then that the lament of the merchants follows that of the kings in Rev. 18 (cf. also 18.3). This reinforces the supposition that John sees the merchants as a powerful and important group within the socio-political structure of the empire. John's high ranking of the μεγιστᾶνες after βασιλεῖς may reflect a common usage of the word in the sense of *nobles*: cf. 2 Chron. 36.18; 1 Esd. 3.9; 4.33; Prov. 8.15-16; Sir. 39.4, Jon. 3.7; Jer. 24.8; 25.18-19; Dan. 5.2-3; *Pss. Sol.* 2.30-32; Mk 6.21; P Leid W[vi.39] (MM, p. 393). Perhaps a fitting translation in Rev. 18.23 would be *magnates* (BAGD, p. 498).

82. E.g. Beckwith, *Apocalypse*, p. 732: 'The judgment here meant, as defined in the following words, is that of making war on the forces of the Beast'; see also Mounce, *Revelation*, p. 344, who understands Christ's judging as 'righteous retribution about to be enacted upon the beast and his followers'.

sphere: the ungodly. In this case there appears to be an element of discontinuity between John's application and the sense of the original text of Isaiah. In Isa. 11.2-4a the messianic king, endowed with the ideal qualities for ruling impartially, 'judges' the poor in the positive sense of seeking justice on their behalf.

An alternative view advanced by Holtz emphasizes the judicial rather than the penal significance of שפט/κρίνω and regards Christ's *judging* here as a positive activity expressed towards the salvation community.[83] Like Isaiah, John presents the messianic shoot as the ideal king (19.16) whose principal tasks are judging his people and making war against his enemies. These he performs in accordance with the divine standard of justice and righteousness. Not only is this theory in harmony with the Isaiah model, but it falls in line with other Jewish interpretations of Isa. 11.4a.[84]

Even so, this does not come across as the obvious sense of the text in Rev. 19.11 in its setting. The difficulty of this view lies in separating *judging* and *making war* as contrasting activities (positive and negative) which effect two distinct groups (the righteous and the wicked). There is bound to be some ambiguity because the process of judging invariably involves two opposing parties. Therefore, it follows that a judgment made *in favour* of one group necessarily includes a corresponding judgment *against* another group, and vice-versa.[85] The question is—which aspect does John emphasize here?

When we take into account the controversy scheme and judicial language which the prophet employs throughout the book, it is difficult to avoid the conclusion that Christ's *judging* in 19.11 may include both ideas.[86] But it does not necessarily follow that the emphasis here

83. 'κρίνειν ἐν δικαιοσύνῃ umschreibt das heilschaffende Handeln des Christus an seiner Gemeinde, nicht sein strafendes Gericht über die Gottwidrigen' (*Christologie*, p. 170); followed also by Rissi, *Future*, p. 22; cf. Müller, *Offenbarung*, p. 326.

84. *Pss. Sol.* 17.26, 29, 32; 1QSb 5.21. 4QpIsaᵃ 8–10, 21 implies a negative judgment with the sword, but the relation of pesher to lemma is uncertain.

85. This is the case in Isa. 11.4a and b; 1QSb 5.21-25; *Pss. Sol.* 17.22-32; and esp. Dan. 7.22-27: 'Judgment was given for the saints... and his [the fourth beast's] dominion shall be taken away to be consumed and destroyed'.

86. Rev. 6.9-11; 12.7-12; 16.7; 18.5-8; 19.2. Especially interesting is the relationship of anticipation and fulfilment between 6.10 and 19.2, where the twofold effect of judgment is clearly evident.

is on the positive result on behalf of the community. That may be only implicit. It is more natural to assume that John accents here the negative side of judgment—the judgment *against* his enemies.[87] In this way *judging* and *making war* are complementary ideas, with the former indicating the judicial decision-making process and the latter the punitive action taken on the basis of the decision.

87. Cf. Prigent, *L'Apocalypse*, p. 292. These enemies include those in the churches who disregarded the prophetic warnings of Christ (2.16, 22-23; 3.3); Sweet, *Revelation*, p. 282.

Chapter 7

ISAIAH IN REVELATION 20–22

Although there are few substantial verbal allusions to Isaiah in Revelation 20, J.W. Mealy has offered compelling evidence that the content and order of events in Rev. 19.17–20.10 follow closely the eschatological outline of the so-called 'Isaiah Apocalypse' (Isa. 24–27).[1] He argues that the many similarities between Ezekiel 38–39 and Isaiah 24–27 allowed John to interpret and compare one with the other, blending their prophetic message into a single eschatological scenario of events. Since there is already abundant evidence that John is in the habit of collating OT texts around themes (as was argued at length in Chapter 2 above), the possibility of a similar procedure here only adds weight to the cumulative evidence which Mealy provides. Recognition of such a dependence on Isaiah 24–27 here helps to strengthen previously suggested connections to this OT passage (e.g. Rev. 4.4) and may warrant re-evaluation of other proposed allusions to the Isaiah Apocalypse.

Keeping in mind this biblical substructure, it is important to recognize that various motifs from Revelation 20, particularly in vv. 11-15, anticipate the development of Isaiah texts in Revelation 21. In fact, the revelation of salvation which begins with Rev. 21.1 is inextricably bound up with all that has gone before it. As a vision of *renewal* 21.1–22.5 can only be fully appreciated against the backdrop of the previous series of visions of *removal*, influenced to a great extent by the judgment prophecies of Isaiah and Ezekiel:[2]

---

1. *After the Thousand Years: Resurrection and Judgment in Revelation 20* (JSNTSup, 70; Sheffield, 1992), pp. 99-101, 133-35, 137-38, 142. The possible use of Isa. 61.6 in 20.6 has been discussed earlier (pp. 113-16).
2. In 19.11–21.1 a series of seven visions introduced by καὶ εἶδον follows in rapid succession. Rev. 21.1 is not formally set apart from this series by μετὰ ταῦτα, but is nevertheless distinctive, since it forms the introduction to the last and most developed vision in the series. See further on the structure Yarbro Collins, *Combat Myth*, pp. 39-41.

Removal of Babylon (16.19–19.5)
Removal of the beast, the false prophet and their followers (19.10-21)
Removal of Satan (20.1-3, 7-10)
Removal of the first heaven and earth (20.11)
Removal of Death and Hades (20.14)

The elimination of everything which threatens the messianic community and stands in opposition to the divine Creator is a necessary prerequisite to the uniting of the heavenly and earthly communities and the universal establishment of God's kingdom.

I have already outlined in Chapter 2 the structural and thematic divisions of 21.1–22.5. From the perspective of biblical antecedents this larger section falls into two main units with subsections:

1. *21.1-8*   Oracles of renewal and presence
2. *21.9–22.5*   New Jerusalem oracles:
   a. *21.9-21*   Architectural traditions
   b. *21.22–22.5* The temple-city

In the first and third sections (21.1-8; 21.22–22.5), it is Isaiah which dominates the biblical substructure, while Ezekiel texts preponderate in the second section (21.9-21).[3] A more detailed analysis of these passages/units and the Isaiah traditions within them will now be undertaken.

Revelation 21.1-2a → Isaiah 65.17, 18

Revelation	Isaiah	
καὶ εἶδον οὐρανὸν καινὸν	כי הנני בורא שמים חדשים	ἔσται γὰρ ὁ οὐρανὸς[4]
καὶ γῆν καινήν	וארץ חדשה	καινὸς καὶ ἡ γῆ καινή,
ὁ γὰρ πρῶτος οὐρανὸς	ולא תזכרנה	καὶ οὐ μὴ μνησθῶσι
καὶ ἡ πρώτη γῆ ἀπῆλθαν...	הראשנות...כי הנני	τῶν προτέρων...ὅτι ἰδοὺ
καὶ...Ἰερουσαλὴμ καινὴν	בורא את־ירושלם	ἐγώ ποιῶ Ιερουσαλημ
εἶδον καταβαίνουσαν ἐκ		
τοῦ οὐρανοῦ ἀπὸ τοῦ θεοῦ		

We can begin by noting that John's threefold renewal scheme in vv. 1-2 coincides with the unique subject outline of Isa. 65.17-18: a

---

3.   The recognition of Isaiah and Ezekiel as the main prophetic foundation for the events of John's final vision was already acknowledged by the earliest extant commentator on Revelation: Justin, *Dial.* 80–81.

4.   α΄σ΄θ΄ read ἰδοὺ γὰρ ἐγὼ κτίζω οὐρανοὺς καινούς.

new heavens, earth and Jerusalem. The first clause, καὶ εἶδον οὐρανὸν καινὸν καὶ γῆν καινήν, follows closely the Hebrew text of Isa. 65.17a, both in word order and in the omission of articles.[5] The second parallel clause however, ὁ γὰρ πρῶτος...ἀπῆλθαν, while retaining the basic function of Isa. 65.17b of explaining the relationship of old to new, shares few verbal or structural similarities with the Isaiah passage. It is natural to expect here that John's reformulation has been influenced by the apocalyptic traditions of the early Christian community, where similar phrases occur.

> ὁ οὐρανὸς καὶ ἡ γῆ παρελεύσονται (Mk 13.31 par.)
> ἕως ἂν παρέλθῃ ὁ οὐρανὸς καὶ ἡ γῆ (Mt. 5.18; cf. Lk. 16.17)[6]

An even closer, though partial, parallel is found in *1 En.* 91.16: [יתחזון חדתין יין] ושמין קדמין בה יעברון ושמא 'And the first heaven in it shall pass away, a [new] heaven [shall appear]'. The close correspondence between Rev. 21.1b and *1 En.* 91.16 is one of several parallels which has led J.T. Milik to the conclusion that John had 'first hand knowledge' of *1 Enoch*, probably in a Greek version.[7] An important difference between the two passages, however, is that *1 En.* 91 says nothing of the removal and re-creation of the earth.[8] Whether or not John formed his 'passing away' phraseology under the influence of *1 En.* 91.16 or early Christian traditions, the presence of a cluster of allusions to Isa. 65.16-20a in Rev. 21.1-4 suggests that on the whole he was building his message directly on the prophetic foundation.

While the majority of commentators accept that John is here

---

5.   In contrast to LXX 65.17 and the recapitulation of the prophecy in Isa. 66.22; Ozanne, 'Influence', p. 142.

6.   These traditions are of course not necessarily based on Isa. 65.17. The Gospel texts probably reflect Isa. 51.6, while a similar teaching in Heb. 12.26-27 builds on Hag. 2.6, 21 (and perhaps Isa. 66.22). It is also interesting to note that whereas the whole Christian tradition employs παρέρχομαι (including 2 Cor. 5.17 and 2 Pet. 3.10), John adopts ἀπέρχομαι. This fact may account for the presence of παρῆλθεν in several MSS of Rev. 21.1.

7.   *The Books of Enoch* (Oxford, 1976), p. 199; Aramaic text and translation, pp. 266-67. In his commentary on *1 Enoch*, M. Black is more hesitant in supposing direct dependence and asks, 'Is Rev. 21.1 alluding to this verse?' (*The Book of Enoch or 1 Enoch* [Leiden, 1985], p. 294).

8.   The similarities and differences between Rev. 21.1 and *1 En.* 91.16 are discussed in more detail by Black in 'The New Creation in 1 Enoch', in *Creation, Christ and Culture: Studies in Honour of T.F. Torrance* (ed. R.W.A. McKinney; Edinburgh, 1976), pp. 13-21, esp. 16-18. Cf. also *Gos. Thom.* 11.

alluding to Isa. 65.17, there is some disagreement concerning the scope of the new heaven and earth prophecy. Does John expect a destruction and completely new re-creation of the cosmos,[9] or simply a renewal of the existing universe?[10] The original intention of the anonymous post-exilic prophet is of little help in this case, since even modern interpreters are divided over the cosmic significance of this OT oracle.[11] Earlier formulations of Third Isaiah's prophecy likewise reflect the same ambiguity and fall into similar categories.

1. Those which expect a *renewal* of the existing heavens and earth: *Jub.* 1.29 (cf. 4.26); *1 En.* 45.4-5.[12]
2. Those which expect a complete destruction and *re-creation*: *1 En.* 91.16; *LAB* 3.10; 2 Pet. 3.7-13.[13]

Although John does not adopt the cataclysm language of 2 Peter, and characteristically refrains from the cosmic speculation typical of apocalyptic eschatology, the casual reader of 20.11–21.5 would certainly be left with the impression that a universal destruction and re-creation is in view. A closer look at the language and context does nothing to dispel this opinion. Rev. 21.1 takes up 20.11 and makes clearer what was already stated there regarding the fate of the heaven and earth: '*No place* was found for them', that is, they passed away (ἀπῆλθαν); John's choice of καινός rather than νεός, and πρῶτος instead of πρότερος further heightens the discontinuity between new

---

9. So Charles, Comblin, Roloff, Müller, Kraft, Günther, Prigent, Vögtle, Rissi, and Wikenhauser.

10. Swete, Sweet; Beckwith and Mounce regard the evidence as ambiguous.

11. Günther, *Der Nah- und Enderwartungshorizont*, pp. 201-202; Vögtle, *Das Neue Testament*, pp. 51-55.

12. *4 Ezra* 7.75 is occasionally placed in this category, but there is no mention there of heaven and earth and no clear allusion to Isa. 65 (cf. 7.26, 31; 8.52). The same can be said for *2 Bar.* 32.6 (cf. 51.7-16 and 73-74), and 1QS 4.25 (cf. 1QH 13.11-12). Kraft would include the Greek translator of Isaiah (LXX) here, since in 65.17 he avoids translating ברא and transfers the original divine speech to the mouth of the prophet (*Offenbarung*, p. 263).

13. As for Mk 13.31; Lk. 21.33; Mt. 5.18; 24.35, each testify that heaven and earth shall pass away, but only Mt. 19.28 mentions a *renewal* (παλιγγενεσία). But whether this means re-creation or renewal is disputed. A similar ambiguity surrounds Heb. 12.26-28. Vögtle discusses all these texts at length, though his tendency to regard most of these examples as simply metaphors of judgment is not in every case compelling (*Das Neue Testament*, esp. pp. 76-89, 156-66).

and old, making anything less than a completely new creation incommensurate with the radical nature of the salvation event which 21.1 inaugurates.[14]

The desire to emphasize a sudden and decisive new beginning which originally led Third Isaiah to adopt creation language was born of a life-situation and concerns similar to John's: a prophet trying to inspire the hope of a weary and struggling community. In these circumstances the creation model offered a sense of immediacy, permanence and divine destiny which the Exodus model of Second Isaiah lacked. The latter was adequate to illustrate themes of *redemption* but less well suited for the description of *inheritance*.

John may not elaborate on the new heavens and earth, but this does not mean they are an incidental part of his description. In relation to what has gone before it, the announcement of a new heavens and new earth provides a formal introduction to the vision of final salvation even as their passing away served as a preface to the final judgment (20.11). In relation to what follows, Rev. 21.1 forms the inclusive framework within which the main item of interest can be discussed: the New Jerusalem.[15] As such it expresses in cosmological language what God Himself will shortly confirm in broader terms: 'Behold, I make *all things* new' (21.5a).

Revelation 21.2a → Isaiah 52.1

Revelation	Isaiah	
τὴν πόλιν τὴν ἁγίαν Ἰερουσαλήμ	ירושלם עיר הקדש	Ιερουσαλημ πόλις ἡ ἁγία

The same phrase occurs in Rev. 21.10, and without Ἰερουσαλήμ in 11.2 and 22.19. While the title of Jerusalem as the *Holy City* may have originated with Second Isaiah (it also appears in 48.2), from the Maccabean period onward it became a standard nationalistic agnomen for Jerusalem among Palestinian and non-Palestinian Jews alike.[16] For

---

14. Cf. Cremer, *BTL*, pp. 321-22. A more detailed argument for the re-creation view is given by Vögtle, *Das Neue Testament*, pp. 115-16.

15. Müller, *Offenbarung*, p. 349; Vögtle, *Das Neue Testament*, p. 119.

16. Neh. 11.1, 18; Isa. 66.20 LXX; Joel 4.17 LXX; Tob. 13.10 (B A; Dan. 9.24; 1 Macc. 2.7; 2 Macc. 3.1; 15.14; 3 Macc. 6.5; Pr. Az. 5; Philo, *Leg. All.* 347; *Somn.* 2.246; 4Q504 4.12; Mt. 4.5; 27.53; Josephus, *Ant.* 4.70; 20.118; cf. 11QT 47.13; *Pss. Sol.* 7.4.

this reason, most commentators have rightly been hesitant to suggest any literary dependence here.[17] Having said this, there are two factors which increase the probability that John may have had Isa. 52.1 specifically in mind. In the first place, he does not use the title here in reference to the earthly city, but to the heavenly Jerusalem, the ideal city of prophecy and promise.[18] Secondly, in Rev. 21.27 he applies another cultic motif from Isa. 52.1 to the New Jerusalem: 'But nothing unclean shall enter it'. If, as seems likely, John understood the Isaiah passage as a prophecy concerning eschatological Jerusalem, it should not be too surprising if he identified the New Jerusalem with the Holy City of Isa. 52.1.

Revelation 19.7-9; 21.2b → Isaiah 61.10

Rev. 19.7-9	*Isa. 61.10 MT*
χαίρωμεν καὶ ἀγαλλιῶμεν	שׂוֹשׂ אָשִׂישׂ ביהוה
καὶ δώσωμεν τὴν δόξαν αὐτῷ,	תגל נפשׁי באלהי
ὅτι ἦλθεν ὁ γάμος τοῦ ἀρνίου	כי הלבישׁני בגדי ישׁע
καὶ ἡ γυνὴ αὐτοῦ ἡτοίμασεν ἑαυτὴν	מעיל צדקה יעטני
καὶ ἐδόθη αὐτῇ ἵνα περιβάληται	כחתן יכהן פאר[19]
βύσσινον λαμπρὸν καθαρόν	וככלה תעדה כליה
τὸ γὰρ βύσσινον τὰ δικαιώματα	
τῶν ἁγίων ἐστίν... μακάριοι οἱ εἰς τὸ	
δεῖπνον τοῦ γάμου τοῦ ἀρνίου	
κεκλημένοι	

LXX
καὶ εὐφροσύνη εὐφρανθήσονται ἐπὶ κύριον.
ἀγαλλιάσθω ἡ ψυχή μου ἐπὶ τῷ κυρίῳ·

17. Only Charles, Ozanne and Gangemi expressly connect it to Isa. 52.1, while Swete finds the inspiration in Dan. 9.24 θ′ (*Apocalypse*, p. 133). Charles states confidently, 'the very phrase... "The holy city, Jerusalem" (xxi.10) is borrowed directly from Isa. lii.1' (*Lectures on the Apocalypse*, p. 15).
18. Rissi, *Future*, pp. 55-56.
19. Instead of 'As a bridegroom priests it with a garland', 1QIsaᵃ has 'As a bridegroom, as a priest with a garland'. Brownlee supposes this to be a 'sectarian' addition, but it may simply be an attempt to make sense of a difficult reading ('Messianic Motifs', p. 201). A similar modification is found in the Targum.

Rev. 21.2b
'Ιερουσαλὴμ καινὴν εἶδον...
ἡτοιμασμένην ὡς νύμφην
κεκοσμημένην τῷ ἀνδρὶ αὐτῆς.

ἐνέδωσε γάρ με ἱμάτιον σωτηρίου
καὶ χιτῶνα εὐφροσύνης
ὡς νυμφίῳ περιέθηκέ μοι μίτραν
καὶ ὡς νύμφην κατεκόσμησέ με
κόσμῳ.

Within the hymnic pericope of Rev. 19.5-9, vv. 7-9 announce the wedding of the Lamb and the *preparation* of his bride. This passage prepares for and anticipates Rev. 21.2, where the bride is *introduced*, and 21.9-21, where the bride is *described*. In all three places John builds on OT traditions that use marriage symbolism to describe the relationship between Yahweh and his faithful people. This procedure follows a pattern similar to that employed with the description of Harlot-Babylon, where the main development (chs. 17–18) was preceded by a summary statement which contained the same OT substructure (14.8-11).[20] A variety of other structural parallels between the Babylon appendix (chs. 17–18) and the New Jerusalem appendix (chs. 21–22) have been outlined above and show that John consciously and consistently plays one against the other, by adopting similar introductory phraseology, thematic sequences and verbal patterns. It is thus appropriate that the bride theme is introduced immediately following the hymnic celebration of the harlot's judgment (19.1-4).

The influence of Isa. 61.10 on Rev. 21.2b has long been acknowledged by commentators.[21] In view of this, it is surprising that the possibility of a similar inspiration in the earlier parallel passage of 19.7-9 has been left relatively unexplored. Part of the reason for this is that in Revelation 19 commentators have generally been concerned with and distracted by the presence of traditions related to the eschatological wedding parables found in the Gospels, especially Matthew.[22] These affinities are not to be denied. But, on the other hand, they do

20. Recognized also by D'Aragon, *JBC*, II, p. 489; Prigent, *L'Apocalypse*, p. 282. In addition, a variety of formal parallels points to an antithetic relationship between 14.6-13 and 19.5-10 (e.g. 14.6 // 19.5; 14.13 // 19.9; cf. 14.14-20 // 19.11-21). The bulk of this section (pp. 231-53) appears in '"His Bride has Prepared Herself": Revelation 19–21 and Isaian Nuptial Imagery', *JBL* 109 (1990), pp. 269-87, and is republished here by permission of the Society of Biblical Literature.

21. P. van Bergen, 'Dans l'attente de la nouvelle Jérusalem', *LuViSup* 45 (1959), pp. 1-9; Trudinger, Ozanne, Comblin; R. Batey, *New Testament Nuptial Imagery* (Leiden, 1971), p. 57; D. Aune, *ISBE*, I, p. 547.

22. Vos, *Synoptic Traditions*, pp. 163-74; Schüssler Fiorenza, *Revelation*, p. 104; Holtz, *Christologie*, p. 190.

not account for all the various strands of marriage imagery which John employs. A breakdown of those elements of wedding symbolism that appear in Rev. 19.7-9 and 21.2 betrays instead a synthesis of OT and early Christian traditions, with Isa. 61.10 offering several parallels.

1. *Rev. 19.7bα.* The eschatological wedding (γάμος) in which the Messiah is bridegroom (νυμφίος—though John does not specifically use this word of Christ): Mt. 22.1-13; 25.1-13 (cf. Mk 2.19-20 par.; 2 Cor. 11.2; Eph. 5.22-23; Jn 3.29).

2. *Rev. 19.7bβ; 21.2, 9; 22.17.* The people of God as the bride (γυνή, νύμφη): Isa. 61.10 (cf. 62.4-5; Hos. 2; 2 Cor. 11.2; Eph. 5.22-33).

3. *Rev. 19.7bβ; 21.2b.* The bride being prepared (ἑτοιμάζω) and adorned (κοσμέω): Isa. 61.10 (cf. 49.18).

4. *Rev. 19.8a, 14.* The bride divinely granted (ἐδόθη αὐτῇ) a wedding garment: Isa. 61.10.

5. *Rev. 19.9a.* The wedding meal (δεῖπνον τοῦ γάμου): Mt. 22.1-13 (using ἄριστον) (cf. Mt. 26.9; *4 Ezra* 9.47).

6. *Rev. 19.9a.* The invited guests (οἱ κεκλημένοι): Mt. 22.1-13.

Elsewhere in Revelation where John has transmitted early Christian traditions, they have almost always appeared in close combination with parallel OT traditions.[23] Rarely does the prophet present distinctly Christian *testimonia* on their own authority, independent of some related OT foundation. It is consistent with this pattern that in the present case we find a similar integration of old and new combining direct prophetic statement with later Christian development. However, it is important to note that, after its introduction (19.7-9), when the bride theme is taken up again (21.2), and developed (21.9-21), the OT connection prevails and identifiable early Christian traditions fade from view.

This makes it all the more important to recognize the *introductory* function of 19.7-9 in relation to the presentation of the Bride–New Jerusalem of Revelation 21.[24] Although in the latter passage the bride

23. E.g. Rev. 6.12-17 and 14.14-20.
24. *Contra* Holtz (*Christologie*, pp. 186-87), who, on the basis of variations in terminology between 19.7-9 and 21.2, questions whether the two passages should be closely connected. Such differences, however, are typical of John's method of thematic recapitulation; cf. Caird, *Revelation*, p. 234.

may be *described* primarily on the basis of OT motifs, the nuptial imagery should not be *explained* in isolation from the combination of OT and early Christian tradition found in the hymnic preamble of 19.7-9. With this understanding of the complementary relationship between Rev. 19.7-9 and 21.2–22.5 in mind, we can now move on to discuss in more detail the extent and nature of the Isaiah allusions contained in these two passages.

a. *Revelation 19.7a* χαίρωμεν καὶ ἀγαλλιῶμεν...ὅτι...Various parallels to this introductory call to praise have been noted by commentators, e.g. Ps. 118.24 (נגילה ונשמחה), and Mt. 5.12a (καίρετε καὶ ἀγαλλιᾶσθε, ὅτι...). Charles brings together Rev. 19.6b and 7 and compares Ps. 96.1(97.1) ὁ κύριος ἐβασίλευσεν, ἀγαλλιασθω ἡ γῆ, εὐφρανθήτωσαν...[25] However, the relevance of this latter option is diminished somewhat by the fact that 19.6b contains the ground for the preceding word of praise (ἀλληλουϊά), and is thus syntactically distinct from 19.7, where the call to praise is followed by a ὅτι-clause of its own which contains the ground for praise.

It would seem more natural to see Rev. 19.7 as John's adaptation of Isa. 61.10a which offers a similar structure, diction and theme. There, as in Revelation, an introductory expression of praise to God (using שיש and גיל, which are commonly translated with χαίρω and ἀγαλλιάω respectively) is followed by the ground of praise (כי) which contains not only marriage imagery, but a similar clothing allegory as well.

b. *Revelation 19.7bβ* καὶ ἡ γυνή αὐτοῦ
Rev. 21.2 ἡτοιμασμένην ὡς νύμφην κεκοσμημένην τῷ ἀνδρὶ αὐτῆς
Rev. 21.9 τὴν νύμφην τὴν γυναῖκα τοῦ ἀρνίον
Rev. 22.17 ἡ νύμφη[26]

---

25. *Revelation*, I, p. lxxv.
26. A few MSS (א[2] *gig co Apr*) read νύμφη for γυνή in 19.7. The use of γυνή here in anticipation of the wedding follows Jewish convention, where *engagement* (ארש; Mish. ארס; μνηστεύω) served as a formal and legally binding starting point of a marriage, which was then consummated with the *wedding* (משתה; γάμος); Deut. 22.23-24; Mt. 1.18-25; *Jos. Asen.* 21.1 'It does not befit a man to sleep with his wife [γυνή] before the wedding [πρὸ τῶν γάμων]' (*OTP*, II, p. 241); Greek text from C. Burchard, 'Ein vorläufiger griechischer Text von Joseph und Aseneth',

Although a similar idea appears in 2 Cor. 11.2 and Eph. 5.22-33, in the NT only Revelation appears to use νύμφη of the Christian community.[27] This is not to say that the application of this symbol to the church (whether earthly, eschatological or both) is in every instance one of formal equivalence, any more than that the interpretation of the New Jerusalem image can be limited to a single frame of reference. But it is still best taken as a relational metaphor, whose primary referent is the salvation community. The use of marriage imagery in general to illustrate various aspects of the relationship between God and his people is found in several OT prophetic writers, but appears to have been especially popular in the Isaianic school. Of the dozen or so OT passages where figurative marriage terminology is employed, more than half come from Isaiah 40–66.

1. engagement (ארש): Hos. 2.21-22; (כלולה) Jer. 2.2
2. bride (כלה): Isa. 49.18; 61.10; 62.5
3. wife (אשה): Ezek. 16.32; Isa. 54.6
4. Yahweh as bridegroom (חתן): Isa. 62.5 (cf. 61.10)
5. Yahweh as husband: (איש) Hos. 2.18; (בעל) Isa. 54.5; Jer. 3.14; 31.32
6. To marry/be married (בעל): Isa. 62.4-5

Not only is Isaiah represented in five of the six categories, but it alone utilizes the term *bride* in this special spiritual sense.[28] Furthermore, only Isaiah employs marriage imagery in a consistently positive manner to the *future* relationship between Yahweh and his faithful remnant as symbolized by the personified Zion-Jerusalem.[29] This

DBAT 14 (1979), pp. 2-53. Cf. also *Jos. Asen.* 21.3; 23.3; *IDB*, III, p. 284.

27. Though cf. Jn 3.29 and Feuillet, 'Le festin des noces de l'agneau et ses anticipations', *EspVie* 97 (1987), pp. 353-62, who argues for a special affinity between the marriage imagery of Revelation and the Gospel of John.

28. Of course, an allegorical interpretation of the Song of Solomon, which speaks of the bride throughout, would offer another possible inspiration for this idea. (e.g. *Cant. R.* 4.10.1; *Deut. R.* 2.37; *Num. R.* 13.2). For the earliest evidence of such an approach, see *IDB*, IV, pp. 421-22; P. Vuilliaud, *Le Cantique des Cantiques d'après le tradition juive* (Paris, 1925).

29. Although the identity of the speaker in 61.10 is not readily apparent, that it is Zion-Jerusalem can easily be inferred from the surrounding context (esp. 62.1). The Targum makes this clear by adding 'Jerusalem hath said' as an introduction to 61.10. Cf. R.N. Whybray, *Isaiah 40–66* (NCB; London, 1975), p. 245. in *4 Ezra* 7.26 the better MS tradition (Lat Syr) speaks of the New Jerusalem as 'the bride...even

eschatological perspective and collective symbol system help to explain Isaiah's particular suitability as a model for John's evocation of the Bride–New Jerusalem. To suggest, then, as Kraft has done, that John has used the marriage imagery of Ezekiel 16 to describe the New Jerusalem in Rev. 21.2 is fundamentally to misunderstand his use of OT prophecy.[30] Ezekiel 16 is a negative portrayal of unfaithful earthly Jerusalem which stands as the antithesis of the eschatological temple and city of Ezekiel 40–48. John clearly recognizes this contrast, for in Rev. 17.16 he uses the parallel passage of Ezek. 23.29, 25 (cf. 16.39-41) to describe Harlot-Babylon. It is therefore most unlikely that he would apply Ezekiel 16 to the New Jerusalem. As was made clear in the thematic outlines in Chapter 2, John is not simply describing the New Jerusalem with random OT motifs, but with prophetic texts specifically concerned with the glorious eschatological Jerusalem.

c. *Rev. 19.8 (cf. v. 14)* καὶ ἐδόθη αὐτῇ ἵνα περιβάληται βύσσινον λαμπρὸν καθαρόν, τὸ γὰρ βύσσινον τὰ δικαιώματα τῶν ἁγίων ἐστίν. There may not be much in the way of close dictional correspondence between this sentence and Isa. 61.10, but the conceptual similarities are striking and unique. Both texts refer to the clothing of the salvation community collectively and emphasize that the garment is a gift from God: 'He has clothed me' // 'it was granted her to be clothed'. More significant still is the fact that in both passages the clothing is symbolic of a similar spiritual quality.

Isa. 61.10: the robe = righteousness
Rev. 19.8b: the fine linen (garment) = righteous deeds

The difference between *righteousness* and *righteous deeds* involves

the city appearing'. But most scholars regard this as corrupt, perhaps even influenced by Rev. 21.1-2, and prefer the Armenian reading, 'the city which now is not seen shall appear'; so Metzger *OTP*, I, p. 53; G.H. Box, *The Ezra-Apocalypse, Being Chapters 3–14 of the Book Commonly Known as 4 Ezra (or II Esdras)* (London, 1912), p. 114, among others. While internal evidence favours this choice (e.g. the Lat-Syr reading upsets the parallelism, and no such idea occurs in the later, more developed Zion vision of 9.38–10.59), it is questionable whether this is enough to overcome the external MS support. Metzger himself says of the Armenian version that it is 'of little value in reconstructing the original text' (p. 518). The recent edition of P. Geoltrain (in Philonenko [ed.], *La Bible Ecrits intertestamentaires*, p. 1420) accepts the Latin reading.

30. *Offenbarung*, p. 263.

only a small change in form, since צדקה in the plural means *righteous acts*. And δικαίωμα does occasionally translate the singular in the LXX.[31] If indeed Isa. 61.10 lies behind both the clothing metaphor in 19.8a *and* its interpretation in 19.8b, it would suggest that the latter is part of the original development, and not a secondary gloss as some commentators have suggested.[32]

d. *Revelation 19.7bβ* καὶ ἡ γυνὴ αὐτοῦ ἡτοίμασεν ἑαυτὴν. *Rev. 21.2b* ἡτοιμασμένην ὡς νύμφην κεκοσμημένην τῷ ἀνδρὶ αὐτῆς. Of all the various motifs that Revelation has in common with Isa. 61.10, it is the simile of the bride 'adorned' in Rev. 21.2b that exhibits the closest dictional correspondence. A virtually identical rendering of the reflexive כלה תעדה with a passive participle is found in Aquila: ὡς νύμφην κοσμουμένην.[33] A remarkably close parallel occurs in the description of Aseneth in *Jos. Asen.* 4.2: κεκοσμημένην ὡς νύμφην θεοῦ, though the exact significance of θεοῦ here is a matter of debate.[34]

Whether or not the reflexive phrase of 19.7bβ (ἡτοίμασεν ἑαυτήν) reflects another, more literal, reading of the Hebrew ('adorns herself') is questionable. In 19.7bβ, ἡτοίμασεν itself has no antecedent in Isa. 61.10, but serves an important function as a linkword with Rev. 21.2b, where the nature of the preparation receives further definition.

31. E.g. 2 Sam. [Kgdms] 19.29; Prov. 8.20 (B); Ezek. 18.21 (A); cf. BAGD, p. 198; BDB, p. 842. There is no possibility of connection between βύσσινος (*fine linen*) and Hebrew מעיל or בגד. Both Hebrew words are strictly generic terms for clothing with no indication of quality. John's use of βύσσινος here stems rather from the Harlot–Bride parallelism, and is used first of Babylon in 18.16, where the description was probably inspired by Ezek. 16.10-13, 16-18. Beckwith notes in τὰ δικαιώματα another contrast with the harlot: τὰ ἀδικήματα, 18.5 (*Apocalypse*, p. 727).

32. E.g. Charles, Müller; *contra* Caird. The attribution of λαμπρός (*bright*) to the bride's attire may have been suggested by Isa. 62.1, which continues the theme of 61.10 and speaks of the *brightness* (נגה) of Jerusalem's righteousness (cf. Rev. 15.6).

33. Symmachus likewise gives a passive construction (ὡς νύμφην περικεί-μενην), while the LXX brings the phrase in line with the active subject–object clauses in 61.10a and is quite different (ὡς νύμφην κατεκόσμησέ με).

34. Burchard, 'Text', p. 7; *OTP*, II, p. 206 n. 4a; M. Philonenko, *Joseph et Aséneth: Introduction, texte critique, traduction et notes* (SPB, 13; Leiden, 1968), p. 141. Cf. Achille Tatius 3.7.5 ὥσπερ Αιδωνει νύμφη κεκοσμημένη ('as a bride adorned for Hades'); Hermas, *Vis.* 4.2.1.

However, given the thematic relationship between 19.7-9 and 21.2, and the presence of at least some verbal affinities (γυνή = νύμφη, ἑαυτήν), the influence of Isa. 61.10 on 19.7bβ, as well as on 21.2b, seems likely. Overall, while the dictional connections between Rev. 19.7-8 and Isa. 61.10 are in individual cases doubtful or inexact, the concentration of various parallel terms and concepts within the single theme of marriage adds a cumulative force to the proposed allusion. Recognition of a structural and thematic relationship between Rev. 19.7-9 and 21.2-21 further strengthens the probability of this biblical link.

Before discussing the broader implications of John's nuptial imagery, it is necessary to treat one further Isaiah allusion which forms the third and final part of the bride construct.

Revelation 21.18-21 → Isaiah 54.11-12

Revelation	Isaiah MT
καὶ ἡ ἐνδώμησις τοῦ τείχους αὐτῆς	הנה אנכי מרביץ בפוך אבניך
ἴασπις καὶ ἡ πόλις χρυσίον καθαρὸν	ויסדתיך בספירים
ὅμοιον ὑάλῳ καθαρῷ. οἱ θεμέλιοι τοῦ	ושמתי כדכד שמשתיך
τείχους τῆς πόλεως παντὶ λίθῳ τιμίῳ	ושעריך לאבני אקדח
κεκοσμημένοι... καὶ οἱ δώδεκα πυλῶνες	וכל גבולך לאבני חפץ
δώδεκα μαργαρῖται, ἀνὰ εἷς ἕκαστος τῶν	
πυλώνων ἦν ἐξ ἑνὸς μαργαρίτου.	
καὶ ἡ πλατεῖα τῆς πόλεως χρυσίον	
καθαρὸν ὡς ὕαλος διαυγής	

Isaiah LXX
ἰδοὺ ἐγὼ ἑτοιμάζω σοὶ ἄνθρακα τὸν λίθον σου
καὶ τὰ θεμέλιά σου σάπφειρον
καὶ θήσω τὰς ἐπάλξεις σου ἴασπιν
καὶ τὰς πύλας σου λίθους κρυστάλλου
καὶ τὸν περίβολόν σου λίθους ἐκλεκτούς

An interesting tradition history lies behind the interpretation of these two verses of Isaiah, which, while providing helpful insights into John's usage, at the same time requires careful evaluation. A comparison of those texts which make up this history of interpretation is complicated particularly by the vague and ambiguous nature of the terminology contained in the original building oracle of Isaiah. This applies both to the precious materials employed and the structural components that they adorn. To help unclutter the accompanying discussion, and to facilitate easy reference, I will present the various traditions in chart form, along with an assessment of the individual motifs in the order in which they appear in Revelation.[35]

Isa. 54.11-12 (MT)	LXX	Tob. 13.16-18a	5QNJ	Rev. 21.18-21	Targ. Isa.
1. stones antimony	stone carbuncle	streets carbuncle, Ophir-stone	streets white stone	streets pure gold	pavement-stones antimony
2. foundations sapphires	foundations sapphire	—	—	foundations precious stones	foundations jewels
3. battlements כדכד?	battlements jasper	battlements pure gold	—	—	timbers pearls
4. gates ?carbuncles	gates crystal stones	doors sapphire, emerald	gate sapphire	gates pearls	gates carbuncles
5. border precious stones	wall precious stones	wall precious stone	—	ἐνδώμησις (of wall) jasper	border precious stones

a. *Revelation 21.18a* καὶ ἡ ἐνδώμησις τοῦ τείχους αὐτῆς ἴασπις. The central architectural feature of John's city is the wall, which is mentioned no fewer than six times (21.12, 14-15, 17-19) and is divided into two parts: (i) οἱ θεμέλιοι τοῦ τείχους (21.14, 19), and (ii) ἡ ἐνδώμησις τοῦ τείχους (21.18a). Although the exact etymology and meaning of ἐνδώμησις remain obscure, the context in which John uses it suggests two options.[36] Since the θεμέλιοι obviously

35. For the text of Tobit consult R. Hanhart, *Septuaginta: Tobit* (Göttingen, 1983). I have followed the longer recension (Sinaiticus and Old Latin) which has received recent support in the discovery of fragments of Tobit at Qumran (see Schürer, III.1, pp. 224-25). Both Schürer and Hanhart (p. 15) apparently failed to notice that Milik, in *The Books of Enoch* (pp. 163, 186, 191, 197) furnishes five examples from the Aramaic fragments, with which readers can make their own comparison. In an example from our chapter (13.12), the Aramaic reads די ימללון מלא קשא, which is paralleled exactly by S La (οἳ ἐροῦσιν λόγον σκληρόν) against BA (οἱ μισοῦντες σε). Cf. Milik, *Ten Years of Discovery in the Wilderness of Judaea* (London, 1959), pp. 31-32. For 5QNJ see Beyer, *Die aramäischen Texte*, pp. 214-21 and for the Targum, Stenning, pp. 183-84.

36. The issue is further complicated by a variant reading in the bulk of the Byzantine tradition which has ἐνδόμησις rather than ἐνδώμησις. Whether or not the two different spellings even represent the same word is not entirely clear. MM

refer to that which forms the foundation or base of the wall, the ἐνδώμησις must in some way be connected with that part of the wall which is built on and rises above the foundation. Thus ἐνδώμησις may denote either the *material* of the upper wall,[37] or the (upper) *structure* of the wall in general (as opposed to its foundations).[38] In any case, it is not likely that John is referring to some unique feature of the wall (e.g. battlements of jasper—see §3 in chart above), since Rev. 21.18 appears to be a general summary statement giving the building materials employed for the city and its wall, following their measuring in 21.16-17.

The ἐνδώμησις of the wall is said to be made of jasper. When we take into account that a few verses earlier John calls jasper a 'most precious stone' (21.11; cf. 4.3), there seems to be closer affinity here between Revelation and Tob. 13.17b, 'and all your walls with precious stone', than between Revelation and Isa. 54.12, which has plural 'stones'. By itself this minor similarity carries little significance, but, in the light of stronger connections to Tobit that will emerge in the

(p. 212) takes them as one word, but LS (pp. 561-62) and BAGD (p. 264) imply a distinction (though the latter ends up conjecturing the same meaning for ἐνδώμη σις which LS gives to ἐνδόμησις!). The grammars are no less confusing. Moulton regards ἐνδόμησις as stemming from a false etymology (II, p. 73), and takes it from ἐν and δωμάω (II, p. 307; cf. B.F. Westcott and F.J.A. Hort [eds.], *The New Testament in the Original Greek* [Cambridge: Cambridge University Press, 2nd edn, 1886], II, Appendix, p. 159). Robertson, on the other hand, derives ἐνδόμησις from ἐνδομέω and accepts ἐνδώμησις as a variant spelling (pp. 152, 201). Despite all this ambiguity it seems preferable to accept ἐνδώμησις as the correct reading here and allow that it has something to do with construction (LS gives *enclosing within a wall*, BAGD, *interior structure*, prob. = *construction*, hence *material*). To the sources listed in the dictionaries can be added Papyrus Dura 19.15 (88/89 CE) which supports the spelling ἐνδόμησις, though unfortunately the context adds little clarity to the lexical discussion.

37. So Beckwith, Müller.

38. The versions and Latin Fathers tend to support the second option (cf. Hoskier, II, p. 600), and it is followed by Charles and others. Since John himself makes a distinction between the θεμέλιοι and the ἐνδώμησις of the wall, it seems most unlikely that the latter is also some kind of foundation, as Mounce and BAGD suggest (*Revelation*, p. 381; BAGD, p. 264). Cf. Beckwith, *Apocalypse*, p. 762; Müller, *Offenbarung*, p. 359 ('nicht "Unterbau"'). A third option presented by Swete (*Apocalypse*, p. 290) and followed by Prigent (*L'Apocalypse*, pp. 340-41) holds that the wall is merely *inlaid* with jasper.

remaining elements of Rev. 21.18-21, it may be more than the result of chance.

b. *Revelation 21.19a* οἱ θεμέλιοι τοῦ τείχους τῆς πόλεως παντὶ λίθῳ τιμίῳ κεκοσμημένοι. The foundations of the city wall were first introduced in 21.14 where they were said to be twelve in number and inscribed with the names of the twelve apostles of the Lamb (cf. Eph. 2.20). Whereas the foundations are associated with the city generally in Isa. 54.11 and the other dependent texts, John assigns them a more specific role in connection with the wall of the city.[39] Instead of sapphire alone, the twelve foundation stones of the New Jerusalem are adorned with *every precious stone*, of which sapphire is just one of many.

For the enumeration of the twelve jewels in Rev. 21.19b-20 most commentators agree that John shifts here to the gem tradition of the high priest's breastplate in Exod. 28.15-21 (cf. 39.8-14), with Ezek. 28.13 usually cited as a secondary parallel.[40] But no one appears to have noticed that John's introduction to the list of gems (παντὶ λίθῳ τιμιῳ κεκοσμημένοι) follows closely the introduction to Ezekiel's list (כל אבן יקרה מסכתך). It may be, therefore, that the order of influence should be reversed, and that John begins with Ezekiel and supplements with Exodus. In any case, he has moved, at least temporarily, away from Isaiah to other traditions. To Isaiah 54 he returns in Rev. 21.21.

c. *Revelation 21.21a* καὶ οἱ δώδεκα πυλῶνες δώδεκα μαργαρῖται. From Rev. 21.12 we learn that the city also has twelve gates with twelve angelic sentries, and that upon the gates are written the names of the twelve tribes of Israel. In the following verse (21.13), the configuration of the gates according to the four points of the compass is outlined. Much of this tradition is inspired by Ezekiel 40–48. But concerning the compositional makeup of the gates, Ezekiel says nothing; and so in Rev. 21.21a John returns to his adaptation of Isa. 54.11-12.

Each of the twelve gates of the New Jerusalem is said to be made of

---

39. Instead of יסדתיך, 1QIsaᵃ 54.11 has the nominal form יסודותיך, but the sense is left relatively unchanged. Heb. 11.10 also mentions the foundations of a heavenly city.

40. For a treatment of John's gem list and a review of past theories, see W.W. Reader, 'The Twelve Jewels of Revelation 21.19-20: Tradition History and Modern Interpretations', *JBL* 100 (1981), pp. 433-57.

a single pearl. Is this association John's own innovation on the basis of Isa. 54.12b, or does it stem from contemporary Jewish eschatological speculation? Because of the uncertainty that typically surrounds the etymology and meaning of many ancient gem-names, opportunities for conjecture frequently presented themselves to early translators and interpreters of the biblical record. This is particularly the case with Isa. 54.12ab, where three of the four principal terms are obscure.

> And I will make your שמשתיך (of) כדכד
> And your gates (of) stones of אקדח

The first two Hebrew words are only used twice in the OT, and the third (אקדח), with which we are particularly concerned, is a *hapax legomenon*. In such circumstances, two main options were open to those working with the text; either admit one's ignorance and provide a suitable substitute, or offer a conjecture based on whatever information might be known or obtained about the word in question.[41] Fortunately, in the present instance the interpretative history of אקדח is fairly well defined and can shed some light on the way John himself may have approached the text.

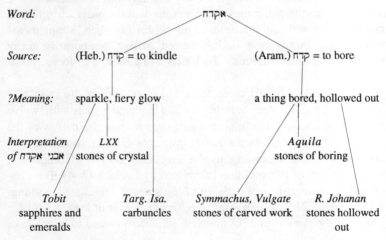

Word:		אקדח		
Source:	(Heb.) קדח = to kindle		(Aram.) קדח = to bore	
?Meaning:	sparkle, fiery glow		a thing bored, hollowed out	
Interpretation of אבני אקדח	*LXX* stones of crystal		*Aquila* stones of boring	
Tobit sapphires and emeralds	*Targ. Isa.* carbuncles	*Symmachus, Vulgate* stones of carved work	*R. Johanan* stones hollowed out

As is natural, most interpreters related אקדח to the nearest cognate root, קדח. But since this word has one meaning in Hebrew and another

---

41. A third alternative is simply to transliterate the word in question, as Jerome has done (*ecda*), KB, I, p. 80.

in Aramaic, two distinct lines of development ensued.[42]

At this point the Hebrew genealogy has reached its full potential, but the Aramaic stemma is open-ended and invites yet another stage of interpretation to answer the question: What is meant by *stones hollowed out*?[43] Since the rest of the building oracle in Isa. 54.11-12 employs costly materials, it would be natural to assume that the stones spoken of here are precious stones. Now, to ask what is a precious stone that is often bored or hollowed out seems to imply an obvious answer. For then, as now, pearls were highly prized and were commonly drilled and strung together in necklaces.[44]

As has often been noted, the association of pearls with the gates of the future Jerusalem is also found in rabbinic tradition, from which the testimony of R. Johanan (Palestine †279) is usually quoted:

> The Holy One, blessed be He, will in the time to come bring precious stones and pearls (טובות ומרגליות) which are thirty [cubits] by thirty and will cut out from them [openings] ten [cubits] by twenty, and will set them up in the gates of Jerusalem (*b. B. Bat.* 75a).[45]

42. For the following list I have utilized the lexical discussions of BDB, p. 869; KB, I, p. 80; Jastrow, p. 1315; *EncJud*, XIII, col. 1011; cf. M. Bauer, *Edelstein-kunde* (Leipzig, 3rd edn, 1932), pp. 523ff. R. Johanan's interpretation of 54.12 is found in *Midr. Pss.* 87.2 and *Pes. K.* 18.5, where it is introduced with the lemma 'and Thy gates of stones hollowed out'; W.G. Braude, *The Midrash on Psalms* (New Haven, 1959), II, p. 75; cf. p. 492 n. 5; W.G. Braude and I.J. Kapstein, *Pĕsikta dĕ—Rab Kahăna* (London, 1975), p. 219. *Targ. Isa.* does have *pearls* in the previous line (54.12a) as a conjecture for the obscure כדכד. 1QIsa[a] reads אוקדה, with the waw supralinear, but the meaning of this addition is unclear.

43. Even at this stage the translator could be satisfied at having provided a sense which fit very well with the idea of city gates, i.e. 'I will make... your gates of (precious) stones hollowed out'. The interpreter, on the other hand, would probably want to go further.

44. Pliny, *H.N.* 9.54 (106), 'The first place therefore and the topmost rank among all things of price is held by pearls'; Aelian, *N.A.* 10.13 'The pearl, it seems, is like a stone (λίθῳ)'; Theophrastus (quoted in Athenaeus, *Deip.* 3.93) 'Among stones (λιθῶν) which are much admired is the so-called *margaritês*... with it are made the costliest necklaces'; Pliny (*H.N.* 9.58 [117]) also mentions Lollia Paulina (the consort of Gaius) at a betrothal banquet being 'covered with emeralds and pearls interlaced alternately and shining all over her head, hair, ears, neck and fingers'. These were spoils from the *eastern* provinces. For archaeological examples from the period, see R.A. Higgins, *Greek and Roman Jewelry* (Berkeley, CA, 1980 [1961]), esp. p. 181 and plate 55a. Cf. Philostratus, *Vita Ap.* 3.53.

45. Other variations of Johanan's words are found in *b. Sanh.* 100a; *Midr. Pss.*

It is important to note that this and similar haggadic traditions (none of which predates 200 CE) are generally presented as *expositions* of Isa. 54.12, though to what extent this is the compiler's doing is not always clear.[46] Whether or not these interpretations go back to John's day is not really necessary to prove, since, as the above construct shows, he could easily have come to such a conclusion on the basis of the text of Isa. 54.12b alone.

The tradition of the 'pearly gates' in Rev. 21.21 is therefore probably not simply the invention of John's fertile imagination, nor even an innovative substitution in the face of textual difficulty, but rather a well-reasoned and comprehensive interpretation of Isa. 54.12b.[47] From this exegetical base proceeds a final haggadic embellishment: 'Each of the gates [was] made of a single pearl'.

d. *Revelation 21.21b* καὶ ἡ πλατεῖα τῆς πόλεως χρυσίον καθαρὸν ὡς ὕαλος διαυγής. The pericope of the building materials of the New Jerusalem (21.18-21) concludes with the observation that the 'street of the city was pure gold'.[48] Commentators have tended to gloss quickly over this line, without taking into consideration the source of the

87.2; and *Pes. K.* 18.5. In the first three (including *b. B. Bat.* 75a), his testimony is related to the gates of Jerusalem generally, while in the last only the east gate of the temple and its two wickets are referred to. Interestingly, Johanan provides the measurements of the gates, something which John evidently had in mind (21.15), but for some reason left out.

46. Collections of rabbinic exposition of Isa. 54.11-12 are found in *Midr. Pss.* 87.1-2 and *Pes. K.* 18.5, which include a variety of pearl traditions. Various other Jewish and Near Eastern pearl legends are gathered together in E. Burrows, 'The Pearl in the Apocalypse', *JTS* 43 (1942), pp. 177-79.

47. Only Caird (*Revelation*, p. 277) specifically upholds a connection: 'The Hebrew *'eqdah*... [John] takes to mean pearls'. Sweet is less direct: 'The Jews took the "carbuncles" of Isa. 54.12 to be pearls' (*Revelation*, p. 306). Both statements are only indirectly true however, since nowhere is אקדח itself taken to mean pearls, but the phrase אבני אקדח is *interpreted* as denoting pearls.

48. Some commentators (e.g. Charles, Caird) take ἡ πλατεῖα as generic 'streets', but there is very little precedent for this, either in the OT or in John's usage (Rev. 11.8; 22.2). A comparison of the plan of 5QNJ, which has several smaller streets of 67 cubits width, but one main street of 92 cubits passing through the middle of the city, suggests that John particularly has in mind this central thoroughfare (cf. 22.2). The adjective ὕαλος often means 'radiant' when used with metals or gems, and since διαυγής can designate both crystal and glass we may wish to translate 'as radiant crystal' (LS, pp. 417, 1840).

imagery. But there is much to suggest that this final architectural feature, like that of the wall, foundations and gates, had its inspiration in the building oracle of Isa. 54.11-12, though not directly, but probably as it has been interpreted in Tob. 13.16-17.

In the first place, the street motif is the only architectural feature in Rev. 21.18-21 that has not been mentioned in the two preceding units of 21.12-14 (introduction) and 21.15-17 (measuring).[49] That it is included here suggests that it was part of a source which John adopts in 21.18-21 for the composition of the city and its constituent parts. Secondly, the addition of streets to the eschatological city blueprint was first made specific by the author of Tobit, on the basis of an interpretation of Isa. 54.11b.[50] Although it may have been possible for John to come to a similar understanding of Isa. 54.11b on his own, there are two further reasons why this is less likely than the suggestion that he is here dependent on Tobit.

First of all, Isa. 54.11b *begins* the list of architectural features of the future Jerusalem, but both John and the author of Tobit have placed the street tradition last in their outline. Now while it may be granted that both authors could have come to a similar interpretation of Isa. 54.11b independently (i.e. that the 'stones' spoken of in 54.11b refer to the streets of the city), it is most unlikely that each would also have taken the first element in Isaiah's description and moved it to the end of their building inventories. It is more natural to assume that John's inclusion of the street motif and its position presuppose the interpretation of Isa. 54.11b given in Tob. 13.17a.[51]

Second, when we turn to consider John's association of the street with 'pure gold' (χρυσίον καθαρόν), here again the evidence points to the influence of Tobit. This is not to say that the author of Tobit himself explicitly makes such a connection (at least as far as the Greek

---

49. Apart from ἡ ἐνδώμησις, which is connected with the wall.

50. All the versions of Tobit agree in reading αἱ πλατεῖαι–ἄνθρακι-ψηφολογηθήσονται, of which πλατεῖαι interprets Hebrew אבניך, ἄνθρακι corresponds to בפוך (as in LXX), and the verb ψηφολογηθήσονται parallels מרביץ... (אבניך) (from ψῆφος and *λογέω; cf. ψηφοθετέω, 'to lay down a stone'). The Targum reflects a similar interpretation in its addition of רצפתיך, 'I will set the stones of *your pavement* with antimony'. John's change of πλατεῖαι (= רחבות?) to the sg. πλατεῖα is probably intentional (see above n. 48).

51. Tobit's adaptation of Isa. 54.11-12, and specifically the street theme, appears also to have influenced the New Jerusalem vision of 5QNJ (see above Chapter 2 n. 73).

translations show). But the vocabulary and word order of Tob. 13.16b-17a provide a unique opportunity for making just such a connection.

οἱ πύργοι Ιερουσαλημ χρυσίῳ οἰκοδομηθήσονται
καὶ οἱ προμαχῶνες αὐτῶν
χρυσίῳ καθαρῷ· αἱ πλατεῖαι Ιερουσαλημ
ἄνθρακι ψηφολογηθήσονται
καὶ λίθῳ Σουφιρ.

Making this interpretation work grammatically is, of course, another matter and cannot be achieved without upsetting the surrounding syntax in some way. We might, for example, make a break after αὐτῶν and take καὶ οἱ προμαχῶνες αὐτῶν with the first χρυσίῳ, but this destroys the obvious parallelism, and a καί would then be needed before the second χρυσίῳ.[52]

Even if this punctuation were accepted, more problems would be created in the following clause, where the last line would lose its subject—unless it were understood as a continuation and expansion of the preceding sentence:

With pure gold the streets of Jerusalem [will be built],
With carbuncle and stone of Ophir will they be inlaid.

All these difficulties, however, presuppose a Greek text which faithfully represents its Hebrew or Aramaic *Vorlage*. Depending on word order, vocabulary, the presence or absence of prepositions, conjunctions and the rest, the syntactical limitations and relationships of the Greek text may prove to be more ambiguous or flexible in the Semitic original.[53] The recent availability of the Tobit manuscripts from Qumran, which contain a large Aramaic fragment of Tob. 13.12–14.3, has not shed any further light on this question.[54]

52. This sentence in Tobit (οἱ πύργοι... οἱ προμαχῶνες αὐτῶν) corresponds roughly to Isa. 54.12a שמשתיך כדכד ושמתי, though whether χρυσίον is an interpretation of or substitution for the somewhat obscure כדכד is unclear (cf. BDB, p. 461; Jastrow, p. 614).
53. One Old Latin MS of Tobit (La^x) actually reads *et plateae tuae sternentur auro mundo* ('and your streets will be paved with pure gold'), but this must certainly be an assimilation to the tradition of Revelation.
54. 4QTob^aram 1. According to J. Strugnell (in a lecture delivered at the *Symposium on the Manuscripts from the Judaean Desert* (University College London, 11–12 June 1987), publication of the Tobit and other Apocrypha fragments was projected for vol. X of *DJD* (1989/90), but as of this writing this edition has not

Despite these uncertainties, the juxtaposition of 'pure gold' and 'the street(s) of Jerusalem' in both Tobit and Revelation seems too convenient to be incidental, particularly when there is already some evidence that Tobit's interpretation of Isa. 54.11-12 has influenced other facets of the description in Rev. 21.18-21.

Altogether, an analysis of the preceding four elements of Rev. 21.18-21 suggests that John draws not only on the New Jerusalem prophecy of Isa. 54.11-12, but also on Tob. 13.16-17, which reaffirms and extends the original oracle of Second Isaiah.[55] Building on this double foundation, he combines their basic ingredients with his own colourful detail to achieve a creative synthesis of past and present prophecy.

With the foregoing redactional analysis in mind, we may now ask for *what purpose* are the traditions relating to the precious building materials of the New Jerusalem employed, and how does this unit (Rev. 21.18-21) fit into the wider visionary framework and thematic development of John's book? It is here that we can return to our original discussion of the bride motif.

Nuptial imagery is at the heart of John's evocation of the New Jerusalem. And as is typical of weddings, the bride occupies the centre of attention. The visionary drama of the bride unfolds in three

appeared. A microfiche of the plates containing these fragments has only recently been made available.

55. Beckwith and Wikenhauser are among the few commentators to acknowledge John's direct use of Tobit. Recognition of this allusion renders obsolete the repeated negative appraisals of Charles, 'of the books which we designate the Apocrypha, there is, so far as I am aware, no indubitable evidence that he has laid them under tribute even in a single passage... John passed by the Apocrypha simply because it was almost wholly lacking in the prophetic element... our author shows no acquaintance with the Apocrypha' (*Lectures on the Apocalypse*, p. 73). The use of Tobit as Scripture in the early (eastern) churches is first attested certainly with Polycarp (*Phil.* 10.2), bishop of Smyrna a generation after John addressed the church there. It is reasonable to assume that this practice had some precedent in earlier Jewish-Christian circles, of which John then may form an important witness. R.T. Beckwith cites *Did.* 1.2 // Tob. 4.15 as an earlier example, but besides there being little dictional resemblance, negative formulations of the Golden Rule are too common to warrant drawing a parallel in this case (*The Old Testament Canon of the New Testament Church and its Background in Early Judaism* [London, 1985, p. 388]; cf. F. Zimmermann, *The Book of Tobit* (New York, 1958), pp. 159-60. Further examples of the Christian use of Tobit, and a helpful bibliography are found in Schürer, III, I, p. 227.

progressive stages of development. Rev. 19.7-9 shows the planning and final preparations stage: a formal wedding announcement is given; the marriage supper is arranged; the guest list is finalized. The ceremony is about to begin, for the bride 'has prepared herself' and awaits her entrance. Her moment of glory arrives in 21.2 where she descends as the New Jerusalem 'prepared as a bride adorned for her husband'. This debut is immediately followed in 21.3 by a reciprocal covenant promise which is ultimately patterned after Near Eastern marriage contracts: 'and they shall be his people[s], and God himself shall be with them [and be their God]'.[56] The third and final stage of the bride theme comes in 21.18-21, where the description of her adornment, anticipated in 21.2, 9 is finally presented. All three units 19.7-9, 21.2 and 21.18-21 are linked to each other by connecting words: ἑτοιμάζω (19.7) → ἑτοιμάζω—κοσμέω (21.2) → κοσμέω (21.19).

That Rev. 21.18-21 forms an integral part and a continuation of the bride scheme is overlooked by most commentators, but this conclusion is sustained by a variety of considerations. In addition to what has already been noted:

---

56. The bracketed elements reflect MS discrepancies, but the context and structure lead one to expect the second parallel clause of the covenant formula. The text is manifestly corrupt (cf. Charles, *Revelation*, II, pp. 207-208, 377; Metzger, *Textual Commentary*, pp. 765-66). Compare the mutual formula from an Elephantine marriage contract: 'She is my wife and I her husband from this day forever' (A.E. Cowley, *Aramaic Papyri of the Fifth Century BC* [Oxford, 1923], pp. 44-46); and the similar declaration from a Murabba'at contract (117 CE) 'you will be my wife... and as for me, I will feed and clothe you, from this day onwards' (*DJD*, II, pp. 110-12). It is not surprising then that the adapted covenant formula 'I will be their God, and they shall be my people' is often found in prophetic writers along with marriage imagery, e.g. Hos. 1-2; Jer. 31; cf. Ezek. 16; M. Greenberg, *Ezekiel 1-20* (AB, 20; Garden City, 1983), pp. 254, 277-78.

There is however, some tension caused here by John's fusion of OT and early Christian marriage symbolism. While he takes up the Christian idea of the Messiah as bridegroom (Rev. 19.7; 21.2, 9), John does not completely relinquish the OT focus on the special relationship between God and his people. The relevance of the *bridegroom* image appears to centre in the event of redemption and its corollary, the parousia. For in the New Jerusalem, the privileges of eschatological union seem coextensive, whether between God and the community or Christ and the community. A similar ambiguity is found in *Jos. Asen.* 4.2, where Aseneth is adorned as 'a bride of God', though Joseph is the bridegroom (*OTP*, I, p. 206).

1. The description of the bride adorned (21.18-21) is the anti-image of the harlot adorned (17.4; 18.16). There is in outward appearance little difference between the two, and therefore it is probably incorrect to suppose that the harlot's splendorous attire is in and of itself a sign of wickedness. The distinction is one of inward character and motive. Harlot-Babylon entices people to become involved in an evil system while the Bride–New Jerusalem draws people to its glory in order to worship the true God.[57]

2. The New Jerusalem prophecy of Isa. 54.11-12, which serves as John's principal model for 21.18-21, is itself part of a larger oracle that employs marriage imagery, and may also be taken as a symbolic representation of the personified city as a wife gloriously adorned for her husband.[58]

3. By his summary statement in Rev. 21.2b, 'prepared as a bride adorned', John shows himself conscious of the fact that the description of the bride clothed in white linen (19.8) and decked with gold, precious stones and especially pearls (21.18-21) reflects contemporary wedding customs among royalty and the affluent.[59] The most intriguing parallel

---

57. The seductive power of jewelry is well illustrated in *T. Jud.* 12.2-3; cf. also Ezek. 16.8-18, which has influenced John's presentation of Harlot-Babylon.

58. The use of antimony and jewels in 54.11-12 'may have been chosen here to suggest the image of Zion as a splendidly groomed woman' (Whybray, *Isaiah 40–66*, p. 188); 'In this verse the profile of Zion, Yahweh's bride, "made up" with eye-paint shines through the picture of her as a city (cf. Rev. XXI.2)' (R. North, *The Second Isaiah* [Oxford, 1964], p. 252). More detailed discussions of the context and symbolism of Isa. 54 can be found in R. Martin-Achard, 'Esaïe LIV et la nouvelle Jérusalem', in J.A. Emerton (ed.), *Congress Volume, Vienna 1980* (VTSup, 32; Leiden, 1981), pp. 238-62, esp. 253-57; R. Lack, *La symbolique du livre d'Isaïe* (AnBib, 59; Rome, 1973), pp. 195, 220-22, 225; W.A.M. Beuken, 'Isaiah LIV: The Multiple Identity of the Person Addressed', *OTS* 19 (Leiden, 1974), pp. 29-70.

59. Pliny (*Letters* 5.16) mentions a father preparing for his young daughter's wedding, referring to 'the money he was to have laid out upon clothes, pearls, and jewels for her marriage'. In *T. Jud.* 13.5 Judah's father-in-law decks his daughter in gold and pearls in anticipation of her marriage; cf. also Cant. 1.10-11; Isa. 3.16-24; Ezek. 16.8-18; Ps. 45.13-15; Hermas, *Vis.* 4.2.1-2; 1 Tim. 2.9; 1 Pet. 3.3; L. Friedländer, *Roman Life and Manners under the Early Empire* (London, 7th edn, 1908), I, p. 235. On this level of meaning, the precious stones of the foundations interspersed with the pearls of the gates form a beautiful necklace which adorns the bride (cf. the example in Higgins, *Greek and Roman Jewelry*, p. 181,

occurs in the Hellenistic romance of Joseph and Aseneth, where Aseneth's bridal panoply is described in detail:

> And Aseneth... brought out her first robe, (the one) of wedding, like lightning in appearance,[60] and dressed in it. And she girded a golden and royal girdle around (herself) which was made of precious stones. And she put bracelets on her fingers... and precious ornaments she put around her neck in which innumerable costly (and) precious stones were fastened, and a golden crown she put on her head, and on that crown... was a big sapphire stone, and around the big stone were six costly stones.[61]

When taken together with the symbolization of Aseneth as a 'city' (15.7; 16.6; 17.6; 19.8-9) with 'walls' (15.7; 19.5; 22.13), 'foundations' (22.13) and 'pillars' (17.6; cf. Rev. 3.12), the nuptial imagery of Joseph and Aseneth has been seen to offer a close analogy to John's presentation of the Bride–New Jerusalem. But despite these similarities, there is little evidence to support the view that Aseneth is an allegorical or even typological figure of the New Jerusalem.[62]

Aseneth is not simply a *city*, but a *city of refuge*, and attains this position by virtue of her repentance, apart from her role as a bride. As such, she represents the archetypal mother (16.16 μητρόπολις) of all who turn in repentance from idolatry and lawlessness to worship the living God. The physical and emotional steps of her conversion (chs. 10–17) constitute the ideal paradigm for all subsequent Gentile proselytes. Little or no eschatological significance is attached to this image, and the author reveals elsewhere that his expectation of future inheritance is a spiritual and heavenly rest (8.9; 15.7; 22.13).[63]

plate 55a, and the quotation from Pliny in n. 44 above).

60. Perhaps a βύσσινη στολή as in 3.6.

61. *OTP*, II, p. 232 (18.5-6); cf. 15.10 and the dressing scene of 3.6–4.1. Joseph, the bridegroom, is referred to as 'the firstborn son of God' (21.4; cf. 6.3-5; 13.13-14; 23.10), and Aseneth as 'the bride of the great king's firstborn son' (21.20). On this basis, E. Stauffer regarded Joseph as a messianic figure whose marriage to Aseneth symbolized the union between God's city—Zion—and the Messiah (*TDNT*, I, p. 657); Cf. T. Holtz, 'Christliche Interpolationen in "Joseph und Aseneth"', *NTS* 14 (1967–68), p. 491 n. 4.

62. *Contra* Stauffer (*TDNT*, I, p. 657); and U. Fischer, *Eschatologie und Jenseitserwartung im hellenistischen Diasporajudentum* (BZNW, 44; Berlin, 1978), pp. 115-20. Fischer's view is rejected by Burchard (*OTP*, II, p. 189) and Schürer (III.1, p. 548 n. 64).

63. Burchard, *OTP*, II, p. 190; *contra* Fischer, *Eschatologie*, pp. 118-20. Fischer's appeal to Zech. 2.15 LXX (p. 117), which lies behind Aseneth's title and

But even if Aseneth bears little or no relation to the New Jerusalem, the bridal traditions and building imagery employed still provide useful background material for setting John's images in context. If Rev. 21.18-21 is to be understood as the final instalment of the bride theme, some implications emerge from the interpretation of the precious materials with which the bride is adorned. When in 19.7 John announces that the bride 'has prepared herself', it is logical to suppose that included in that preparation is not only the fine linen wedding gown of 19.8, but also the bridal trappings of 21.18-21. And since the fine linen of the bride is interpreted by John himself as symbolic of 'the righteous acts of the saints', is it not likely that the glorious adornment of 21.18-21 carries a similar spiritual meaning?

Commentators have come to various conclusions as to the nature of the precious stones symbolism, ranging from a literal interpretation to allegory. These interpretations tend to fall into two broad categories, depending on whether the city of Revelation 21–22 is understood as an entity in itself in some way distinct from the redeemed community,[64] or is wholly a collective symbol of the community, to the exclusion of other physical and spatial realities.[65] So some regard the gem motif as simply poetic hyperbole accenting the beauty and worth of the city generally[66] or emphasizing its qualities of light and brilliance,[67]

the accompanying motto (15.7; 19.5, 8) is misleading. The relevance of this text concerns its prophecy of the ingathering of the Gentiles and not the surrounding motifs relating to the *place* of salvation. Cf. also *Jos. Asen.* 19.8-9 with Amos 7.7 LXX and Mic. 4.7 LXX.

64. Charles, *Revelation*, II, pp. 157-61; Justin, *Dial.* 81; Irenaeus, *Adv. Haer.* 5.34.4; cf. Mounce, *Revelation*, p. 370. Helpful discussions of the relationship of the city image to the community are found in Rissi, *Future*, pp. 55-56; and Holtz, *Christologie*, pp. 191-95.

65. R.H. Gundry, 'The New Jerusalem: People as Place, not Place for People', *NovT* 29 (1987), pp. 254-64. J.M. Ford, 'The Heavenly Jerusalem and Orthodox Judaism', in E. Bammel, C.K. Barrett and W.D. Davies (eds.), *Donum gentilicium: New Testament Studies in Honour of David Daube* (Oxford, 1978), pp. 215-26, who states, 'it is an allegory of the ideal community' (p. 223); Clement of Alexandria, *Pedag.* 2.12.119.1; Origen, *Contra Celsum* 8.19-20.

66. Kraft, *Offenbarung*, p. 272; D. Georgi, 'Die Visionen vom himmlischen Jerusalem in Apk 21 und 22', in D. Lührmann and G. Strecker (eds.), *Kirche* (FS G. Bornkamm; Tübingen, 1980), p. 367. *Contra* Reader, 'The Twelve Jewels of Revelation 21.19-20', pp. 455-56.

67. Beckwith, *Apocalypse*, p. 762; Caird, *Revelation*, p. 274; cf. *LAB* 26.13-15.

whereas others relate it to the perfected saints as the spiritual building-blocks of the eschatological community.[68]

That the symbolism evokes several levels of meaning may well be intentional, and a spiritual interpretation of the bridal imagery or other facets of the New Jerusalem does not exclude the possibility that John's eschatological hope includes a literal earthly city. However, it seems best to conclude that in the main John is here working within the circle of tradition that likens people or a community to a building or temple.[69] He has combined this idea, which generally has no precious building materials motif, with OT prophecies of Jerusalem restored in glory and features of Near Eastern temple construction. For, as was argued earlier, John's city is a temple-city, and the redeemed eschatological community is the spiritual temple in which God and the Lamb dwell and are worshiped. Thus, when viewed through the prism of building imagery, the costly ingredients of the city may represent the eternal glory, purity and durability of the perfected community.

But when viewed from the perspective of nuptial imagery, the glorious bridal attire and ornaments of the New Jerusalem reach back from the future into the present and serve as a symbolic testimony to the faithfulness of the earthly community.[70] Just as the fine linen of the bride serves as a metaphor for the 'righteous deeds of the saints' (19.8; cf. 3.4-5), so also her bridal ornaments are collectively emblematic of the spiritual fidelity and holy conduct of those in the churches who 'overcame'. The fact that Rev. 21.2 and 21.18-21 are separated from 19.7-9 by the millennium does not belie or contradict their interrelationship, for everything that the bride could do *to prepare herself* had to be done *before* the parousia, as the exhortations of

68. Swete, *Apocalypse*, pp. 293-94; J.M. Ford, 'The Jewel of Discernment (A Study of Stone Symbolism'), *BZ* NS 11 (1967), pp. 109-16.

69. To the many examples provided by Ford ('The Jewel of Discernment'), add the discussions of 4QpIsa[d] by J.M. Baumgarten, 'The Duodecimal Courts of Qumran, Revelation, and the Sanhedrin', *JBL* 95 (1976), pp. 59-78, esp. pp. 65-71 (reprinted with corrections in *Studies in Qumran Law* [SJLA, 24; Leiden, 1977], pp. 145-71); M.P. Horgan, *Pesharim: Qumran Interpretations of Biblical Books* (CBQMS, 8; Washington, DC, 1978), pp. 125-31; Rissi, *Future*, p. 49; and Martin-Achard, 'Esaïe LIV', pp. 257-58.

70. I find Gundry's literalistic interpretation of the precious stones as a material reward and future compensation for the earthly poverty of the saints unconvincing ('The New Jerusalem', p. 261).

the seven letters make clear. This explains the placement of Rev. 19.7-9 immediately before the parousia (19.11-21) and further corroborates its introductory function. The eschatological union of the bride (19.7-9, 14; 21–22) and bridegroom (19.11-21; 20.4-6) consummates the relationship between Christ and his church first portrayed in Revelation 1–3, which begins with a vision of Christ adorned (1.12-20), followed by his admonitions to the church to prepare herself for his appearing (chs. 2–3). Her successful preparation ends the difficult period of engagement and occasions the joyous announcement: 'the marriage of the Lamb has come' (Rev. 19.7b).[71]

Revelation 21.4a → Isaiah 25.8ab

Revelation	Isaiah	
καὶ ἐξαλείψει πᾶν δάκρυον	בלע המות לנצח	κατέπιεν ὁ θάνατος ἰσχύσας,
ἐκ τῶν ὀφθαλμῶν αὐτῶν	ומחה אדני יהוה	καὶ πάλιν ἀφεῖλεν ὁ θεὸς πᾶν
καὶ ὁ θάνατος οὐκ ἔσται ἔτι	דמעה מעל כל פנים	δάκρυον ἀπὸ παντὸς προσώπου

The declaration of the presence of God with men in Rev. 21.3 is followed immediately in 21.4 by the implications of his presence for the negative vicissitudes of human existence. Both verses mark the transition into a new era which was already anticipated in 7.14-17, where the same biblical testimony was employed. What was there the closing pledge of divine comfort 'and God will wipe every tear from their eyes' (7.17b—Isa. 25.8b) becomes here the introductory promise of God's consolation, expanded by the addition of Isa. 25.8a 'and death shall be no more'.[72]

Taking into account the fuller version of Isa. 25.8b in Rev. 7.17b,

---

71. Sweet, *Revelation*, p. 301. While Christ's adornment in Rev. 1 is not necessarily that of a bridegroom, this does not alter the fundamental relationship of anticipation and fulfilment between Rev. 1–3 and 19–22. It is only natural that John reserve the nuptial imagery for the latter stage, where it serves to underline the community's transition from temporary hardship and faithful preparation to eternal glory and companionship with its Lord.

72. John's peculiar habit of utilizing elements of OT texts in reverse order is found also in 6.13-14 (Isa. 34.4) and 7.16-17 (Isa. 49.10); Ozanne, *Influence*, p. 144. The influence of Isa. 25.8a here is recognized by Wikenhauser, Caird, Rissi, Sweet, Prigent and Müller.

which includes ὁ θεός after ἐξαλείψει, a dictional comparison can be made.

1. Like the LXX, John renders אדני יהוה by ὁ θεός and the collective דמעה with πᾶν δάκρυον, while the verb ἐξαλείψει follows closely the Hebrew מחה, in contrast to LXX ἀφεῖλεν.[73]

2. Instead of 'from every face' he substitutes 'from their eyes', thereby directing the promise more closely to his interest group and giving it a more personal reference.

3. In the second clause, καὶ ὁ θάνατος οὐκ ἔσται ἔτι may be a paraphrase of Isa. 25.8a, 'He will swallow up death forever',[74] or more likely, John has incorporated the 'no death' prophecy of 25.8 into the verbal framework of Isa. 65.19-20 which dominates the remainder of 21.4.[75]

Not only will God relieve the hurt caused by life's suffering ('wipe away tears'; cf. Mt. 5.4), but he will remove those factors which brought about the suffering. By John's day the abolition of death in the new age was a fairly standard feature of Jewish and Christian eschatology, with Isa. 25.8 forming the central proof text.[76] In Revelation, however, it is more than simply a piece of conventional apocalyptic baggage. As the negative corollary to the promise of eternal life, it is an appropriate expectation to set before those whom

---

73. σ´ also has ἐξαλείψει; cf. Charles, *Revelation*, I, pp. 217-18.

74. Following the majority tradition (LXX, θ´,Syr, 1 Cor. 15.54c) which takes המות as the subject rather than the object of בלע (MT, α´, σ´). And on the possibility of οὐκ ἔσται ἔτι as a negative equivalent of לנצח, Charles notes, 'whereas Aquila and Theodotion incorrectly render לנצח as an Aramaic phrase by εἰς νῖκος and the LXX by ἰσχύσας, our author gives the right sense in a periphrastic form' (*Revelation*, II, 208). Cf. the textual discussion in Conzelmann, *1 Corinthians*, pp. 292-93.

75. Thus compare 21.4b καὶ...οὐκ ἔσται ἔτι...οὔτε...οὐκ ἔσται ἔτι with Isa. 65.19b-20a עוד...יהיה לא...ו...עוד...ולא. The introduction of 65.20 would be particularly appropriate since this verse speaks about life and death in the New Jerusalem. The need to bring in Isa. 25.8a at this point is dictated by the fact that death is still a possibility in Third Isaiah's scenario (65.20). The contradiction between 25.8 and 65.20 was also recognized by the rabbis, and John's conflation may reflect an early response to this problem (*b. Pes.* 68a; *Gen. R.* 26.2).

76. 1 Cor. 15.54; *4 Ezra* 8.52-54; *2 Bar.* 21.22-23; Justin, *Dial.* 45.4; *m. M. Qat.* 3.9; *b. M. Qat.* 28b; *b. Pes.* 68a; *Exod. R.* 16.21; 30.3; *Deut. R.* 2.30; *Lam. R.* 1.13.41; *Eccl. R.* 1.4.3; cf. *Gos. Truth* 42.20-21; *Melch.* 9.14.9.

John repeatedly calls to be 'faithful unto death' (Rev. 2.10, 13; 6.9, 11; 11.7; 12.11; 13.10, 15; 18.24).

There is, of course, a distinction between death personified (that is, Death and Hades as a place of the dead—1.18; 6.8; 20.13-14) and the human experience of death (2.10; 12.11; 21.4), though the elimination of the former in 20.14 necessarily assumes the end of the latter in 21.4.[77]

Revelation 21.4b → Isaiah 65.19b-20a; (35.10; 51.11)

Revelation	Isa. 65.19b-20a	
[καὶ ὁ θάνατος οὐκ ἔσται ἔτι]	ולא ישמע בה עוד	καὶ οὐκέτι μὴ ἀκουσθῇ
οὔτε πένθος οὔτε κραυγὴ	קול בכי וקול זעקה	ἐν αὐτῇ φωνὴ κλαυθμοῦ
οὔτε πόνος οὐκ ἔσται ἔτι	לא יהיה משם קוד...	οὐδὲ φωνὴ κραυγῆς. καὶ οὐ μὴ γένηται ἐκεῖ...

Isa. 35.10; 51.11

ונסו יגון ואנחה   ἀπένδρα ὀδύνη καὶ λύπη καὶ στεναγμός

Similarities in theme, structure and vocabulary between Isa. 65.19-20a and Rev. 21.4b suggest that John has now returned to the New Jerusalem prophecy of Isaiah 65 with which he began his final vision. In fact, it appears that the larger passage of Isa. 65.16-20a provided the basic format and inspiration for Rev. 21.1-4, into which related texts and traditions were integrated by John.[78]

Rev. 21.1-4	*Isa. 65.16-20a*
And I saw a new heaven and a new earth, for the first heaven and the first earth had passed away... and I saw the... new Jerusalem... and there shall no longer be death nor mourning nor crying nor shall there be pain any longer for the former things have passed away.	For behold, I create new heavens and a new earth; and the former things shall not be remembered... for behold, I create Jerusalem... and there shall be heard in it no more... weeping and... crying no more shall there be... [for the former troubles are forgotten].

77. Rissi, *Future*, p. 67; Müller, *Offenbarung*, p. 351.
78. The use of Isa. 65.16c as an *inclusio* in 21.4d further confirms such a procedure. This text will be discussed next.

Inasmuch as Isa. 65.19-20a accounts for virtually everything in 21.4b except the word πόνος,[79] there is no justification whatsoever for citing this allusion as secondary to Isa. 35.10, as do the majority of commentators.[80] In my opinion, it seems superfluous to even mention Isa. 35.10 at all, since it offers little basis for comparison with Rev. 21.4, either in terminology or context.[81]

Revelation 21.4d → Isaiah 65.16c (43.18)

Revelation	*Isa. 65.16b*	
[ὅτι] τὰ πρῶτα ἀπῆλθαν	כי נשכחו הצרות	ἐπιλήσονται γὰρ τὴν θλῖψιν
	הראשנות	αὐτῶν τὴν πρώτην
	Isa. 43.18	
	אל תזכרו ראשנות	μὴ μνημονεύετε τὰ πρῶτα

Concerning the biblical antecedent of this phrase Charles states, '...that τὰ πρῶτα ἀπῆλθαν is to be taken immediately in connection with 'Ἰδοὺ καινὰ ποιῶ πάντα is obvious in itself', and he regards the inspiration for this combination as Isa. 43.18-19.[82] He then proceeds to use this as a basis for rearranging the text and 'restoring' the 'original' order by returning the phrase to its supposed rightful place after 21.5a:

> And he that sat upon the throne said,
> *The former things have passed away*;
> Behold, I make all things new.[83]

This transposition indeed yields a very smooth and logical reading, but there is every indication that this was not John's original intent. Charles's error proceeds from the faulty premise that Rev. 21.4d is

---

79. πένθος // בכי and κραυγή // זעקה; πόνος has no parallel and is probably added by John, though still using the verbal framework of Isa. 65.
80. E.g. Charles, Rissi, Vos, Lohmeyer and N[26]. Many others do not even mention Isa. 65.19 here. Note the LXX of 35.10 has three elements where the MT has only two.
81. יגון in Isa. 35.10 and 51.11 is translated by πόνος in one passage (Jer. 20.16 LXX), but this is hardly compelling evidence. However, this closing phrase of Isa. 35.10 is found in other descriptions of a future renewal: e.g. 1QH 11.26; *Apost. Const.* 8.41.2, 5; *Num. R.* 23.14.
82. *Revelation*, II, pp. 202-203.
83. *Revelation*, II, p. 443 n. 3, pp. 376, 201-203.

based on Isa. 43.18 and thus should belong with the divine statement of 21.5b, which is clearly drawn from Isa. 43.19. Upon closer examination however, it is much more likely that the phrase in question continues the dependence on Isaiah 65 in 21.1-4 and serves as a comprehensive summary of the preceding statements of abrogation. A variety of factors point to Isa. 65.16c as the primary inspiration behind Rev. 21.4d, as opposed to either 43.18 or the similar 65.17.

1. Whereas Isa. 43.18 is a command, 65.16 is a declaration introduced by a causal conjunction (כי), as in Rev. 21.4d.[84]
2. In 65.16, the *nifal* perfect of שכח (*forget*) accords with the completed state of action implied in ἀπῆλθαν, in contrast to 65.17, which has the imperfect of זכר (*remember*). Furthermore, 'are forgotten' offers a closer parallel and an easier transition to 'have passed away' than does 'shall not be remembered' (65.17b) or 'remember not' (43.18).[85]
3. The context of Isa. 65.16, which announces the elimination of the former *troubles* suits perfectly the role of 21.4d as a summary of the removal of the troubles of 21.4bc which are based on 65.19.[86]

Even without ὅτι, Rev. 21.4d must carry some explanatory significance in relation to what precedes it, for John is careful to separate it from what follows by a new introduction and a change of speaker. Thus the words [ὅτι] τὰ πρῶτα ἀπῆλθαν conclude the indirect revelatory speech of the 'voice from the throne' begun in 21.3, while the first person speech of 21.5, ἰδοὺ καινὰ ποιῶ πάντα, is clearly to be taken as the inaugural address of God himself.

Having said this, because of the strong thematic links between Isa.

84. As Mounce notes, there is little textual support for ὅτι here, though both N²⁶ and *UBSGNT* have retained it (with some reservation) (*Revelation*, p. 373 n. 16). But its accidental omission in an early exemplar is possible through confusion with the preceding word ἔτι—Metzger, *Textual Commentary*, p. 766.

85. Though the reformulation of the זכר clauses in both 43.18 and 65.17 with עבר/παρέρχομαι is already well attested in both Jewish and Christian circles: 2 Cor. 5.17 τὰ ἀρχαῖα παρῆλθεν; *1 En.* 91.16 ושמין קדמין בה יעברון; Mk 13.31 par. (cf. Mt. 5.18) ὁ οὐρανὸς καὶ ἡ γῆ παρελεύσονται; 2 Pet. 3.10 οἱ οὐρανοὶ ...παρελεύσονται; cf. *Did.* 10.6. John's ἀπέρχομαι shows independence from the uniform Christian Greek tradition and may be his own rendering of a Semitic version. Ozanne thinks John knew and modified 2 Cor. 5.17 ('Influence', p. 144).

86. Rissi, *Future*, p. 58. *Exod. R.* 23.11 applies 65.16 to the messianic age.

65.16-17 and 43.18-19,[87] Rev. 21.4d may function as both the formal conclusion to Rev. 21.1-4 and the transition or bridge to the divine statement of 21.5, passing from one OT renewal text to another by means of their common language and shared prophetic perspective. Because of these affinities, which John probably recognized, one cannot exclude entirely the influence of Isa. 43.18. But it must be seen as secondary to 65.16, forming a small but important link in a chiastic agenda which moves from new → old // old → new, and from the particular to the universal.[88]

A	21.1-2	New: heavens, earth, Jerusalem (Isa. 65.17-18)
B	21.1, 4bc	Old: heavens, earth, death, mourning, weeping, pain (Isa. 65.17; 25.8; 65.19)
B′	21.4d	Old: (all) the former things passed away (Isa. 65.16)

$$\downarrow$$
Isa. 43.18
$$\downarrow$$

| A′ | 21.5a | New: all things made new | (Isa. 43.19) |

Revelation 21.5a → Isaiah 43.19a

Revelation	Isaiah
ἰδοὺ καινὰ ποιῶ πάντα	הנני עשה חדשה ἰδοὺ ποιῶ καινά

2 Cor. 5.17-18a
ἰδοὺ γέγονεν καινά. τὰ δὲ πάντα...

The high point of Rev. 21.1-8 comes with the divine proclamation of 21.5 'Behold, I make all things new', based on Isa. 43.19a. The setting for this announcement extends back to the judgment pericope of 20.11-15, for the full significance of divine renewal cannot be appreciated apart from the previous acts of divine removal. There the confrontation between the created order and the direct presence of 'he who sits on the throne' resulted in the dissolution of the physical

87. That Third Isaiah is building on the words of his predecessor is acknowledged by many commentators. The parallels include 43.18a, 'remember not the former things' // 65.17b; 'the former things shall not be remembered'; 43.19, 'behold, I am doing a new thing' // 65.17a *'behold, I create new...'*; cf. P. Stuhlmacher, 'Siehe, ich mache alles neu', *LR* 18 (1968), pp. 3-18.

88. Kraft, Prigent and Sweet cite both Isa. 65.16 and 43.18. The 'former things' of Isa. 43.18 refer especially to the situation of the community in Babylon (43.14-17).

universe and the judgment of human beings. Here, 'he who sits on the throne' issues the creative word which brings a completely new beginning, and turns non-existence into new existence.[89]

Just as John can leave out a word from his source to emphasize the comprehensive nature of the removal (*troubles* from Isa. 65.16), so also he can add one to show the corresponding magnitude of renewal (πάντα to Isa. 43.19). That he conceives this eschatological event in terms of a new creation, a second Genesis, may be inferred from Rev. 4.11b, where God's role in the first creation is expressed in similar language: σὺ ἔκτισας τὰ πάντα, and by the attendant *Urzeit–Endzeit* titles of 21.6, 'I am the Alpha and Omega, the beginning and end'.[90]

Whether or not John's ποιῶ carries a futuristic sense as in Isaiah is debatable. God's declaration of γέγοναν in the continuation of 21.5 suggests rather that his words are to be taken within the chronological perspective of the vision-event and emphasize fulfilment rather than anticipation.[91] This does not necessarily reduce the paraenetic force of the passage.

In comparison with 2 Cor. 5.17, where the same OT passage is invoked, it has commonly been observed that John and Paul have very little in common in their respective interpretations of Isa. 43.18-19. Whereas the prophet understands the new creation as an event yet unfulfilled, one which encompasses the future renewal of both human beings and their environment, the apostle uses the same vocabulary to describe the present spiritual transformation of those who are 'in Christ'.[92] But as Prigent notes, Isa. 43.18-19 on its own invites a 'realized' application, and one might wonder whether Paul would treat Isa. 65.17-25 in the same manner.[93] John on the other hand, interprets 43.18-19 in the light of 65.16-19 and relates both prophecies to the

---

89. 'Er hat das erste Wort gesprochen, "Es werde Lichte!" Er spricht nun das Schlusswort' (E. Schmitt, quoted by Brütsch, *Offenbarung*, III, p. 28).

90. *Contra* Kraft, *Offenbarung*, p. 264.

91. *Contra* Lohmeyer, and Müller, *Offenbarung*, p. 352; cf. Thompson, *The Apocalypse and Semitic Syntax*, p. 32.

92. Cf. Gal. 6.15; *Barn.* 6.13. For a detailed discussion, consult W. Grimm, *Die Verkündigung Jesu und Deuterojesaja* (ANTJ, 1; Bern, 2nd edn, 1981). Caird, however, sees the announcement of 21.5 as the cumulative result of a process of renewal begun in the earthly community (*Revelation*, pp. 265-66).

93. *L'Apocalypse*, p. 329; and 'Le temps et le Royaume dans l'Apocalypse', in Lambrecht (ed.), *L'Apocalypse johannique*, p. 234.

same eschatological event which follows the parousia, millennium and final judgment.[94]

Revelation 21.6b; 22.17b → Isaiah 55.1

Revelation	Isa. 55.1	
ἐγὼ τῷ διψῶντι δώσω	הוֹי כל צמא	οἱ διψῶντες,
ἐκ τῆς πηγῆς τοῦ ὕδατος	...לכו למים	πορεύεσθε ἐφ' ὕδωρ...
τῆς ζωῆς δωρεάν (21.6b)	שברו בלוא כסף	καὶ πίετε ἄνευ ἀργυρίου
καὶ ὁ διψῶν ἐρχέσθω,	Jn 7.37b, 38b	
ὁ θέλων λαβέτω ὕδωρ	ἐάν τις διψᾷ ἐρχέσθω πρός με	
ζωῆς δωρεάν (22.17b)	καὶ πινέτω...ποταμοὶ ἐκ τῆς κοιλίας	
	αὐτοῦ ῥεύσουσιν ὕδατος ζῶντος	

Despite differences in form, speaker and function, Rev. 21.6b and 22.17b share a common core of verbal components and may be evaluated together. However, determining a specific antecedent for these two passages is somewhat complicated by the possibility that John is adopting the conventional vocabulary of a living water tradition which was already current in Johannine circles.[95] In the case of the similar saying in Jn 7.37b, the difficulty of pinning down OT sources is well known, and should warn us against drawing hasty conclusions in the present instance.[96]

Many commentators have accepted an allusion to Isa. 55.1 in Revelation mainly on the strength of the opening address τῷ διψῶντι

94. A similar eschatological interpretation of Isa. 43.19 is contained in 1QS 4.25 where the 'new creation' (עשׂות חדשׁה) follows the 'time of visitation', 'the determined end' and 'the appointed time of judgment' (4.16, 18, 26). After this, humanity will receive 'all the glory of Adam' (4.23).

95. Besides Jn 7.37b, cf. 4.10-15; 6.35; and *Odes Sol.* 30.1-2: 'Fill for yourselves water from the living spring of the Lord... and come all you thirsty and take a drink, and rest beside the spring of the Lord' (*OTP*, II, p. 762).

96. Reim, *Studien*, pp. 56-81, 163, 193, 226; J.N. Freed, *The Old Testament Quotations in the Gospel of John* (NovTSup, 11; Leiden, 1965), pp. 21-37. To illustrate the broad spectrum of opinion, Reim sees Isa. 55.1-3 in Jn 7.27 as an 'obvious allusion' (p. 163); B. Lindards regards it as 'strongly reminiscent' of Isa. 55.1 (*The Gospel of John* [NCB; London, 1972], p. 298); Freed opts for a combination of texts which includes Isa. 55.1 (p. 37); and Bultmann and E. Haenchen do not mention Isa. 55.1 at all (*The Gospel of John: A Commentary* [Oxford, 1971]; *John 2: A Commentary on the Gospel of John, Chapters 7–21* [Hermeneia; Philadelphia, 1984]). Surprisingly, in their detailed treatments, neither Reim nor Freed ever discusses or mentions the Revelation texts.

(δώσω) // ὁ διψῶν (ἐρχέσθω).⁹⁷ Without supporting evidence, however, this feature is not really distinctive enough to confirm an allusion, since thirsting as a spiritual metaphor is not uncommon, and the use of a substantive participle followed by a future or imperative verb is John's standard approach in formulating eschatological promises and exhortations.⁹⁸ More convincing evidence may be obtained by comparing individual elements of the second passage (22.17b) with the text of Isa. 55.1.

    a. ὁ διψῶν ἐρχέσθω // כל צמא לכו
    b. ὕδωρ // למים
    c. δωρεάν // בלוא כסף

It is the last parallel involving δωρεάν which is the most significant and changes the character of the allusion from possible to probable. δωρεάν, an infrequently used adverb, means *as a gift, without payment*, and corresponds closely to Isaiah's *without money*.⁹⁹ In Revelation the word occurs only in these two passages (21.6b; 22.17b), where the influence of Isa. 55.1 is suspected. Together with the other dictional affinities, this detail offers a good basis for accepting Isa. 55.1 as one of the biblical influences lying behind the living water sayings of Rev. 21.6b and 22.17b.¹⁰⁰

The living water promise of Rev. 21.6 forms the first part of a two-part paraenetic summary in 21.6-8 which contains both a final divine promise and warning (τῷ διψῶντι belongs the living water; τοῖς δειλοῖς etc. belongs the lake of fire). The promise follows the same structural pattern as the eschatological rewards of the letters

97. E.g. Charles, Lohmeyer, Ozanne, Holtz, Beasley-Murray, Sweet, Müller and Roloff; *contra* Prigent. Schüssler Fiorenza includes Isa. 55.1 among a variety of OT texts (*Revelation*, p. 100).

98. E.g. Pss. 42.2; 63.1; 143.6; Mt. 5.6; Rev. 2.7, 17 (τῷ νικῶντι δώσω); 2.11, 26; 3.5, 12, 21 (ὁ νικῶν...[δώσω]); 2.7 etc. (ὁ ἔχων οὖς ἀκουσάτω); 13.18 (ὁ ἀδικῶν ἔχων νοῦν ψηφισάτω); 22.11 (ὁ ἀδικησάτω κτλ); 22.17a (ὁ ἀκούων εἰπάτω...ὁ θέλων λαβέτω).

99. BDB, p. 209. Although δωρεάν generally corresponds to Hebrew חנם, it occurs in parallel with כסף אין/ἄνευ ἀργυρίου in LXX Exod. 21.11; Isa. 52.3; cf. 2 Sam. (Kgs) 24.24; 1 Chron. 21.24. Ozanne and Holtz also note this connection ('Gott in der Apokalypse', in Lambrecht (ed.), *L'Apocalypse johannique*, p. 258 n. 65).

100. For the background to the *springs* and *living water* see the discussion of 7.17 above (pp. 170-74), and Ezek. 47.1-12; Zech. 14.8.

(Rev. 2–3), except that here God is the speaker.[101]

This promise has two parts: the present human need (thirst), and the future divine compensation (living water). The theme of the people of God thirsting and the divine provision of water is one of the favourite metaphors of salvation used by Second Isaiah (41.17-18; 43.19-20; 44.3-4; 48.21; 49.10), based on the wilderness experiences of Israel in the desert.[102] John has already used one of these passages (Isa. 49.10) in 7.16-17 and the beginning of another (43.19) just before the living water promise of 21.6. The relationship of anticipation and fulfilment between Rev. 7.14-17 and 21.1-8 suggests that the living water traditions found in these two passages are related in meaning.

Since in 21.6-7 the living water is part of the overcomer's inheritance and forms an antithetic parallel to the lake of fire as the inheritance of the wicked (21.8), there can be little doubt that 'living water' serves as a symbol of eternal life, which has its source in God (21.1).[103]

This leaves the final question of who is meant by 'the one thirsting'. It cannot mean the *unbeliever* here, because this destroys the contrast with 21.8. Neither is it likely to designate the *not-yet-martyr*, as Lohmeyer suggested, for this is incompatible with the inclusive perspective of the eschatological index of Rev. 11.18, which anticipates a reward for the saints both great and small.[104] The division of human destiny into two categories suits a more general collocation of

101. In none of the rewards of the letters does Christ promise the gift of living water (although he does promise the right to eat from the tree of life in 2.7). And nowhere is the quenching of thirst related to Christ, but rather God. The Lamb may *guide* them *to* the springs of living water, but in contrast to the Gospel of John (and Paul, 1 Cor. 10.4), he is not himself the spring (but cf. 22.1). Cf. Schüssler Fiorenza, *Revelation*, p. 100.

102. Oddly enough, Isa. 55.1-2 is the only thirsting metaphor in Second Isaiah which does not fall clearly into this category, but it is still a salvation oracle addressed to the struggling exilic community. Westermann remarks, 'the address in v. 1a is clearer—those concerned are hungry and in need. This corresponds to the usual address in Deutero-Isaiah's proclamation of salvation, where Israel in exile is addressed in similar terms' (*Isaiah 40–66*, p. 283).

103. The earliest known interpretation of Isa. 55.1 in Sir. 51.24-25 gives it a wisdom setting, which anticipates the later rabbinic identification of the water with the Torah: *b. Suk.* 52b; *b. Qid.* 30b; *Gen. R.* 54.1; 66.1; 84.16; *Exod. R.* 2.5; 25.8; *Num. R.* 1.7; *Deut. R.* 7.3; *Cant. R.* 1.2, 3; cf. *Targ. Isa.* 55.1.

104. *Offenbarung*, p. 168. Any special attention to the martyrs is given in the millennium (20.4-6).

the righteous versus the wicked, or the faithful in contrast to the unfaithful.

We may perhaps go further and suggest that the 'thirst' of the believers here is not so much a symbol of their *desire* for God as it is emblematic of their *weary condition*, which is the result of earthly faithfulness. According to the allied passage in Rev. 7.16, the present time of tribulation is one which involves 'hunger' and 'thirst' for those desiring to live faithful lives in the face of daily struggles and temptation. That 'thirst' will only be fully assuaged in the new age (Rev. 7.17; 21.6), and not by spiritual communion in the present.

Both the identification of 'the one thirsting' with the believer and the deferred nature of the promise make it difficult to reconcile this passage with the use of the same imagery in Rev. 22.17b. Whereas Rev. 21.6b is an eschatological promise given by God to the believer, 22.17b is a present invitation delivered by the prophet, ostensibly to the interested unbeliever. For in the preceding lines the Spirit, the bride and the hearer apparently are counted as part of the 'in-group' who join in the parousia call of ἔρχου, while the *one thirsting* appears to be summoned as an outsider to come and take the water of life.[105]

But this reading of Rev. 22.17 is incompatible with John's understanding of the living water as an eschatological gift for the believer who conquers through suffering—an understanding which is expressed in three earlier passages (Rev. 7.17; 21.6; 22.1). Furthermore, the rhetorical arrangement of 22.17 does not necessarily imply a sharp distinction between the *hearer* and the *one thirsting*, so that the one refers to a believer and the other an unbeliever. As opposed to a three–one subject division (i.e. Spirit–bride–hearer → one thirsting), the structure supports a two–two scheme, with the *hearer* and the *one thirsting* being called to respond *individually*, as the Spirit and the bride have already proclaimed *corporately*.[106]

We may reduce the tension between Rev. 22.17 and 21.6 even further by emphasizing John's expectation of imminence, and by seeing the final invitation as part of an 'inaugurated eschatology'. In this way,

---

105. *Contra* Charles, who, because of his dissection of the various Jerusalem traditions must take all the ἔρχου invitations as directed to unbelievers seeking the truth rather than to Christ (*Revelation*, II, pp. 179-80). This view is made difficult by 22.20. Cf. also Mounce, *Revelation*, p. 395.

106. Cf. Satake, *Gemeindeordnung*, pp. 76-81; and Holtz, *Christologie*, pp. 199-201. Note the relation of the hearer to the Spirit in the letters (Rev. 2–3).

the promise of 22.17 is similar in perspective to 22.14-15 where entrance to and exclusion from the future Holy City has present significance. Such a dual focus probably had its origins in a cultic setting.[107]

Revelation 21.12b → Isaiah 62.6a

Revelation	Isaiah	
καὶ ἐπὶ τοῖς πυλῶσιν	על חומתיך ירושלם	καὶ ἐπὶ τῶν τειχέων σου,
ἀγγέλους δώδεκα[108]	הפקדתי שמרים	Ιερουσαλημ, κατέστησα
	כל היום וכל הלילה	φύλακας ὅλην τὴν ἡμέραν
	תמיד לא יחשו	καὶ ὅλην τὴν νύκτα

Angels have had important roles all the way through John's book, as vision attendants, cultic functionaries, agents of judgment, and the like; fulfilling their duties in the spheres of heaven, earth, and even in between (Rev. 14.6). It is not surprising to find then that angels likewise play a part in the final evocation of the New Jerusalem. And not simply as part of the visionary framework, but as permanent features of the city itself.

A possible inspiration for the idea of the angelic gatekeepers has been suggested in Isa. 62.6a, where watchmen are appointed on the walls of Jerusalem.[109] Since commentators both ancient and modern have understood these watchmen to be angels, it is not unlikely that a similar interpretation was known to John.[110] Even so, the two passages diverge on almost every other particular. In Isaiah the watchmen are set *on the walls*, while in Revelation they serve *at the gates*.[111] In

107. Whether this cultic setting can be narrowed down even more precisely to the Eucharistic celebration is debated; cf. Satake, *Gemeindeordnung*, pp. 78-79; Roloff, *Apokalypse*, pp. 212-13; Schüssler Fiorenza, *Revelation*, p. 100; and more generally Aune, *The Cultic Setting of Realized Eschatology* (NovTSup, 28; Leiden, 1972).

108. This line is omitted in some important witnesses: A 051 2030 2050 2377 pc t syh arm, but this is obviously traceable to homoioteleuton (δώδεκα καὶ... δώδεκα καί).

109. Commentators who accept an allusion include Schlatter, Rissi, Lohmeyer and Georgi; others cite it as possible: Swete, Mounce, Sweet; *contra* Prigent.

110. R. Nehemiah (c. 150 CE) states 'for the very ministering angels... were made by God the custodians of Israel. Who are they? Michael and Gabriel; as it says: *I have set watchmen upon thy walls, O Jerusalem*' (*Exod. R.* 18.5, cf. *Pes. K.* suppl. 6.2); Duhm, Whybray, Kissane; *contra* Fohrer; cf. Westermann.

111. Despite the fact that John does not always preserve strict case distinctions in his use of prepositions (Mussies, *Morphology*, pp. 100-101), there is no reason to

Isaiah, they are temporary lookouts watching for the coming salvation of Yahweh, whereas John's angelic gatekeepers appear to function as permanent sentries who protect the Holy City from impurity.[112] Because of these differences and the existence of other passages which could have suggested angelic guardians at the entrance of God's dwelling with humanity (Gen. 3.24; cf. Ezek. 41.25), the proposed allusion to Isa. 62.6a must remain inconclusive.

Revelation 21.22–22.5 → Isaiah 60, 52
In the final pericope of the New Jerusalem vision (Rev. 21.22–22.5) John shifts from architectural imagery to a picture of life in the city itself. The outward physical description gives way to an inward view of the Holy City and its citizens. With this change of perspective comes a corresponding change in biblical foundations. From the building oracle of Isaiah 54 which dominated Rev. 21.18-21, John now turns to the Zion prophecy of Isaiah 60, with its emphasis on the relationship between the glorious future Jerusalem and the nations. For one who is consciously building on New Jerusalem prophecies, the transition from Isaiah 54 to Isaiah 60 is a natural one. For since none of the prophecies in Isaiah 55–59 are directed to Zion, these two chapters are thematically contiguous.[113] Although allusions to Isaiah 60 control this final section, John blends in traditions from other New Jerusalem prophecies as well (Isa. 52; Zech. 14; Ezek. 47).

suggest that ἐπὶ τοῖς πυλῶσιν means anything but 'at the gates' (so KJV, Charles, RSV, NIV); *contra* Beckwith, 'The angels stand upon (ἐπί) the gate towers' (*Apocalypse*, p. 758).

112. Westermann, *Isaiah 40–66*, p. 377; Rev. 21.27; cf. the role of Michael and the angels in expelling from the divine abode those proscribed (Rev. 12.7-9). Against Kiddle–Ross, it is most unlikely that the twelve angels are representatives of the church and connected with the 'stars' of 12.1 (*Revelation*, p. 426).

113. A similar juxtaposition of Isa. 54 and 60 as cognate prophecies is found in Origen, *Comm. Joh.* 10.294 and *Exod. R.* 15.21 (cf. the collection of Isaiah texts in Eusebius, *H.E.* 10.4.47-54). Another example of John's use of OT testimonies in thematic sequence occurs in 21.3 and 10. Here he has anticipated the modern critical scholar (!) and recognized the fact that Ezek. 38–39 are 'misplaced' and that the temple vision of 40.1ff. logically follows on the end of ch. 37. Thus he uses Ezek. 38–39 in Rev. 19–20; then Ezek. 37.27 in 21.3; and then the next very allusion to Ezekiel in Rev. 21.10 takes up Ezek. 40.1! Cf. Mealy, *After the Thousand Years*, pp. 187-88.

Revelation 21.23; 22.5b → Isaiah 60.1-2, 19

Rev. 21.23

καὶ ἡ πόλις οὐ χρείαν ἔχει
τοῦ ἡλίου οὐδὲ τῆς σελήνης
ἵνα φαίνωσιν αὐτῇ, ἡ γὰρ δόξα
τοῦ θεοῦ ἐφώτισεν αὐτήν,
καὶ ὁ λύχνος αὐτῆς τὸ ἀρνίον

Rev. 22.5b

καὶ οὐκ ἔχουσιν χρείαν
φωτὸς λύχνου καὶ φωτὸς ἡλίου,
ὅτι κύριος
ὁ θεὸς φωτίσει ἐπ' αὐτούς

Isa. 60.19 (cf. 60.20ab)

לא יהיה לך עוד השמש לאור יומם   καὶ οὐκ ἔσται σοι ὁ ἥλιος εἰς φῶς ἡμέρας,
ולנגה הירח לא יאיר לך[114]   οὐδὲ ἀνατολὴ σελήνης φωτιεῖ σοι τὴν
νύκτα,
והיה לך יהוה לאור עולם   ἀλλ' ἔσται σοι κύριος φῶς αἰώνιον
ואלהיך לתפארתך   καὶ ὁ θεὸς δόξα σου

Isa. 60.1-2

קומי אורי כי בא אורך   φωτίζου φωτίζου, Ιερουσαλημ, ἥκει γάρ
σου τὸ φῶς,
וכבוד יהוה עליך זרח...   καὶ ἡ δόξα κυρίου ἐπὶ σε ἀνατέταλκεν...
ועליך יזרח יהוה   ἐπὶ δὲ σὲ φανήσεται κύριος,
וכבודו עליך יראה   καὶ ἡ δόξα αὐτοῦ ἐπὶ σὲ ὀφθήσεται.

Rev. 21.23 and most of what follows it is closely related to the momentous announcement which opens this section: the city has no temple (21.22). Because the presence of God is no longer confined to a physical temple, John goes on in v. 23 to relate the corresponding significance of the unrestricted divine glory for the city as a whole. This development was already anticipated in 21.11, where the entire city was seen to possess the glory of God.[115] While most commentators

114. LXX 1QIsaᵃ Targ add *night* after הירח.
115. An even closer relationship between 21.11 and 21.23 could be intended by John if in the former he uses φωστήρ in its primary (?only) sense of *light-bearer, luminary*, as Swete, Farrer and Trench have argued. It is the conventional term used to describe the sun, moon and stars. If so, ὁ φωστήρ αὐτῆς would mean 'that which diffused light to the heavenly city, her luminary or light-giver... [and] what this light-giver was, we learn from v. 23' (R.C. Trench, *Synonyms of the New Testament* [London, 1880], p. 165). But the majority of commentators translate it as *radiance*, citing Anth. Graec. II, 359.7 and 1 Esd. 8.76. Farrer discounts these examples and says *luminary* makes good sense in each case (*Revelation*, p. 216). Even if the meaning *radiance* were attested, it may still be that the more common meaning should be understood in Rev. 21.11 (so Mealy, *After the Thousand Years*, p. 174, and n. 1). Perhaps then the influence of Isa. 60 begins here rather than in 21.23, and provides another example of John's technique of

are content to cite Isa. 60.19 as the inspiration behind 21.23 and 22.5b, a few have recognized that John also draws on related motifs in 60.1-2.[116] Rev. 21.23a is a virtual paraphrase of the parallel sun and moon clauses of Isa. 60.19a, leaving out only the day and night elements since the interchange of day and night is no longer relevant in John's city (21.25b; 22.5a).[117] The second half of the verse (21.23b) follows the basic format of Isa. 60.19b, but adopts the language of 60.1-2 in its first clause, ἡ γὰρ δόξα τοῦ θεοῦ ἐφώτισεν αὐτήν.

As the temple is replaced by the direct presence of both God and the Lamb (21.22), so also the light of the Holy City has a double source in God and the Lamb. Obviously the Isaian oracle itself only contemplates a single luminary, which is God. But for the early Christian interpreter of Isa. 60.19b the synonymous parallelism in the Isaiah text employing both Lord (יהוה = κύριος), and God (אלהים = θεός) offered an open invitation to introduce Christ into the picture. Which is exactly what Origen does in *Contra Celsum* 6.51: 'The word proclaims to the righteous through Isaiah that there will be a restoration with days in which not the sun but the Lord himself shall be to them an everlasting light and God shall be their glory'. That the apologist identifies the *Lord* here with Christ is confirmed in *Comm. Joh.* 10.294, where he even goes so far as to substitute χριστός for κύριος in a quotation of Isa. 60.19b: ἀλλ' ἔσται σοι χριστὸς φῶς αἰώνιον, καὶ ὁ θεὸς δόξα σοι.[118] If this is indeed John's procedure, he has

thematic recapitulation in a pattern of summary and expansion.

116. Brütsch, and Lancellotti, 'Il passo s'inspira senza dubbio ad Is. 60, I s' (*Sintassi ebraica*, p. 53). Such a conflation is also supported by the fact that the very next verse in Revelation (21.24) uses Isa. 60.3.

117. The Targum gives a similar periphrasis of the first line לא תצטרכין // οὐ χρείαν ἔχει... But against Wilcox ('Tradition and Redaction', p. 207), there is no need to infer dependence here. Other texts probably influenced by Isa. 60.19-20 include Zech. 14.6-7; *Sib. Or.* 3.787; esp. the motif of *eternal light*—1QS 4.8; 1QH 6.17-18; 7.25; 12.15; *4 Ezra* 2.35.

118. H. Chadwick, *Origen: Contra Celsum* (Cambridge, 1953), p. 367; SC 157.2, 564. We can trace this interpretation of Isa. 60.19b back even further to Justin in Asia Minor (*Dial.* 113.5), who refers to Christ as οὗτος ἐστιν ὁ ἐν Ἰερουσαλὴμ αἰώνιον φῶς λάμπειν μέλλων (*PG*, VI, col. 737). Similarly Eusebius, *Ps. Comm.* (PG 23 Col. 1016D); cf. *Pesiq. R.* 36.2. John's familiarity with this exegetical technique is supported by two earlier examples where he appears to exploit parallel divine titles (Rev. 1.17 and 6.16).

reversed the order of his source to arrive at the sequence of God–Christ.

Isa. 60.19b (LXX)   *Rev. 21.23b*
ἀλλ' ἔσται σοι κύριος φῶς αἰώνιον   ἡ γὰρ δόξα τοῦ θεοῦ ἐφώτισεν αὐτήν,
καὶ ὁ θεὸς δόξα σου   καὶ ὁ λύχνος αὐτῆς τὸ ἀρνίον

In implementing this transposition and designating the Lamb as the city's *lamp* and God in effect as its *light* John is probably not intending to express any clear idea of subordination of Christ to God.[119] The distinction between lamp and light is rhetorical rather than theological, being the result of the parallelism. This is confirmed by Rev. 22.5, where God alone supplants the light of both the sun and the lamp.[120]

Neither is John making a cosmological statement. Thus it goes beyond his purpose to suppose that the glory of God lights only the city while the sun and moon remain to light the rest of the earth,[121] or that God takes the place of the sun and Christ of the moon.[122] While it may be that John's evocation of God and the Lamb as the luminaries of the New Jerusalem can be understood on more than one level, the primary purpose of the imagery is to emphasize the resplendent nature of the divine glory and the effect of its immediate presence on the city. The light is the visible sign and confirmation of God's life-giving presence, diffused throughout the city unrestricted by temple walls.[123] Now is fulfilled the final phrase of the *trisagion* which John left off in Rev. 4.8: 'The whole earth is filled with his glory'.

119. So also Beckwith, Holtz and Schüssler Fiorenza. In the Gospel of John, the Baptist is called a *lamp* (λύχνος, 5.35), but Christ is always referred to as the *light* (φῶς, 1.4-9; 3.19-21; 8.12; 9.5; 12.35-36, 46; cf. 1 Jn 2.8; Eph. 5.14).
120. Lamp is commonly used as a synonym for light in parallel constructions, e.g. Ps. 119.105; Prov. 6.23; 13.9; and in Prov. 20.27 the LXX even translates with φῶς rather than λύχνος. Cf. Rev. 1.16c.
121. *Contra* Charles (*Revelation*, II, pp. 171-72).
122. As Bousset supposes (*Offenbarung*, p. 451; cf. Beasley-Murray, *Revelation*, p. 327; Holtz, *Christologie*, p. 198 n. 3). In Rev. 1.16 Christ's glorious appearance is compared to the sun rather than the moon. Cf. *Odes Sol.* 11.13: 'And the Lord (is) like the sun upon the face of the land' (*OTP*, II, p. 745).
123. John consistently describes divine glory by analogy with light: 1.16; 18.1; 21.11; Roloff, *Offenbarung*, pp. 206-207. Cf. *Targ. Isa.* 60.2 'The Shekinah of the Lord shall dwell in Thee'.

Revelation 21.24 → Isaiah 60.3 (5, 11, 13)

Revelation	Isaiah	
καὶ περιπατήσουσιν τὰ ἔθνη	והלכו גוים	καὶ πορεύσονται βασιλεῖς
διὰ τοῦ φωτὸς αὐτῆς,	לאורך	τῷ φωτί σου
καὶ οἱ βασιλεῖς τῆς γῆς	ומלכים	καὶ ἔθνη τῇ
φέρουσιν τὴν δόξαν αὐτῶν εἰς αὐτήν	לנגה זרחך	λαμπρότητί σου

With Rev. 21.24 John progresses from the installation of the divine glory in the Holy City (// Isa. 60.1-2, 19-20) to the effect of the city's exalted position on the nations and kings of the earth (// Isa. 60.3-16). Up to and including the word βασιλεῖς he retains the basic vocabulary of Isa. 60.3, but modifies the sense through subtle changes. The addition of the article to *nations* and *kings*, and the further expansion of the latter with τῆς γῆς brings the OT prophecy in line with John's special categories of reference (*the nations*: Rev. 2.26; 11.2, 18; 12.5; 14.8; 15.3-4; 16.19; 18.3, 23; 19.15; 20.3, 8; 21.24, 26; 22.2; *the kings of the earth*: Rev. 1.5; 6.15; 17.2, 18; 18.3, 9; 19.19; 21.24).[124]

In the first clause (21.24a), περιπατέω would be the expected translation of הלך *if* the latter were used in the sense of 'to walk', but in this case it means 'to go, proceed' (ergo LXX πορεύομαι). Thus, along with the change of preposition, John subtly transforms the meaning of Isaiah's statement from 'nations will come to your light' to 'the nations will walk by its light'.[125]

The dependence of the nations on the light of the New Jerusalem in the new age is a deliberate antithesis of the former relationship between the nations and Babylon. Whereas the nations once received their direction and inclination from the evil city (Rev. 14.8; 18.3, 23),

124. Despite the theological problems posed by the presence of the nations and kings in the New Jerusalem, one should not interpret them apart from John's consistent use of these categories as collective symbols designating those formerly in opposition to God's kingdom. They are political terms of reference which should not be completely spiritualized. Even if they are somewhat idealized, they are not abstract. John's 'world' was geographically and politically defined. For more detailed discussion of this difficulty, consult Mounce, *Revelation*, pp. 384-85; Beasley-Murray, *Revelation*, p. 328; Sweet, *Revelation*, p. 308; Caird, *Revelation*, p. 279; Müller, *Offenbarung*, p. 363; Comblin, 'Liturgie', p. 16. Cf. the unique theory of Rissi, *Future*, pp. 73-74, 78.

125. Tob. 13.11 (S OL) also builds on this passage of Isaiah, but the sense is left unchanged. Cf. the metaphorical use of περιπατεῖν ἐν τῷ φωτί/τῇ ἡμέρᾳ (Rom. 13.13; Jn 8.12; 11.9; 12.35; 1 Jn 1.7; Eph. 4.17; 5.8).

now they rely for guidance on the divine glory. Whereas they once trampled the Holy City (11.2), now they walk in its light. This eschatological reorientation of the nations fulfils the expectation of Rev. 15.4 that 'all the nations shall come and worship before you'.

Turning to the second parallel clause of 21.24b, 'the kings of the earth will bring their glory into it', John forgoes the parallelism of Isa. 60.3 and instead links the subject of 60.3 with a motif drawn from the general scenario which follows in Isa. 60.5-16. There is no verse in Isa. 60 which specifically relates kings to the bringing of δόξα.[126] Nevertheless, because Rev. 21.24 begins on the basis of Isaiah 60 and v. 25 continues on that basis, it seems fairly likely that the phrase is a combination of ideas associated with both the kings and nations in Isaiah 60.

Kings
60.10b   And their kings shall minister to you
60.16b   You shall suck the breast of kings

Nations
60.5d   The wealth of nations shall come to you
60.11c   That men may bring to you the wealth of nations
60.13a   The glory of Lebanon shall come to you

Of these texts, Isa. 60.5, 11 appear to have had the most influence, and John uses the latter again in 21.26, where he renders חיל ('wealth') as δόξα.[127] The 'glory of kings' denotes generally the outward splendour of royal wealth and the visible symbols of kingly authority.[128]

What John intends to convey by the picture of kings bringing their glory into the New Jerusalem is essentially the same as Third Isaiah's purpose: to announce the future reversal of earthly structures of power and authority and to emphasize the universal sovereignty of the kingdom of God.[129] Moreover, as with the nations in the previous line (21.24a), there is also an implicit contrast with Babylon's former control of the kings of the earth (Rev. 17.18), and the latter's collabo-

126.   Though close parallels are found in Pss. 68.30 and 72.10.

127.   חיל in Isa. 60.11 means *wealth*, but כבוד can also designate *abundance, riches* (Ps. 49.17-18; Nah. 2.10; Isa. 10.3; 61.6; 66.11-12; cf. 60.13). For the possibility of interchange between the two terms compare חיל גוים (60.5, 11; 61.6) with כבוד גוים (66.12), and the parallelism of 61.6b.

128.   Dan. 4.36; 5.20; Esth. 1.4, 6-7; Bar. 5.6; 1 Macc. 10.58-60 (a king entering a city with δόξα); Mt. 6.29, Lk. 12.27.

129.   Schüssler Fiorenza, *Priester*, p. 355.

ration in the monopoly of political and economic power (18.9-10).
The obeisance of the earthly kings to the divine presence enthroned
in the New Jerusalem is thus the eschatological counterpart of the
visionary drama played out earlier in Rev. 4.4, 10 and 11.15-16,
where the twenty-four elders step down from their thrones, cast down
their golden crowns before God's throne and worship him.

Revelation 21.25-26 → Isaiah 60.11

Revelation	*Isaiah*	
καὶ οἱ πυλῶνες αὐτῆς	ופתחו שעריך תמיד	καὶ ἀνοιχθήσονται αἱ πύλαι σου διὰ
οὐ μὴ κλεισθῶσιν ἡμέρας,	יומם ולילה לא יסגרו	παντός, ἡμέρας καὶ νυκτὸς οὐ κλεισθήσονται
[νὺξ γὰρ οὐκ ἔσται ἐκεῖ	והיה...לא לילה	ἔσται...οὐ νύξ *Zech. 14.7*]
καὶ οἴσουσιν τὴν δόξαν καὶ τὴν τιμὴν τῶν ἐθνῶν εἰς αὐτήν	להביא אליך חיל גוים	εἰσαγαγεῖν πρὸς σὲ δύναμιν ἐθνῶν

In these two verses a clear allusion to Isa. 60.11 is interrupted by an
explanatory clause in Rev. 21.25b which is probably inspired by Zech.
14.7.[130] Instead of taking up the positive statement in the first part of
Isa. 60.11, 'your gates shall be open continually', John opts for the
negative parallel clause which follows, 'day and night they shall not be
shut' (Isa. 60.11b; cf. Rev. 3.7-8). But instead of using the 'day and
night' phrase in its idiomatic sense of *continually* (as he does everywhere else—Rev. 4.8; 7.15; 12.10; 14.11; 20.10), John appears to
acquire a sudden concern for literalism and realizes that the addition
of καὶ νυκτός here would be inconsistent with his program of a city
with perpetual light. Therefore, cutting off abruptly at ἡμέρας, he
adds a short note to explain the omission, bringing in here the phrase
from Zech. 14.7.[131]

---

130. 'There will be continuous day... not day and night, for at evening time
there shall be light' (Zech. 14.7). John uses Zech. 14.11 a few verses later (22.3a).
Beasley-Murray and Kiddle–Ross also accept this connection, while Farrer regards it
as an adaptation of Isa. 60.20 (*Revelation*, p. 221).

131. But it is obvious that the point of the gloss is more than just a passing
comment. It is important enough to warrant repetition on its own in 22.5a, and fits in
with John's emphasis on the abrogation of the old world (21.1b, 4). Some of the
versions (sah[2/4] boh[f] arm eth) add καὶ νυκτός here, but apart from this the MS
testimony is very uniform, which is surprising, considering the text's disjointedness

This sudden break is certainly very awkward, and one can think of a variety of alternatives by which John could have avoided this confusion. But in the end it matters little, for his intention is clear enough: the normal procedure of shutting the city (and temple) gates at nightfall is irrelevant in a city where God's light shines eternally.

In Isaiah, the purpose of the continually open gates is to accommodate the never-ending flow of wealth which the nations bring for the rebuilding of the city and temple. In Revelation, the interjection of the explanatory clause disturbs the original syntactical relationship between Isa. 60.11a and b, and John is compelled to change the infinitive of purpose (להביא) to a finite verb καὶ οἴσουσιν (though still leaving out a stated subject). But despite the interruption, it is likely that Rev. 21.26 should still be closely connected with v. 25a, and that John retains here the essential idea of Isaiah of a steady pilgrimage of nations flowing into the Holy City bringing their tribute.[132]

Whereas the pilgrims of Isaiah bring in the 'wealth of nations', John expands the offerings to include 'the glory and the honour of nations'. Exactly what is meant by *glory and honour* here depends on the perspective from which the expression is viewed. In the language of prophecy the phrase may be taken (as in Isaiah) to mean physical offerings, in which case there may be an implicit comparison with the wealth of the nations received by Babylon in Revelation 18.[133] However, from a liturgical point of view, *glory and honour* form part of the conventional vocabulary of spiritual worship.[134] Taken from this angle, the oblation of the nations in Rev. 21.26 may function as the

and the multiple conjectures of modern commentators.

132. For the pilgrimage motif here see above Chapter 2 n. 78, and Comblin, 'Liturgie', p. 15 and n. 28. Isa. 60.11b is one of several allusions to Isa. 60 which appear in 1QM 12 and 19, but there the promise is extended to include all the cities of Judah. Other possible allusions are found in Hag. 2.7-8; Zech. 14.14; cf. Tob. 13.11; *Sib. Or.* 3.772-73; *Pss. Sol.* 17.31; Mt. 2.11.

133. So also Lohmeyer, Brütsch and Sweet. The semantic relationship of חיל to כבוד/δόξα was discussed above in n. 127.

134. *Glory and honour*: Pss. 8.5; 28.1 (LXX); 95.7 (LXX); Job 37.22 (LXX); 1 Macc. 14.21; Rom. 2.7, 10; Heb. 2.7, 9; Rev. 4.9, 11. *Honour and glory*: 1 Tim. 1.17; 2 Pet. 1.17; Rev. 5.12-13. However, the combination of glory and honour is not always completely abstract. It can also refer to the outward splendour which accrues from material wealth, Exod. 28.2; 2 Macc. 5.16. Cf. Hag. 2.7-8; Beckwith, *Apocalypse*, pp. 763-64.

earthly counterpart to the heavenly doxologies of Revelation 4–5.[135] Since elements from both Revelation 4–5 and 17–18 converge in this final vision it is likely that John has left the image purposely ambiguous.

Revelation 21.27a → Isaiah 52.1 (35.8)

Revelation	Isa. 52.1	
καὶ οὐ μὴ εἰσέλθῃ	כי לא יוסיף יבא	οὐκέτι προστεθήσεται διελθεῖν
εἰς αὐτὴν πᾶν κοινόν	בך עוד ערל וטמא	διὰ σοῦ ἀπερίτμητος καὶ ἀκάθαρτος

	Isa. 35.8	
	לא יעברנו טמא	καὶ οὐ μὴ παρέλθῃ ἐκεῖ ἀκάθαρτος

From Isa. 60.11 in Rev. 21.25-26 John now moves directly to another Zion prophecy found in Isa. 52.1, which has probably already influenced his use of the title Holy City. Whereas Isaiah 60 speaks positively of what will enter the glorious future city, Isa. 52.1 stipulates that which cannot and will not enter the perpetually open gates. A similar phrase occurs in Isa. 35.8, but the diction and context clearly favour the use of Isa. 52.1 here.[136]

John's κοινόν corresponds to Isaiah's טמא (*unclean*) as a contrast to קדוש (*holy*); to which he characteristically adds πᾶν.[137] The extension of the ban on *anything unclean* from the temple precincts to the entire city is closely paralleled in the Temple Scroll.

135. But even amidst the catalogues of supposedly spiritual virtues in Rev. 4–5 the Lamb is said to be worthy to receive *wealth* (5.12 πλοῦτος = Hebrew חיל). Thus the issue is not as clear-cut as Comblin makes it out to be: 'Les nations n'apportent ici ni richesses, ni chameaux, ni or, ni encens, ni troupeaux, ni bois précieux, mais seulement un homage' ('Liturgie', p. 15 n. 28).

136. *Contra* Kraft and Müller, who accept the influence of both passages. The two texts (Isa. 35.8 and 52.1) do appear to be conflated in 1QH 6.20-21, but there distinct vocabulary from both passages occurs.

137. This cultic usage of κοινός appears to be exclusively Jewish and displaced חל/βέβηλος of the LXX; cf. Lev. 10.10; 1 Macc. 1.47, 62; Mk 7.2, 5; Acts 10.14; Rom. 14.14; BAGD, p. 438; MM, p. 350; Cremer, *BTL*, p. 362. For John's additions of πᾶν, see above Chapter 4 n. 104; cf. MG, III, p. 196.

And the city which I will hallow by settling my name and my temple within it, shall be holy and clean of *any unclean thing* [כל טמאה // πᾶν κοινόν] with which they may be defiled; everything that is in it shall be clean, and all that will be brought to it shall be clean.[138]

As in the above injunction, John's use of the neuter πᾶν κοινόν is probably intended as a comprehensive proscription which covers both unclean objects and persons.[139] Nonetheless, it is clear from the following specific categories (Rev. 21.27b) and the contrasted οἱ γεγραμμένοι that he has in mind mainly unholy people. This is reinforced by the parallel passages of 21.8 and 22.15, which reveal that, while John may adopt the language of the cult, the actual conditions for exclusion from the Holy City are based on moral, rather than ritual, impurity.

As with these related exhortations (Rev. 21.7-8; 22.14-15), the eschatological setting of 21.27 serves primarily a paranaetic function, reaching back to the present situation of the community.[140] John's pattern for the ideal community in Revelation 21–22, which no evildoer shall violate, is anticipated by the exhortations of the letters (Rev. 2–3), where the churches are admonished to root out those practising falsehood and wickedness and break off fellowship with them. Thus the original intent of Isa. 52.1 has been little changed: 'Deutero–Isaiah here expresses the same concern as Ezekiel (Ezek. 44.9) for the inviolable holiness of the new community'.[141]

Revelation 22.5b → Isaiah 60.2; Numbers 6.25

Revelation	*Isaiah*	
ὅτι κύριος ὁ θεὸς	ועליך יזרח יהוה	ἐπὶ δὲ σὲ φανήσεται κύριος, καὶ
φωτίσει ἐπ᾽ αὐτούς	וכבודו עליך יראה	ἡ δόξα αὐτοῦ ἐπὶ σὲ ὀφθήσεται

Num. 6.25

יאר יהוה פניו אליך   ἐπιφάναι κύριος τὸ πρόσωπον αὐτοῦ ἐπὶ σέ

Most of Rev. 22.5ab and its relationship to Isaiah 60 has already been

---

138. 11QT 47.36; cf. cols. 45–48; Yadin, *Temple Scroll*, I, pp. 289-90; II, p. 193; CD 12.1-2; 1QSa 2.4-11; Ezek. 43.12; *Jub.* 1.28.

139. BDB, pp. 379-80; Charles, *Revelation*, II, p. 174; Kraft, *Offenbarung*, p. 273; Lohmeyer, *Offenbarung*, p. 175.

140. This is recognized by many commentators, e.g. Schüssler Fiorenza, Sweet, Prigent, Roloff and Müller.

141. Whybray, *Isaiah 40–66*, p. 164.

discussed above in conjunction with 21.23. Although the repetition of the divine light theme here forms an *inclusio* with 21.23, its application shifts in focus from the city (αὐτήν) to its inhabitants (αὐτούς). For this and other reasons some commentators have suggested that the phrase 'the Lord God will shine upon them' goes beyond Isaiah 60 and alludes to the priestly blessing of Num. 6.25, 'The Lord make his face to shine upon you'.[142]

From a dictional point of view, there is little which favours the use of Num. 6.25 over Isa. 60.2. Even so, the similarities between the two OT passages does not exclude the possibility that John has in mind both texts.

The priestly blessing of Num. 6.24-26 was widely current in Jewish liturgical practice and is also found in the prayer of a Christian contemporary of John: Clement of Rome.[143] And not only does its cultic setting accord well with the context of Rev. 21.22–22.5 and John's emphasis on believers as priests, but also Rev. 22.4 has close affinities with Num. 6.25 and 27. The interpretation of Num. 6.25 as an *eschatological* promise associated with the end-time presence of God with his people could easily be effected by conflation with Isa. 60.1-2.[144] By combining the impersonal promise to Zion of Isa. 60.1-2 with the personal blessing of Num. 6.25, John can relate the glory of God's presence both to the Holy City (αὐτήν 21.23) and to its holy citizens (αὐτούς 22.5).

In drawing together the various allusions to Isaiah 60 in Rev. 21.22–22.5, it is important to keep in mind the role of temple tradi-

---

142. So Lohmeyer, Beasley-Murray, Sweet and Müller. Charles suggests instead the shortened form of the blessing in Ps. 118.27, and is followed by Holtz (*Revelation*, II, pp. 210-11; *Christologie*, pp. 205-206). In addition, Charles translates φωτίζειν in 22.5 transitively, 'For the Lord God shall cause (His face) to shine upon them', rather than the intransitive 'shall shine upon them' (II, p. 444 and n. 4). The verb can be taken either way, but the first obviously offers a closer parallel to Num. 6.25. None of these commentators takes into account the influence of Isa. 60.1-2.

143. Pss. 4.7; 67.2b; 118.27; Sir. 50.19-21; 1QS 2.1-4; 1QSb 3.5, 25; cf. 4.27-28; 1QH 4.5; *EncJud*, XIII, cols. 1060–63; Schürer, II, pp. 453-54, 458; *1 Clem.* 60.3.

144. As is attested in *Sifre Num.* 40 'The Lord make his face to shine upon thee. R. Nathan said [It means] the light of the Shekina (which will come in the Messianic age), as it says (Isa. lx.1) "Arise, shine, for thy light has come..."' (P. Levertoff, *Midrash Sifre on Numbers* [London, 1926], p. 32); similarly *Num. R.* 11.5.

tions in this section. In 21.22, which sets the tone for the whole pericope, the concept of a divine dwelling determined by humanly made
boundaries is done away with. As a result, holy space is no longer
defined by the presence of the temple, but is now coterminous with the
unrestricted presence of God, and is at the same time coextensive with
the living space of God's people as a whole. This is the only way to
make sense of the statement 'the Lord God is its temple and the
Lamb'. Cultic service no longer revolves around the temple but
around the direct presence of God, and thus the temporary inter-
mediaries of God's glory (temple–sun–moon) are no longer necessary.

Therefore, just because John's Holy City has no temple building
does not mean he is abrogating temple functions as well. It has already
been pointed out that he compensates for the absence of the temple by
extending temple motifs to the city as a whole. The use of Isaiah 60
fits well into this scheme, for the latter passage likewise is taking up
cultic images when it speaks of God's glory resting on the city, the
tribute of kings and nations for the house of God, and pilgrims
streaming through the gates of the festival city.[145] Finally, in the light
of Ben Sira's testimony that the priestly blessing of Numbers 6 was
recited at the conclusion of the temple service (Sir. 50.19-21), the
closing synthesis of Isa. 60.1-2, 19 and Num. 6.25, 27 in Rev. 22.4-5
provides a fitting benediction to John's vision of the temple-city.

Revelation 22.12 → Isaiah 40.10; 62.11

Revelation	Isa. 40.10	
ἰδοὺ ἔρχομαι ταχύ,	יבוא...הנה אדני יהוה	ἰδοὺ κύριος...ἔρχεται...
καὶ ὁ μισθός μου μετ' ἐμοῦ	הנה שכרו אתו	ἰδου ὁ μισθὸς αὐτοῦ μετ' αὐτοῦ
ἀποδοῦναι ἑκάστῳ ὡς	ופעלתו לפניו	καὶ τὸ ἔργον ἐναντίον
τὸ ἔργον ἐστὶν αὐτοῦ		αὐτοῦ

	Isa. 62.11	
	הנה ישעך בא	ἰδού σοι ὁ σωτὴρ παραγίνεται
	הנה שכרו אתו	ἔχων τὸν ἑαυτοῦ μισθὸν
	ופעלתו לפניו	καὶ τὸ ἔργον πρὸ προσώπου αὐτοῦ

1 Clem. 34.3
ἰδοὺ ὁ κύριος, καὶ ὁ μισθὸς αὐτοῦ
πρὸ προσώπου αὐτοῦ, ἀποδοῦναι
ἑκάστῳ κατὰ τὸ ἔργον αὐτοῦ

---

145. Schüssler Fiorenza also emphasizes the cultic setting of Isa. 60 (*Priester*,
pp. 161-63).

In the series of closing exhortations in Rev. 22.6-21, vv. 12-13 form a unit which corresponds closely to its introductory counterpart in Rev. 1.7-8. Here the announcement of imminence and retribution is one of several I-speeches delivered by Christ himself through the medium of his angelic representative (1.1; 22.6, 16). The saying in v. 12 can be broken down into three parts, only one of which has any clear connection to Isaiah.

1. ἰδοὺ ἔρχομαι ταχύ. The exact same phrase occurs in Rev. 22.7, and without ἰδού in 22.20. Similar statements of Christ are found in Rev. 2.16, 3.11 and 16.15. It is found nowhere else in early Christian literature. In two of these cases (2.16; 16.15) the 'I come' sayings serve as warnings, while in the remaining examples they are either meant as encouragement (3.11; 22.20) or are left ambiguous (22.7, 12). Because of the frequency with which this formula occurs in Revelation, and the variety of settings in which it is employed, it must remain doubtful whether it is inspired by the introduction to the reward clause in Isa. 40.10 ἰδοὺ κύριος...ἔρχεται. It may simply be a product of early Christian prophetic speech.

2. καὶ ὁ μισθός μου μετ' ἐμοῦ. There is little question that this phrase ultimately goes back to Isaiah 40 or 62 אתו שכרו.[146] But even though the diction in both Isaiah passages is identical, several factors make 62.11 the more attractive option. For one thing in Isa. 40.10 the rewarder is the Lord God, but in 62.11 Third Isaiah's reapplication of his predecessor's words paves the way for a messianic interpretation.

> Behold, your salvation comes
> Behold, his reward is with him.

Associating the task of rewarding with Christ is made even more natural by the LXX, which renders *salvation* as *saviour* (ὁ σωτήρ). Jewish-Christian exploitation of this variation for Christological purposes is attested already in the conflation of Isa. 62.11 with Zech. 9.9 in Mt. 21.5.

In addition, Isa. 62.11 is better suited to the idea of an eschatological reward because in 40.10 the reward is merely a figure for the returning exiles. But whether or not the (τὸν) μισθόν which Christ promises here includes both reward and punishment is unclear.[147] In

---

146. So Lohmeyer, Beckwith, Ozanne, Trudinger, Caird, Kraft, Beasley-Murray, Prigent and Müller, citing predominantly Isa. 40.10.

147. *Contra* Beckwith (*Apocalypse*, p. 776) and Vos (*Synoptic Traditions*,

the eschatological index of Rev. 11.18, which anticipates the events of 20.11-15, the giving of a *reward* (τὸν μισθόν) applies only to the saints. 3. ἀποδοῦναι ἑκάστῳ ὡς τὸ ἔργον ἐστὶν αὐτοῦ. This phrase is not from Isaiah, but its connection with the previous reward clause raises questions about the origin of the saying in Rev. 22.12 as a whole.[148] Because of the very similar combination of texts in *1 Clement* 34, Kraft has suggested that the saying may belong to traditional Christian paraenesis.[149] Vos, on the other hand, argues at length that John is here dependent on the logion attributed to Jesus in Mt. 16.27: μέλλει γὰρ ὁ υἱὸς τοῦ ἀνθρώπου ἔρχεσθαι...καὶ τότε ἀποδώσει ἑκάστῳ κατὰ τὴν πρᾶξιν αὐτοῦ.[150] All this adds up to the likelihood that John is not working with Isaiah directly in Rev. 22.12, but takes over an existing saying in which the OT texts had already been combined and applied to the future judgment.

pp. 175-77), who regard it as both good and bad recompense. Cf. Mt. 16.27; 1 Cor. 3.10-15; 2 Cor. 5.10.

148. The two most likely sources for this clause are Ps. 62.13 (61.13) or the LXX of Prov. 24.12. Paul uses the latter in Rom. 2.6. Cf. Jer. 17.10; Sir. 35.22; 2 Tim. 4.14; *2 Clem.* 11.6.

149. *Offenbarung*, p. 279; also Prigent, *L'Apocalypse*, p. 354. Though in *1 Clement* the agent is God; cf. *Barn.* 21.3.

150. *Synoptic Traditions*, pp. 174-78 ('John is alluding to the saying of Jesus as reported in Matt. 16:27', p. 176).

Chapter 8

SUMMARY AND CONCLUSIONS:
JOHN'S USE OF ISAIAH—RESULTS OF ANALYSIS

A. *Classification of Allusions*

As was set out in the introduction, one of the goals projected for the examination of Isaiah allusions in Revelation was to be able to determine, with some degree of confidence, to what extent the book of Isaiah is and *is not* employed in the composition of John's prophecy. To this end, on the basis of the detailed evaluations of Chapters 3–7, I have ranked each proposed allusion according to one of three categories: certain/virtually certain, probable/possible or unlikely/doubtful. The resultant chart (found on the following page) will serve as both a starting place and reference point from which a variety of conclusions, corrections and proposals may be drawn.

We can begin with a general summary. Of the approximately 73 potential Isaiah allusions examined, 41 were judged to be authentic; 9 were judged probable, though not certain; and, in the last column, 23 were classed as doubtful.[1] While it is likely that, in individual cases, some will read the evidence differently and dispute the position of certain texts, it appears to me doubtful that any example could ever move up or down more than one ranking. That is, it is unlikely that a 'doubtful' text will ever become a 'certain' text, and vice versa. In any case, a comparison of these results with the estimates of previous commentators suggests that, on the whole, the selection and winnowing process has not been over-rigorous. Swete counts 46 allusions to Isaiah,

---

1. These totals do not include repetitions, nor have I separated individual motifs within a single verse or literary unit if they have been employed consecutively. Thus e.g. Isa. 6.2a, 3a in Rev. 4.8 is counted as one allusion. A census according to independent elements would raise the total of certain allusions by about 10.

and Lestringent accepts 47, which compares closely to my combined total of certain and probable texts (50).[2]

Isaiah Allusions in Revelation

Certain/Virtually Certain Revelation—Isaiah		Probable/Possible Revelation—Isaiah		Unlikely/Doubtful Revelation—Isaiah	
1.16b/2.12, 16/19.15a, 21	11.4b	1.16b/2.12, 16/19.15a, 21	49.2	1.1	1.1
1.17b/2.8/ 22.13	44.6 *et al.*	3.12a	22.23	1.1-3	56.1-2
2.17	65.15/62.2	4.4	24.23	1.4b/3.1	11.2
3.7b	22.22	6.12	50.3	4.5/5.6	
3.9b	60.14/49.23	7.14b	1.18b	1.5a	55.4
3.9c	43.4	7.15b	4.5-6	1.5c	40.2
3.14a	65.16	16.1a, 17b	66.6a	1.11a	30.8
4.8	6.2a, 3a	21.2a	52.1	1.19a	48.6
5.5b/22.16b	11.10	21.12b	62.6a	5.1	29.11
6.13	34.4			5.6	53.7
6.14a	34.4aß			7.2a	41.2, 25
6.15b, 16b	2.19, 10			8.5	6.6
7.16-17a	49.10			11.2b	63.18
7.17b	25.8b			11.8b	1.10
12.2, 4b	26.17			11.9b	53.9
12.5-6	66.7-8			12.1ff.	27.1
14.8a/18.2a	21.9			12.1-2, 5	7.14
14.10b-11a/ 19.3b	34.9-10a			12.9/8.10- 11/9.1	14.12-15
14.19c-20a/ 19.13a, 15c	63.1-3			12.12a	44.23/49.13
15.8	6.1c, 4b			14.5a	53.9
17.2a/ 18.3b, 9b	23.17b			14.10a	51.17
18.2b	13.21/34.11, 13b-14			16.12	11.15-16
18.7b-8a	47.7-9			16.16	14.13
18.23c	23.8			20.6b	61.6a
19.7-8/21.2b	61.10				
19.11c	11.4a				

2.   *Apocalypse*, p. cliii n. 1; *Essai sur l'unite de la révélation biblique*, p. 148. Tenney allows 79 allusions to Isaiah, which comes close to my total of proposed allusions (73); but he is obviously listing any suggested parallel, with no concern for verification (*Interpreting Revelation*, p. 104).

Certain/Virtually Certain		Probable/Possible	Unlikely/Doubtful
19.17–20.10	24–27		
21.1-2a	65.17, 18b		
21.4a	25.8ab		
21.4b	65.19-20a		
21.4d	65.16c/		
	(43.18)		
21.5a	43.19a		
21.6b/22.17b	55.1		
21.18-21	54.11-12		
21.23/22.5b	60.1-2, 19		
21.24	60.3, 5, 11		
21.25-26	60.11		
21.27a	52.1		
22.12	62.11/40.10		

As a basis for further research, the advantages of this delimiting approach are twofold. First, the elimination of doubtful parallels and the corresponding confirmation of certain texts paves the way for a better appreciation and evaluation of those Isaiah passages which lie at the heart of John's prophetic message. Secondly, more conviction can be attached to conclusions based on these accepted texts.

B. *Thematic Arrangement of Certain Allusions*

Using the list of certain allusions as a base, it is now possible to narrow the field of application even further by first gathering these texts in order of their appearance in Isaiah, and then breaking them down into thematic categories. The first procedure reveals that the 41 texts involved derive from approximately 23 principal sections of Isaiah, with four passages standing out as especially prominent.

2.19, 10	23.8, 17	44.6	**60.1-3, 5, 11, 14, 19**
6.1-4	(24–27)	47.7-9	61.10
11.4, 10	25.8	49.10, 23	62.2, 11
13.21	26.17	52.1	63.1-3
21.9	**34.4, 9-11, 13-14**	54.11-12	**65.15-20a**
22.22(-23)	43.4, (18), 19	55.1	66.7-8

Even at this stage, one can begin to discern patterns of selection and outlines of topical interest. Final definition is obtained by organizing these passages according to the thematic classifications outlined in Chapter 2.[3]

1. *Visionary experience and language*: Isa. 6.1-4
2. *Christological titles and descriptions*: Isa. 11.4, 10; 22.22; 44.6; 65.15
3. *Eschatological judgment:*
   a. Holy war and Day of the Lord: Isa. 2.19, 10; 34.4; 63.1-3
   b. Oracles against the nations: Isa. 13.21; 21.9; 23.8, 17; 34.9-14; 47.7-9
4. *Eschatological salvation*:
   a. Salvation oracles in anticipation: Isa. 65.15/62.2; 61.10; 60.14/49.23; 43.4; 49.10; 25.8b
   b. Oracles of renewal: Isa. 65.15-20a; 25.8ab; 43.(18), 19; 55.1
   c. New Jerusalem oracles: Isa. 52.1; 54.11-12; 60.1-3, 5, 11, 19

Not only does it appear that these Isaiah texts are consciously *selected* according to subject, but they are also *applied* according to subject. Thus Isa. 6.1-4 is reserved for the visionary framework (Rev. 4.8; 15.2), while Isa. 2.19, 10, 34.4 and 63.1-3 all correspond to passages dealing with the parousia and final battle, despite the fact that this involves three separate units lying chapters apart from each other (Rev. 6.12-17; 14.14-20; 19.11-21). John's use of Isaian oracles against the nations is limited to prophecies against Harlot-Babylon (14.8-11; 17.1–19.4), while various salvation oracles are employed in passages anticipating the eschatological renewal (Rev. 2–3; 7.15-17; 19.5-9), as well as the vision of renewal itself (21.1-8). And finally, John's description of the New Jerusalem (Rev. 21.9–22.5) takes much of its inspiration from Isaiah's prophecies concerning the future restoration and glory of Zion-Jerusalem.[4] In contrast to these clusters of Isaiah texts, it is striking that, apart from Isa. 26.17 and 66.7-8 in Revelation 12, no certain or even probable allusions to Isaiah are found in Revelation 8–13.

---

3.   I have left out only the reward passage of Isa. 62.11/40.10 and the birth texts of Isa. 26.7 and 66.7-8, though even these last two reflect topical selection.

4.   The remark of M. Goulder, 'It is quite rare for Isaiah to dominate a whole unit in the way that Ezekiel does', clearly does not accord with the facts ('The Apocalypse as an Annual Cycle of Prophecies', *NTS* 27 [1980–81], p. 348). Isaiah texts dominate in the Philadelphia letter (3.7-13), as well as in Rev. 21.1-8, 18-21 and 21.22–22.5.

C. *Exegetical and Literary Techniques*

In spite of the fact that John's use of Isaiah, and the OT in general, is to a large extent allusive, there is abundant evidence to show that the Jewish-Christian prophet was familiar with a variety of exegetical and literary devices, and employed these consistently and purposefully in his handling of the OT material. In the following list I have included both obvious and apparent examples of interpretational methodology. Most of these examples are discussed in more detail in Chapters 3–7.

a. *Repetition of OT texts*. This is a distinctive feature of John's approach, which extends also to his use of other OT books. Individual motifs from Isaiah which are reused one or more times include 11.4b (5×), 44.6 (3×), 23.17b (3×), 11.10 (2×), 25.8b (2×), 63.1-3 (2×), 21.9 (2×), 34.10 (2×), 61.10 (2×), 55.1 (2×) and 60.1-2 (2×). These biblical recapitulations appear to be sender–receiver signals which are designed to alert the reader to certain fundamental associations within the rhetorical framework of the vision-report. In this capacity, they serve three basic functions:

1. To create anticipation of something to come (Isa. 25.8b in Rev. 7.17b and 21.4a; Isa. 55.1 in Rev. 21.6b and 22.17b), and, conversely, to emphasize a warning of something to come (Isa. 11.4b in Rev. 1.16b etc. and 19.15a, 21; Isa. 21.9 in Rev. 14.8a and 18.2a).

2. As a connecting link between thematic units divided by intervening material, especially in a relationship of summary and expansion (Isa. 63.1-3 in Rev. 14.19c-20 and 19.13, 15; Isa. 21.9 in Rev. 14.8 and 18.2; Isa. 61.10 in Rev. 19.7-9 and 21.2).

3. As a reprise emphasizing continuity and/or fulfilment (i.e. inclusio: Isa. 44.6 in Rev. 1.17b and 22.13; ?Isa. 11.10 in Rev. 5.5b and 22.16b; Isa. 34.10 in Rev. 14.11a and 19.3; Isa. 60.1-2 in Rev. 21.23 and 22.5b).[5]

b. *Combination of two or more texts by analogy*. This is one of John's favourite techniques, which involves the bringing together of different

---

5. On the wider use of *inclusio* in Revelation, see A. Satake, 'Inklusio als ein beliebtes Ausdrucksmittel in der Johannesapokalypse', *AJBI* 6 (1980), pp. 76-113.

texts on the basis of common subject matter (i.e. thematic analogues) and/or vocabulary (e.g. catchword). With regard to the Isaiah allusions in Revelation, the examples of this procedure fall into two categories:

1. *Conflation* of two or more texts into one integral whole: Isa. 11.4b + Ps. 2.8-9 (Rev. 19.15); Isa. 11.4b + Isa. 49.2 (Rev. 1.16b etc.); Isa. 66.7 + Ps. 2.9 (Rev. 12.5); Isa. 63.2-3 + Joel 4.13 (Rev. 14.19-20; 19.15c); Isa. 60.1-2 + Num. 6.25 (Rev. 22.5a); Isa. 60.19 + 60.1-2 (Rev. 21.23); Isa. 24–27 + Ezek. 38–39 (Rev. 19–20).

2. *Correlation* of two or more texts which retain their independence: Isa. 61.10 + Isa. 54.11-12 (Rev. 19.7-9→21.18-21).

c. *Exploitation of Hebrew parallelism for christological purposes (e.g. interpreting OT κύριος as Christ).* Isa. 44.6 (Rev. 1.17b etc.); Isa. 2.19, 10 (Rev. 6.16b); Isa. 60.19 (Rev. 21.23); ?Isa. 65.16 (ὁ ἀμήν 3.14a).

d. *Bridging two passages together by means of a third which shares common elements.* Isa. 60.14 → *Isa. 49.23* → Isa. 43.4 (Rev. 3.9); Isa. 65.16 → *Isa. 43.18* → Isa. 43.19 (Rev. 21.4-5).

e. *Clarification and augmentation of an obscure text by means of a more developed parallel text.* Isa. 54.11-12→Tob. 13.16-18a (Rev. 21.18-21); or, similarly, *explanation* or *resolution* of a theological difficulty introduced by one passage by the juxtaposition of another: Isa. 60.11→Zech. 14.7 (Rev. 21.25)

f. *Interpretative handling of ambiguous Hebrew roots (etymologization).* אמן in Isa. 65.16 (Rev. 3.14a), and אקדח in Isa. 54.12 (Rev. 21.21).

g. *Extending the scope of a passage by subtle additions.* ἔτι to Isa. 49.10 (Rev. 7.16); πᾶν to Isa. 49.10, 25.8 and 52.1 (Rev. 7.16b, 17c; 21.4a, 27a); and πάντα to Isa. 43.19 (Rev. 21.5).

When we keep in mind John's use of *gematria* (computation of numerical value of letters) in Rev. 13.18, it should come as no surprise to find similarities between some of the above examples and

Jewish hermeneutical principles, such as are exemplified in later rabbinic rules of interpretation (*middôt*).[6] Some of the more obvious parallels are category b, with $g^e z\bar{e}r\hat{a}$ $\check{s}\bar{a}w\hat{a}$ (*inference from analogy*), and category e, with $k\bar{a}y\hat{o}s\hat{e}$' $b\hat{o}$ $b^e m\bar{a}q\hat{o}m$ '$a\d{h}\bar{e}r$ (deduction from another passage). The repeated application of these and other exegetical techniques further strengthens the conclusion that the Jewish-Christian prophet does not treat the OT Scriptures in an *ad hoc* manner, but consistently employs accepted hermeneutical procedures. Many of these examples are no doubt the result of his Jewish heritage,[7] but some can only be explained on the basis of John's exalted christological perspective (e.g. category c).

From the viewpoint of exegetical methodology, with few exceptions, it would be difficult to distinguish the prophet from his Jewish contemporaries. This fact makes it necessary to draw a distinction between John's christological presuppositions and his exegetical praxis. Certainly the latter serves the former, but this does not necessarily mean that the former always dictates the latter. Therefore, we must take issue with the oft-quoted opinion of Feuillet that Revelation is simply 'une relecture de l'Ancien Testament à la lumière de l'événement chrétien', if by 'relecture' he means to imply the interpretative *process* as well as the *result*.[8]

In light of the above conclusions, such a statement is an unhelpful overgeneralization which obscures the fact that much of the OT interpretation and applications in Revelation could as easily be attributed to a non-Christian Jew with messianic and/or nationalistic concerns. This is especially evident in the anti-Roman propaganda of Revelation 17–18, where John's use of OT desolation motifs is remarkably similar to the approach of the author of 4Q179 (Chapter 6 n. 68), and in the application of Babylon oracles to Rome, a procedure adopted also by the Jewish Sibyl (Chapter 6 n. 77). To be sure, the fulfilment of messianic hopes in Jesus had a profound effect on John's reading of

6. For the various lists of *middôt*, see H.L. Strack, *Einleitung in Talmud und Midrasch* (München, 6th edn, 1976), pp. 95-109; on the question of the earliest use of such principles, see G.J. Brooke, *Exegesis at Qumran: 4QFlorilegium in its Jewish Context* (JSOTSup, 29; Sheffield, 1985), pp. 6-44.

7. Schlatter, *Das Alte Testament*, pp. 104-108; Hartman, *Prophecy Interpreted*, pp. 109-12.

8. *L'Apocalypse*, p. 65; cf. Farrer, *Revelation*, p. 30, who states that Jesus is the 'halacha' by which to understand the OT.

the OT, but this does not mean that he suddenly abandoned one method of interpretation in favour of another, or that christological awareness was an overriding determinant in *all* his exegesis.

A more significant and fundamental misunderstanding of John's office and use of the OT is displayed by those commentators who find prophetic activity and authority incompatible with exegetical activity. This faulty premise leads to a variety of superficial judgments concerning the prophet's use of Scripture. The following quotations from Schüssler Fiorenza and Vos are indicative of this sort of position.

> [John] does not interpret the OT but uses its words, images, phrases, and patterns as a language arsenal in order to make his own theological statement... [He] never refers to the OT as authoritative Scripture... John's task is not exposition and interpretation of the OT prophets but prophetic proclamation about many peoples, kings, and nations. The author of Rev. is not bent on the exposition and explication of the OT as authoritative Scripture.[9]

> The Old Testament material is never employed to support an argument, to buttress an apology, or to give authoritative basis for a particular teaching. Rather, John merely employs the thought and terminology of the Old Testament as the garb in which to clothe his New Testament vision. The disregard for the various contexts of the Old Testament material... as well as the general practice of combining words and phrases from various and diverse Old Testament passages support the proposition that it is mainly the Old Testament concepts which John is *employing* and not the passages which he is *quoting*.[10]

Clearly these evaluations stand in stark contrast with the results of this study. Even though the issues involved here have already been dealt with generally in Chapter 2, they are important enough to warrant further comment. The evidence adduced in support of the above statements can be divided into two main categories.

1. *John is not interpreting the OT, because he does not use quotation formulae, uses Scripture anthologically, and does not follow the OT context.*

In response to these assertions it can be said first of all that none of them can be accepted as an objective criterion by which to decide the issue of interpretation versus non-interpretation. The absence of

9. *Revelation*, pp. 135-36; cf. pp. 102, 137.
10. *Synoptic Traditions*, pp. 51-52; similarly Halver, *Der Mythos*, p. 15.

introductory formulae is hardly a satisfactory guide in such matters, since the great majority of OT usage in the NT and elsewhere lacks such formal indicators.[11] We must also make a distinction between an author quoting Scripture for a general audience or group of readers unfamiliar with his particular theological concerns, and the situation of John, whose approach to the OT cannot have been completely unknown to the communities in which he served, regardless of whether or not they always agreed with him. In such biblically oriented conventicles, all that is needed are a few key words of an OT passage to trigger associations and remind the hearers of themes and biblical topoi with which they are probably already familiar.[12]

As for the question of contextual fidelity, this is certainly a very subjective area. What constitutes the standard for determining the 'correct' or 'original' interpretation? Do we measure John's application of an OT text against modern commentaries, a consensus of scholars, or model interpretations in early Judaism or Christianity? Even if he does use a passage atomistically, does this mean that his use is not interpretation? It is unlikely that the prophet himself would agree with such a judgment. Of course John makes adaptations and alterations in applying the older prophecies to his situation—but then again, what early Jewish or Christian exegete does not?[13] In any case, as far as the present study is concerned, there have been very few instances where John has strayed far from the 'obvious' meaning of Isaiah, whatever that may be.[14] The alternative conclusion—that the

11. See above, Chapter 2 n. 4.

12. Hartman, *Asking for a Meaning*, p. 96-101; cf. B. Lindars, *New Testament Apologetic* (London, 1961), p. 19; and Boring, *Sayings*, p. 99, who accepts that John's use of the OT points to a community 'intensively occupied with Scripture'. We may infer from Rev. 2.20, where John accords the prophetess Jezebel a teaching function, that he himself also undertook such duties (cf. *Did.* 11.10-11; 15.1).

13. H. Braun, 'Das Alte Testament im Neuen Testament', *ZTK* 59 (1962), pp. 16-31.

14. For a similar evaluation in regard to other NT books, see C. Westermann, 'Prophetenzitate im Neuen Testament', *EvT* 27 (1967), pp. 307-17; and, in relation to certain apocalyptic texts, see Hartman, *Prophecy Interpreted*, p. 126: 'Practically 100% of the OT passages to which allusion is made "fit", i.e. they have not been lifted out of their contexts and have not had their meanings radically altered'. For more useful material on this issue, see P. Grech, 'The "Testimonia" and Modern Hermeneutics', *NTS* 19 (1972–73), pp. 318-24; and T. Holtz, 'Zur Interpretation des Alten Testaments im Neuen Testament', *TLZ* 99 (1974), cols. 19-32, esp. col. 26.

prophet simply uses the OT as a religious thesaurus to pad his visions with conventional symbolism and rhetoric—is, in my opinion, completely unconvincing and at odds with the facts. This leads us to the second issue.

2. *John does not interpret the OT because he is a prophet, and such activity would be inconsistent with his special claim of authority and the title of the book: 'The Revelation of Jesus Christ'.*
Schüssler Fiorenza in particular elicits support for this thesis in a quote by K. Stendahl, who asserts that 'the prophetic spirit creates; it does not quote in order to teach or argue'.[15] While there is some measure of truth in this statement, it fails to take into account that the 'prophetic spirit' does not necessarily create *ex nihilo*. One need only look to the exilic and post-exilic prophets to see that the reuse, reformulation and actualization of previous prophetic testimony was in no way considered incompatible with a prophet's call and inspiration.[16] Especially in the prophetic school tradition the legacy of unfulfilled oracles remained important, with the adept almost being obligated to take up the words of his or her predecessors and bring them to completion through inspired reinterpretation or reapplication.[17]

We have already seen that John considers himself as part of a revelatory continuum which stretches from God's OT messengers to the prophetic circle within which he is probably a leading figure. Rev. 10.7 in particular reveals that he did not view his message as a 'solo' effort, for the mystery which is about to be fulfilled is one which God revealed to his servants the Prophets, and not simply to his servant John. This corporate revelatory perspective is upheld again immediately following the final vision in Rev. 22.6, where John is told that 'the Lord, the God of the spirits of the prophets, has sent his angel to show his servants what must soon take place'.

15. *Revelation*, p. 136.
16. A variety of trenchant observations on the subject of 'mantological exegesis' can be found in Fishbane, *Biblical Interpretation*; e.g. on the reuse of earlier oracles by Ezekiel (pp. 463, 477), by the Isaiah school (pp. 495-98), and the author of Dan. 9–12 (pp. 493-95, 515). Cf. also P. Grech, 'Interprophetic Re-Interpretation and Old Testament Eschatology', *Augustinianum* 9 (1969), pp. 235-65.
17. 'Nothing so much characterizes the hermeneutical issue of biblical oracles as the concern to *close* divine predictions which have remained open' (Fishbane, *Biblical Interpretation*, p. 465).

The very fact that John calls previous prophetic testimony a *mystery*, and yet can go on to say that it is about to be fulfilled, witnesses to his interaction with previously revealed traditions and shows an awareness of his role as a prophetic interpreter. A similar understanding of a relationship between the present revelation of mysteries and the interpretation of past prophetic testimony is found in the writings of Paul, who refers to his gospel 'according to the revelation of the mystery which was kept secret for long ages but is now disclosed and *through the prophetic writings is made known to all nations*' (Rom. 16.25-26; cf. Gal. 1.12; Eph. 3.3-5). As Fishbane has aptly stated, 'the secret of the final days was inscribed in the entrails of the older exoteric prophecies'.[18] By means of a Revelation of Jesus, John became the 'high priest' and prophet who handled them, interpreted them, and delivered their message to the expectant community.[19]

Thus, not only can an understanding of John's use of the OT offer guidelines for the modern exegete; it can also perhaps tell us something about the formation of the book itself and its prehistory, which may be divided into at least three stages:

1. pre-visionary influences
2. actual vision experiences
3. post-visionary redaction

Based on the results of Chapter 2 and John's thematic application of the OT, it seems likely that his book was the result of a gradual process of development which began with a political-religious crisis such as the community's conflicts with Roman authority (cf. Rev. 2.13) and led to eschatological speculation around chief themes, such as the Beast and the Harlot.[20] This in turn would lead naturally to the

18. Fishbane, *Biblical Interpretation*, p. 495.

19. 'Er fühlt sich als Fortsetzer und abschliessender Ausleger der alttestamentlichen Prophetie' (Kraft, *Offenbarung*, p. 16); similarly Rissi, *Future*, p. 55.

20. The collection and interpretation of OT texts around special themes is, of course, not unique to the author of Revelation. Hartman (*Prophecy Interpreted*) has uncovered a similar procedure in the composition of the synoptic apocalypse, and several Qumran documents likewise reflect a thematic approach; e.g. 4QFlor, 4QTest, 11QMelch (Brooke, *Exegesis at Qumran*, pp. 219, 311-23), and especially 4QTanh. This last work may be described as a 'thematic pesher' which gathers together passages from Isa. 40–54 dealing with the consolation of Zion. Fishbane labels this method 'taxemic exegesis' (*Biblical Interpretation*, p. 433 and n. 24).

development and juxtaposition of their respective anti-images: the Lamb and the Bride. There is little disagreement that John has built these contrasts into the structure of his book, so that the authorization scheme of Revelation 12–13 (Dragon and the Beast) parallels Revelation 4–5 (God and the Lamb), and is followed by the opposition of their corporate representatives in Revelation 17–18 (Harlot-Babylon) and Revelation 21–22 (Bride–New Jerusalem). In the pre-visionary stage, these primary images had probably already been connected with specific biblical models and had been given basic definition through exegetical and prophetic activity within the community. In turn, these foundational images and the texts associated with them provided the substrate and inspiration for the visionary experience itself. And in the last stage, narrations of the visionary kernels were redacted and given final definition in accordance with the same OT models.

Whether or not this compositional theory can withstand more detailed scrutiny, it is not necessary to conclude from this study that John's book is purely a literary product.[21] Nor has it been my intention to suggest that every sentence is the result of biblical interpretation.[22] But recognition of an exegetical and hermeneutical prehistory to the final product which we call the Book of Revelation is critical for its understanding. For all that Revelation is visionary, it is not *ad hoc*. And for all that its use of Scripture is at times implicit, it is not superficial. John certainly expected his readers to appreciate the exegetical foundation of his visions.[23] His interpretation of Isaiah in particular was clearly one of the more important pre-visionary influences which provided the substance and inspiration for the vision experience and for its final redaction.

21. On the question of authentic visionary experience versus literary activity, compare the discussions of Lindblom, *Gesichte und Offenbarung*, pp. 206-39; Hartman, *Prophecy Interpreted*, pp. 104-12; and Rowland, *Christian Origins*, pp. 62-65.

22. For discussion of the 'mental matrix' of mantological exegesis see Fishbane, *Biblical Interpretation*, p. 521-24; and Hartman, *Prophecy Interpreted*, 104-11.

23. Caird, *Revelation*, p. 11; cf. M. Fishbane, 'Revelation and Tradition: Aspects of Inner-Biblical Exegesis', *JBL* 99 (1980), pp. 359-61.

BIBLIOGRAPHY

Ambrogio, C. de, *L'Apocalisse* (2 vols.; Turin, 1964).

Ash, J.L., 'The Decline of Ecstatic Prophecy in the Church', *TS* 37 (1976), pp. 227-52.

Audet, J.-P., *La Didaché, Instructions des Apôtres* (Paris, 1958).

—'Literary Forms and Contents of a Normal Εὐχαριστία in the First Century', TU 73 (1959), pp. 643-62.

Aune, D.E., *Prophecy in Early Christianity and the Ancient Mediterranean World* (Grand Rapids, 1983).

—*The Cultic Setting of Realized Eschatology* (NovTSup 28; Leiden, 1972).

—'The Use of PROPHĒTĒS in Josephus', *JBL* 101 (1982), pp. 419-21.

Aus, R.D., 'The Relevance of Isaiah 66.7 to Revelation 12 and 2 Thessalonians 1', *ZNW* 67 (1976), pp. 252-68.

Ball, C.J., 'Had the Fourth Gospel an Aramaic Archetype?', *ExpTim* 21 (1909–10), pp. 92-93.

Barnes, E., 'Ezekiel's Denunciation of Tyre (Ezek. xxvi–xxviii)', *JTS* 35 (1934), pp. 50-54.

Barrett, C.K., 'The Lamb of God', *NTS* 1 (1954–55), pp. 210-18.

Bartina, S., '"Una espada salía de la boca de su vestido" (Ap. 1, 16; 2, 16; 19, 15, 21)', *EstBib* 20 (1961), pp. 207-17.

Batey, R., *New Testament Nuptial Imagery* (Leiden: Brill, 1971).

Bauckham, R.J., 'The Book of Revelation as a Christian War Scroll', *Neot* 22 (1988), pp. 17-40.

—*Climax of Prophecy: Studies on the Book of Revelation* (Edinburgh: T. & T. Clark, 1993).

—'The Eschatological Earthquake in the Apocalypse of John', *NovT* 19 (1977), pp. 224-33.

Bauer, M.H., *Edelsteinkunde* (Leipzig, 3rd edn, 1932).

Bauer, W., *Orthodoxy and Heresy in Earliest Christianity* (London, 1972).

Baumgarten, J.M., 'The Duodecimal Courts of Qumran, Revelation, and the Sanhedrin', *JBL* 95 (1976), pp. 59-78.

Beale, G.K., *The Use of Daniel in Jewish Apocalyptic Literature and in the Revelation of St John* (Lanham, 1984).

—'The Origin of the Title "King of Kings and Lord of Lords" in Revelation 17.14', *NTS* 31 (1985), pp. 618-20.

Beasley-Murray, G.R., *The Book of Revelation* (NCB; London, 1974).

Becker, J., *Gottesfurcht im Alten Testament* (AnBib, 25; Rome, 1965).

—'Erwägungen zu Fragen der neutestamentlichen Exegese', *BZ* NF 13 (1969), pp. 99-102.

Beckwith, I.T., *The Apocalypse of John* (New York, 1919).

Beckwith, R.T., *The Old Testament Canon of the New Testament Church and its Background in Early Judaism* (London, 1985).

Bergen, P. van, 'Dans l'attente de la nouvelle Jérusalem', *LuViSupp* 45 (1959), pp. 1-9.

Berger, K., 'Apostelbrief und apostoliche Rede—Zum Formular frühchristlicher Briefe', *ZNW* 65-66 (1974-75), pp. 207-19.

—*Die Amen-Worte Jesu* (BZNW 39; Berlin, 1970).

Bergmeier, R., 'Altes und Neues zur "Sonnenfrau am Himmel" (Apk 12). Religionsgeschichtliche und quellenkritische Beobachtungen zu Apk 12,1-17', *ZNW* 73 (1982), pp. 97-108.

Betz, O., 'Donnersöhne, Menschenfischer und der Davidische Messias', *RevQ* 3 (1961-62), pp. 41-70.

Beuken, W.A.M, 'Isaiah LIV: The Multiple Identity of the Person Addressed', *OTS* 19 (Leiden, 1974), pp. 29-70.

Beyer, K., *Die aramäischen Texte aus die Toten Meer* (Göttingen, 1984).

Bietenhard, H., *Die himmlische Welt im Urchristentum und Spätjudentum* (WUNT, 2; Tübingen, 1951).

Black, M., *The Book of Enoch or 1 Enoch* (Leiden, 1985).

—'The New Creation in 1 Enoch', in *Creation, Christ and Culture: Studies in Honour of T.F. Torrance* (ed. R.W.A. McKinney; Edinburgh, 1976), pp. 13-21.

—'The Throne-Theophany Prophetic Commission and the "Son of Man": A Study of Tradition-History', in *Jews, Greeks, and Christians* (ed. R. Hamerton-Kelly and R. Scroggs; Leiden, 1976), pp. 57-73.

Blevins, J.L., 'The Genre of Revelation', *RevExp* 77 (1980), pp. 393-408.

Bori, P.C., 'L'estasi del profeta: Ascensio Isaiae 6 e l'antico profetismo cristiano', *CNS* 1 (1980), pp. 367-89.

Boring, M.E., *Sayings of the Risen Jesus* (SNTSMS, 46; Cambridge, 1982).

—'The Apocalypse as Christian Prophecy: A Discussion of the Issues Raised by the Book of Revelation for the Study of Early Christian Prophecy', in *SBL Seminar Papers for 1974* (2 vols.; Missoula, 1974), II, pp. 43-62.

—'The Unforgivable Sin Logion Mark III 28–29 (Matt. XII 31-32/Luke XII 10): Formal Analysis and History of Tradition', *NovT* 18 (1976), pp. 258-79.

Bornkamm, G., 'Die Komposition der apokalyptischen Visionen in der Offenbarung Johannis', *ZNW* 36 (1937), pp. 132-49.

Boussett, W., *Die Offenbarung Johannis* (Göttingen, 6th edn, 1906).

Box, G.H., *The Ezra-Apocalypse, being Chapters 3–14 of the Book Commonly Known as 4 Ezra (or II Esdras)* (London, 1912).

Boyd, W.J.P., 'I am Alpha and Omega (Rev 1, 8; 21, 6; 22, 13)', *SE*, II (= TU 87 [1964], pp. 526-31.

Brandon, S.G.F., *The Fall of Jerusalem and the Christian Church* (London, 1957).

Braude, W.G., *The Midrash on Psalms* (2 vols.; New Haven, 1959).

Braude, W.G., and I.J. Kapstein, *Pĕsikta dĕ-RaB Kahăna* (London, 1975).

Braun, H., *Qumran und das Neue Testament* (2 vols.; Tübingen, 1966).

—'Das Alte Testament im Neuen Testament', *ZTK* 59 (1962), pp. 16-31.

Brockelmann, C., *Lexicon Syriacum* (Halle, 2nd edn, 1928).

Broeck, R. van den, *The Myth of the Phoenix according to Classical and Early Christian Traditions* (Leiden, 1972).

Brongers, H.A., 'Der Zornesbecher', *OTS* 15 (1969), pp. 177-92.

Brooke, G.J., *Exegesis at Qumran: 4Q Florilegium in its Jewish Context* (JSOTSup, 29; Sheffield, 1985).

Brown, R., *The Epistles of John* (AB, 30; London, 1982).

Brownlee, W.H., 'Messianic Motifs of Qumran and the New Testament', *NTS* 3 (1956–57), pp. 195-210.

—*The Meaning of the Qumran Scrolls for the Bible* (New York, 1964).

Bruce, F.F., *1 & 2 Thessalonians* (Waco, 1982).

—'The Spirit in the Apocalypse', in *Christ and Spirit in the New Testament* (ed. B. Lindars and S.S. Smalley; Cambridge, 1974), pp. 333-44.

Brütsch, C., *Die Offenbarung Jesu Christi: Johannes-Apokalypse* (3 vols.; ZBK; Zürich, 2nd edn, 1970 [1955]).

Buchanan, G.W., 'The Word of God and the Apocalyptic Vision', *SBLASP* (1974), pp. 183-92.

Bultmann, R., *The Gospel of John: A Commentary* (Oxford, 1971).

—*The Second Letter to the Corinthians* (Minneapolis, 1985).

Burchard, C., 'Ein vorläufiger griechischer Text von Joseph und Aseneth', *DBAT* 14 (1979), pp. 2-53.

Burney, C.F., *The Aramaic Origin of the Fourth Gospel* (Oxford, 1922).

Burrows, E., 'The Pearl in the Apocalypse', *JTS* 43 (1942), pp. 177-79.

Butterworth, G.W., *Clement of Alexandria* (LCL; London, 1939).

Caird, G.B., *A Commentary on the Revelation of St John the Divine* (New York and London, 1966).

Cambier, J., 'Les images de l'Ancien Testament dans l'Apocalypse de Saint Jean', *NRT* 77 (1955), pp. 113-22.

Campenhausen, H. von, *Ecclesiastical Authority and Spiritual Power in the Church of the First Three Centuries* (London, 1969).

Carmignac, J., E. Cothenet and H. Lignée, *Les textes de Qumran traduits et annotés* (2 vols.; Paris, 1961, 1963).

Casey, J.S., 'Exodus Typology in the Book of Revelation', unpublished PhD dissertation (Southern Baptist Theological Seminary, 1981).

Cerfaux, L., 'La vision de la femme et du dragon de l'Apocalypse en relation avec le Protévangile', *ETL* 31 (1956), pp. 21-33.

Cerfaux, L. and J. Cambier, *L'Apocalypse de Saint Jean lue aux chrétiens* (LD, 17; Paris, 1955).

Chadwick, H., *Origen: Contra Celsum* (Cambridge, 1953).

Charles, R.H., *A Critical and Exegetical Commentary on the Revelation of St John* (2 vols.; Edinburgh, 1920).

—*Lectures on the Apocalypse: The Schweich Lectures* (London, 1922).

—*Studies in the Apocalypse* (Edinburgh, 1913).

Chevallier, M.A., *L'esprit et le Messie dans le Bas-Judaisme et le Nouveau Testament* (Paris, 1958).

Chilton, B., *The Glory of Israel* (JSOTSup, 23; Sheffield, 1983).

Clements, R.E., *Isaiah 1–39* (NCB; London, 1980).

Cohen, G.D., 'Esau as Symbol in Early Medieval Thought', in *Jewish Medieval and Renaissance Studies* (ed. A. Altmann; Cambridge, 1967), pp. 19-48.

Collins, A. Yarbro, *The Apocalypse* (NTM, 22; Dublin and Wilmington, DE, 1979).

—*The Combat Myth in the Book of Revelation* (HDR, 9; Missoula, MT, 1976).

—'Revelation 18; Taunt-Song or Dirge?', in *L'Apocalypse johannique et l'Apocalyptique dans le Nouveau Testament* (ed. J. Lambrecht; Gembloux, 1980), pp. 185-204.

Collins, J.J., 'Pseudonymity, Historical Reviews and the Genre of the Revelation of John', *CBQ* 39 (1977), pp. 329-43.

Comblin, J., 'La liturgie de la nouvelle Jérusalem (Apoc xxi. 1–xxii. 5)', *ETL* 29 (1953), pp. 5-40.

—*Le Christ dans l'Apocalypse* (Tournai, 1965).

Conzelmann, H., *1 Corinthians: A Commentary on the First Epistle to the Corinthians* (Philadelphia, 1975).

—*Primitive Christianity* (London, 1973).

Cothenet, E., 'Les prophètes chrétiens comme exégètes charismatiques de l'Ecriture', in *Prophetic Vocation in the New Testament and Today* (ed. J. Panagopoulos; NovTSup, 45; Leiden, 1977), pp. 77-107.

—'Les prophétes chrétiens dans l'Evangile selon saint Matthieu', in *L'Evangile selon Matthieu: Rédaction et Théologie* (ed. M. Didier; Gembloux, 1972), pp. 281-308.

—'Prophétisme dans le Nouveau Testament', *DBSup* 8 (1972), cols. 1222-1337.

Court, J.M., *Myth and History in the Book of Revelation* (London, 1979).

—'The Didache and St Matthew's Gospel', *SJT* 34 (1981), pp. 109-20.

Cowley, A.E., *Aramaic Papyri of the Fifth Century BC* (Oxford, 1923).

Cruz, V., *The Mark of the Beast: A Study of ΧΑΡΑΓΜΑ in the Apocalypse* (Amsterdam, 1973).

D'Aragon, J.-L., 'The Apocalypse', in *The Jerome Biblical Commentary* (2 vols. in one, ed. R.E. Brown *et al.*; London, 1969), II, pp. 467-93.

Dautzenberg, G., *Urchristliche Prophetie: Ihre Erforschung, ihre Voraussetzungen im Judentum und ihre Struktur im ersten Korintherbrief* (Stuttgart, 1975).

Delling, G., *Der Kreuzestod Jesu in der urchristlichen Verkündigung* (Göttingen, 1972).

—'Zum gottesdienstlichen Stil der Johannes-apokalypse', *NovT* 3 (1959), pp. 107-37.

Dietrich, E.L., 'Das religiös-emphatische Ich-Wort bei den jüdischen Apokalyptikern, Weisheitlehrern und Rabbinen', *ZRGG* 4 (1952), pp. 289-311.

Dittmar, W., *Vetus Testamentum in Novo* (Göttingen, 1903).

Dix, G.H., 'The Seven Archangels and the Seven Spirits', *JTS* 28 (1927), pp. 233-50.

Dodd, C.H., *The Bible and the Greeks* (London, 1925).

—*The Interpretation of the Fourth Gospel* (Cambridge, 1968).

Dornsieff, F., *Das Alphabet in Mystik und Magie* (Leipzig–Berlin, 1922).

—'Das Rotas Opera Quadrat', *ZNW* 36 (1937), pp. 222-38.

Draper, J.A., 'The Heavenly Feast of Tabernacles: Rev. 7.1-17', *JSNT* 19 (1983), pp. 133-47.

Driver, G.R., 'Isaiah I–XXXIX: Textual and Linguistic Problems', *JSS* 13 (1968), pp. 36-57.

Dumbrell, W.J., *The End of the Beginning: Revelation 21–22 and the Old Testament* (Homebush, 1985).

Dunn, J.D.G., 'Prophetic "I"-Sayings and the Jesus Tradition: The Importance of Testing Prophetic Utterances within Early Christianity', *NTS* 24 (1977–78), pp. 175-98.

—*Unity and Diversity in the New Testament* (London, 1977).

Dürr, L., *Die Wertung des göttlichen Wortes im alten Testament und im antiken Orient* (Leipzig, 1938).

Eissfeldt, O., *The Old Testament: An Introduction* (Oxford, 1974).

Elliott, J.H., *The Elect and the Holy* (NovTSup, 12; Leiden, 1966).

Ellis, E.E., 'Prophecy in the New Testament Church—and Today', in *Prophetic*

Vocation in the New Testament and Today (ed. J. Panagopoulos; NovTSup, 45; Leiden, 1977), pp. 46-57.

—*Prophecy and Hermeneutic in Early Christianity: New Testament Essays* (WUNT, 18; Tübingen, 1978).

Ernst, J., *Die eschatologischen Gegenspieler in den Schriften des Neuen Testaments* (Regensburg, 1967).

Everson, A.J., 'The Days of Yahweh', *JBL* 93 (1974), pp. 329-37.

Farrer, A., *A Rebirth of Images* (Glasgow, 1948).

—*The Revelation of St John the Divine* (Oxford, 1964).

Fekkes, J., III, '"His Bride has Prepared Herself": Revelation 19–21 and Isaian Nuptial Imagery', *JBL* 109 (1990), pp. 269-87.

Feuillet, A., 'La Femme vêtue du soleil (Ap 12) et la glorification de l'Epouse du Cantique des Cantiques (6, 10). Réflexions sur le progrès dans l'interprétation de l'Apocalypse et du Cantique des Cantiques', *NovVet* 59 (1984), pp. 36-67.

—*L'Apocalypse: Etat de la question* (StudNeot, 3; Paris et Bruges, 1963).

—'L'exode' de Jésus et le déroulement du mystère rédempteur d'aprés S. Luc et S. Jean', *RevThom* 77 (1977), pp. 181-206.

—'Le festin des noces de l'agneau et ses anticipations', *EspVie* 97 (1987), pp. 353-62.

—'Le Messie et sa Mère d'après le chapitre xii de l'Apocalypse', *RB* 66 (1959), pp. 55-86.

—'Les vingt-quatre vieillards de l'Apocalypse', *RB* 65 (1958), pp. 5-32.

Fiorenza, E. Schüssler, 'Composition and Structure of the Book of Revelation', *CBQ* 39 (1977), pp. 344-66.

—*Priester für Gott* (Münster, 1972).

—'Redemption as Liberation: Apoc 1.5f. and 5.9f.', *CBQ* 36 (1974), pp. 220-32.

—*The Book of Revelation: Justice and Judgment* (Philadelphia, 1985).

Fischer, U., *Eschatologie und Jenseitserwartung im hellenistischen Diasporajudentum* (BZNW 44; Berlin, 1978).

Fishbane, M., *Biblical Interpretation in Ancient Israel* (New York, 1985).

—'Revelation and Tradition: Aspects of Inner-Biblical Exegesis', *JBL* 99 (1980), pp. 343-61.

Fishwick, D., 'On the Origin of the Rotas-Sator Square', *HTR* 57 (1964), pp. 39-53.

Fitzmyer, J.A., 'The Use of Explicit Old Testament Quotations in Qumran Literature and in the New Testament', *NTS* 7 (1960–61), pp. 297-333.

Foerster, W., 'Die Heilige Geist im Spätjudentum', *NTS* 8 (1961–62), pp. 117-34.

Fohrer, G., *Die Symbolischen Handlungen der Propheten* (ATANT, 54; Zürich, 1953).

Ford, J. Massyngberde, 'The Heavenly Jerusalem and Orthodox Judaism', in *Donum gentilicium: New Testament Studies in Honour of David Daube* (ed. E. Bammel, C.K. Barrett and W.D. Davies; Oxford, 1978), pp. 215-26.

—'The Jewel of Discernment (A Study of Stone Symbolism)', *BZ* NF 11 (1967), pp. 109-16.

—*Revelation* (AB, 38; Garden City, 1975).

Francis, F.O., 'Humility and Angelic Worship in Col. 2.18', in *Conflict at Colossae* (ed. F.O. Francis and W.A. Meeks; Missoula, 1975), pp. 163-95.

Freed, J.N., *The Old Testament Quotations in the Gospel of John* (NovTSup, 11; Leiden, 1965).

Friedländer, L., *Roman Life and Manners under the Early Empire* (4 vols.; London, 7th edn, 1908–1913).

Friedländer, M. (ed.), *The Commentary of Ibn Ezra on Isaiah* (4 vols.; London, 1873).

Fuchs, H., *Der geistige Widerstand gegen Rom in der antiken Welt* (Berlin, 2nd edn, 1964).

Gangemi, A., 'L'utilizzazione del Deutero–Isaia nell' Apocalisse di Giovanni', *Euntes Docete* 27 (1974), pp. 109-44, 311-39.

Gaston, L., *No Stone on Another: Studies in the Significance of the Fall of Jerusalem in the Synoptic Gospels* (Leiden, 1970).

Gelin, A, *L'Apocalypse dans Bible Pirot* (Paris, 1938).

Georgi, D., 'Die Visionen vom himmlischen Jerusalem in Apk 21 und 22', in *Kirche*, (Festschrift G. Bornkamm; ed. D. Lührmann and G. Strecker; Tübingen, 1980), pp. 351-67.

Guelich, R.A., *The Sermon on the Mount* (Waco, TX, 1982).

Giblin, C.H., 'Structural and Thematic Correlations in the Theology of Revelation 16–22', *Bib* 55 (1974), pp. 487-504.

Gibson, E.C.S., *The Old Testament in the New Testament* (London, 1907).

Giet, S., *L'Apocalypse et l'histoire* (Paris, 1957).

Gillet, L., 'Amen', *ExpTim* 56 (1944–45), pp. 134-36.

Goldstein, J.A., *II Maccabees* (AB, 41A; Garden City, 1983).

Gollinger, H., *Das 'Grosse Zeichen' von Apokalypse 12* (SBM, 11; Würzburg, 1971).

Goppelt, L., *TYPOS* (Grand Rapids, 1982).

Gottwald, N.K., *Studies in the Book of Lamentations* (London, 1954).

Goulder, M., 'The Apocalypse as an Annual Cycle of Prophecies', *NTS* 27 (1980–81), pp. 342-67.

Gray, G.B., *A Critical and Exegetical Commentary on the Book of Isaiah I–XXVII* (Edinburgh, 1912).

Grech, P., 'The "Testimonia" and Modern Hermeneutics', *NTS* 19 (1972–73), pp. 318-24.

—'Interprophetic Re-Interpretation and Old Testament Eschatology', *Augustinianum* 9 (1969), pp. 235-65.

Greenberg, M., *Ezekiel 1–20* (AB, 20; Garden City, 1983).

Grelot, P., 'L'exégèse messianique d'Isaïe LXIII,1–6', *RB* 70 (1963), pp. 371-80.

Grimm, W., *Die Verkündigung Jesu und Deuterojesaja* (ANTJ, 1; Bern, 2nd edn, 1981).

Grudem, W., *The Gift of Prophecy in 1 Corinthians* (Washington, DC, 1982).

Gundry, R.H., 'The New Jerusalem: People as Place, not Place for People', *NovT* 29 (1987), pp. 254-64.

—*The Use of the Old Testament in St Matthew's Gospel* (NovTSup, 18; Leiden, 1967).

Gunkel, H., *Die Propheten* (Göttingen, 1917).

Günther, H.W., *Der Nah– und Enderwartungshorizont in der Apokalypse des heiligen Johannes* (Würzburg, 1980).

Habel, N., 'The Form and Significance of the Call Narrative', *ZAW* 77 (1965), pp. 297-323.

Hadorn, W., *Die Offenbarung des Johannes* (THKNT, 18; Leipzig, 1928).

Haenchen, E., *John 2: A Commentary on the Gospel of John Chapters 7–21* (Herm.; Philadelphia, 1984).

Hahn, F., 'Die Sendschreiben der Johannesapokalypse', in *Tradition und Glaube* (ed. G. Jeremias, H.-W. Kuhn and H. Stegemann; Göttingen, 1971), pp. 357-94.

Hall, S.G., 'Melito in the light of the Passover Haggadah', *JTS* NS 22 (1971), pp. 29-46.

Halver, R., *Der Mythos im letzten Buch der Bibel* (Hamburg, 1964).

Hanhart, R., *Septuaginta: Tobit* (Göttingen, 1983).

Hanson, J.S., 'Dreams and Visions in the Graeco–Roman World and Early Christianity', in *Aufstieg und Niedergang der römischen Welt* (18; Berlin, 1971–72), pp. 401-18.

Hillers, D.R., *Treaty Curses and the Old Testament Prophets* (Rome, 1964).

Holm-Nielsen, S., *Hodayot: Psalms from Qumran* (Aarhus, 1960).

Holtz, T., *Die Christologie der Apokalypse des Johannes* (TU, 85; Berlin, 1962).

—'Gott in der Apokalypse', in *L'Apocalypse johannique et l'apocalyptique dans le Nouveau Testament* (ed. J. Lambrecht; Gembloux, 1980), pp. 247-65.

—'Christliche Interpolationen in Joseph und Aseneth"', *NTS* 14 (1967–68), pp. 482-97.

—'Zur Interpretation des Alten Testaments im Neuen Testament', *TLZ* 99 (1974), cols. 19-32.

Horgan, M.P., 'A Lament over Jerusalem (*4Q179*)', *JSS* 18 (1973), pp. 222-34.

—*Pesharim: Qumran Interpretations of Biblical Books* (CBQMS, 8; Washington, DC, 1978).

Horsley, R.A., with J.S. Hanson, *Bandits, Prophets, and Messiahs: Popular Movements at the Time of Jesus* (San Francisco, 1985).

Hoskier, H.C., *Concerning the Text of the Apocalypse* (2 vols.; London, 1929).

Hunzinger, C.H., 'Babylon als Deckname für Rom und die Datierung des 1. Petrusbriefes', in *Gottes Wort und Gottes Land* (ed. H.G. Reventlow; Göttingen, 1965), pp. 67-77.

Hurtado, L., 'Revelation 4–5 in the Light of Jewish Apocalyptic Analogies', *JSNT* 25 (1985), pp. 105-24.

Jenkins, F., *The Old Testament in the Book of Revelation* (Grand Rapids, 1972).

Jeremias, J., 'Har Magedon (Apc 16, 16)', *ZNW* 31 (1932), pp. 73-77.

Jones, B.W., 'More about the Apocalypse as Apocalyptic', *JBL* 87 (1968), pp. 325-27.

Jörns, K.P., *Das hymnische Evangelium* (SNT, 5; Gütersloh, 1971).

Kaiser, O., *Isaiah 13–39* (OTL; London, 1974).

Kallas, J., 'The Apocalypse—an Apocalyptic Book?', *JBL* 86 (1967), pp. 69-80.

Karrer, M., *Die Johannesoffenbarung als Brief: Studien zum ihrem literarischen, historischen, und theologischen Ort* (Göttingen, 1986).

Kassing, A.T., *Die Kirche und Maria: Ihr Verhältnis im 12. Kapitel der Apokalypse* (Düsseldorf, 1958).

Kelly, H.A., 'The Devil in the Desert', *CBQ* 26 (1964), pp. 190-220.

Kiddle, M., and M.K. Ross, *The Revelation of St John* (London, 1940).

Kissane, E.J., *The Book of Isaiah* (2 vols.; Dublin, 1941).

Knibb, M. [and R.J. Coggins], *The [First and] Second Book of Esdras* (CBC; Cambridge, 1979).

Koch, K., 'Vom profetischen zum apokalyptischen Visionsbericht', in *Apocalypticism in the Mediterranean World and the Near East* (ed. D. Hellholm; Tübingen, 1983), pp. 413-46.

—*The Growth of the Biblical Tradition* (London, 1969).

Kraft, H., *Die Offenbarung des Johannes* (Tübingen, 1974).

Kraft, R.A., 'Barnabas and Didache', in *The Apostolic Fathers: A Translation and Commentary* (ed. R.M. Grant; New York, 1965), vol. III.

Krämer, M., 'Hütet euch vor den falschen Propheten. Eine überlieferungs-
    geschichtliche Untersuchung zu Mt. 7, 15-23/Lk 6, 43-46/Mt 12, 33-37', *Bib* 57
    (1976), pp. 349-77.

Lack, R., *La symbolique du livre d'Isaie* (AnBib, 59; Rome, 1973).

Lake, K., *The Apostolic Fathers* (2 vols.; LCL; London, 1912).

Lambrecht, J., (ed.), *L'Apocalypse johannique et l'apocalyptique dans le Nouveau
    Testament* (Gembloux, 1980).

Lancellotti, A., 'L'Antico Testamento nell' Apocalisse', *RB* 14 (1966), pp. 369-84.

—*Sintassi ebraica nel greco dell' Apocalisse*. I. *Uso delle forme verbali* (Assisi, 1964).

Lauchli, S., 'Eine Gottesdienststruktur in der Johannesoffenbarung', *TZ* 16 (1960),
    pp. 359-78.

Leiser, B.M., 'The Trisagion of Isaiah's Vision', *NTS* 6 (1959–60), pp. 261-63.

Lestringant, P., *Essai sur l'unité de la révélation biblique* (Paris, 1942).

Levertoff, P., *Midrash Sifre on Numbers* (London, 1926).

Licht, J., 'An Ideal Town Plan from Qumran—The Description of the New Jerusalem',
    IEJ 29 (1979), pp. 45-59.

Lincoln, A.T., *Paradise Now and Not Yet* (Cambridge, 1981).

Lindars, B., *The Gospel of John* (NCB; London, 1972).

—*New Testament Apologetic* (London, 1961).

Lindblom, J., *Gesichte und Offenbarung: Vorstellungen von göttlichen Weisungen und
    übernatürlichen Erscheinungen im ältesten Christentum* (Lund, 1968).

—*Prophecy in Ancient Israel* (Oxford, 1962).

Lohmeyer, E., *Die Offenbarung des Johannes* (HNT, 16; Tübingen, 2nd edn, 1953).

Lohse, E., *Die Offenbarung des Johannes* (NTD, 11; Göttingen, 1960).

—*Märtyrer und Gottesknecht* (Göttingen, 1963).

Long, B.O., 'Reports of Visions among the Prophets', *JBL* 95 (1976), pp. 353-65.

Lührmann, D., *Das Offenbarungsverständnis bei Paulus und in Paulinischen
    Gemeinden* (WMANT, 16; Neukirchen, 1965).

Lust, J., 'The Order of the Final Events in Revelation and in Ezekiel', in *L'Apocalypse
    johannique et l'apocalyptique dans le Nouveau Testament* (ed. J. Lambrecht;
    Gembloux, 1980), pp. 179-83.

Maalstad, K., 'Einige Erwägungen zu Jes. XLIII 4', *VT* 16 (1966), p. 514.

Maier, J., *The Temple Scroll* (Sheffield, 1985).

Malherbe, A.J., 'The Inhospitality of Diotrephes', in *God's Christ and his People:
    Studies in Honour of Nils Alstrup Dahl* (ed. J. Jervell and W.A. Meeks; Oslo,
    1977), pp. 222-32.

March, W.E., 'Prophecy', in *Old Testament Form Criticism* (ed. J.H. Hayes; San
    Antonio, 1974), pp. 141-77.

Marconcini, B., 'L'utilizzazione del T.M. nelle citazioni isaiane dell' Apocalisse', *RivB*
    24 (1976), pp. 113-35.

Martin, R.P., *The Spirit and the Congregation* (Grand Rapids, 1984).

Martin-Achard, R., 'L'oracle contre Shebnâ et le pouvoir des clefs, Es. 22, 15–25', *TZ*
    24 (1968), pp. 241-54.

—'Esaia 47 et la tradition prophétique sur Babylone', in *Prophecy; Essays Presented
    to Georg Fohrer on his 65th Birthday* (ed. J.A. Emerton; Berlin and New York,
    1980), pp. 83-105.

—'Esaïe LIV et la nouvelle Jérusalem', in *Congress Volume, Vienna 1980* (ed.
    J.A. Emerton; VTSup, 32; Leiden, 1981), pp. 238-62.

Massaux, E., *Influence de l'Evangile de saint Matthieu sur la littérature chrétienne avant saint Irénée* (Gembloux, 1950).

McKelvey, R.J., *The New Temple* (London, 1969).

McNamara, M., *The New Testament and the Palestinian Targum to the Pentateuch* (AnBib 27; Rome, 1966).

Mealy, J.W., *After the Thousand Years: Resurrection and Judgment in Revelation 20* (JSNTSup, 70; Sheffield, 1992).

Melton, L.D., 'A Critical Analysis of the Understanding of the Imagery of City in the Book of Revelation' (PhD dissertation, Southern Baptist Theological Seminary, 1970).

Metzger, B., *A Textual Commentary on the Greek New Testament* (UBS, 1981).

Michel, O., 'Spätjüdisches Prophetentum', in *Neutestamentliche Studien für Rudolf Bultmann* (ed. W. Eltester; Göttingen, 1954), pp. 60-66.

Michl, J., *Die 24 Ältesten in der Apokalypse des Hl. Johannes* (München, 1938).

Milik, J.T., *The Books of Enoch* (Oxford, 1976).

—*Ten Years of Discovery in the Wilderness of Judaea* (London, 1959).

Miller, M.P., 'Targum, Midrash and the Use of the Old Testament in the New Testament', *JSJ* 2 (1971), pp. 29-82.

Minear, P., 'False Prophecy and Hypocrisy in the Gospel of Matthew', in *Neues Testament und Kirche* (ed. J. Gnilka; Freiburg, 1974), pp. 76-93.

—*New Testament Apocalyptic* (Nashville, 1981).

Mollat, D., 'Apocalisse ed Esodo', in *S. Giovanni: Atti della XVII settimana biblica* (Brescia, 1964), pp. 346-61.

Montgomery, J.A., 'The Education of the Seer of the Apocalypse', *JBL* 45 (1926), pp. 70-80.

Morgen, M., 'Apocalypse 12, un targum de l'Ancien Testament', *Foi et Vie* 80 (1981), pp. 63-74.

Morris, L., *Apocalyptic* (Grand Rapids, 1972).

Morrow, F.J., 'The Text of Isaiah at Qumran' (PhD dissertation, Catholic University of America, 1973).

Mounce, R.H., *The Book of Revelation* (NICNT; Grand Rapids, 1977).

Müller, H.P., 'Die Plagen der Apokalypse. Eine formgeschichtliche Untersuchung', *ZNW* 51 (1960), pp. 268-78.

—'Formgeschichtliche Untersuchungen zu Apc. 4f.' (PhD thesis, Heidelberg, 1962).

Müller, U.B., *Die Offenbarung des Johannes* (ÖTK, 19; Gütersloh, 1984).

—*Prophetie und Predigt im Neuen Testament: Formgeschichtliche Untersuchungen zur urchristlichen Prophetie* (Gütersloh, 1975).

Mullins, T.Y., 'New Testament Commission Forms, Especially in Luke–Acts', *JBL* 95 (1976), pp. 603-14.

Mussies, G., *The Morphology of Koine Greek as Used in the Apocalypse of John: A Study in Bilingualism* (NovTSup, 27; Leiden, 1971).

Musurillo, H., *The Acts of the Christian Martyrs* (Oxford, 1972).

Naveh, J., and S. Shaked, *Amulets and Magic Bowls* (Jerusalem, 1985).

Nestler, E., 'Was Montanism a Heresy?', *Pneuma* 6 (1984), pp. 67-78.

Newsom, C., *Sons of the Sabbath Sacrifice: A Critical Edition* (HSS, 27; Atlanta, 1985).

Nickelsburg, G.W.E., *Resurrection, Immortality and Eternal Life in Intertestamental Judaism* (Cambridge, MA and London, 1972).

Nielsen, K., *Incense in Ancient Israel* (VTSup, 38; Leiden, 1986).

Nikolainen, A.T., 'Der Kirchenbegriff in der Offenbarung des Johannes', *NTS* 9 (1962–63), pp. 351-61.

Nikolasch, F,. *Das Lamm als Christussymbol in den Schriften der Väter* (Vienna, 1963).

Nolan, B.M., *The Royal Son of God* (Göttingen, 1979).

North, R., *The Second* Isaiah (Oxford, 1964).

Osten-Sacken, P. von der, '"Christologie, Taufe, Homologie"—Ein Beitrag zu Apc Joh 1, 5f.', *ZNW* 58 (1967), pp. 255-66.

Ottley, R.R., *The Book of Isaiah according to the Septuagint* (2 vols.; Cambridge, 2nd edn, 1909/1906).

Ozanne, C.G., 'The Influence of the Text and Language of the Old Testament on the Book of Revelation' (PhD thesis, University of Manchester, 1964).

Panagopoulos, J. (ed.), 'Die urchristliche Prophetie: Ihr Charakter und ihre Funktion', in *Prophetic Vocation in the New Testament and Today* (Leiden, 1977), pp. 1-32.

—(ed.), *Prophetic Vocation in the New Testament and Today* (NovTSup, 45: Leiden, 1977).

Penar, T., *Northwest Semitic Philology and the Hebrew Fragments of Ben Sira* (Rome, 1975).

Philonenko, M., *Joseph et Aséneth: Introduction, texte critique, traduction et notes* (SPB, 13; Leiden, 1968).

Philonenko, M., and A. Dupont-Sommer (eds.), *La Bible Ecrits intertestamentaires* (Paris, 1987).

Ploeg, J. van der, *Le rouleau de la guerre* (Leiden and Grand Rapids, 1959).

Plöger, O., 'Prophetisches Erbe in den Sekten des Frühen Judentums', *TLZ* 79 (1954), cols. 291-96.

Pohl, A., *Die Offenbarung des Johannes*, I (Wuppertal, 1969).

Polk, T., *The Prophetic Persona* (JSOTSup, 32; Sheffield, 1984).

Preston, R.H., and A.T. Hanson, *The Revelation of Saint John the Divine* (London, 1949).

Price, S.R.F., *Rituals and Power: The Roman Imperial Cult in Asia Minor* (Cambridge, 1984).

Prigent, P., *Apocalypse 12: Histoire de l'exégèse* (BGBE, 2; Tübingen, 1959).

—*Apocalypse et liturgie* (CT, 52; Neuchâtel, 1964).

—*L'Apocalypse de Saint Jean* (CNT, 14; Paris, 1981).

—'Le temps et le Royaume dans l'Apocalypse', in *L'Apocalypse johannique et l'apocalyptique dans le Nouveau Testament* (ed. J. Lambrecht; Gembloux, 1980), pp. 231-45.

Rad, G. von, *Old Testament Theology* (3 vols.; Edinburgh, 1965).

—'The Origin of the Concept of the Day of Yahweh', *JSS* 4 (1959), pp. 97-108.

Reader, W.W., 'The Twelve Jewels of Revelation 21.19-20: Tradition History and Modern Interpretations', *JBL* 100 (1981), pp. 433-57.

Reiling, J., 'Prophecy, the Spirit and the Church', in *Prophetic Vocation in the New Testament and Today* (ed. J. Panagopoulos; NovTSup, 45; Leiden, 1977), pp. 58-76.

—*Hermas and Christian Prophecy: A Study of the Eleventh Mandate* (Leiden, 1973).

Reim, G., *Studien zum Alttestamentlichen Hintergrund des Johannes-evangeliums* (Cambridge, 1974).

Reventlow, H.G., *Problems of Biblical Theology in the Twentieth Century* (London, 1986).

Rissi, M., *The Future of the World* (London, 1972).

Robertson, A.T., *A Grammar of the Greek New Testament* (Nashville, 1934).

Roloff, J., *Die Offenbarung des Johannes* (Zürich, 1984).

Rordorf, W., and A. Tuilier, *La doctrine des douze apôtres* (SC, 248; Paris, 1978).

Rosenbloom, J.R., *The Dead Sea Isaiah Scroll* (Grand Rapids, 1970).

Rosenthal, F., 'Nabataean and Related Inscriptions', in *Excavations at Nessana*, I (ed. H.D. Colt; London, 1962), pp. 198-210.

Rousseau, F., *L'Apocalypse et le milieu prophétique du Nouveau Testament: Structure et préhistoire du texte* (Paris, 1971).

Rowland, C., *The Open Heaven* (London, 1982).

—*Christian Origins* (London, 1985).

Russell, D.S., *The Method and Message of Jewish Apocalyptic* (Philadelphia, 1964).

Russell, J.B., *Satan: The Early Christian Tradition* (Ithica, 1981).

Saake, H., 'Paulus als Ekstatiker', *NovT* 15 (1973), pp. 153-60.

Sand, A., *Das Gesetz und die Propheten: Untersuchungen zur Theologie des Evangeliums nach Matthäus* (Regensburg, 1974).

Satake, A., *Die Gemeindeordnung in der Johannesapokalypse* (WMANT, 21; Neukirchen, 1966).

—'Inklusio als ein beliebtes Ausdrucksmittel in der Johannes-apokalypse', *AJBI* 6 (1980), pp. 76-113.

Schäfer, P., *Die Vorstellung vom Heiligen Geist in der rabbinischen Literatur* (München, 1972).

Scherrer, S., 'Revelation 13 as an Historical Source for the Imperial Cult under Domitian' (PhD dissertation, Harvard, 1979).

Schilling, R., *Rites, Cultes, Dieux de Rome* (Paris, 1979).

Schlatter, A., *Das Alte Testament in der johanneischen Apokalypse* (BFCT, XVI/6; Gütersloh, 1912).

Schlütz, K., *Isaias 11, 2 (die sieben Gaben des hl. Geistes) in den ersten vier christlichen Jahrhunderten* (ATA, 11.4.9; Aschendorff, 1932).

Schmid, J.S., *Studien zur Geschichte des griechischen Apokalypse–Textes* (3 vols.; München, 1955).

Schmidt, J.M., *Die jüdische Apokalyptic* (Neukirchen–Vluyn, 1969).

Schmidt, K.L., 'Lucifer als gefallene Engelmacht', *TZ* 7 (1951), pp. 161-79.

Schnackenberg, R., 'Zum Begriff der "Warheit" in den beiden kleinen Johannesbriefen', *BZ* NF 11 (1967), pp. 253-58.

Schoedel, W.R., *Ignatius of Antioch* (Herm.; Philadelphia, 1985).

Schürer, E., *The History of the Jewish People in the Age of Jesus Christ* (rev. edn, ed. G. Vermes, F. Miller and M. Goodman; 3 vols.; Edinburgh 1973–1987).

Schweizer, E., *Matthäus und seine Gemeinde* (Stuttgart, 1974).

—'Observance of the Law and Charismatic Activity in Matthew', *NTS* 16 (1969–70), pp. 213-30.

—*The Letter to the Colossians* (London, 1982).

Scott, J.A., 'The Meaning of the Verb βάπτω, βαπτίζω', *ClassJ* 16 (1920–21), pp. 53-54.

Shea, W.H., 'The Location and Significance of Armageddon in Rev. 16.16', *AUSS* 18 (1980), pp. 157-62.

Shepherd, M.H., *The Paschal Liturgy and the Apocalypse* (London, 1960).

Silberman, L.H., 'Farewell to 'O 'AMĤN. A Note on Rev. 3, 14', *JBL* 82 (1963), pp. 213-15.

Skehan, P., 'Isaias and the Teaching of the Book of Wisdom', *CBQ* 2 (1940), pp. 289-99.

Smend, R., *Die Weisheit des Jesus Sirach* (Berlin, 1906).

Smith, D. Moody, 'The Use of the Old Testament in the New', in *The Use of the Old Testament in the New and Other Essays: Studies in Honor of W.F. Stinespring* (ed. J.M. Efird; Durham, N.C., 1972), pp. 3-65.

Spicq, C., *Les Épitres Pastorales* (Paris, 4th edn, 1969).

Spittler, R.P., 'The Limits of Ecstasy: An Exegesis of 2 Corinthians 12.1-10', in *Current Issues in Biblical and Patristic Interpretation* (ed. G.F. Hawthorne; Grand Rapids, 1975), pp. 259-66.

Staehelin, J., *700 Parallelen, die Quellgründe der Apokalypse* (Bern, 1961).

Stanton, G., *The Interpretation of Matthew* (London, 1983).

Stenning, J.F., *The Targum of Isaiah* (Oxford, 1949).

Steuernagel, C., 'Die Strukturlinien der Entwicklung der jüdischen Eschatologie', in *Festschrift für Alfred Bertholet zum 80* (ed. W. Baumgartner, O. Eissfeldt, K. Elliger and L. Rost; Tübingen, 1950).

Strack, H.L., *Einleitung in Talmud und Midrasch* (München, 6th edn, 1976).

Stuhlmacher, P., 'Seihe, ich mache alles neu', *LR* 18 (1968), pp. 3-18.

Sweet, J., *Revelation* (London, 1979).

Swete, H.B., *The Apocalypse of St John* (London, 1911).

Taylor, V., *The Names of Jesus* (London, 1953).

Tenney, M.C., *Interpreting Revelation* (Grand Rapids, 1957).

Theissen, G., *Sociology of Early Palestinian Christianity* (Philadelphia, 1978).

—'Wanderradikalismus: Literatursoziologische Aspekte der überlieferung von Worten Jesu im Urchristentum', *ZTK* 70 (1973), pp. 245-71.

Thompson, L., 'Cult and Eschatology in the Apocalypse of John', *JR* 49 (1969), pp. 330-50.

Thompson, S., *The Apocalypse and Semitic Syntax* (Cambridge, 1985).

Thompson, W.G., 'An Historical Perspective in the Gospel of Matthew', *JBL* 93 (1974), pp. 243-63.

Torrey, C.C., 'Armegeddon (Apoc 16, 16)', *HTR* 31 (1938), pp. 237-48.

—*Documents of the Primitive Church* (New York, 1941).

Toy, C.H., *Quotations in the NT* (New York, 1884).

Trench, R.C, *Synonyms of the New Testament* (London, 1880).

Trevett, C., 'Prophecy and Anti-Episcopal Activity: A Third Error Combatted by Ignatius?', *JEH* 34 (1983), pp. 1-18.

Trites, A.A., *The New Testament Concept of Witness* (Cambridge, 1977).

Trudinger, L., 'O 'AMĤN (Rev. III.14), and the Case for a Semitic Original of the Apocalypse', *NovT* 14 (1972), pp. 277-79.

—'Some Observations concerning the Text of the Old Testament in the Book of Revelation', *JTS* NS 17 (1966), pp. 82-88.

—'The Text of the Old Testament in the Book of Revelation' (PhD dissertation, Boston University, 1963).

Turner, N., *A Grammar of New Testament Greek. IV. Style* (Edinburgh, 1976).

Unnik, W.C. van, 'A Formula Describing Prophecy', *NTS* 9 (1962–63), pp. 86-94.

—*Het Godspredikaat 'Het Begin en het Einde' bij Flavius Josephus en in de Openbaring van Johannes* (Amsterdam, 1976).

—'1 Clement 34 and the "Sanctus"', *VC* 5 (1951), pp. 204-48.

Urbach, E.E., 'מתי פסקה הנבואה?' ('When Did Prophecy Disappear?') *Tarbiz* 17 (1945–46), pp. 1-11.

Vanhoye, A., 'L'utilisation du livre d'Ezéchiel dans l'Apocalypse', *Bib* 43 (1962), pp. 436-76.

Vermes, G., *Scripture and Tradition in Judaism: Haggadic Studies* (SPB, 4; Leiden, 1961).

—*The Dead Sea Scrolls in English* (London, 3rd edn, 1987).

Vögtle, A., *Das Neue Testament und die Zukunft des Kosmos* (Düsseldorf, 1970).

—'Mythos und Botschaft in Apokalypse 12', in *Tradition und Glaube: Das frühe Christentum in seiner Umwelt* (Festgabe K.G. Kuhn; ed. G. Jeremias, H.-W. Kuhn and H. Stegemann; Göttingen, 1971), pp. 395-415.

Vos, L.A., *The Synoptic Traditions in the Apocalypse* (Kampen, 1965).

Vriezen, T.C., 'Prophecy and Eschatology', in *Congress Volume, Copenhagen 1953*, VTSup, 1; Leiden, 1954), pp. 199-229.

Vuilliaud, P., *Le Cantique des Cantiques d'aprés le tradition juive* (Paris, 1925).

Walker, N., 'The Origin of the "Thrice-Holy"', *NTS* 5 (1958–59), pp. 132-33.

Weinel, H., *Die Wirkungen des Geistes und der Geister im nachapostolischen Zeitalter bis auf Irenäus* (Freiburg, 1899).

Weizsäcker, C. von, *The Apostolic Age* (London, 1895).

Westermann, C., *Isaiah 40–66* (London, 1969).

—*Basic Forms of Prophetic Speech* (Philadelphia, 1967).

—'Prophetenzitate im Neuen Testament', *EvT* 27 (1967), pp. 307-17.

Whale, P., 'The Lamb of John: Some Myths about the Vocabulary of the Johannine Literature', *JBL* 106 (1987), pp. 289-95.

Whybray, R.N., *Isaiah 40–66* (NCB; London, 1975).

Wikenhauser, A., *Die Offenbarung des Johannes* (RNT, 9; Regensburg, 3rd edn, 1959).

Wilcox, M., 'Tradition and Redaction of Rev. 21, 9-22, 5', in *L'Apocalypse johannique et l'apocalyptique dans le Nouveau Testament* (ed. J. Lambrecht; BETL, 53; Gembloux, 1980), pp. 205-15.

Wildberger, H., *Jesaja* (2 vols.; Neukirchen, 1965–72).

Williams, F.E., *Nag Hammadi Codex I: Introduction, Texts, Translations, Indices* (ed. H.W. Attridge; Leiden, 1985).

Wilson, R.R., 'Prophecy and Ecstasy: A Reexamination', *JBL* 98 (1979), pp. 321-37.

Wolff, C., *Jeremia im Frühjudentum und Urchristentum* (TU, 118; Berlin, 1976).

Wolff, H.W., 'Die Begründungen der prophetischen Heils- und Unheilsspruche', *ZAW* 52 (1934), pp. 1-22.

—*Dodekapropheton 1: Hosea* (BKAT, 14; Neukirchen, 1961).

—*Jesaja 53 im Urchristentum* (Berlin, 2nd edn, 1950).

Woude, A.S. van der, *Die messianischen Vorstellungen der Gemeinde von Qumran* (Assen, 1957).

Yadin, Y., *The Temple Scroll* (3 vols.; Jerusalem, 1984).

Zaehner, R.C., *The Bhagavad-gītā* (Oxford, 1969).

Zahn, T., *Die Offenbarung des Johannes* (2 vols.; Leipzig, 1924–26).

Zimmerli, W., *Ezekiel* (2 vols.: Herm.; Philadelphia, 1979).

Zimmerman, F., *The Book of Tobit* (New York, 1958).

INDEXES

INDEX OF REFERENCES

OLD TESTAMENT

JEWISH LITERATURE

JOURNAL FOR THE STUDY OF THE NEW TESTAMENT

Supplement Series